TERRORISM:
Interdisciplinary
Perspectives

TERRORISM:
Interdisciplinary Perspectives

Edited, with an Introduction, by
Yonah Alexander
and
Seymour Maxwell Finger

with a Foreword by
Hans J. Morgenthau

HV
6431
.T47

Copublished in cooperation with
The Ralph Bunche Institute on the United Nations
City University of New York
and
The Institute for Studies in International Terrorism
State University of New York
by
The John Jay Press
New York

Second Printing, 1978

Library of Congress Cataloging in Publication Data
Main entry under title:

Terrorism: interdisciplinary perspectives.

    Bibliography: p.
    Includes index.
    a. Terrorism — Addresses, essays, lectures.
I. Alexander, Yonah.   II. Finger, Seymour Maxwell, 1915-
HV6431.T47   301.6'33   77-7552

U.S.A. ISBN 0-89444-004-7   0-89444-006-3 (pb.)

Manufactured in the United States of America

Table of Contents

Hans J. Morgenthau:
Foreword

Terrorism presents established governments with a number of problems unprecedented in modern history. Traditionally, governments have possessed a monopoly of organized physical violence which they would use against other governments monopolistically endowed in a similar way or against individual citizens violating the legal order. It is new in modern history that a group of citizens would band together, challenging the monopoly of organized violence in the hands of the government.

One does not need to have in mind the possibility of civil war if the challenge on the part of citizens is large and well organized enough. The very fact that a group of citizens would dare not just to violate the legal order but to challenge its validity points to a drastic and, in modern history, unprecedented weakening of the authority of the government. It also points up the dilemma a government faces when confronted with terrorist demands it has to come to terms with: is it going to yield to the terrorists' demands in order to stave off threats to the lives and property of some of its citizens, thereby encouraging new terrorist demands, or is it going to reject those demands at the risk of jeopardizing those same lives and property? How is the government to react to this challenge to its authority? Obviously, there can be no simple and easy answer to that question. More particularly, there can be no answer to that question which uses the modes of thought and action with which the period since the end of the Napoleonic wars has acquainted us, in order to solve the problems of the late 20th century. As the experience of organized armed citizens laying down conditions for the government to fulfill on the threat to the lives and property of other citizens is novel, so must the reaction of the government to such a challenge be novel.

It is the great merit of this collection of essays to consider the issues raised by contemporary terrorism in this spirit of unprecedented novelty and thereby to contribute significantly to the solution of the issues raised.

June 3, 1977

Yonah Alexander
Seymour Maxwell Finger:
Introduction

According to newspaper accounts, a psychopathic "lovesick loner" has spread terror through the New York metropolitan area for many months. He has allegedly shot to death five young women with shoulder-length hair and one man and has wounded seven other people in eight separate shootings. In most of the incidents the murderer fired at innocent victims while they were sitting in parked cars. The manhunt for the ".44 caliber killer" ended with the arrest of David Berkowitz in August.

At the Thunder Bay District Jail in Ontario, Canada, four knife-wielding prisoners held seven hostages, demanding a public inquiry into the prison system and demanding speedier court trials. After an assistant prosecutor talked to the prisoners, heard their grievances, and aparently promised them immunity, the hostages were freed unharmed.

In Japan, an unidentified hijacker carrying a toy pistol attempted to force the pilot of an All-Nippon 727 airliner carrying 173 passengers to fly from Tokyo to the northern city of Sendai. The pilot refused the hijacker's demand and returned the plane to Tokyo. When the plane landed the hijacker killed himself by swallowing cyanide in the plane's washroom.

These and countless other instances of socially disruptive behavior including criminal or pathological elements are indeed a form of private "terrorism" utilized by perpetrators to achieve rational or irrational personal objectives. However, "terrorism" in its public or ideological and political senses has a completely different meaning in terms of its nature and implications. It is clearly illustrated by the following cases selected at random from world-wide press coverage in 1976 and 1977:

Eight incendiary devices started small fires in three Manhattan department stores. Fuerzas Armadas de Liberacion Nacional (F.A.L.N.), the Puerto Rico pro-independence group, claimed responsibility for the fires, and in a letter found in a public telephone booth, F.A.L.N. stated: "At no time will we let any corporation or the colonial government of Puerto Rico attempt to mine our natural resources. This also includes any offshore drilling for petroleum." The letter also demanded the release from U.S. jails of five imprisoned Puerto Rican Nationalists who had been convicted of violent criminal acts.

Fourteen South Moluccans living in the Netherlands, seeking independence for their islands from Indonesia, seized a Dutch train and a school, taking more than 160 hostages. After more than two weeks of negotiations with the Netherlands government, a hundred hostages were released. After twenty days, the rest of the hostages were liberated through an assault by the Dutch Marines. Six terrorists and two hostages were killed during the assault.

Members of the Movement for the Self-Determination and Independence of the Canary Archipelago, known as M.P.A.I.C., the initials of its name in Spanish, placed a bomb in a florist's shop at the Las Palmas Airport in the Canary Islands. The explosion wounded eight persons and forced two 747 jets, one American and one Dutch, to be diverted from Las Palmas to the Island of Tenerife where, on the fog-bound Los Rodeos airstrip, the planes collided, killing almost 600 people.

In Karlsruhe, West Germany, assassins riding a motor-cycle pulled up from behind a limousine stopped at a traffic light, sprayed it with sub-machine gun fire, and escaped. Killed in the attack were Siegfried Buback, West Germany's Chief Prosecutor and his driver; another official was critically wounded. The Ulrike Meinhof Action Committee claimed responsibility for the murders apparently because Buback had been leading proceedings against leaders of the Baader-Meinhof Group, urban anarchists dedicated to the overthrow of capitalism and the present parliamentary system in West Germany.

Members of the Zimbabwe African National Union, seeking black majority rule in Rhodesia, killed seven white Roman Catholic missionaries at St. Paul Mission. Four nuns, two priests and a lay brother were shot. The attackers escaped.

Along a mountain road in Lebanon four unidentified gunmen chased a car in which Kamal Jumblatt, the leftist and Druze leader, was being driven homeward. They opened fire, killed Jumblatt, his bodyguard and his driver, and fled. Subsequently, Jumblatt's followers killed some 200 Christian villagers to avenge the assassination of their leader.

The foregoing acts of violent behavior — characterized by a technique of perpetrating random and brutal intimidation, coercion, or destruction of human lives and property, and used intentionally by subnational groups, operating under varying degrees of stress, to obtain realistic or illusory goals — are symtomatic of what we consider "terrorism" to be.

Indeed, we seem to have entered an "age of terrorism," the pattern of which is unlike any other period in history when ideological and political violence occurred. The major reason for this contemporary phenomenon lies in the very nature of modern civilization itself. The present complex technological society is extremely vulnerable to unsuspected and ruthless attacks of terrorism, because transportation centers, communication facilities, oil fields and refineries, and factories cannot always be protected against the random acts of small groups of dedicated and determined terrorists.

Second, highly sophisticated weapons, like heat-seeking missiles which can be fired from light shoulder launchers, are now relatively easy for various terror movements to obtain. It is also likely that in the future these groups will have access to biological, chemical, and nuclear instruments of death and destruction.

Third, the availability of the most modern warfare capabilities to terror groups challenges the stability of an orderly human society. Their newly found power transforms subnational groups, ordinarily regarded as "powerless," into parties with formidable strengths. They are often capable of creating states within states, thereby undermining the ability of legitimate governments to rule or ultimately to survive.

Fourth, the advances of science and technology are slowly turning all of modern society into a potential victim of terrorism, with no immunity for the non-combatant segment of the world population, nor for those nations and peoples who have no direct connection to specific grievances motivating acts of violence or to particular conflicts. Because of the unrestricted and indiscriminate character of terrorism, innocent civilians are increasingly subject to daily risk anywhere in the world.

Fifth, communication and transportation opportunities have enabled an international network of terrorism to develop with a certain degree of centralized organizational structure. Collaboration among ideologically linked groups and even among those without a common philosophy or political interest has developed relationships involving financing, training, supply of combat materials, propaganda facilities, refuge bases, organizational assistance, attacks by proxy, and joint attacks. This pattern of "comradeship" is inevitably expanding the areas of international violence.

Sixth, as the world is shrinking through the revolution in communications, terrorists are assured extensive publicity for their wanton acts and enunciated causes. Because terrorism is essentially violence for effect and is targeted not only against immediate victims but is directed at a wide audience as well, terrorists are making a conscious and deliberate effort to use the media for intimidation and blackmail. The immediacy and diffusion of acts of terror through the electronic media have consequently produced great psychological effects far beyond the area of terrorism. Another major consequence of extensive media coverage of ideological and political violence is the exportation of terroristic techniques and inspiration to other terrorist groups.

In addition to factors inherent in the modern industrial system, several broad causative circumstances have substantially contributed to our "age of terrorism," including the confrontations between the East and West as well as between ideologies of the left and right; the rise in ethnic, linguistic, racial, religious, and national consciousness of groups throughout the world, manifested in extreme cases by the actions of the contending factions in Northern Ireland, Lebanon, the Philippines, and Ethiopia; the intensification of resistance by dependent peoples struggling for their liberation and a legitimate right to self-determination; growth of opposition by citizens to repressive regimes and dictators ruling their countries; the revolution of the rising expectations waged to correct the North-South economic disequilibrium. What complicates the conditions that breed terrorism is the fact that members of the state system sometimes actually support political and ideological violence. Iraq, Libya, Somalia, Uganda, and South Yemen have supplied terrorists with money, weapons, medicines, communication facilities, intelligence information, and fake identification and passports. They have also provided terrorists with training and "safe havens." As long as subnational groups receive assistance from sympathetic states, terrorism will be a viable activity.

Governments, at least in liberal democracies face another dilemma caused by terrorism. Although they are aware of the dangerous and seriously disruptive effects of terrorism upon the

quality of life in and outide of their countries, they are often
inhibited from taking the necessary steps to deal effectively with
the problem due to considerations of civil liberties or state
policy. In a democratic society any contemplated measure to
deter crime or terrorism must be weighed against the potential
damage to the rights, including due process, of law-abiding
citizens. Qualms about capital punishment must be weighed
against the fact that imprisonment of terrorists for murder often
serves as a stimulant for new acts of terrorism aimed at
obtaining the release of jailed terrorists. State policy may also
hamper efforts to deal with terrorism. In France, the government
decided to release Abu Daoud, a leader in the Black September
movement accused of participating in the killing of Israel's
atheletes at the Munich Olympics in 1972, despite France's
adherence to the European Convention on the Suppression of
Terrorism. The decision helps to undermine the credibility of
conventions and, consequently, their deterrence.

The United Nations, reflecting the ideological and political
differences among member states has been unable to take
appropriate measures to cope with terrorism. The Ad Hoc
Committee on International Terrorism of the General Assembly
was unable to reach a universal consensus on the definition of
the term "terrorism," and could not agree on possible strategies
to deal with the problem.

However, the International Civil Aviation Organization
(I.C.A.O.), a specialized agency of the United Nations System,
has developed three important international conventions against
aerial hijacking and other threats to the safety of air travel.
Unfortunately, the effectiveness of these conventions has been
drastically reduced, because some states which have not ratified
the conventions continue to provide safe havens for hijackers. A
proposal by the Federal Republic of Germany for an
international convention against the taking of hostages is
currently before a committee of the U.N. General Assembly.

Recognizing the seriousness and complexity of terrorism, we
have asked a group of colleagues and scholars in various
disciplines to examine the manifold aspects of "terrorism" —
past, present, and future — from the perspectives of their own
disciplines. Their often very different approaches to terrorism
have been recorded in this volume so that a dialogue on the
meaning, causes, consequences, and control of all forms of
terrorist action may begin. As catalysts to the process, the Ralph
Bunche Institute on the United Nations, City University of New
York, and the Institute for Studies in International Terrorism,

State University of New York, convened a three-day conference in New York City, June 9-11, 1976, assisted by a grant from the Rockefeller Foundation.

The authors wish to express their gratitude to the Rockefeller Foundation and to the two Institutes; their generous support made this volume possible. These institutions bear no responsibility for the views and findings in this volume; contributors bear sole responsibility for their own observations and conclusions, as do we, the editors.

The editors also wish to thank the authors who have contributed to this volume and to add their gratitude to the following acknowledgments which individual authors wish to make.

Baljit Singh would like to thank Iwao Ishino, Director of the Institute for Area and Comparative Studies at Michigan State University for his support and encouragement in the completion of his paper.

Robert A. Friedlander wishes to thank the *Israel Yearbook on Human Rights* for permission to reprint his paper in this volume. The paper appeared in Volume VI of the *Israel Yearbook on Human Rights*, 1976.

David C. Rapoport is indebted to the National Institute of Mental Health for providing a grant (5 RO 1 MH 205-222-2) which enabled him to complete his work and paper.

Jay Mallin wishes to thank *Air University Review* for permission to include his paper in this book. The paper appeared in the January-February issue of that journal.

H. H. A. Cooper's paper appeared originally in *Chitty's Law Journal*, Vol. 24, No. 7, 1976, and permission to include the paper in this volume is gratefully acknowledged.

TERRORISM:
Interdisciplinary
Perspectives

I.
DEFINITIONAL
AND
HISTORICAL
PERSPECTIVES

Baljit Singh:
An Overview

Sigmund Freud has argued that civilization, with its institutional restraints and the repression of human nature, guarantees discontent. His vision of the human condition suggests that society must be continually prepared to accept change and expand human freedoms or must face many forms of resistance as an unavoidable reaction for its intransigence.

The agents of change, however, are often victimized by society which tends to label them as traitors and treats their ideas and actions as dangerous threats to civilization itself. The most dangerous element in a situation of change is not that a resister is victimized or killed for his ideas or acts but that it is often done without recognizing it or saying so and is hidden behind the mask of a "penal code." Resistance and violence, thus, may well have begun with Creation and may not end even on judgment day.

There is almost an infinite variety of violence of anti-social nature — homicide, acts of vandalism, arson, destructive rage, or other expressions of an essentially irrational urge to strike at someone or something. Political violence, on the other hand, occurs in acts designed to bring about social and political change both among and within nations.

Political violence may be grouped into two types: 1. conventional wars and intervention, that is, those actions that are related to achieving national objectives and that essentially fall within the Napoleonic mode, and 2. unconventional, an unimaginative category that encompasses all varieties of political

warfare from subversion to guerrilla warfare and draws inspira-
tion from such diverse sources as Sun-Tsu's *The Art of War*;
Kautilya's *Arthasastra*; Clausewitz's *On War*; Lenin's *Partisan
Warfare*; Mao Tse Tung's *On the Protracted War*; T. E.
Lawrence's *Seven Pillars of Wisdom*; and Carlos Marighella's
Minimanual of the Urban Guerrilla.

This paper attempts to provide an overview of the phenomenon of political terrorism. Within this framework, it is my
contention that political resistance and violence are not mere
symptoms of some psychic disorder among the individual
resisters but, in reality, are deep manifestations of a general
disequilibrium in human organization.

Political terrorism comprises only one type of violent
activity subsumed under the general heading of unconventional
warfare. Furthermore, the scope of political terrorism has
expanded radically through history. Perhaps the best known
terrorists of yesteryear belonged to the Arab world's "Society
of the Assassins." (1) The Assassins were founded some 900
years ago by the religious teacher Hassan Ibn Sabah. Their
Arabic name, *Hashshasin*, sprang from the terrorists addiction
to hashish. Because of their activities as killers, the word,
assassination, came to mean political murder. The Assassins
were a religious-political group whose power rested on the
membership of *fedawi* (devoted ones) who killed at the
command of their religious leader, believing that killing the
unrighteous guaranteed their own salvation and assisted in
overthrowing a corrupt order.

The Assassins remained a powerful force in the Arab world
for 200 years and pitted their new weapon against their
religious and political opponents, the Turkish military forces
and Sunni Islam. Ultimately, they were destroyed by Mongol
invaders, but two of their organizational practices — 1. popular
agitation or their attempts to spread their beliefs among the
populace and 2. a strict code of secrecy among all members of
the organization — have an exceptionally modern ring.

Political terrorism as an instrument of power came of age
during the French Revolution of 1793-1794. Despite some
indiscriminate killings during the early phases of the Revolution, a *policy* of revolutionary terror evolved clearly with the
Jacobins. (2) Robespierre, Saint-Just, and the Committee of
Public Safety played a vital role in the organization and
direction of what came to be known as the Reign of Terror.
As Fromkin has remarked:

Robespierre had coerced a nation of 27 million people into accepting his dictatorship. His followers sent many thousands either to jail or to their deaths; one scholar's estimate is 40,000 deaths and 3,000,000 arrests. Yet when retribution came and Robespierre and his group of supporters were executed, it turned out that in all there were only 22 of them. (3)

By no means is this the entire story of political terror during the French Revolution. The important point, however, is that a political group which should have been weak when judged objectively could wield such disproportionate amount of power. What made such a development possible can be explained only by analyzing the phenomena of terror.

Terror incorporates two facets: 1. a state of fear or anxiety within an individual or a group and 2. the tool that induces the state of fear. Thus, terror entails the threat or use of symbolic violent acts aimed at influencing political behavior.

Despite its long history of use in many countries, political terror failed to score any significant successes after the French Revolution until 1921 when the British were forced to bow to the terrorist campaign in Ireland and granted that country independence under the terms of the Irish Treaty. The period between the Irish Treaty and the end of World War II saw little political terrorism, except as an adjunct to conventional warfare. The Germans, Russians, Yugoslavs, Japanese, French, British, and even Americans, all engaged in some type of terrorist activity. The scope of it, however, was rather limited, and the objectives were well-defined.

Following World War II, political terrorism reemerged on the international scene. With notable exceptions in Cyprus and Algeria, it became one of the many tools used within the larger arena of nationalist movements for independence. From its minimal application in India to a substantial reliance upon it in Algeria, Cyprus, and Kenya, political terrorism encompassed a wide range of activities, including intimidation, abduction, sabotage, selective assassination, and indiscriminate killing.

During the 1960s, political terrorism appears to have entered into another phase. Perhaps the two most significant qualitative changes were: 1. its trans-national character and 2. its emergence as a self-sufficient strategy — that is, terrorists attempted to operate independently of the larger political arena. Several developments help explain this new direction.

The growth of political terrorism into a trans-national

phenomena has been greatly facilitated through a revolution in communication — radio, satellite television, air travel, and tourism. Terrorist acts committed in the remotest parts of the world now receive instant coverage and their "propaganda by deed" is exploited to full advantage. The growth in international tourism has radically changed the composition of passengers aboard international airlines. Consequently, skyjackings emerged as tempting activities for contemporary political terrorists. Table 1 (4) illustrates the rapid escalation in skyjackings until international action through increased security measures, extradition agreements, and tough-minded responses to terrorist demands forced a decline.

Terrorism's emergence as a self-sufficient tool to achieve political objectives is largely due to the vulnerability of our modern urban civilization. While Mao Tse Tung emphasized rural, peasant-based guerrilla warfare and thought in terms of an ultimate, armed and open revolutionary conflict to attain victory, today's urban guerrillas view the modern city as the new battleground. Carlos Marighella in his *Minimanual of the Urban Guerrilla* (5) exhibits considerable insight into the delicate nature and the interrelationship of vital services in our modern cities. He also provides a detailed list of terror tactics and their most efficient usage, including political kidnapping, selective assassination, bombing, hijackings, and bank robbery.

Whether this new form of political terror will ever "succeed" in attaining its vague objective of destruction of "the giant industrial-financial-economic-political-cultural-military-police-complex" that guards and perpetuates "fascism . . . colonialism . . . the dictatorship . . . the North American Businessmen," (6) remains to be seen, but the *Minimanual* does detail the new vulnerabilities of modern urban civilization and suggests new techniques to be marshalled against it.

The strategies and tactics employed by political terrorists are generally directed at three groups: the populace, the regime in power, and the terrorist organization itself. The overall objectives of these strategies and tactics are to: 1. gain popular support, 2. disrupt and destroy the military and psychological strength of the regime, and 3. achieve internal stability and growth.

If we accept the premise that political terror is primarily aimed at the psyche rather than at "military hardware" *per se*, a carefully selected assassination of an "important but unpopular" public official may boost terrorists' morale, create sympathy among the populace, and provoke the regime to adopt

TABLE I

UNLAWFUL SEIZURE AND INTERFERENCE WITH COMMERCIAL AIRCRAFT

Year	Attempted or completed seizures	Attempted or completed sabotage	Persons affected	Countries involved	Fatalities	Injuries
1930						
1967	79†		...	...	...	...
1968	35†		...	...	...	...
1969	80	5	4,489	52	6	33
1970	74	22	5,011	47	92	42
1971	51	18	4,016	33	113	15
1972	73	43	4,942	45	185	108
1973	33	19	2,278	47	205	83
1974	25	14	1,942	23	171	40
1975 (through 5 March)	7	3	...	12	...	...
Totals*	343	124	22,678	....	772	321

† Incomplete Data

*1969-1975

repressive measures that further alienate the populace.

Jay Mallin has suggested the following five basic, short-term objectives (tactics) as those most commonly employed by political terrorists: 1. morale building within the ranks, 2. advertising the movement, 3. disorientation and psychological isolation of the populace, 4. elimination of opposing forces, and 5. provocation of the government. (7)

These objectives are closely interrelated and are mutually reinforcing. Nascent terrorist groups often attempt to accomplish multiple objectives through a single act. George Habash of the Popular Front for the Liberation of Palestine (P.F.L.P.) once remarked that "The main point is to select targets where success is 100% assured. . . . You should see how my people react to a successful operation! Spirits shoot sky-high." (8) A successful operation therefore may not only build morale within the ranks and advertise the movement, but it may also help achieve the long-term objective of gaining popular support.

Political terrorism essentially is *propaganda by deed.* Consequently, advertising the movement becomes an integral part of its tactics. The weak, who generally resort to terrorism as a weapon, have a great need for their cause to be widely noticed. Ramdane Abbane of the Algerian F.L.N. succinctly summarized this tactic when he said:

> Is it better for our cause to kill ten of our enemies in a remote village where this will not cause comment, or to kill only one man in Algiers where the American press will get hold of the story the next day? . . . . We must ensure that people learn about our struggle. (9)

During the past few years the communication media has reported a wide variety of politically motivated terrorist acts designed both to gain publicity and to build organizational morale. The P.F.L.P.'s simultaneous skyjacking and subsequent destruction of four international airliners in September 1970, the Palestine Liberation Organization (P.L.O.) Commando's seizure of a Jewish high school at Maalot in May 1974 resulting in the death of two dozen children, and the death of some twenty innocent pedestrians in May 1974 when stolen cars packed with time bombs exploded in downtown Dublin, are but a few grim reminders of this tactic. However, to create a favorable image, such acts must be carefully targeted and efficiently executed, otherwise they may create an unfortunate first impression of the group and antagonize the populace. The so-called Symbionese Liberation Army's mindless abduction of Patricia Hearst followed by confused political rhetoric and material demands, exemplifies the latter result.

Another important objective of political terrorism is the disorientation and psychological isolation of the individuals in the populace. The tactic of inducing an atmosphere of fear and general nervousness is designed to detach the individual from his social context "whereby he has only himself upon whom to rely and cannot draw strength from his customary social supports." (10) To create a disrupted psychological behavior through inducing a state of fear and anxiety among the populace, terrorists engage in random, intense, and unpredictable violent acts. These tactics create an atmosphere of ever-present danger to the public's physical safety and tend to undermine its confidence in the ability of the regime to maintain stability and order. When a regime continually fails to maintain order, the populace is forced to accept whatever protection, cohesion, or guarantees may be extended by the terrorists. In their search for stability and safety, the populace submits to a new authority structure that can alleviate their anxieties, as they did in Algeria, Cuba, and Northern Ireland. In such a situation, however, the terrorists' authority to govern is highly tenuous, and they must continually engage in acts of terror to remain in control, thereby repeatedly testing their resourcefulness. Since excessive acts of physical violence to induce fear and psychological disorientation can be both costly and often are counterproductive, they generally occur with heavy doses of propaganda, the main purpose of which is to break the bonds that exist between the populace and the incumbent regime. Fear, anxiety, and psychological disorientation among the populace greatly contribute to undermining a regime's authority and its ability for effective control.

The individual political terrorist, on the other hand, articulates himself through group participation. Group acts enhance his sense of political purpose and direction, his dignity and identity. Individual consciousness is welded into a group ideology that provides needed social and political supports.

Most political terrorists themselves lead a life of uncertainty and strain. Power struggles, factional fights, ideological debates, strategy disputes and discipline problems are common within these clandestine organizations. The need for obedience to commands and conformity in the organization often requires enforcement action, generally the actual physical liquidation of wavering members. The Irish Republican Army and Black

September, for instance, have consistently eliminated dissident members. A similar fate also awaits enemy agents, reformers, and collaborators. The objective of all these acts is to demonstrate, both within and outside the group, the determination and the uncompromising stance of the leadership. In Algeria "executions of the traitors" by the F.L.N. far exceeded the number of French killed during the period of conflict. (11)

Elimination of any large numbers of opposing forces, especially security and administrative personnel, usually comes during the more advanced stages of a terrorist movement. However, specific acts of terrorism are directed at selected individuals to demonstrate an organization's growing strength and momentum and to paralyze and exhaust the regime. The Viet Cong, during one later stage of their movement, are reported to have systematically killed more than 5,000 and kidnapped some 7,000 government officials within a period of one year. (12) Such assassinations underscore both the strength of the organization and the danger of association with the regime.

The most important tactic in terrorist strategy to gain popular support and to discredit an incumbent regime may be provoking the government into adopting countermeasures, preferably repressive ones. Fidel Castro successfully forced Batista to take desperate repressive actions. Batista's responses probably contributed more towards his loss of support in Cuba than the actual battlefield victories of Castro's group. (13)

The terrorists also believe that provoking a government into taking repressive measures induces a breakdown in social norms and helps create conditions for public disaffection and alienation. If such an atmosphere can be sustained over a period of time, it can be exploited to the terrorists' psychological and political advantage.

In summary, the strategy, tactics, and objectives of political terrorists are highly interrelated and mutually reinforcing. According to Fromkin:

> It is an uncertain and indirect strategy that employs the weapon of fear in a special sort of way in which to make governments react. . . Fright can paralyze the will, befuddle the mind, and exhaust the strength of an adversary. Moreover it can persuade an opponent that a particular political point of view is taken with such deadly seriousness by its few adherents that it should be accommodated, rather than suffering the casualties

year after year in a campaign to suppress it. (14)

The dominant forms of political terrorism today are but a reflection of the politics of our time. As the national independence movements were the natural products of colonialism, the contemporary political terrorists symbolize, often mistakenly, resistance against discrimination, exclusion, suppression, and abusive power and privilege all too manifest in social, economic, ethnic, cultural, and political spheres of society.

Over 2,000 years ago, the Indian scholar-statesman, Kautilya, (15) articulated the following four interdependent instruments to achieve human and social well being: *Dharma* (Law or Duty), *Artha* (Resources), *Kama* (Relations or Desire), and *Moksha* (Spiritual Deliverance). According to Kautilya, these four instruments of human existence must remain in harmonic balance if society and its polity are to remain integrated and continue to prosper.

In contemporary terms, Kautilya's observations signify the importance of the maintenance of a proper balance between individual rights and freedoms and societal needs and aspirations. Only when a balance exists between these elements can we expect the attainment of popular well being, social peace, and an integrated social and political order.

> The task of creation and sustenance of an integrated social order so essential for peaceful progress of human societies, can be said to pervade . . . three vital fields of human knowledge compressed into Knowledge of Dharma or law and legal relations, Knowledge of Artha or resources and economic relations and Knowledge of Kama or inter-individual and inter-social cultural relations. Without these, society would simply drift into dissolution. (16)

Kautilya's ideal social order has remained a mere illusion throughout recorded human history and the struggle of the "Declasses," "Outs" and "Have-nots" against the "Classes," "Ins" and "Haves" has changed little since the dawn of civilization. (17) The modern resisters, however, appear to be better organized and more numerous.

The contemporary agitational political terrorism, in its broadest dimensions, symbolizes outrage and frustration against the inequities in *Dharma*, *Artha*, and *Kama* and the irrelevance of *Moksha.* That is, as long as laws, resources, and human dignity remain the preserve of some or even many but not all, resistance against such a state of affairs will surely continue in Northern Ireland, the Middle East, Africa, Latin America, or the United States of America.

I have attempted to demonstrate the futility of discussing political terrorism outside the general context of the organization of power in society and polity. Although often the ugly and brutal side of politics, all political terrorism is not necessarily either ignoble or irrational. The contemporary terrorist certainly does not fit the stereotyped mold of either the *Hashshasin* of 900 years ago or the "common criminal" of today. (18) The sociological and psychological research dealing with the individual actors who participate in this form of political violence is sketchy at best. This much, however, is known: most contemporary terrorists, or at least the leading figures among them, are persons of intellect and come from comfortable socio-economic backgrounds. This is true of most of the present-day groups including the *P.L.O.*, Uruguayan *Tupamaros,* the Brazilian disciples of Marighella, the West German *BaderMeinhoff*, the Japanese Red Army, and the I.R.A.

J. B. Bell's discussion of the individual terrorist suggests an intriguing and somewhat unorthodox portrait. (19) The following three general characteristics summarize his observations: 1. To operate effectively as a terrorist, one must have a high moral sense, truly abhor murder, and enter upon violence with regret. 2. Pure opportunism, murder without ideology and without restraint leads to crime, not political change. 3. The ideal assassin does not so much kill as consciously execute his victim, who may not be his major target.

Horowitz, although not providing a systematic profile of the individual terrorist, identifies the following useful hypotheses where further social-behavioral research may provide additional knowledge: (20) 1. A terrorist is a person engaged in politics who makes little, if any, distinction between strategy and tactics on the one hand and principles on the other. 2. A terrorist is prepared to surrender his own life for a cause considered transcendant in value. 3. A terrorist is a person who possesses both a self-fulfilling prophetic element and a self-destructive element. 4. A terrorist is a person for whom all events are volitional and none are determined. 5. A terrorist is young, most often of a middle-class family background, usually male, and economically marginal. 6. A terrorist performs his duties as an avocation. 7. The terrorist distinguishes himself from the casual homicide in several crucial respects: he murders systematically rather than at random; he is symbolic rather than passionate (that is, he is concerned with scoring political points rather than responding to personal provocation); his actions are usually well planned rather than spontaneous. 8. The terrorist by definition does not distinguish between coercion and terrorism because he lacks access to the coercive mechanisms of the state. 9. A terrorist, through the act of violence, advertises and dramatizes a wider discontent. 10. A terrorist believes the act of violence will encourage the uncommitted public to withdraw support from the regime, and hence make wider revolutionary acts possible by weakening the resolve of the opposition. 11. A terrorist may direct his activities against the leadership of the opposition by assassinating presidents and political leaders; such terrorists usually tend to function alone in the service of an often poorly defined ideology rather than within a political movement. 12. A terrorist does not have a particularly well defined ideological persuasion.

As stated earlier, Horowitz's portrait of a modern political terrorist, though not very systematic and even contradictory in places, does provide a useful checklist for further investigation.

I began this paper with the psychology of the individual and his resistance to societal oppression and controls. My discussion, however, has been in terms of group activity. This apparent anomaly may cause the reader to wonder about the thrust of my reasoning. Simply stated, all frustration and resistance fundamentally are highly individual feelings or experiences, but for them to be meaningful, they need to be operationalized. Group activity and organization make this transition possible and provide the distinction between anti-social acts and political resistance.

Political terrorism occurs as the result of a conscious decision by ideologically inspired groups to strike back at what their members may perceive as "unjust" within a given society or polity. The answers to contemporary political terrorism, therefore, would have to be found within this larger social, economic, political, and psychological context.

NOTES

(1) See: Christopher Dobson, *Black September: Its Short Violent History*, New York: Macmillan Publishing Co., Inc., 1974, pp. 6-8.

(2) See: Donald Green, *The Incidence of Terror during the French Revolution*, Cambridge, Mass.: Harvard University Press, 1935, and George LeFebvre, *The French Revolution from its Origins to 1793*, London: Routledge and Kegan Paul, 1965.

(3) David Fromkin, "The Strategy of Terrorism," *Foreign Affairs*,Vol. 53, No. 4, July 1975, pp. 684-685.

(4) *Fifth United Nations Congress on Prevention of Crime and the Treatment of Offenders* — working paper on "Changes in Forms and Dimensions of Criminality — Transnational and National," No. A/CONF. 56/3 (English), August 19, 1975, p. 37.

(5) Reprinted in Robert Moss, *Urban Guerrilla Warfare*, London: International Institute for Strategic Studies, 1971.

(6) Carlos Marighella, *Minimanual of the Urban Guerilla, Ibid.*

(7) Jay Mallin, *Terror and Urban Guerrillas*, Coral Gables, Fla.: University of Miami Press, 1971, p.9.

(8) *Ibid.*, p. 46.

(9) Moss, supra note 5, p. 210.

(10) Harry Eckstein, *International War*, New York: Free Press, 1964, p. 83.

(11) J. Bowyer Bell, *The Myth of the Guerrilla*, New York: Knopf, 1971, p. 80.

(12) Moss, supra note 5, p. 133.

(13) Andrew Scott, *Insurgency*, Chapel Hill: University of North Carolina Press, 1970, p. 311.

(14) David Fromkin, supra note 3, p. 686.

(15) For a detailed discussion of Kautilya's ideas see: R. Shamasastry (tr.), *Kautilya's Arthasastra*, Mysore, 1951, Books I & IV. A shorter analysis is available in T. N. Ramaswamy, *Essentials of Indian Statecraft — Kautilya's Arthasastra for Contemporary Readers*, New York: Asia Publishing House, 1962, pp. 5-16.

(16) T. N. Ramaswamy, supra note 15, p. 8.

(17) For a detailed historical perspective on this subject, see: Max Nomad, *Aspects of Revolt*, New York: The Noonday Press, 1959.

(18) Much has been made of these two types in Dobson, supra note 1, and the working papers of the *Fifth United Nations Congress on Prevention of Crime and the Treatment of Offenders*, Geneva: August 1975, (Mimeo).

(19) See: J. Bowyer Bell, "Assassination in International Politics," *International Studies Quarterly*, 16:1, March 1972, pp. 78-80.

(20) Irving L. Horowitz, "Political Terrorism and State Power," *Political and Military Sociology*, Spring 1973, pp. 148-150.

Jordan J. Paust:
A Definitional Focus

It is not the purpose here to provide an in-depth analysis of definitional criteria, but it is nevertheless felt that the absence of a working definition of terrorism could lead to the sort of confusion or ambiguity carried on too often in the General Assembly or the literature. Here, the focus on definitional criteria is not founded on the misconceptions that groups of words will dictate decisions (1) or that rules can protect us from ourselves; nor is it based on a deference to a "mechanical arrogance of abstractions." (2) It lies rather in the view that the impossibility of absolute precision does not necessarily render complete confusion desirable, (3) and that a definition can be extremely useful to guide decision-makers to relevant policy, or at least to a comprehensive consideration of varying claims to authority in varying contexts of terroristic process with greater insight into context, greater rationality in choice, greater overall policy realization, and greater efficacy during the process of authoritative response. (4)

DEFINITIONAL CRITERIA

The Secretary-General's report on international terrorism reflects the need for a definitional approach by attempting to articulate certain basic definitional components. (5) These include: 1. terror outcome, 2. instrumental or "immediate" victims, 3. primary targets ("population" or "broad groups" and others), 4. violence, and 5. political purpose.

The 1937 Convention on Terrorism and subsequently scholars nave identified other components of the process of terrorism. (6) The 1937 Convention emphasized: 1. willful or intentional act, 2. terror purpose ("calculated to create a state of terror in the minds of the primary target"), 3. an outcome of death, grievous bodily harm or loss of liberty to a set of instrumental targets (e.g., heads of state, their families, public servants), 4. an outcome of damage to or destruction of public property as instrumental targets, and 5. acts "calculated to endanger the lives of the members of the public." These criteria are sometimes helpful and sometimes far less so. What seems lacking in each approach is sufficient awareness of different phases of the process of terrorism. Awareness of the process of terrorism can allow greater attention to components of a definition that, taken together, will more usefully mirror the process of terrorism and provide a descriptive approach to definition.

PHASES OF THE TERRORISTIC PROCESS

In short, one must seek to understand what is happening to whom, where, when, how, why and with what outcomes and effects. Or, as some of us (of the (McDougal-Lasswell jurisprudential orientation) prefer to state in thinking about terrorism and its legal permissibility or impermissibility, it is highly desirable to have the sort of comprehensive awareness of the process of terrorism obtained by consideration of the following factors: 1. The types of *participants* engaged in the terroristic process as precipitators, instrumental targets, primary targets, spillover victims, and so forth, 2. The *objectives* of the participants and other relevant subjectivities (identifications, demands, expectations), 3. The *situations* of actual interaction (i.e., territorial, temporal and institutional arenas), 4. The types of *resources* (base values) at the disposal of each type of participant, including analysis of their value positions (e.g., positions of power, well-being, wealth, respect, enlightenment, skill, affection, and rectitude), 5. The particular tactics or *strategies* of terror utilized (e.g., assassination, taking of hostages, bombings, injury to property, aircraft hijacking), 6. The *outcomes* of the terroristic process, and 7. The *effects* of terroristic process upon the serving of all relevant legal policies. (7) Such policies can be overly generalized in terms of world public order values and those of human dignity, as has been recognized in the U.N. Charter and elsewhere. (8)

This comprehensive approach to the problem of terrorism will most definitely invoke consideration of the varied types of participants and situations as well as certain general categories of terrorism such as state terrorism, institutionalized terror, private terrorism, supra-national ideologic terrorism, etc. Moreover, it is also necessary to consider the varied types of expectation, demand, and aspiration in a multi-ideologic world, particularly when seeking to identify empirically the patterns of authority and control (or practice) which do, and will, combine as "law" in social process.

Another important recognition that is necessary for a rational discussion is that a description of terrorism as terrorism does *not* answer the legal question: is this form of terrorism illegal? Just because we identify a particular act or process as "terroristic" does not provide an answer to the more important question of whether or not the particular conduct and results are legally permissible. For example, the problems inherent in defining once and for all the concept of "aggression" have little to do with the type of definition of terrorism. "Aggression" is impermissible per se; it is the conclusion of illegality which attaches to certain conduct and results. Terrorism, however, may be permissible or impermissible, depending upon the actual features of context and whether it serves or thwarts the legal policies at stake in any given interaction. Consequently, entirely different definitional needs are involved, posing two separate intellectual tasks: description of process and decision as to permissibility.

Moreover, we cannot realistically approach this question by trying to define away certain types of terrorism as if they did not exist; this particular approach (to define nothing) is most unhelpful. To meet the need, I offer a definitional approach that is objective. It does not "answer" the question of permissibility, nor does it advance any particular politicized preference. Instead, it is useful for defining the process of terrorism that can occur in any setting, with any underlying motive, against any target, etc. Much of the reasoning behind the need for this approach has already been publicized (and published); however, in any comprehensive focus upon the terroristic process, the following factors should be carefully considered: 1. precipitators, 2. perspectives, 3. acts involving the threat or use of violence, 4. instrumental targets (human and non-human), 5. primary targets and secondary targets, 6. incidental or spill-over victims, and 7. the result of such terror which coerces the primary target into a given behavior or attitude.

Terrorism is therefore viewed as a form of violent strategy, a form of coercion utilized to alter the freedom of choice of others. Terrorism, thus defined, involves the intentional use of violence or the threat of violence by the precipitator(s) against an instrumental target in order to communicate to a primary target a threat of future violence. The object is to use intense fear or anxiety to coerce the primary target into behavior or to mold its attitudes in connection with a demanded power (political) outcome.

In a specific context the instrumental and primary targets could well be the same person or group. Also, terror can be caused by an unintended act, but the community does not seem to perceive such activity as "terrorism"; nor does it seek to regulate terror caused by conduct which does not include intense coercion or acts and threats of violence. Additionally, the instrumental target need not be a person; attacks on power stations, for example, can produce a terror outcome in the civilian population of the community dependent upon the station for electricity.

There must be a terror outcome, or the process could hardly be labeled as terrorism. There are fine lines for juridicial distinction to be made between fear and intense fear outcomes, although in many cases the type of strategy could well be prohibited under different normative provisions of the law of war. For example, an attack upon or hijacking of a civil aircraft in the zone of armed conflict which produces no terror outcome among the crew, passengers, or others may nevertheless violate prohibitions against attacks upon noncombatants or the taking of hostages as well as new international treaty norms governing hijacking. These kinds of attacks cannot properly be referred to as terrorism (perhaps attempted terrorism in some cases), and present definitions which refer merely to "acts of violence," "repressive acts," "violent acts of a criminal nature" (full of circuitous ambiguity per se), and "a heinous act of barbarism" are strikingly incomplete. Terrorism can also be precipitated by governments, groups, or individuals; consequently, any exclusion of one or more sets of precipitators from the definitional framework is highly unrealistic. Equally unrealistic are definitional criteria which refer to "systematic" uses of violence; terrorism can occur at an instant and by one act. Indeed, the law of war already makes no distinction between singular or systematic terroristic processes, governmental or nongovernmental precipitations, or governmental and nongovernmental targets. If distinctions in permissibility result, it is usually the result of a conscious policy choice and not a definitional exclusion.

Similarly unhelpful definitional criteria include: "unjust" activity, atrocious conduct, arbitrariness, irrationality, indiscrimination, selectivity and unexpectedness.

In this regard, it may be helpful to consider some overly broad approaches to definition in legal prescription. One approach has been taken by the State of Texas. In 1973 the Texas legislature enacted an offense of "Terroristic Threat" to punish those who threaten to commit

> any offense involving violence to any person or property with intent to 1. cause a reaction of any type to this threat by an official or volunteer agency organized to deal with emergencies; 2. place any person in fear of imminent serious bodily injury; or 3. prevent or interrupt the occupation or use of a building; room; place of assembly; place to which the public has access; place of employment or occupation; aircraft; automobile, or other form of conveyance; or other public place. (9)

It seems most curious, however, that such offenses are punishable merely as a misdemeanor, (10) and that terror outcome is not required for "terroristic threat." Only subsection two requires some production of fear outcome; the other subsections merely require an official or volunteer agency "reaction" or the prevention of enjoyment of public facilities. Perhaps this approach to definition lends itself more fairly to the penalty, since the possibilities of violative conduct are very broad and could be nearly innocuous in some cases (as a phone threat to punch the Mayor of Houston in the nose), but the legislative approach is far too vague and broad for useful guidance in approaches to definition or sanction. If terrorism is meaningfully to survive as a separate offense, there must be some awareness of the need for terror outcome — outcome which is the primary factor separating terrorism from more "normal" acts of murder, assault, etc. It cannot be overemphasized that definitional approaches which relate merely to "acts of violence," the "threat or use of violence," "repressive acts," and similar categoriza-tions (11) are strikingly incomplete and unhelpful in terms of meaning and effective guidance for decision. Further, such approaches ignore the critical need for a focus upon the use of intense fear or anxiety for coercion of a primary target into behavior or attitudinal patterns sought in connection with a demanded power outcome. Such approaches, blind as they are to the terror process, will be unhelpful in guiding us to realistic and effective responses to terrorism. A more rational approach to solution, with greater chance for international adoption, would utilize a definitional approach like the one suggested in a paper on private sanction measures and would make terroristic threat, with terror outcome, punishable as a felony.

A brief comparison of foreign legislation in this area may also highlight certain points made previously. In the vast majority of cases, foreign law does not seek to create a new, separate crime of terrorism. In other cases, it seems sufficient for foreign governments to expand censorship and detention powers under an anti-terror/anti-subversion label without a new crime of terrorism. Most governments utilize martial law powers, expand military jurisdiction, create new security courts or procedures, or operate by police or military decree on an ad hoc basis. These approaches are usually overly broad and would be unconstitutional if adopted in the United States. Also, several states have adopted sweeping measures for detention, search, media control, and other powers in the name of anti-terror without defining terrorism or with such a broad definition as to include almost any anti-government utterance or conduct. (12)

Whenever an attempt is made to define terrorism under foreign law, the definitional approach is too broad for U.S. purposes (i.e., they over regulate and/or proscribe in an unconstitutionally vague manner). The Czechoslovakian Penal Code takes the simple approach by proscribing the "terrorizing" of another person. (13) Although presumably more specific than most (since a "terrorizing" outcome or effect would seem to be required), this approach may be overly broad. It does not seem conditioned by requirements of "intentional" activity or violent acts (i.e., unintentional conduct and conduct or threats of conduct of a non-violent nature may also be prohibited, especially in view of communist theories of "objective" crime which do not adhere to Western mens rea requirements). What seems to be a Czechoslovakian requirement of terror outcome or effect is nearly mirrored in all other definitional attempts with the exception of the Soviet Union. However, the need for "terror" outcome or effect has been diluted. What is required for "terrorism" in these countries is some threat or state of "alarm, fear or terror." (14) In my opinion, a state of public "alarm" or "fear" not equated with intense fear or terror should not be regulated under a "terrorism" label. Thus, these provisions are too broad and may well be constitutionally suspect if adopted in the United States. The Soviet penal provision is very broad; it does not require any fear, alarm, or terror outcome. (15)

Most definitional approaches are also more restrictive than the proposal in Annex A with regard to the types of conduct utilized to produce the proscribed public or private alarm. (16) They seem needlessly restrictive in focus. A requirement of a threat or use of violence would seem sufficient to cover all delimiting factors, with one possible exception. For example, typical lists of means utilized to produce public alarm include: use of weapons, explosives, incendiary materials, poisonous gases, toxins, infectuous microbe agents, and other devices capable of harming the public. (17) All of these seem covered by the "threat or use of violence" factor in Annex A, and the broader phrase seems preferable so as not to exclude any particular mode not in a list approach. What might cause difficulty, however, is the question whether a "threat or use of violence" includes the use of poison and microbes. I think it does, (18) and to be safe, the phrase, "or threat or use of poisons or microbes," could be added.

With regard to the "threat" versus "attempt" problem considered previously, each foreign definitional approach includes prohibitions of threat or is sufficiently broad to include any "act" (i.e., threat, attempt, etc.) which produces prohibited outcomes. The only exception is the U.S.S.R. Its penal code requires a "killing" or "grave bodily injury," thus presumably excluding attempts to kill or threats to kill. (19) It should also be noted that only three states limit their definitional approach by some reference to the political objectives of the terrorists, although many states without a definition seem aware of the need to differentiate between political terrorism and non-political terrorism like that of the Mafia. Nicaragua and Mexico require a purpose to disturb the public order, cause unrest in the land (Nicaragua), attempt to damage the authority of the state (Mexico), or to pressure the authorities to make a decision (Mexico). (20) The U.S.S.R. requires a "purpose of subverting or weakening the Soviet regime." (21) Again, it seems very useful to distinguish between political and non-political motivation, but the specific "political" effects detailed by Mexico, Nicaragua and the U.S.S.R. would not need to be copied or listed in any U.S. legislation. Finally, it is simply noted that the most comprehensive approach toward definition is that of the Mexico Penal Code; it contains most of the elements of a definitional focus that this author finds useful, (22) but it is still too broad in its prohibition of "alarm" and "fear" producing acts.

At the other extreme are attempts to define away certain forms of state or insurgent terrorism as if they did not exist.

Underlying most of the efforts to exclude certain forms of terrorism from community review by definitional exercise may be attempts by claimants or sympathizers to place their preferred types of terrorism in a class of "non-terrorism" which, presumably, would remain permissible for all time in all forms, regardless of consequences. Some seek a definitional exclusion of claims in favor of the use of terror against colonial regimes during a people's quest for self-determination or against fascist and totalitarian regimes. However, definitional exclusion does not seem likely to contribute to efforts to exclude entire contexts of social violence from legal regulation, as in the unsuccessful attempts to exclude: situations of violence against "aggressors," struggles of self-determination, violence against "oppressors," and "guerrilla wars." (23)

Many of these efforts appear to stem from an unnecessary confusion about questions concerning the permissibility of an initiation of armed struggle and the types of tactics used during an armed struggle. (24) The strategy of an argument involving permissibility is: the law is against us; it might change; so why don't we wait? However, what *is* the state of the law? Are there shared legal policies at stake which could guide decisions in cases of self-determinative terror (25) or in cases of terror against colonial, fascist and/or totalitarian regimes? Naturally certain acts of state and private terrorism cannot be treated in the same way, but how shall we deal with each of them? Why is it so difficult for us to face the problem of terrorism in guerrilla warfare (which most definitely is *not* always a matter of "internal" concern or effect), particularly when Article 33 of the 1949 Geneva Convention on Civilians flatly states that terrorism is prohibited? (26) I disagree that a clear-cut separation of terrorism and "guerrilla activities" is always possible or desirable. (27) It is only too evident that states, state-guerrillas, belligerent-guerrillas, insurgent-guerrillas, or other private groups or persons can make use of terroristic strategy. Accordingly, categories such as "guerrilla" or "self-determination" should not be used simplistically to exclude from consideration the various types of terrorist strategy that can occur within or with such forms of social interaction. We should distinguish situations, but we should not exclude them at the outset of our inquiry by definitional exercise as, for example, in investigating the intertwined aspects of a variety of labels and events (e.g., "guerrilla," state terrorism, self-determination, aircraft hijacking, "oppression," diplomatic assassination or kidnapping, etc.) in connection with terrorism and the Middle East conflict. (28)

NOTES

(1) See: McDougal and F. Feliciano: *Law and Minimum World Public Order*, 1961, pp. 56-57, 62-63, 103, 119, 148-58.
(2) *Id.* at 57, n. 136.
(3) *Id.*, p. 62. Also see: F. Cohen, "Transcendental Nonsense and the Functional Approach," 34 *Columbia Law Review* Vol. 809, 1935.
(4) *Id.*, pp. 57, 62-63, 102, 119, 148-58. Increased complexity and interdependence have antiquated the reliance on multifarious national interpretations of what policies and other factors are involved in the process of international terrorism. They have also made irrelevant the confusion now evident in the international community, which seems to have resulted from a lack of definitional framework in recent proposals. A comprehensive awareness of fact and legal policies at stake, instead provides more realistic attention both to terrorism as a process of coercion and to appropriate responses to terrorism. See: J. Paust, "Responses to Terrorism: A Prologue to Decision Concerning Measures of Sanction," *Stanford Journal of International Studies*, Vol. 12, 1977, and J. Paust, "A Survey of Possible Legal Responses to International Terrorism: Prevention, Punishment and Cooperative Action," *Georgia Journal of International and Comparative Law*, Vol. 5, No. 431, 1975.
(5) See: 1972 U.S. Doc. A/C.6/418, pp. 6-7.
(6) Another factor which seemed to apply to all acts of terrorism was a requirement that acts be "directed against a State" (which most likely was designed to exclude terrorization by governments of their own people and other incidents involving non-state targets). See also: 1972 U.N. Doc. A/C. 6/418, pp. 6-7, 10-16, 39 n.1. A survey of several definitional components can be found in Hutchinson, "The Concept of Revolutionary Terrorism," *Journal of Conflict Resolution*, Vol. 16, 1972, p. 383 [hereinafter cited as Hutchinson]. Factors identified by Hutchinson include: 1. international conduct, 2. terror purpose, 3. "political" purpose, 4. violent conduct (act or threat), and 5. terror outcome (production of intense fear or anxiety). Other factors identified by Hutchinson which the present author finds marginally useful include: 1. "systematic" use or "consistent pattern," 2. atrocious or shocking conduct, 3. arbitrariness, 4. selectivity of targets, 5. indiscriminate affection of targets, 6. irrationality, and 7. immoral or "unjust" activity. In a study on political violence, Eugene Walter describes the process of terrorism as involving three main elements: 1. an

act or threat of violence, 2. an emotional outcome, and
3. production of "social effects." He also identifies three types
of participants: source, victim, and targets. See: E. Walter:
Terror and Resistance, 1969: pp. 5, 7-11.

(7) For an explanation of the utility of these seven factors,
see: McDougal and Feliciano: *Law and Minimum World Public
Order*, 1961; Lasswell and McDougal, "Criteria for a Theory
about Law," *Southern California Law Review*, Vol. 44, 1971,
p. 362; J. N. Moore: "Prolegomenon to the Jurisprudence of
Myres McDougal and Harold Lasswell," *Virginia Law Review*,
Vol. 54, 1968, p. 662. A recent use of such phase analysis
categories, to organize the process of coercion initiated through
use of the Arab "oil weapon," appears in Paust and Blaustein,
"The Arab Oil Weapon — A Threat to International Peace,"
American Journal of International Law, Vol. 68, 1974, p. 410.

(8) See also: M. McDougal: "Human Rights and World Public
Order: Principles of Content and Procedure for Clarifying General
Community Policies," *Virginia Journal of International Law*,
Vol. 14, 1974, p. 387; J. J. Paust: "Human Rights and the
Ninth Amendment: A Form of Guarantee," *Cornell Law Review*,
Vol. 60, 1975, p. 231.

(9) Texas Penal Code, Section 22.07(a), effective Jan. 1,
1974.

(10) *Id.*, Section 22.07(b).

(11) Also see: Nicaragua Penal Code, Article 499(a), (b) and
(d), making a person who possesses tear gas or who *threatens*
"to harm" persons or organizations by mail, phone or other
media a "terrorist criminal"; U.S.S.R. Penal Code, Special Part,
Chapter One (Crimes against the State), Article 66 ("Terrorist
Act"), killing or causing grave bodily injury to authority figures
"for the purpose of subverting or weakening the Soviet regime,"
and Article 67, killing or causing grave bodily injury to a
representative of a foreign state "for the purpose of provoking
war or international complications."

(12) See: laws and decrees re: Brazil (Decree Law No. 898,
Sept. 1969, art. 28), Chile, Costa Rica (Title XVII, art. 372),
France, Italy, Federal Republic of Germany, South Africa, Spain,
United Kingdom. Many have antiterrorist decrees, statutes and
acts *without* a definition of terrorism. *But see:* Spanish Penal
Code, Art. 261 ("with the intention of terrorizing the
inhabitants . . .").

(13) Penal Code, Sections 93/94.

(14) El Salvador Criminal Code, art. 400 (utilizing weapons,
explosives, etc.); Austria Penal Code, art. 99 (threat with intent

to create "fear and alarm"); Bolivia Penal Code, Bk. II, Title 1, Chapt. 3, art. 133 ("intimidate or terrorize . . . stir up uprisings and disorders . . . raise shouts of alarm . . ."); Lebanon Penal Code, Art. 314 ("all deeds the objective of which is to create a state of alarm" committed with use of certain weapons, toxins, etc.); Mexico Penal Code, Chpt. VI (alarm, fear or terror by violent means, certain weapons, toxins, etc.); and Nicaragua Penal Code, Art. 499 (for the purpose of disturbing public order, or sowing or causing unrest). See also: Canada Penal Code (crime of "intimidation").

(15) U.S.S.R. Penal Code, special Part, Chapter 1, art. 66. Furthermore, the restrictive focus on state or public figures as targets is nearly outside the scope of this paper — no attention is paid to attacks on property or to the vast majority of other non-protected persons.

(16) Not included here are: Austria, Bolivia, Czechoslovakia and the U.S.S.R.

(17) Included here are: Lebanon, Mexico, Nicaragua and El Salvador.

(18) Also see: Mexico Penal Code, Chapter VI ("any *other* violent means," emphasis added).

(19) Even if another provision regulates attempts to violate Article 66 of the Penal Code, Special Part, Chapter 1, it would appear that a "threat" not amounting to an actual attempt to kill or injure would not be proscribed.

(20) See: supra note 14.

(21) See: supra note 19.

(22) *Compare* the Mexican Penal Code provision *with* definitional factors identified in J. Paust, "Some Thoughts on 'Preliminary Thoughts' on Terrorism," *American Journal of International Law*, Vol. 68, 1974, p. 502 and in this paper.

(23) For a more detailed analysis and explanation, see: Paust: "Terrorism and the International Law of War," *Milwaukee Law Review*, Vol. 64, 1974, p. 1. It should be emphasized that legal prohibition of specific terroristic strategies will not in any way prohibit a right to engage in permissible violence to promote self-determination, to oppose "aggression," or to wage "guerrilla" warfare. Professor De Visscher sets out an incomplete list of relevant policies for detailed consideration of the permissibility of initiations of armed violence to ensure self-determination. In addition to Article 51 of the Charter, Articles 1 and 2(4) are also relevant, as is the authoritative interpretation of Article 2 found in the U.N. General Assembly Declaration on Principles of International Law Concerning Friendly Relations and Co-

operation among States in Accordance with the Charter of the United Nations (Res. 2625, 25 U.N. GAOR, Supp. 18 at 122-124, 1970, U.N. Doc. A/8028.

See also: Paust & Blaustein: "War Crimes Jurisdiction and Due Process: A Case Study of Bangladesh," 1974, supra note 4; W. M. Reisman: Nullity and Revision, 1971; and E. Suziki: *Self-Determination and World Public Order: Community Response to Group Formation*, unpublished J.S.D. thesis, 1974, Yale Law School.

(24) See: Paust: "Terrorism," supra note 23.

(25) It should be noted that a basic incompatibility exists between terror and self-determination. See: supra note 9.

(26) 75 U.N.T.S. 287. See also: supra note 9.

(27) See: supra note 23; Paust, "Law in a Guerrilla Conflict: Myths, Norms and Human Rights," *Israel Yearbook on Human Rights*, Vol. 3, 1973, p. 39.

(28) See: Symposium: "International Terrorism in the Middle East," *Akron Law Review*, Vol. 7, 1974.

Robert A. Friedlander:
The Origins of International Terrorism

The dramatic rise of international terrorism during the past decade and its concomitant political and psychological impact have produced a contemporary crisis of near global proportions. Recent terrorist activities have not just been limited to a specific number of countries, nor have they been characteristic of a particular region or the resulting manifestation of notoriously oppressive regimes. The terrorist phenomenon, as reflected almost daily in the news media, is worldwide, and its innocent victims can be found among every class and nationality. Although a genuine and continuing threat to world public order exists, international opinion is deeply divided as to the cause of terrorism and is distressingly uncertain as to its remedy.(1)

Disagreement within the world community regarding the nature of the threat presented and the failure to agree upon effective remedial action results in part from confusion over both the origins and the composition of international terrorism. It has become commonplace to assert that a precise definition is lacking and that a working model has yet to be developed.(2) Nevertheless, by placing terror-violence in its proper legal and historical context, a clearer and more effective perspective can be attained. The purpose of this paper, therefore, is neither to propose solutions nor to assess responsibility, but merely to adhere to the wry dictum of a noted twentieth-century philosopher that "[t]hose who cannot remember the past are condemned to repeat it."(3)

The word, "Terrorism," derives from the era of the French Revolution and the Jacobin dictatorship which used terror as an instrument of political repression and social control.(4) The so-called Reign of Terror during the early 1790s was thus a state-directed activity, domestic in inspiration and in execution.(5) Not until the Revolution was exported to the rest of Europe by means of military conquest did the twin policies of intimidation and retribution become international in scope. Injuries inflicted as a matter of public policy by other European governments, whatever their politics upon local populations, proved to be, regretably, among the most enduring of Revolutionary legacies.(6)

Terrorism, like the Revolution, has been cast in both a domestic and international mold. Moreover, the Jacobin terror relied on the exercise of governmental power rather than upon the individual act. State terrorism, therefore, was and is an integral part of the terrorist concept,(7) although both the individual terrorist and group activists predate the Revolutionary Era. Group terrorism can be traced back to the end of the Middle Ages; the solitary terrorist appeared with the rise of the nation-state.

As a political weapon, terrorism was first extensively utilized during the twelfth and thirteenth centuries by a secret medieval dissident Islamic religious order, popularly known as the *Assassins.* The term itself is derived from the Arabic and translates literally as "hashish-eater" or "one addicted to hashish."(8) This group of sectarian Moslem fanatics, who often acted under the influence of intoxicating drugs, was employed by its spiritual leaders to spread terror in the form of violence and murder among prominent Christians and other religious enemies. These zealots were, in effect, the first terrorist armed bands, and their fearsome activities entered European folklore by way of the returning Crusaders and the writings of Marco Polo. Ultimately, they were destroyed by the Mongol invaders, but their use of murder as a political instrument provided a grim inheritance for the modern world.(9)

It has become almost an historical truism to say that state violence when directed against the individual engenders a like response. Organized group action using terrorist means for political ends against selected targets on a randomized basis also had its origins in the Revolutionary Era. The harsh Napoleonic invasion of the Spanish Peninsula spawned a popular retributative movement which in turn introduced a new concept of modern warfare—the guerrilla.(10) "A guerrilla war is a people's war," proclaimed Che Guevara in the mid-twentieth century,(11) and this definition applies to the origins of spontaneous armed protest through selective violence. Attacks mounted by the Spanish *guerrillas* against the French occupation army were

tained by British financial and military aid, thereby in-
ternationalizing the indigenous counter-terror movement. The Penin-
sular War, as it came to be called, provided in tactics, strategy, and
values an instructive model for future revolutionary arenas.(12)

The terrorist, acting alone, motivated by personal or political
passion, is not an unfamiliar figure in recorded history. Murder and
violence as methods for effecting radical change were common to the
ancient world,(13) but the rise of the nation-state and the theory of absolute sovereignty added a new dimension to the relations of men and
society. Centralization of political structures during the formative
period of the national state was directly linked to the extension of
monarchical power at the expense of competing institutions, particularly the Church. Since sixteenth and seventeenth century mon-
archs by virtue of their royal office exercised international authority
as well as national leadership, the growth of sovereign perogatives effectively undermined prevailing institutional relationships and shook
the foundation of post-Reformation society. Unleashed by the forces of
centralized government, the new economic and political dynamism had
its greatest effect upon religious orthodoxy and social order. Protest
by both the defenders of reaction and the proponents of extremist
reform was quickly forthcoming, and one result was a philosophic
justification for individualized attacks against the monarch himself as
the visible symbol of the new statism.

Assassination, utilized as both an ideological statement and a
political weapon, long predates the politicization of terror-violence in
the modern world. "Among the Florentines," writes historian Carl
Burckhardt, "tyrannicide was a practice universally accepted and approved."(14) By the late sixteenth century the doctrine of tyrannicide
was openly expounded as the legal and moral rationale for private
resistance to sovereign authority and the abuse of public power. The
most influential opponent of political despotism was the Jesuit
scholar, Juan de Mariana whose study *De Regis Institutione* (1599)
was officially banned and burned by French authorities.(15) A half-
century later the British poet and political theorist, John Milton,
raised the defense of tyrannicide to justify the deposition and
execution of Charles I. According to Milton, "[t]yrannicide, that is the
killing of a tyrant, is not only lawful, but also laudable."(16)

The legal legacy of the tyrannicide doctrine can be found in the
protections granted to chiefs-of-state beginning in the mid-nineteenth
century. The rapid growth of a European-wide revolutionary tradition
in the decades following the Congress of Vienna influenced Western
European governments to modify their position on granting asylum to
offenders of political crimes.(17) The *attentat* clause, resulting from an
attempt upon the life of the French Emperor Napoleon III, and later

broadened as a result of the assassination of the American President James Garfield, placed a reservation upon the so-called political offense exception in international law for the purpose of preserving societal order.(18) Murder of a head of state or any members of his family was designated as a common crime, and this concept has been incorporated into Article 3 of the 1957 European Convention on Extradition.(19) Political assassination became formally associated with terrorist activities through the Geneva Convention on Terrorism of 1937.(20)

Equating an act of insurrection, rebellion, or political protest, however misguided, with the idea of terror-violence has produced more confusion than clarification. The creation of a specially protected class of governmental officials has had the effect of legitimizing all regimes under the protective cover of anti-terrorist statutes. The real issue is how to develop a workable legal standard that will distinguish between permissable revolutionary activity and prohibited criminality in public international law.

For centuries pirates have been declared *hostis humani generis* (common enemies of humanity), and piracy has long been designated as "an offense against the law of nations."(21) Universal jurisdiction over captured offenders is granted to all states, as pirates are held in fact to be outlaws before the world.(22) From the Paris Declaration of 1856 to the Geneva Convention of 1958, numerous treaties and agreements have dealt more or less effectively with acts of terror-violence on the high seas. By way of analogy, one may well ask whether the rash of aerial highjackings during the past fifteen years, beginning with the first commercial plane commandeered to Cuba in 1961, can be designated as aerial piracy, and if so, do the same penalties apply? As with most international legal questions, the answers are at best tentative. Many legal scholars and commentators have adopted the term, "air piracy", and relate it, directly or indirectly, to international terrorism.(23) Nonetheless, any application of sanctions based upon the law of piracy is a matter of considerable debate, and the existence of universal norms is open to question. To quote Professor McWhinney: "What the record indicates is. . . .[a] default of any really concerted energetic international control action. . . ."(24)

The uncertain relationship of piracy and skyjacking to international terrorism is paralleled by the historic confusion among the legal community as to the nature of political crimes. The landmark British case dealing with the subject, *In Re Castioni* (1890), remains with some modification the contemporary British standard. In order for the offender not to be subject to an extradition request, the crime in question must have occurred during a political revolt or disturbance and formed part of, or have been incidental to, that same revolt or disturbance.(25) Canada, on the other hand, has adopted a more rigorous approach. Murder, even if for an arguably political cause, is deemed to be a common crime, and the elements of a political act are very narrowly drawn, so that mere political considerations will not provide a valid excusing condition.(26) The United States only recognizes a political offense exception to the extradition request of another government if there is in force a specific extradition treaty or convention with the requesting state which allows for that exemption.(27) The prevailing view in civil law countries is best summed up by the holding of the Chilean Supreme Court that "the principles of public international law. . .do not admit that any ordinary crime is converted into a political one solely because of its ultimate objectives."(28)

One distinguished scholar proposes a broad definitional approach to political crime—"an act directed against the security of the state."(29) Another suggests that whatever the agreed-upon political standard of the moment, the norm itself is constantly changing.(30) A third seeks to distinguish between a *political* act and a *terrorist* act, arguing that the former is largely *mala prohibita* (a prohibited evil), while the latter is *mala in se* (evil by its very nature).(31) Perhaps the confusion arises from the fundamentally political nature of terror-violence. Whatever the reason, political terrorism is now a global phenomenon identified with the spread of ideological violence which in turn threatens the very existence of a minimum world public order.(32)

Sergei Nechayev wrote in the summer of 1869: "We come from the people, our skins wounded by the present regime. . . We have an entirely negative plan, which no one can modify: utter destruction."(33) Revolutionary terrorism assumed its classic form in nineteenth century Russia with the creation of the *Zemlya i Volya* (Society of Land and Liberty) in 1876 and the *Narodnaya Volya* (People's Will) in 1879. These two groups were in program and in action terror organizations which had for their primary purpose the transformation of Russian society and government by assassination politics. Tyrranicide had once again become a political weapon. Government violence was to be met with popular violence, and terror became an integral part of the Russian societal process.(34) The formation of the Socialist-Revolutionary Party in the last decade of the nineteenth century helped to institutionalize assassination as political protest. The "Basic Theses" of the party program were that terror would not only be a means of disorganizing the Tsarist regime, but would also "serve as a means of propaganda and agitation which will display itself before the eyes of the whole people ... and which will bring alive other revolutionary forces."(35) It likewise brought alive the *Okhrana*

(Tsarist secret police) which unleashed a program of counter-terror that continued until the outbreak of World War I.(36)

Russian revolutionary terror was internal in theory and practice, but it provided both the model and the inspiration for its twentieth century successors, and its protagonists spoke the language of the F.L.N., the I.R.A., and the P.L.O. Kaliayev, the terrorist-hero of Camus' play, *The Just Assassins,* a fictional adaptation of historical events, rationalized that he threw bombs at tyranny and not at humanity. His most fervent wish is "to shed my blood to the last drop, or blaze up like tinder in the flare of an explosion and leave not a shred of me behind." To throw a bomb is in effect to die for an ideal—"that's the only way of proving oneself worthy of it. It's our only justification."(37)

An external manifestation of revolutionary terrorism, utilized as an unofficial instrument of national foreign policy as well as a deadly weapon of political protest, was the Union or Death Society, popularly known as the Black Hand. This was a secret Serbian revolutionary organization whose primary aim was to bring about the union with Serbia of unredeemed Serbian nationals and territory. As was so often the case with revolutionary terror groups, the end justified the means. Transnational assassination would lead the way to the creation of a Greater Serbia by paralyzing Serbian oppressors.(38) The Black Hand also precipitated the coming of the First World War. The assassination of the Austrian Archduke Franz Ferdinand on June 28, 1914, by Gavrilo Princip, a nineteen-year old terrorist trained by the Black Hand, was literally a shot heard around the world.(39) Transnational terror had now been inextricably intertwined with nationalist movements.(40) Princip's shots were more explosive than he ever dreamed. A Greater Serbia would be created by the Treaty of St. Germain (1919) under the name of Yugoslavia, and, ominous for the rest of the twentieth century, self-determination in the guise of national liberation movements would become literally a license to kill.(41)

The role of terrorist as liberationist was soon brought before the English-speaking world by the creation of the Irish Republican Army (I.R.A.) and the outbreak of the Anglo-Irish War following the British general elections of 1918. The Irish revolutionary republican government unleashed a guerrilla campaign of cold-blooded murder, and the British government retaliated in kind.(42) From January 1919 until May 1921, Ireland provided a classic illustration of the U.N. Secretariat's 1972 admonition: "As violence breeds violence, so terrorism begets counter-terrorism, which in turn leads to more terrorism in an ever-increasing spiral."(43) In the case of Ireland, however, terrorism also begat independence.

A recurrence of transnational political violence during the 1930s, dramatized by the twin slaying in Marseilles of King Alexander of Yugoslavia and French Foreign Minister Louis Barthou, along with the assassination of the Austrian Chancellor Englebert Dollfus that same year (1934), resulted in the calling of a conference by the League of Nations to deal with the resurgent problem of international terrorism.(44) The Geneva Conference of 1937 produced two Conventions—one for the Prevention and Repression of Terrorism, and the other for the Creation of an International Criminal Court.(45) However, the two Conventions failed to obtain a sufficient number of ratifications and, consequently, never entered into force. It appears that the December 14, 1973, U.N. General Assembly·Convention on Prevention and Punishment of Crimes against Internationally Protected Persons, Including Diplomatic Agents, will meet a similar fate.(46)

The word, "totalitarianism," has been added to the political lexicon of the twentieth century as a result of Nazi barbarism and Stalinist despotism. These two systems represent state terrorism carried to its furthermost illogical extremity. "If lawfulness is the essence of non-tyrranical government and lawlessness is the essence of tyrrany," writes Hannah Arendt, "then terror is the essence of totalitarian domination."(47) Both Nazi Germany and Soviet Russia during the 1930s and the 1940s practiced genocide and humanicide on a scale unprecedented and unimagined in all human history.(48) The systematic terrorism inflicted by the Nazis upon the inhabitants of conquered European countries was an organized, total terror that would bring about at the end of World War II the formulation of a legal doctrine of crimes against humanity by the Nuremberg Tribunal.(49) Conversely, the Resistance throughout war-torn Europe cannot be termed terrorism in either the legal or the historical sense. In fact, the Resistance was the true heir of the Spanish *guerrillas* who rose against Napoleon I. The Resistance also was the progenitor of the post-1945 guerrilla movements in the Afro-Asian world.(50)

By the end of the World War II, the ideology of terror and the perpetration of terror-violence had become a permanent part of the twentieth century historical process. It remains one of the ironies of history that the first significant outbreak of terrorist activity and state repression following the end of World War II began in Palestine and the Middle East. Jewish terror engendered British counter-terror, and Arab terrorism directed against Jewish targets inevitably followed. The warning of Frantz Fanon, major theorist of the Algerian independence movement, still holds true: "National liberation . . . is always a violent phenomenon."(52)

Not surprisingly, given the sovereignty explosion(53) and prevailing power alignments, there has been almost a total lack of agreement on either the cause or the cure of international terrorism.(54) The cult of violence has become by default a ritual substitute for the use of reason in the political arena. Although there is widespread acknowledgment of the necessity for dealing with political terror-violence,(55) there has been almost no sense of international urgency toward creating viable juridical procedures and implementing effective legal controls.(56) Consequently, despite the lessons of the past and the portents of the future, power politics and ideological militance continue to make a mockery of the law of nations.

NOTES

(1)See: Report of the *Ad Hoc* Committee on International Terrorism, 28 GAOR, Supp. 28, U.N. Doc. A/9028 (1973), especially "annex," pp. 21-34, hereinafter cited as *Ad Hoc* Committee: Report.

(2)Cf. Dugard, "Towards the Definition of International Terrorism," *American Journal of International Law*, Proceedings, Vol. 67, 1973, p. 94; Franck and Lockwood, "Preliminary Thoughts Towards an International Convention on Terrorism," *American Journal of International Law*, Vol. 68, 1974, pp. 69, 72-82; U.N. Secretariat, Measures to Prevent International Terrorism Which Endangers or Takes Innocent Human Lives or Jeopardizes Fundamental Freedoms, and Study of the Underlying Causes of Those Forms of Terrorism and Acts of Violence Which Lie in Misery, Frustration, Grievance and Despair, and Which Cause Some People to Sacrifice Human Lives, Including Their Own, in an Attempt to Effect Radical Changes, U.N. Doc., 1972: A/C.6/418 at 6-10, hereinafter cited as U.N. Secretariat: Draft Study; *Ad Hoc* Committee: Report, supra note 1, p. 5; Hannay, "International Terrorism: The Need for a Fresh Perspective," *International Lawyer*, Vol. 8, 1974, p. 268; Tran-Tam, "Crimes of Terrorism and International Criminal Law," in *A Treatise on International Criminal Law*, edited by Bassiouni and Nanda, 1973, pp. 490-91; Fromkin, "The Strategy of Terrorism," *Foreign Affairs*, Vol. 54, 1975, p. 683. Baxter, "A Skeptical Look at the Concept of Terrorism," *Akron Law Review*, Vol. 7, 1974, p. 380, argues that the very term international terrorism "is imprecise; it is ambiguous; and above all, it serves no operative legal purpose." Singh, "Political Terrorism: An Overview," a paper presented to the 34th Annual Meeting of the Midwest Political Science Association, April 29-May 1, 1976, Chicago, Illinois, demonstrates that terrorism is largely political in motivation, selective in design, and effective in result.

(3)Santayana, *Life of Reason*, 1906, p. 284.

(4)11*Oxford English Dictionary,* Vol. II, 1933, p. 216. This general definition is also provided: "A policy intended to strike with terror those against whom it is adopted; the imployment of methods of intimidation; the fact of terrorizing or condition of being terrorized." *Ibid.* See also: Lefebvre, *The French Revolution,* Vol. II trans. by Stewart and Friguglietti, 1964; Sydenhem: *The French Revolution,* 1965; Thompson, *Napoleon Bonaparte: His Rise and Fall,* 1952; Gottschalk, *The Era of the French Revolution,* 1929; Gershoy, *The French Revolutionn and Napoleon,* New ed., 1964.

(5)Excellent analyses of Jacobin policies and the origins of the Terror can be found in Palmer, *Twelve Who Ruled,* 1941; Brinton; *The Jacobins,* 1930; Brace: *Bordeaux and the Gironde,* Reprint ed., 1968; Sydenham: *The Girondins,* 1961.

(6)See: Lefebvre, *Napoleon,* trans. by Stockhold and Anderson, 1969; Bruun, *Europe and the French Imperium-1799-1814,* 1938; Thompson, supra note 4.

(7)Concern over international terrorism in the form of the unlawful exercise of state power did not abate with the end of World War II and the Nuremberg Trials. See, for example: International Law Commission, Draft Code of Offences against the Peace and Security of Mankind, U.N. Doc. A/CN.4/25 (1950), and Friedmann, "Some Impacts of Social Organization on International Law," *American Journal of International Law,* Vol. 50, 1956, pp. 475, 493-495, which from the vantage point of the 1950s views international terrorism as a governmentally organized activity; Tran-Tam, supra note 2, at 490-500, which is a Saigon-oriented reaction to the Vietnamese conflict of the mid-1960s; and *Ad Hoc* Committee, Report, supra note 1, especially the Algerian draft proposal at pp. 23-25, which maintains that "[t]he motivation of 'individual terrorism' is a subject for study in sociology, psychology, genetics and other contemporary human sciences," whereas state terrorism should be the sole concern of the international community. Taken together, the proposed definitional standards set forth by the participating member states primarily reflected their own national policies and attitudes, particularly with reference to Indochina, the Middle East, and decolonization. A detailed conceptual framework for state terrorism and its practical application can be found in the first three chapters of Walter, *Terror and Resistance,* 1969, while both individual and group action is carefully analyzed through a series of case studies in Crozier, *The Rebels,* 1960, and Moss, *The War for the Cities,* 1972. May, "Terrorism as Strategy and Ecstasy," *Social Research,* Vol. 41, 1974, p. 277, divides terrorism into a "regime of terror" (state) and a "siege of terror" (individual and group).

(8)*Oxford English Dictionary*, supra note 4, at p. 499.

(9)*Ibid.* For a detailed account of these early terrorists, see: Hodgson, *The Order of Assassins*, 1960. Short statements can be found in Von Grunebaum, *Medieval Islam*, 2d ed., 1953, pp. 198-199n, and Hurwood, *Society and the Assassin: A Background Book on Political Murder*, 1970, pp. 1-13, 189-201. One hardly needs to point out that religious dogma combined with political fanaticism has been a potent force during the past three decades in Middle East politics.

(10)Napier, *History of the War in the Peninsula*, 1886, pp. 23 *et seq.* and Carr, *Spain 1808-1939*, 1966, p. 109. Guerrilla is actually the diminutive form of the Spanish word *guerra* and literally translated means "little war."

(11)Guevara, "Guerrilla Warfare: A Method," from *Venceremos!* ed. by Gerassi, 1968 pp. 266, 267.

(12)The literature on guerrilla warfare and its related areas is both extensive and still growing. However, the following provide a general overview: Stone, *Legal Controls of International Conflict*, 1954, pp. 547-570; Schwarzenberger, *International Law and Order*, 1971, pp. 219-236; Crozier, supra note 7; Larteguy, *Les Guerilleros*, 1967; Mallin, *Terror and Urban Guerrillas*, 1971; Oppenheimer, *The Urban Guerrilla*, 1969; Bell, *The Myth of the Guerrilla: Revolutionary Theory and Practice*, 1971; Gann, *Guerrillas in History*, 1971; Singh and Mei, *The Theory and Practice of Modern Guerrilla Warfare*, 1971; Ellis, *A Short History of Guerrilla Warfare*, 1976; Farer, "The Laws of War 25 Years after Nuremberg," *International Conciliation*, Vol. 583, May, 1971; Draper, "The Status of Combatants and the Question of Guerilla Warfare," *British Yearbook of International Law*, Vol. 45, 1971, p. 173; R. Clutterbuck, *Protest and the Urban Guerrilla*, 1973; Moss, supra note 7; Paust, "Law in a Guerrilla Conflict; Myths, Norms and Human Rights," *Israel Yearbook on Human Rights*, Vol. 3, 1973, p. 39. Veuthey, "La Guerilla: Le Probleme du Traitement des Presonniers," *Annales d' Etudes Internationales*, Vol. 3, 1972 pp. 119, 120n observes that other current synonyms for guerrilla warfare include peoples' war, war of resistance, revolutionary war, partisan warfare, war of insurrection, and subversive warfare. Dinstein, "Terrorism and Wars of Liberation Applied to the Arab-Israeli Conflict: An Israeli Perspective," *Israel Yearbook on Human Rights*, Vol. 3, 1973, pp. 78, 85 argues that guerrillas who adhere to the laws of war "have nothing in common with terrorists: they are simply irregular troops."

(13)See particularly: MacDowell, *Athenian Homicide Law in the Age of the Orators*, 1963.

(14)Burckhardt, *The Civilization of the Renaissance in Italy: An Essay*, Vol. 1, Phaidon ed., 1965, p. 38.

(15)Cf. Kutner, "Due Process of Rebellion," *Valpariso Law Review*, Vol. 7, 1972, pp. 5-7; Durant, *The Age of Reason Begins*, 1961, pp. 627-629.

(16)Milton, *Tenure of Kings and Magistrates*,1648. See generally: Jaszi and Lewis, *Against the Tyrant: The Tradition and Theory of Tyrranicide*, 1957; Kutner,supra note 15. However, cf. *contra*, Hobbes, *Leviathan: Or the Matter, Forme and Power of a Commonwealth Ecclesiastical and Civil*, 1651, chap. xviii, which was used as a justification for both Cromwell's Protectorate and Charles II's Restoration. See also: Locke, *Second Treatise on Government*, 1690, chap. xix, who concludes that abuse of power should be punished by forfeiture of sovereign authority. Kadish, "Respect for Life and Regard for Rights in the Criminal Law," *California Law Review*, Vol. 64, 1976, pp. 871, 884-888, in a modern view stresses the "fundamental freedom" of the individual "to preserve himself against aggression," no matter what authority is granted to the state.

(17)Bassiouni, *International Extradition and World Public Order*, 1974, pp. 370-375.

(18)*A Digest of International Law*, ed. by Moore, reprint edition, 1970 Vol. 4, pp. 352-353; Deere, "Political Offenses in the Law and Practice of Extradition," *American Journal of International Law*, Vol. 27, 1933, pp. 247, 252-254; Schultz, "The General Framework of Extradition and Asylum;" Bassiouni and Nanda, supra note 2, p. 316. Rubin, "International Terrorism and International Law," a paper presented to the Ralph Bunche Institute Conference on International Terrorism, June 10, 1976, New York City, raises the issue of "differing traditions and treaty interpretations."

(19)Eur. T.S., No. 24, December 13, 1957, reprinted in Bassiouni and Nanda, supra note 2, pp. 409-416.

(20)See: *infra*, note 45.

(21)Cf. Moore opinion in The Lotus, P.C.I.J., Ser. A, No. 10, 1927, p. 70; Story opinion in *U.S. v. Smith*, 5 Wheat. 153, 160-161, 1820; Brownlie, *Principles of Public International Law*, 2d ed., 1973, pp. 236-244.

(22)Feller, "Jurisdiction over Offenses with a Foreign Element," in Bassiouni and Nanda, supra note 2, at 32-33.

(23)Cf. Joyner, *Aerial Highjacking as an International Crime*, 1974, pp. 1-115; McWhinney, *The Illegal Diversion of Aircraft and International Law*, 1975, pp. 5-6, 111-120; Agrawala, *Aircraft Highjacking and International Law*, 1973, pp. 74-78; Emanuelli, *Les Moyens de Prevention et de Sanction en Cas d'Action Illicite contre l' Aviation Civile Internationale*, 1974, pp. 76-83; Sundberg, "Piracy and Terrorism" in Bassiouni and Nanda, supra note 2, pp. 472-290; Shubber, "Is Highjacking of Aircraft Piracy in International Law?" *British*

Yearbook of International Law, Vol. 43, 1969, p. 153; Shepard, "Air Piracy: The Role of the International Federation of Air Pilots Association," *Cornell International Law Journal*, Vol. 3, 1970, p. 81; Dinstein, "Criminal Jurisdiction over Aircraft Highjacking," *Israel Law Review*, Vol. 7, 1972, p. 195. The special problems posed by the language of the 1958 Geneva Convention on the High Seas is examined by Rubin, "Is Piracy Illegal?" *American Journal of International Law*, Vol. 70, 1976, p. 92.

(24)McWhinney, supra note 23, p. 116. See also: Emanuelli, supra note 23, pp. 77-81; Joyner, supra note 23, pp. 230-248; Agrawala, supra note 23, pp. 77-78; Sundberg, supra note 23, pp. 473-474. Schwarzenberger, supra note 12, p. 283, doubts "whether, in many cases of highjacking, the condition of Article 15 of the [Geneva] Convention can be fulfilled."

(25)*In Re* Castioni, 1 Q.B. 149 [1891]. See also: *In Re* Meunier, 2 Q.B. 415 [1894]; *Ex Parte* Kolczynski, 1 Q.B. 540 [1955]; *Regina v. Governor of Pentonville Prison, ex parte* Tzu-Tsai Cheng, 2 All E.R. 204 [1973]. Cf. comment, *Cambridge Law Journal*, Vol. 32, 1973, p. 181.

(26)See *In Re* State of Wisconsin and Armstrong, 28 D.L.R. 3d 513 [1972], and *In Re* Federenko, 20 Man. L.R. 22 [1910]. Cf. the 1972 statement of the Canadian Ministry of Foreign Affairs that "[t]he legitimacy of a cause does not itself legitimize the use of certain forms of violence, especially against the innocent." Quoted by Green, "The Nature and Control of International Terrorism," *Israel Yearbook on Human Rights*, Vol. 4, 1974, pp. 134, 163.

(27)*U.S. v Artukovic*, 170 F Supp. 383 [1959]. Cf. *Gallina v. Fraser*, 177 F. Supp. 356 [1959]; aff'd. 278 F. 2d 77 [1960]; cert. denied 364 U.S. 851 [1960].

(28)Quoted by "In the Matter of Extradition of Hector Jose Campora and Others," *American Journal of International Law*, Vol. 58, 1957, pp. 690, 695. Cf. *In Re* Kaphengst [1929-1930], Ann. Dig. 292, No. 188 (Switz. 1930); E.S.B. I,456, 457 (Switz. 1930). See also: *In Re* Ktir, 87 E.S.B. I, 134 (Switz. 1961); *American Journal of International Law*, Vol. 56, 1962, p. 224 and *In Re* Kavic, Bjelonovic and Arsenijevic, 39 *I.L.R.* 371 (1952).

(29)Cf. Garcia-Mora, "The Nature of Political Offenses: A Knotty Problem of Extradition Law," *Virginia Law Review*, Vol. 48, 1962, p. 1226.

(30)Evans, "Reflections upon the Political Offense in International Practice," *American Journal of International Law*, Vol. 57, 1963, p. 1. The problem is well-stated by noted psychoanalyst Erich Fromm: "[t]he successful revolutionary is a statesman, the unsuccessful one a criminal." Fromm, *Escape from Freedom*, Paperback ed., 1965, p. 286.

(31)Kittrie, "Terrorism and Political Crimes in International Law," *American Journal of International Law,* Proceedings, Vol. 67, 1973, pp. 87, 104.

(32)Friedlander, "Terrorism and Political Violence: Some Preliminary Observations," *International Studies Notes,* Vol. 2, 1976, p. 1. See also Friedlander, "Sowing the Wind: Rebellion and Terror-Violence in Theory and Practice," *Denver Journal of International Law and Politics,* Vol. 6, 1976, p. 83. Cf. Szabo, "Political Crimes: A Historical Perspective," *ibid.,* Vol. 2, 1972, p. 7, who argues that "[f]rom a strictly judicial point of view, the politcal crime is impossible to define. . .

(33)Quoted by Venturi, *Roots of Revolution: A History of the Populist and Socialist Movements in Nineteenth Century Russia,* 1966, p. 373.

(34)Cf. *ibid.,* p. 558-708; Wilkinson, *Political Terrorism,* 1974, pp. 60-74; Gross, "Political Violence and Terror in 19th and 20th Century Russia and Eastern Europe," p. 8; *Assassination and Political Violence: A Report to the National Commission on the Causes and Prevention of Violence,* ed. by Kirkham, Levy and Crotty, 1969 pp. 433-441; Hardman, "Terrorism," *Encyclopedia of the Social Sciences,* ed. by Seligman and Johnson, 1935 Vol. 14, pp. 577-579. There are those who insist that Mikhail Bakunin, occasional collaborator of Nechayev and founder of radical anarchism, should be considered as the archetype of revolutionary terrorism. Bakunin's rhetoric was violent but far from original. See especially: Friedrich, *Tradition and Authority,* 1972, pp. 103-108 and Venturi, supra note 33, pp. 36-62. Rapoport, "The Politics of Atrocity," Paper presented to the Ralph Bunche Institute Conference on International Terrorism, June 10, 1976, New York City, views modern revolutionary terror as originating from the nineteenth century Russian anarchists. The anarchist view was that hell had to be endured before heaven could be attained. According to the perspective of Britain's Justice Cave at the end of the nineteenth century, "the party of anarchy, is the enemy of all Governments." See: *In Re Meunier,* 2 Q.B. 415, 419 [1894].

(35)Quoted by Wilkinson, supra note 34, p. 64. Hutchinson: "The Concept of Revolutionary Terrorism," *Journal of Conflict Resolution,* Vol. 16, 1972, pp. 383, 385 defines terrorism as being "part of a revolutionary strategy." Thornton: "Terror as a Weapon of Political Agitation," *Internal War: Problems and Approaches,* 78 ed. by Eckstein, 1964, p. 78 claims that "[a]s a general rule, assassination and sabotage are nonsymbolic acts directed at persons and things, respectively. Terror is a symbolic act that may be directed against things or people."

(36)The Socialist Revolutionary terror program was vigorously opposed by V. I. Lenin and the Bolshevik party. See Lenin, *What Is To Be Done? Burning Questions of Our Movement*, 74-77 New World paperback ed., 1969, pp. 74-77. On September 4, 1870, Friedrich Engles wrote to Karl Marx that "[t]error consists mostly of useless cruelties perpetrated by frightened people in order to reassure themselves." Quoted by Conquest: *The Great Terror: Stalin's Purge of the Thirties*, 1968, p. xii.

(37)Camus: "The Just Assassins," *Caligula and Three Other Plays*, trans. by Gilbert, Vintage ed., 1958, pp. 246, 282. See also the excellent study by Footman: *The Alexander Conspiracy: A Life of A.I. Zhelyabov*, Reprint ed., 1974.

(38)A. Dragnich: *Serbia, Nikola Pasic and Yugoslavia*, 1974, pp. 68-80. See also: Stavrianos: *The Balkans Since 1453*, 1958, pp. 464-466.

(39)Fay: *The Origins of the World War*, Vol. 2, 1930, Chaps. 2 and 3; Stavrianos: supra note 38, pp. 548-552.

(40)The term "transnational terrorism" is that of Crozier: *A Theory of Conflict*, 1974, pp. 109-110, which pertains to individual and group action as opposed to state involvement.

(41)Two strong proponents of drawing a precise legal standard separating the essential criminality of terrorism from the basic legitimacy of self-determination are Paust: "A Survey of Possible Legal Responses to International Terrorism: Prevention, Punishment, and Cooperative Action," *Georgia Journal of International & Comparative Law*, Vol. 5, 1975, pp. 431, 459-462 and Novogrod: "Internal Strife, Self-Determination, and World Order," *International Terrorism and Political Crimes*, ed. by Bassiouni, 1975, pp. 98-119.

(42)See: Wilkinson, supra note 34, pp. 83-89; Hachey: "Political Terrorism: The British Experience," *International Terrorism: National, Regional, and Global Perspectives*, ed. by Alexander, 1976, pp. 107-110; Hull, *The Irish Triangle: Conflict in Northern Ireland*, 1976, pp. 32-37; Hardman, supra note 34, p. 577; and especially *Northern Ireland*, Hearings before the Subcommittee on Europe of the House Committee on Foreign Affairs, 92d Cong., 2d Sess., 1972. Between 1920 and 1922 about 300 persons wre killed in what amounted to a mini-civil war among Northern Irish Catholics and Unionists Boyd: *Holy War in Belfast: A History of the Troubles in Northern Ireland*, Paperback ed., 1972, pp. 176-178.

(43)U.N. Secretariat, Draft Study, supra note 2, p. 9.

(44)Novogrod: "Civil Strife and Indirect Aggression," Bassiouni and Nanda, supra note 2, p. 217; Dautricourt: "The International Criminal Court," *ibid.*, pp. 643-644; Finger: "International Terrorism and the United Nations," Alexander, supra note 42, p. 323.

(45)*International Legislation: 1935-1937,* ed. by Hudson, 1972 Vol. 7, pp. 862-893. Prohibited acts of terror-violence included attempts directed against the life, physical well-being, or freedom of heads of state, their spouses, or other government officials if the attack was upon their public office; the impairment of public property; and a general impairment of human lives if made by a citizen of one state against another.

(46)G.A. Res. 3166 (XXVIII), reprinted in *American Journal of International Law,* Vol. 68, 1974, p. 383. See also: Rozakis: "Terrorism and the Internationally Protected Persons in Light of the ILC's Draft Articles," *International and Comparative Law Quarterly,* Vol. 23, 1974, p. 32.

(47)Arendt: *The Origins of Totalitarianism,* New paperback ed., 1973, p. 464.

(48)Conquest, supra note 36, pp. 525-533, estimates a minimum of 20 million deaths directly attributable to Stalin's rule. Cf. the careful analysis in Carmichael: *Stalin's Masterpiece: The "Show Trials" and Purges of the Thirties—The Consolidation of the Bolshevik Dictatorship,* 1975, pp. 184-189. He estimates a total of 7 million political prisoners for 1937-1938, the peak years of the Great Purge. Dawidowicz: *The War against the Jews, 1933-1945,* pp. 402-403, lists approximately 6 million Jews as victims of the Holocaust. See also: Feldman: "Concentration Camps and Extermination Camps," *Holocaust,* ed. by Encyclopedia Judaica, 1974, pp. 96-97, and other estimates cited in Levin; *The Holocaust: The Destruction of European Jewry 1933-1945,* 1968 pp. 715-718. The generally accepted overall figure attributed to Hitler's extermination policies is 10 million deaths. For the impact of state terrorism upon the community of nations, see: address of President Harry S. Truman to the U.N. San Francisco Conference, U.N. Doc. 8, G/5, April 25, 1945.

(49)On the subject of belligerent occupation and the legal rights and duties attached thereto, see: Stone: supra note 12, pp. 684-732; Bassiouni; "Genocide and Racial Discrimination," Bassiouni, supra note 2, pp. 522-532; Bierzanek: "War Crimes: History and Definition," *ibid.,* pp. 559-590; Roling: "The Nuremberg and the Tokyo Trials in Retrospect," *ibid.,* pp. 590-635; Dinstein; "International Criminal Law," *Israel Yearbook on Human Rights,* Vol. 5, 1975, pp. 55, 58-60, 77-78. Aron: *Peace and War: A Theory of International Relations,* 1966, pp. 169-170, argues, as do others, that the Anglo-American zone bombing raids of Germany during World War II were "raids of terror."

(50)Cf., for example, Dedijer; *Unless Peace Comes,* 1968, pp. 18-29, and *National Liberation: Revolution in the Third World,* ed. by Miller and Aya, 1971.

(51)Alexander, "From Terrorism to War: The Anatomy of the Birth of Israel," supra note 42, pp. 232-247; Collins and LaPierre, *O Jerusalem!* Paperback ed., 1973 p. 68-136; Silverberg; *If I Forget Thee O Jerusalem: American Jews and the State of Israel,* Paperback ed., 1972, pp. 293-306, 318-326, 340-352.

(52)Fanon: *The Wretched of the Earth,* Paperback ed., 1968, p. 35.

(53)The phrase is that of Green: "The Ministate: A Navigational Hazard?" Paper presented to the XVII Annual Convention, International Studies Association, February 25-29, 1976, Toronto, Canada.

(54)See *Ad Hoc* Committee, Report, supra note 1.

(55)This belief was shared by most of the participants at the Department of State Conference on International Terrorism, March 25-26, 1976, Washington, D.C. See: Johnson: "Perspectives on Terrorism," Summary Report of Conference on International Terrorism, Department of State, Washington, D.C.

(56)On the possibilities of nuclear blackmail and the growing threat of atomic or biochemical terrorism, cf. Ponte: "Atomizing the World," *Skeptic,* Vol. 14, 1976 p. 33; Woods: "The Possible Criminal Use of Atomic or Biochemical Materials, *Anzas Journal of Criminology,* Vol. 8, 1975, p. 113; Hutchinson: "Terrorism and the Diffusion of Nuclear Power," Paper presented to the XVII Annual Convention, International Studies Association, February 25-29, 1976, Toronto, Canada; "A Special Safeguards Study," Report of U.S. Atomic Energy Commission, 120 *Congressional Record,* Senate, No. 59, 93rd Cong., 2d Sess., 6621-6630, April 30, 1974; "Terrorism: 'Growing and Increasingly Dangerous,'" Interview with Robert A. Feary, Special Assistant to the Secretary of State and Co-ordinator for Combatting Terrorism, *U.S. News & World Report,* September 29, 1975, p. 77. In the United States, potential harm of this type is only partially covered by statute. See 18 USCS, Sec. 2153 (a), which prohibits and penalizes the destruction of war material, war property, and war utilities. See also *ibid.,* Sec. 2157.

David Rapoport:
The Politics of Atrocity

Once upon a time, not very long ago, the term, "terrorist," was tolerably clear to most people, mostly because terrorists told us who they were and what they were doing. In the nineteenth-century, for example, Anarchists proudly called themselves terrorists, traced their lineage at least back to the French Revolution, and sometimes to the Order of Assassins in medieval Islam. Later, Trotsky was not embarrassed to speak of the benefits of the Red Terror. (1) The last group to describe *itself* as a terrorist organization was the one widely known as "The Stern Gang," thirty years ago. (2) Today, the term has so many abusive connotations that no terrorist will ever call himself one publicly, and he will make every effort to pin that term on his enemy.

He who controls the language used to describe a struggle obviously has enormous influence on its outcome. Journalists know about the problems and power of language, and in their efforts to be "fair" and "not take sides" have devised a most unique approach. Several months ago I scanned seven newspaper articles on revolutionary violence in one week. In each piece the rebel was first called a terrorist, which the government prefers, and then a guerrilla, which the rebel prefers. One even wrote of a rebel as a soldier as well — which must have pleased the rebel enormously. In attempting to correct the abuse of language for political purposes, our journalists may succeed in making language altogether worthless.

In the days when language was less corrupted, the difference between terms was much clearer. Military activity was bound by conventions entailing *moral* distinctions between belligerents and neutrals, combatants and non-combatants, appropriate and inappropriate targets, legitimate and illegitimate methods. Guerrilla war was a special kind of military activity, in which hit and disappear tactics to disperse the enemy's *military* forces were employed to wear down and gradually defeat the enemy.

The traditional, distinguishing characteristic of the terrorist was his explicit refusal to accept the conventional moral limits which defined military and guerrilla action. (3) Because a terrorist knew that others did think that violence should be limited, he exploited the enemy's various responses to his outrages. The terrorist perpetrated atrocities and manipulated reactions to them.

This characterization differs somewhat from one many who want to use the term, "terrorist," responsibly might offer. The object of terror tactics, they would say, is to produce terror, a state of fear so intense that those affected become paralyzed or panic-stricken, a state of fear best induced by indiscriminate attacks which teach the lesson that no action taken or status claimed provides immunity. (4) Certainly, all terrorists aim to produce terror at some time in their struggle, but individual underground groups of rebel terrorists are too small to sustain the complete uncertainty necessary to terrorize large portions of any society for very long. Attacked individuals quickly learn how to cope by recognizing danger and enlisting social support. Although terrorists can and may need to paralyze selected, critical organizations, it is still true that their atrocities are generally meant to have other effects, which a good definition of terrorism should accommodate.

The characteristics and possibilities of modern revolutionary terror were first understood in the writings and actions of mid-nineteenth-century Russian Anarchists, particularly Nechaev, Bakunin, and Kropotkin. They were partly inspired by those Czarist Balkan intrigues which employed assassins against Turkish officials. The Turks responded by massacring Christian subjects whose deaths in turn created Christian uprisings, a desire for outside intervention, and war fevers in Russia itself. *Publicity* and *provocation*, not pure terror, were the objectives of Czarist atrocities, and those objectives were incorporated in the more systematic Anarchist efforts to put atrocities at the service of revolution. (6)

Since the beginning of time perhaps, rebels have committed

atrocities to produce paralysis and panic. (7) Only the Messianic religious groups, like the ancient Jewish Sicarri and Zealots prominent in the Great Revolt against Rome, and the Assassins or Fidayeen of medieval Islam, who aimed at redeeming what each believed was a specific Divine promise of a future earthly paradise, used terror in the modern sense. (8)

The religious groups are, however, *sui generis*: they left no record of their thought and therefore were unable to generate a tradition even within their own cultures. The Russian Anarchists are very different and much more significant, for in explaining the various uses of terror and suggesting why modern society had become vulnerable, they created a tradition of thought and action which three successive generations of terrorists have labored to study and improve. (9) Without understanding the Anarchist tradition, no one today can understand the long persistence and likely future of terrorism in our world.

The Anarchist doctrine has four major points. 1. Society is full of latent hostilities and ambivalences, because since the French Revolution people had become aware in some sense of the potentialities for perfection in society (The French Revolution is the functional equivalent of the unredeemed Divine promise for religious groups). 2. Society muffles and diffuses hostilities by devising moral conventions which provide channels for settling some grievances and for securing personal amenities. 3. However, society also undermines its own conventions, because it explains their origin historically. Consequently, History replaces God as our final judge; acts we deem immoral our children will hail as noble efforts essential for humanity's liberation. 4. The quickest and most effective means of destroying conventions is terror. The perpetration of an atrocity frees the terrorist from the paralyzing grip of convention over his soul; it also publicizes his cause and provokes the defenders of society to violate their own norms, thereby generating a massive popular uprising (The functional equivalent in religious terrorism was the contention that the world had to become impossibly bad before it could become unimaginably good).

In one form or another and in various degrees of intensity, all of these assumptions have been present in terrorist movements since 1880; however, of particular concern is the use of atrocities among contemporaries. An atrocity serves two basic purposes. It may produce a variety of social reactions that the terrorist desires, and it also can be a kind of personal therapy. Both ends are often served by the same atrocity, for as Nancy

Ling Perry, the pamphleteer of the Symbionese Liberation Army, wrote, "Revolutionary violence is nothing but the most profound means of achieving internal as well as external violence." (10) Nonetheless, it is clear that the two purposes are conceptually distinct and will be treated separately with brief references to one way the changed political character of the international world has contributed to terrorist successes.

TERROR AS A MEANS TO PRODUCE SOCIAL RESULTS

Revolutionary terror, Kropotkin wrote, is "propaganda by the deed!" A terrorist crime is a crime for publicity. When a bomb explodes, people take notice, and the explosion may draw more attention than a thousand speeches or pictures. If the terror is sustained, more and more people become interested. Many wonder why the atrocities occurred and if the "cause" seems plausible. The perpetrators ultimately may gain sympathy, because citizens, although initially repelled by the act of terrorism, may also feel that the desperation of the weak must have been generated by monstrously unjust circumstances. Terror publicizes grievances, which the terrorist believes would have been unnoticed without his act. All things being equal, the more spectacular the outrage, the more likely it is that the rest of the world will discuss the grievance and perhaps in time recognize the terrorist as the most suitable spokesman for those aggrieved.

The critical factor in generating reactions, of course, is the status of the assailants; the strong are regarded differently than the weak. When a government commits an atrocity against its own citizens, outsiders, particularly in the international world, are likely to become hostile. Usually, a government will seek to suppress evidence of its outrages, while rebels aim to publicize theirs. (11)

Atrocities by rebels have other less conspicuous effects. In every state at least a few individuals dream of destroying the existing order and will be inspired with enthusiasm to seize the provided opportunity to rebel. Others who may have been working for radical change by non-violent means, suddenly find themselves outflanked. In refusing to support the terrorists, the non-violent will be accused of not being truly committed to the cause they have been espousing. Their most immediately convincing defense is to describe the terror as the work of a small band of doomed juveniles or political lunatics, who will perhaps provoke dangerous reactions. (12) If, however, the terror is sustained, those who have been told not to support terrorist methods which cannot work inevitably begin to find the terrorists offering a credible alternative.

In most states police procedures are designed to deal with ordinary criminals during peace time, while armies are constructed for war. The fight against the terrorist approximates neither condition. In the absence of accepted legitimating conventions, responses must be fitful, clumsy, and abusive. The problem of society's reaction to terrorism is summarized in a statement a Cypriot offered his English friend: "Your operation against the terrorist must be conducted across the body of the Cyprus people — like a man who has to hit an opponent through the body of the referee." (13)

If the government's natural responses are not sufficiently provocative, the terrorist can make them more provocative. Nothing enrages moral sensibilities more, and nothing makes one more willing to sanction *any* counter-measure than deliberately indiscriminate murder, especially when people imagine themselves or those they know as potential victims. A systematic assassination campaign, for example, against police officers or their families could probably destroy all police restraint. I.R.A. random bombings stimulated Protestant "Paddy bopping" reprisals, the local term for random assassinations of Roman Catholics. A similar F.L.N. terror produced wild "Arab hunts" when French colonials killed every Moslem they saw and thereby unintentionally strengthened support for the terrorists.

Calculated efforts by Palestinians to attack children drove Israelis to a frenzy, as heart-ripping televised scenes two year ago at Maalot and Kiryat Shemona illustrated. Israeli officials themselves, were assaulted and abused. They pointedly stayed away from the next funeral resulting from terrorism when an enraged mob had incinerated the bodies of dead terrorists — an atrocity to pious Jews and Moslems alike. To the Israelis, the cumulative effect of terrorism was to erode confidence in their government's will to protect citizens.

Atrocities and counter-atrocities increase hatred among everyone, constantly reducing opportunities for a possible political solution that most people could accept. The struggle is taken from those most restrained by conventions and long-run political considerations, and moderates are continually crushed between millstones of blind fury. Whenever serious moves towards a political agreement, short of total victory for one side or another, occur in Northern Ireland or the Middle East one can expect a daring outrage calculated to frustrate them.

The logic of publicity and provocative atrocities is particularly appropriate to "revolutionary-like" situations. Any organized form of violence may lead to acts of pure terror, because even when regulating conventions are understood and accepted, the rage or interest of either party encourages violations. The horrible Dresden fire raids in World War II were either an effort to avenge Rotterdam and Coventry or an attempt to paralyze and panic Germans. Can anyone believe that they were undertaken to provoke sympathy for the Allied cause, or to provoke Germans to burn more Englishmen so that other Englishmen would become enthusiastic about incinerating more Germans?

To speak of the systematic use of terror for publicity and provocation purposes is to presume, of course, that the antagonists in some critical senses share a moral community. The public statements by the terrorist always justify atrocities in defensive terms, as necessary specific responses to particular alleged atrocities of the enemy. (14) Appeals are made to the *same* sets of potential supporters, and victories or defeats depend on how well rebels can turn government's moral restraint or strength into political weaknesses. (15) The restraint of government, on the one hand, provides immunities for the terrorist, but if government abandons restraint, it suffers a different kind of disadvantage in the eyes of interested parties, for the atrocities of the strong always seem more invidious than those of the weak. The best situation for the terrorist may be an irresolute government torn between conflicting popular demands, a government which provides the rebels with some immunities but violates its policy often enough to undermine its claim to be restrained. (16)

Russian Anarchists emphasized that the modern world was vulnerable to terror, because its shame and guilt feelings could be exploited. They also assumed that all contemporary systems in this respect were equally weak. Although the world has experienced three successive generations of terror since the 1880s — each successive one producing better organized groups than its predecessor — success has occurred only in those colonial situations where foreign parties felt a moral commitment to the issues the struggles developed. (It is worth repeating in this context that publicity and provocation terror was first used by the Czars to nourish revolts in the Ottoman Empire in which groups associated with the Russian Church existed.)

Before World War II terrorists were successful in Ireland only; after the war, terrorists often achieved limited successes, although they and their groups were unable to stimulate the popular uprisings anticipated by Anarchist doctrine, occasionally they received sufficient indigenous sympathy to make colonial governments reluctant to retain power, especially because colonial withdrawal was usually possible without greatly endangering a government's constitutional identity. Two new political circumstances also weakened the colonial will to fight. An increased moral ambivalence within metropolitan populations concerning the retention of overseas territories developed, and a significant international desire existed to see Western empires destroyed, a desire which could be mobilized more easily because the United Nations existed. The moral attitudes after World War II were summarized neatly by the Cypriot who told Lawrence Durrell, "Of a stupid man (the peasants) say, 'He thought he could beat his wife, without his neighbors hearing.' In this case the neighbors are your own Labour Party, U.N.O., and many others. We are provoking you to beat us so that our cries reach their ears." (17)

Until recently terrorists first had to demonstrate visible and continuing support among the people they claimed to represent before many foreign states *qua* states would recognize a movement's claims. However, the astonishing sudden rise of the Palestine Liberation Army illustrates that under certain circumstances, the process can be reversed dramatically. Originally, the P.L.O. lacked indigenous support and could not exist on the West Bank after the Six Day War. Foreign sanctuaries guaranteed survival, and P.L.O. political successes came from a brief series of outrages against unarmed individuals at Italian, Greek, and Swiss airports, who were usually citizens of neutral states. Other attacks occurred at Israeli border points where civilians and children were the main targets. These activities encouraged Arab states to abandon Jordan's claims to the West Bank and to recognize the P.L.O. as the Palestinian representative. In the wake of Israel's inability to defeat Syria and Egypt quickly in war and the increased international importance of Arab oil and money, the U.N. could also be induced to recognize the P.L.O. When the U.N. acquiesced, the P.L.O. achieved credibility, and indigenous support materialized for the first time.

The final history of the P.L.O. has not yet been written. The organization still needs foreign sanctuaries, and its confinement to Lebanon which has resulted in the as yet, undecided Lebanese civil war indicates that support by other Arabs is drastically limited, especially when the latter themselves are subject to direct Israeli reprisals.

Nonetheless, the process by which the P.L.O. rose to prominence has set a wholly new precedent in terrorist history. It demonstrates how any group or state in Western Europe can be a politically "relevant" target for a movement which has not gained indigenous support in the territory where its real aims lie. Will the precedent be expanded? Will other movements follow suit, believing that anyone anywhere can be attacked for political advantage? Attempts may very well be made, but none are likely to succeed. The Palestinian situation has had two essential peculiar circumstances: it has rightly or wrongly been understood by many as a product of Western imperialism, and the Palestinian cause has been a central irremovable issue in the domestic politics of other Arab states. Nowhere else, except perhaps in Rhodesia and South Africa, can one now find reasonably convincing analogous cases. Certainly, the Croatians and other European separatist groups who have imitated the Palestinians by hijacking the aircraft of foreign countries to compensate for the lack of visible indigenous support have failed. That Latin American terrorists have not gone to Europe to attempt hijackings emphasizes the very limited applicability of the Palestinian strategy.

In the future, as they have in the past, terrorist movements most likely will be compelled to develop indigenous strength before they can hope to gain international support from a large number of countries. With the disappearance of situations which have been defined as colonial, *because* they are associated with the West, terrorists will find the international situation more difficult to exploit. Specific foreign states, depending upon their interests and special situations, may support a movement in someone else's country. This kind of support, however, is quite different from the deep emotional compulsion to sympathize with terrorists, simply because they rebelled against Western domination, a condition which for three decades has been characteristic of the whole international environment.

In an international context in which states are no longer compelled by a domestic sentiment they cannot control and, therefore, are "free" to choose whom they support and under what circumstances, indigenous strength becomes less important. No terrorist organization in history has ever been closer to toppling a national, as opposed to a colonial government, than the Tupamaros were in Uruguay a few years ago. However, no supportive international aid materialized. The rapid dissolution of the Kurdish terrorist movement when Iran closed its borders — a dissolution which occurred in spite of the fact that the Kurds had deep roots in Iraq — is another indication that the international environment, which made terrorism so important in recent years, may be changing radically.

In *most* circumstances in the forseeable future, terrorists will have to fight national governments or governments which believe they cannot yield without destroying their own constitutional identity. Terrorists, for obvious reasons, have never yet been able to overcome opposition of this kind. (18) Neighboring states will also become more cautious in lending support, because international opinion will tolerate retaliation from national entities, although it would not from colonial powers.

TERROR AS PERSONAL THERAPY

In the original Anarchist doctrine, atrocities served two purposes. They were a means of producing politically favorable reactions in others, and they were ends in themselves, enabling the terrorist to gain self-respect. Different terrorist movements subsequently emphasized one purpose at the expense of the other. The more successful political movements have always stressed terror as a means, and most groups which see terror in expediential terms have functioned in colonial areas where the limited goal of withdrawal was feasible. A terror not sufficiently limited by political calculations in colonial territories can and did promote devastating backlashes which destroyed the movements, as the experiences in Kenya and Malaya during the 1950s indicate.

Arguments about the effectiveness of atrocities are common within a terrorist movement, leading from an original nucleus to proliferation of organizations like Irgun and the Stern Gang, Fatah and P.L.P., I.R.A. Officials and I.R.A. Provisionals. Proliferation usually involves questions of how far terrorists can expand the scope of atrocities without making the will to resist inflexible. In such cases, more moderate elements may accuse more extreme elements as being committed to "terror for its own sake," as the I.R.A. Officials frequently characterize the Provisionals. (19) Usually what is meant in Ireland, and in similar cases, is that the Provisionals have become so blinded by their hatred for Protestants that they cannot understand that they are making Protestants believe that no compromise is conceivable.

Terrorist movements have, however, stressed terror as an end in itself. They are less interesting as political forces, but like the psychotic who reflects in an exaggerated way tendencies not usually noticed in ordinary persons, these terrorist movements should be studied because each teaches something about the necessary makeup of terrorist movements everywhere. (20) Some Anarchist elements in the nineteenth-century were the original representatives of contemporary terrorism, and a few of their many modern counterparts are the Japanese Red Army, the British Angry Brigade, the German Baader-Meinhoff group, and the Weathermen. They have generally operated in nation-states, but as political movements, (21) they have been hopelessly inept. Their millenarian vision seems incomprehensible to anyone else, and their political goal is so completely out of the realm of experience that the groups themselves have no way of understanding when they are closer or further from their goal. Like the religious terrorist, they understand only that Hell must precede Paradise. Lacking standards to judge the political significance of particular atrocities, they are left only with the value of the act itself. Atrocity becomes a substitute for revolution; consequently, action *is* revolution in the slogans associated with such movements — "The Revolution is Now," "Revolution is Joy," "I am the Revolution," "Revolution for the Hell of It," "Revolution: the Highest Trip of All."

The truly bizarre quality of these slogans has not always been grasped, because too many acceptable analogies exist which seem to justify them. Terrorism is a form of conflict, and most people enjoy conflict for its own sake. The delight conflict generates is felt in many situations — in sports, the school, the market place, and finally in war.

One can gain therapeutic value from conflict, especially if a cause seems worthy. One who stands up for his convictions feels more like a person for doing so. Perpetually overcrowded psychiatric facilities emptied during Berkeley's revolutionary days. Never did life seem more interesting or worthwhile.

Nevertheless, serious conflict embraces a variety of concerns. Most people often have good reason to feel ashamed of joy they feel when, for example, the conflict seems unfair, irrelevant to any achievable social object, and indicates that the participants are being consumed by their own hate. The difference between a normal person who enjoys a good fight and the sadist or masochist is that the sadist uses another person *solely* as an instrument for pleasure and the masochist uses himself for that purpose. Incidentally, the relation between sado-masochism and terror is quite close as a casual reading of the Marquis de Sade reveals.

The satisfaction most people get from fighting is related to feelings of respect they feel for the other party, for themselves, and for a cause; these feelings are usually embodied in conventions which are supposed to regulate the conflict even after victory. The complete contempt for such feelings is what makes Bernardine Dohrn's exultation of the Manson family atrocities so extraordinary or peculiar. "Dig it," she commanded. "First they killed the pigs, then they ate dinner in the same room with them, then they even shoved forks in their stomachs. Wild." (22)

As Hegel's essay on terror points out, the ultimate disrespect is to act as though a victim's death had no dignity, no inherent meaning? that killing one can be likened to the slicing of a head of lettuce or to swallowing a drink of water. (23) Not all Anarchists or all terrorists would endorse Dohrn's statement, but if one believes that the value of life or death is determined only by political considerations and by the perpetrator's own benefit, then Dohrn's conclusion for many will always be quite feasible.

The Anarchist terrorist assumes that society is corrupt, and as a member of it, the terrorist is corrupt at least to the extent that one limits oneself by society's conventions. To grasp one's true self, one must break through the boundaries of "normal" actions, thoughts, and feelings.

For Nechaev the terrorists can transcend their own corruption or humanity by becoming literally instruments of the cause, making sure that they will have "no personal inclinations, no attachments, no property and no name ..." To Nechaev all terrorists are "expendable capital," and he is the first revolutionary leader explicitly to urge the treatment of one's own comrades as chattel. (24) The present generation must see as "its only obligation and pleasure the study of the science of demolition with the object of a complete merciless destruction of the whole filthy order." Rostypin urged indiscriminate bombings, which he called "unmotivated terror," because it ignores the personal or human qualities of victims. He justified it as a good method to break forever society's hold on the terrorist. (25)

To make oneself into an instrument was a continuing experimental process to expand the imagination and capacities of terrorists to overcome inner layers of resistance. Nineteenth-century Anarchists called the effort the "de-sanctification process," because it forced one to commit new and more heinous obscenities to test commitment. A similar effort appeared among the Weathermen when they first went underground, involving defecation on tombstones, eating pet animals, and committing homosexual acts on command. (26)

Sensing that the greatest atrocity a terrorist could commit would be to murder a comrade for the sole purpose of proving himself free of guilt, Nachaev's first and only violent act as a terrorist was the organization of a collective ritual murder. It is the central incident in Dostoyevski's novel, *The Possessed*. Several years ago, the Japanese police captured a unit of the Japanese Red Army in which eight of its fourteen members had been tortured and murdered by comrades for offenses indicating a "bourgeois mentality." One member had put her child in paddipads, a second wore lipstick, and a third had risked death when ordered to swerve his speeding truck in order to avoid hitting an animal. When questioned about the appropriateness of the discipline, the survivors who were murderers, said the main purpose was to overcome the sense of shame and to help them become worthy revolutionary leaders!

One does not know how deep the belief in terror as personal therapy is in contemporary groups, and what new levels of atrocities against themselves are even conceivable to terrorists. It may be impossible to make oneself literally nothing but an instrument, but people will keep trying, and we shall be worse off in the process.

NOTES

(1) Leon Trotsky, *Terrorism and Communism*, Ann Arbor, 1961; first published in 1920.

(2) See: Gerald Frank, *The Deed*, New York, 1963.

(3) Although they call themselves guerrillas, some terrorist groups circulate documents designed for actual or potential members which speak of the necessity for terror tactics. See, for example: Carlos Marighela, *For The Liberation of Brazil*, London, 1971, p. 89 and Susan Stern, *With the Weathermen*, New York, 1975, p. 182.

(4) Standard dictionary definitions are uniform. In *Webster's Third New International Dictionary*, 1961: "the use of terror as a means of coercion," terror is "a state of intense fear and apprehension;" in *The American College Dictionary*, 1966: "a state of fear and submission produced by terrorist methods;" in *The Oxford English Dictionary*: "a policy intended to strike with terror against those whom it is adopted." Scholars rarely

depart from this definition. See, for example: J. B. S. Hardman, "Terrorism" in *Encyclopedia of the Social Sciences*, 1939. Although Paul Wilkinson, *Political Terrorism*, London, 1974, p. 16, notes that the distinguishing feature of terrorism as an organized form of violence is the unwillingness to be limited by any convention, the aim remains to produce terror. Jordan J. Paust, "A Survey of Possible Legal Responses to International Terrorism . . ." *Georgia Journal of International and Comparative Law*, Vol. 431, distinguishes between victims and targets of an assault, but does not speak of the various emotional states and reactions which may be intended.

(5) A few studies of government terror exist like Eugene V. Walter, *Terror and Resistance* New York, 1969, and Dallin A. and G. Breslauer, *Political Terrorism in Communist Systems* Stanford, 1970. However, we have no systematic comparison of the originating circumstances, purposes, and strategies of government and rebel terror.

(6) Although the historical importance of the Anarchists is that they understood that pure terror has a limited role in the insurrection process, it is also true that they neglected its potential significance for particulsr objectives. Anarchists, for example, never appreciated the major initial tactical problem of how to cope with the police, and in the end the police destroyed them. On the other hand, every successful terrorist campaign following the strategy of Michael Collins, I.R.A. leader after World War I, paralyzed the police early, usually by systematic assassination policies. For a more extensive discussion of Anarchist terror, see: D. C. Rapoport, *Assassination and Terrorism*, Toronto, 1971, and for a elaboration of the police as a target, see D. C. Rapoport, "Inside the Terrorist Mind," Chicago *Tribune*, "Perspective." November 2, 1975.

(7) Almost invariably the pre-modern terrorist groups were unsuccessful.

(8) For a description of the Fidayeen, see: Marshall Hodgson, *The Order of Assassins*, Gravenhage, 1955 and Bernard Lewis, *The Assassins*, London, 1967. In his final chapter, Lewis very briefly compares the Assassins with other terrorist groups. Josephus provides most of our information on the Sicarii and Zealots in *The Jewish War* and to a lesser extent, in *The Antiquities of the Jews*. Although the secondary sources are useful, no one primarily interested in the general phenomena of terrorism has yet published a study of any of the three groups. D.C. Rapaport, "Terrorism: The Jew as Perpetrator and Victim in the Great Revolt against Rome (forthcoming) com-

pares Zealot and Sicarii strategy and tactics with that of modern groups.

(9) As actual terrorists, the Anarchists were quite inept. But then quite possibly the only successful terrorist movements up to that time were the Sons of Liberty who struck at Tory sympathizers during the American War of Independence and the Ku Klux Klan (early contemporaries of the Russian Anarchists) who contributed to the decision to withdraw Federal troops from the South before their mission had been accomplished during the Reconstruction. Both groups seemed to utilize a traditional terror strategy of generating panic and paralysis. At any rate, no theory on strategy of terror emerged from these groups, because they did their dirty work in secret, and kept their mouths shut afterwards! There is virtually no literature on the Sons of Liberty. Henry B. Dawson's *The Sons of Liberty*, New York: 1859, is a useful but limited piece. Material on the K.K.K. is more plentiful but none suggests a distinctive understanding of terror by the K.K.K. For a convenient introduction, see: W. P. Randel, *The K.K.K.*, London, 1965.

(10) San Francisco *Chronicle*, April 23, 1974.

(11) In the interesting purported N.K.V.D. "Document on Terror" which assesses the effect of Stalinist terror, a major argument is that a government which is *seen* using terror isolates itself in the international arena. The manuscript does not, however, discuss the very different international impact of rebel terror. The document is reprinted in *News from behind the Iron Curtain*, Vol. 3, March, 1952, pp. 43-57.

(12) The leader of the Irgun, an Israeli group in the revolt against British rule, stated the point succinctly: "We were loved or hated — but no longer jeered at. Any underground that passes beyond the stage of inevitable initial ridicule has gone halfway — perhaps the more difficult half of the way — to its goal." Menachem Begin, *The Revolt*, Los Angeles, 1972, p. 121.

(13) Lawrence Durrell, *Bitter Lemons*, London, 1959, p. 224.

(14) When a war begins, each military act (as long as it stays within the boundaries of military convention) does not have to be justified morally. Precisely because conventions are always being violated, terrorists feel compelled to justify each successive action.

(15) An incident in Northern Ireland when I was there drove the point home. British troops and the I.R.A. were exchanging fire. An I.R.A. man was hit; immediately a crowd

of children, none older than seven, dashed on to the street. The troops stopped firing, and the man was pulled away by two women who suddenly appeared, as the troops watched helplessly. Those I questioned said that they could not shoot children, and they added that if a child were hit, the ensuing uproar in England and Ireland would have increased the ability of the I.R.A. to commit atrocities now forbidden to it. One I.R.A. sympathizer described the situation as "the politics of the last atrocity." Another added, "In Belfast a child is often more relevant than a gun; no one who cares for Ireland would stop a child from making a contribution." I wondered aloud whether those who sent the children might sometimes prefer that they die. "Getting the wounded man out is the only thing the Provos care about," was the indignant response. "The final decision belongs to the British: they know the rules." Clearly the respondent cared very much that her view of the action was correct.

(16) Obviously we should expect the strong to be more restrained, if only because we assume that they have other options. But the weak are not always as weak as they claim to be, and they may refuse other options, believing that atrocities are the quickest least costly way to achieve their ends.

(17) *Bitter Lemons*, supra note 13. The strategy of compelling the 'strong' to attack the 'weak' was first developed systematically by the Pankhursts, leaders of the British Suffragetes. See, for example: Trevor Lloyd, *Suffragetes International*, London, 1971.

(18) Israel's case, obviously, contains a mixture of the two contexts. The P.L.O. and many Arabs publicly speak of its existence as a Western military outpost which could be withdrawn by outsiders at will. However, Israelis know that national survival is at stake. Since the resister's attitude ultimately determines the means necessary, the Palestinians would not be able to achieve the destruction of Israel without conventional military arms.

(19) This is a major theme of Maria McGuire's book, *To Take Arms: My Years with the I.R.A. Provisionals*, New York: 1973.

(20) Virtually all terrorists justify violence as personal therapy. By comparison soldiers rarely make this point.

(21) In nation states two kinds of movements predominate: the Anarcho-Marxist variety which always stresses terror as an end in itself and the "secessionists" which are based on an

ethnic minority, i.e., Puerto Rican nationalists, F.A.L.N., whose aim, strategy, and tactics resemble those of movements in colonial areas.

(22) Thomas Powers, *Diana: The Makings of a Terrorist*, New York: 1971, p. 168. A more extensive discussion of the Weathermen's fascination with the Manson family is found in Stern, supra note 3, pp. 202-6.

(23) "Absolute Freedom and Terror," *The Phenomenology of Mind*, New York: 1967, p. 605.

(24) Nechaev's "Revolutionary Catechism" is reprinted in D. C. Rapoport, *Assassination and Terrorism*, supra note 6.

(25) Nechaev represents one response to the Anarchist argument that the revolutionary himself has been corrupted by social conventions. Other nineteenth century Anarchists became what Albert Camus calls "fastidious assassins," killing a selected individual who best symbolized a social evil, and then accepting, indeed seeking, punishment. The fastidious assassin assumed that while existing conventions corrupt him, they have been corrupted in their own right, and that his action will restore their true meaning. A terrorist destroys, but in accepting death himself restores respect for life. This is a strange interesting view, one no longer characteristic of terrorism, although there were elements of the argument in the trial of the two Stern Gang members who assassinated Lord Moyne. See: Camus, *The Rebel*, New York: 1956, p. 164 and Alexander Berkman, *Prison Memoirs of an Anarchist*, Pittsburgh: 1970.

(26) Regardless of the efforts taken, ambivalence remains. When terrorists with hostages, for example, are surrounded, they are rarely able to make good their threats for in *time* personal anxieties and even feelings for their hostages usually lead them to surrender without a fight. Time is the crucial factor in dissolving determination in a hopeless situation.

II.
POLITICAL
AND
STRATEGIC
PERSPECTIVES

James A. Miller:
Political Terrorism, and Insurgency: An Interrogative Approach

Rather than present a personal view or research findings concerning particular manifestations of the problem of "international terrorism," this paper attempts a "big-picture" view of the problem of "international terrorism" which has been creating much concern among scholars, the media, government officials, businessmen, and the general public. A new conceptual approach or model will be introduced for innovatively describing and analyzing not only aspects of "international terrorism" but also aspects of closely related phenomena like political terrorism, insurgency, people's war, and wars of national liberation. The minimum goal of the model is to serve as a conceptual framework within which scholars, the media, government analysts, and businessmen might comfortably and productively converse about a common area of concern.

What exactly is the nature of the problem which prompted the convening in June, 1976 of the conference on "international terrorism" at the City University of New York and similar conferences on the same subject several months earlier at the State Department in March, 1976 and at Glassboro State College in New Jersey in April, 1976? "International terrorism" is a popular "buzz-word" today, but is "international terrorism" a suitable term to delineate a subject for discussion and research? In any academic-oriented endeavor, a critical first step is defining, or delimiting, one's subject matter. As will be seen, the conceptual approach introduced here treats politically-oriented violence by organized groups of individuals.

SUBJECT DELIMITATION

During the winter of 1975-1976, newspapers regularly published stories about phenomena referred to as "insurgency," "political terrorism," "international terrorism," or "guerrilla warfare." The Irish Republican Army held Dutch businessmen as prisoners; incessant street fighting occurred among Christians, Moslems, and Palestinians in Beirut, Lebanon, broken by one ineffective ceasefire after another; terrorist and guerrilla warfare activities by the People's Revolutionary Army (E.R.P.) continued in Argentina; the assassination and kidnapping of foreign diplomats occurred in various European capitals.

Similar activities and events included the widespread negative reactions to the execution in Spain of several Basque extremists convicted of killing policemen; Israeli retaliatory raids against Palestinian refugee camps followed terrorist acts against Israelis. Three insurgent factions were at war in newly independent Angola, with the Soviet and Cuban-supported Popular Movement for the Liberation of Angola (M.P.L.A.) winning and members of the pro-West National Union for the Total Independence of Angola (U.N.I.T.A.) moving to the hills to revert to the classic, protracted rural-based guerrilla pattern. Symbionese Liberation Army (S.L.A.) members Patty Hearst and William and Emily Harris underwent criminal trials in the United States; La Guardia Airport in New York was bombed; the alleged betrayal by the Central Intelligence Agency of the Kurdish insurgency occurred. Meanwhile, terrorist and guerrilla warfare activities continued in oburma, Thailand, Malaysia, Rhodesia, Nambibia, Spanish Sahara, Eritrea, Territory of Afars and Issas, Jamaica, Puerto Rico and other places. All of these events were taking place during the winter following the end of the long and arduous insurgent struggle of the Vietnamese Communists against the French and then the Americans and the South Vietnamese regime for a united, Communist Vietnam.

All of these activities are examples of *political violence.* Nieburg has defined political violence:

> ... acts of disruption, destruction, injury whose purpose, choice of targets or victims, surrounding circumstances, implementation, and/or effects have political significance, that is, tend to modify the behavior of others in a bargaining situation that has consequences for the social system.(1)

If we view "social system" in the broadest sense, political violence may be either domestic and intrastate or international in nature.

One type of political violence, particularly common in the above examples, is *political terrorism.* A form of political violence not having the sanction of the state or group of states toward which it may be directed, political terrorism involves the acts of destroying property, killing, injuring, or kidnapping individuals or threatening to do the same, for the primary purpose of intimidating persons, organizations, governments or groups of states to modify their behavior to comply with the politically-oriented desires of the perpetrators. Specific tactics/offensive methods of political terrorism may include kidnapping, assassination, hijackings, extortion, mutilation, massacre, torture, bombings, arson, bank robberies, and arms thefts.

The model, however, does not focus directly or exclusively upon political terrorism, although this concept remains an integral aspect of the model. Rather, the model is built around the concept of *political violence movement.* It is recognized that political violence may also be perpetrated by individuals or by states. The former might involve an isolated assassination effort; the latter might involve participation in inter-state war or use of the police and military powers of the state to suppress domestic dissent. The focus of the new model, however, is based upon the concept of *political violence movement,* or P.V.M., which may be defined as an organized political group, normally independent of governmental entities, which on a protracted basis deliberately plans and engages in acts of political violence, often including acts of political terrorism, for the normal primary purpose of attaining political aims vis-a-vis political entities such as governments or groups of states.

The model is designed to be applicable in conflicts involving P.V.M.s. A *P.V.M. conflict* thus involves both a P.V.M. and the opposing authorities. The model is symmetrical in that each P.V.M. conflict is viewed from the perspectives of both the P.V.M. and of the authorities.

As noted, a P.V.M. is an *organized political group* that explicitly is organized as a *movement* or aspires to such status. P.V.M.s exist on a sustained, *protracted* basis and are not just "overnight" phenomena. P.V.M.s *deliberately* undertake acts of violence. Inadvertent acts, like an unintended murder are not included in their plans. The *planning* aspect of the definition of a P.V.M. rules out spontaneous uprisings like those of Hungary in 1956. The normal *political aims* of violence by a P.V.M. excludes from coverage by the model violent actions by groups acting because of criminal, psychotic, or other non-political motivations. The so-called "partisan movements" of World War II, which engaged in irregular warfare against occupying enemy forces, may be examined using the model if they were sufficiently *independent* of or separate from the regular forces and government in general.

The model can accommodate movements with a wide variety of goals, strategies and views of revolution and opposition to authority. Movements investigated using the model may include those which desire to revolutionize completely the social, economic, and political fabric of the target regime or those which are dedicated to preserving the status quo or to restoring the old status quo. The model and the definitions and perspectives inherent in it are purposely designed to maximize objectivity and avoid generalizations and categorizations based on subjective positions. The definition of a P.V.M. does not refer to the nationality or geographical location of the members of a P.V.M. or of the victims or targets of P.V.M. violence. This limitation is intended to avoid some of the definitional troubles inherent in efforts to define or distinguish international terrorism from insurgency and other types of political violence.

P.V.M. activity can be distinguished from other forms of political violence involving groups of people. P.V.M. activity is a form of "low-intensity conflict," one of the four forms of warfare, the other three being "limited war" (Korean War), "general war" (World War II), and "total war" (nuclear war). Although international terrorism represents an international dimension of low-intensity conflict, insurgency is an intrastate or domestic aspect. Other types of domestic low-intensity conflict besides insurgency include turmoil, coup d'etat, revolution, and civil war (Figure I). It is useful to mention these terms to clarify what the model does not encompass.

Turmoil is relatively spontaneous, unorganized political violence, generally characterized by low levels of violence and modest aims. It usually involves substantial popular participation, as in violent strikes, riots, and political demonstrations(2). A coup d'etat is a clandestine effort by a small but critical segment of the state apparatus to attempt, without the involvement of the masses, to replace the government leadership with itself.(3) A revolution is a large-scale and prolonged case of low-intensity conflict that succeeds, by insurgency, coup or even civil war, in replacing the incumbents with a regime that initiates a fundamental political, social and economic transformation.(4) Lastly, a civil war results when a coup, revolution, or insurgency is not fully successful, and both sides face off in geographically distinct areas with rival armies.(5) A civil war closely resembles an interstate war, except that in civil war the two warring governmental authorities are fighting within the geographical confines of a single state.(6)

FIGURE I
POLITICAL VIOLENCE MOVEMENT CONFLICTS AND OTHER TYPES OF POLITICAL VIOLENCE

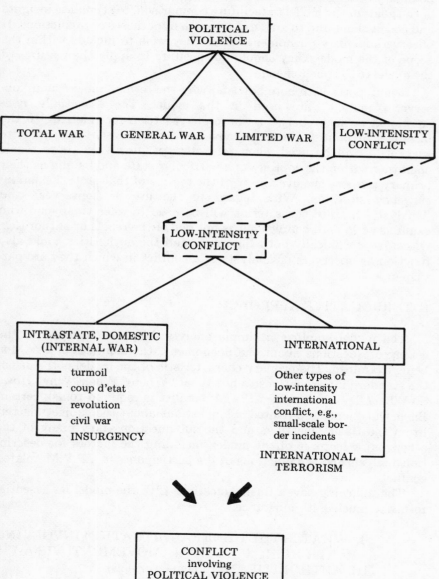

The diversity of movements engaging in political violence — and its subvariant of political terrorism — could well lead to disputes about whether or not a particular movement is a P.V.M. However, any boundary setting weaknesses of the model are not bothersome in light of the goals of the model to facilitate comparison, to stimulate insights and conclusions, and to arrive at research hypotheses or predictions. If observers identify phenomena which they wish to include within the scope of the model, they should not hesitate to apply the features of the model to the phenomena.

It is important to note how and why the terms "rebels" and "observer"/"analyst" are used in the model. The essentially non-emotional term, "rebels," is the preferred term for referring to the members of political violence movements. However, the term, "insurgents," will be used when referring specifically to those rebels operating within the confines of a particular state and having as their primary purpose the overthrow of the regime of that state, i.e., an insurgency situation. With regard to the use of "observer" and "analyst," both of these terms will be used to refer to anyone who examines a P.V.M. conflict but is not one of the rebels or authorities. Of course, technically both the rebels and the authorities could also function as observers or analysts of a conflict in which they are participants.

INTERROGATIVE APPROACH

The model employs a simple analytical approach keyed to the asking of questions about the phenomena, the conflicts of P.V.M.s, being examined. The primary characteristic of the model is the use of the standard interrogatives: Who? What? Where? When? Why? How? So What? The analyst of a P.V.M. conflict is required to ask certain Basic Questions, and related sub-questions about the subject matter. From the Basic Questions and the sub-questions flow many of the other major features of the model, including the factors for description/analysis and the functions of the participants in a P.V.M.-related conflict.

The following seven Basic Questions give the model its essential form and much of its substance:

I. WHAT IS THE GENERAL SITUATION INVOLVING A PARTICULAR POLITICAL MOVEMENT VIS-A-VIS THE AUTHORITIES? (Problem Overview)

II. WHO ARE THE ACTORS IN THE P.V.M. CONFLICT? (Actors)

III. WHERE WITHIN THE INTERNATIONAL P.V.M. SYSTEM DOES THE P.V.M. CONFLICT EXIST OR HAVE RELEVANCE? (Environments/Linkages)

IV. WHY DOES THE P.V.M. CONFLICT EXIST? (Origins/Purposes)

V. HOW DO THE REBELS AND THE AUTHORITIES OPERATE IN THE P.V.M. CONFLICT? (Modus Operandi).

VI. WHEN — IN HISTORY AND TERMS OF THE P.V.M. PROCESS — DOES THE P.V.M. CONFLICT TAKE PLACE? (Phases/Authorities' Response)

VII. SO WHAT? WHAT IS THE SIGNIFICANCE OF THIS P.V.M. CONFLICT IN TERMS OF THE OUT-COME/PRESENT STATUS? (Significance)

The key words or phrases noted in parentheses following each of the Basic Questions represent the general nature of the matters covered by each Basic Question. They and the questions may be used interchangeably. The order of the Basic Questions is based on what appears to be the most convenient manner for presentation. It is assumed that analysis using the model ultimately involves an essentially simultaneous use of each of the Basic Questions. The matters treated by the Basic Questions are all important and overlap considerably. Because the model is designed to be applicable to present, past and potentially future P.V.M.s, the tense in the Basic Questions can, like other aspects of this model, be altered as appropriate.

There are twenty-nine factors of description/analysis, each of which is grouped under one of the Basic Questions (Figure II). Consequently, Basic Question IV (Why?) has two factors: Cause and Ideology. Associated with each of these factors is a sub-question. Thus, for example, sub-question 10, relating to factor 10 reads:

> 10. *Cause:* Why did certain preconditions lead to, or combine with, precipitating events to comprise a "cause" sufficiently compelling to prompt the creation of a P.V.M. and a P.V.M. conflict?

Related to a number of the factors of description/analysis are sub-factors. An example of a sub-factor is "preconditions," which is associated with factor 10: Cause. The Appendix presents all of the Basic Questions, factors of description/analysis, sub-questions, and sub-factors. Since each P.V.M. conflict situation will be different, some factors will be more relevant than others. The analysis of a particular P.V.M. conflict is encouraged to be innovative at all times and to develop additional questions and factors as appropriate to generate conclusions and research questions.

FIGURE II

BASIC QUESTIONS/FACTORS OF DESCRIPTION AND ANALYSIS FOR
EXAMINING POLITICAL VIOLENCE MOVEMENT CONFLICTS

What Factors

[1] Status
[2] Action Decision
[3] Broad Objectives

Who Factors

[4] Leadership
[5] Membership
[6] Actors/Roles

Where Factors

[7] Domestic Environment
[8] International Environment
[9] Political Violence Movement
System/Linkages

Why Factors

[10] Cause
[11] Ideology

How Factors

[12] Strategy
[13] Popular Support

How Factors (Cont)

[14] Organization
[15] Propaganda/Communication
[16] Tactics
[17] Domestic Material Support
[18] International Support
[19] Intelligence
[20] Counterintelligence

When Factors

[21] Subversion/Organization Phase
[22] Terrorism Phase
[23] Guerrilla Warfare Phase
[24] Conventional Warfare Phase

So What Factors

[25] Incentives
[26] Capabilities
[27] Vulnerabilities
[28] Intentions
[29] Law

The twenty-nine factors of description/analysis in the model are designed to encompass, either by themselves or through the sub-factors associated with them, all of the "factors of success," "strategic variables," "principles," "terms of reference," systemic "input and output factors," or areas of research in the writings of practitioners of political violence, authorities, and outside observers. These people are the keys to conducting, combating, and/or describing and analyzing conflicts or elements of conflicts involving political violence movements. In addition, each of the twenty-nine factors may be viewed in terms of the management-type "functions" performed by both the rebels and the authorities in a P.V.M. conflict.

A major element of the interrogative approach is the use of a "systems approach." A "system" can be defined as "a collection of elements defined for a specific purpose."(7)

> But why a "systems approach?" The good analyst recognizes the necessity of carefully defining the *set* of things he is interested in and their interrelationships. When he draws a box around his "system," its parameters are determined by his purpose. We often speak of "a system" as if it has an entity all its own. This is a mistake. Every system is a conceptual creation of a man's mind. . .
>
> The systems approach suggests one other important concept: every system is a subsystem. . .
>
> A good analysis, then, starts with a careful definition of the system under consideration. To make them manageable, most systems so defined must be limited in scope. A proper question . . . is, "Have any critical elements been omitted?"(8)

The new model features an international or world Political Violence Movement System, an analytical construct which encompasses all on-going P.V.M. conflicts and their component elements at a particualr time. Furthermore, each individual P.V.M. conflict may be viewed as a separate system. Considering political violence movements and the opposing authorities in terms of a systems approach may help the outside observer in a number of ways. This approach helps to point out the total subject universe and to identify which elements, events, or influences are to be considered within the scope of the analysis. A systems approach can further the identification of new issues, research questions, and relationships, as well as point out the interrelationships of the various elements in the system. The approach defines influences and impacts relating to both the internal and external environments. Moreover, a systems approach can enhance the efficiency and effectiveness of analysis and perhaps helps avoid piecemealing, fragmentation, duplication, or "reinvention of the wheel."

Apparently, the greatest advantage of a systems approach in considering any subject for study is that it encourages the observer to "think big" and to consider all relevant factors in at least the initial stages of inquiry. Some scholars interested in phenomena relating to P.V.M.s, for example, focus only upon relatively small aspects like the psychology of rebel leaders, the ways in which international law might limit international terrorism, or ways to improve police intelligence. Such studies are indeed necessary; however, at least some scholars should envision and retain the "big picture" of all P.V.M.-related matters and studies. Certainly it is not possible to include within the scope of each academic study of some P.V.M.-related phenomena all aspects of the subject or all of the different academic disciplines. With the systems approach, it does appear that particularly in the case of P.V.M. conflicts, it is necessary for more scholars to think in broad terms and to pay close attention to unfamiliar phenomena, different disciplines, and relevant new research techniques.

The international Political Violence Movement System is therefore an integral part of the model, and consideration of elements of it are prescribed at various points in the process of using the model. The international P.V.M. System basically consists of all known P.V.M.s, the authorities and other actors with whom the P.V.M.s interact, the domestic and international environments, and the various linkages and actions which occur within the system.

Consideration of the major participants in a P.V.M. conflict can be useful in terms of the management and management-related functions which they perform. Examination of the P.V.M. and the authorities in a P.V.M. conflict from the standpoint of management functions can sometimes provide insights and conclusions which might not evolve using only the analytical approaches associated with the new model. The use of functions coincides with the symmetrical approach of the model, recognizing that both the rebels and the authorities are "managing" the conflict and performing various management-related functions. The various management functions, each of which is associated with one of the twenty-nine factors of description/analysis, are illustrated in Figure III. The functions are written in such a way that both sides are performing the same basic functions. However, the outside observer must identify the perspective from which he is viewing the P.V.M. conflict.

MODEL DYNAMICS

Using the new model, the analyst of a particular P.V.M. conflict should generally consider the twenty-nine factors of description/analysis in order. After examining the first twenty-nine factors,

FIGURE III

MANAGEMENT FUNCTIONS AND POLITICAL VIOLENCE
MOVEMENT CONFLICTS

Factors	Management functions
[1] Status	Identify creation of a P.V.M.
[2] Action Decision	Identify the problem/take initial action.
[3] Broad Objectives	Set broad objectives.
[4] Leadership	Direct and control.
[5] Membership	Staff the organization.
[6] Actors/Roles	Cultivate friends vs. foes.
[7] Domestic Environment	Assess domestic environment.
[8] International Environment	Assess international environment.
[9] P.V.M. System/Linkages	Develop "systems approach" or "big picture" perspective.
[10] Cause	Assess cause(s) of problem.
[11] Ideology	Identify/utilize ideology.
[12] Strategy	Plan and implement strategies.
[13] Popular Support	Acquire domestic popular support.
[14] Organization	Develop organization.
[15] Propaganda/Communication	Indoctrinate and communicate.
[16] Tactics	Plan and apply tactics/offensive methods.
[17] Domestic Material Support	Acquire domestic material support.
[18] International Support	Exploit international environment/ linkages.
[19] Intelligence	Develop intelligence network.
[20] Counterintelligence	Develop security network.
[21] Subversion/Organization Phase	Conduct/oppose subversion.
[22] Terrorism Phase	Conduct/oppose terrorism.
[23] Guerrilla Warfare Phase	Conduct/oppose guerrilla warfare.
[24] Conventional Warfare Phase	Conduct/oppose conventional warfare.

FIGURE III

MANAGEMENT FUNCTIONS AND POLITICAL VIOLENCE
MOVEMENT CONFLICTS (Cont)

Factors	Management functions
[25] Incentives	Assess incentives.
[26] Capabilities	Assess capabilities.
[27] Vulnerabilities	Assess vulnerabilities.
[28] Intentions	Assess intentions and plans.
[29] Law	Assess legal-related aspects.

the analyst may want to determine the overall conclusions and research questions about the conflict and to determine the relationship of the conflict to other past and present P.V.M. conflicts. The ability of the analyst to "put it all together" will depend to a large extent on the manner in which data has been organized.

A Worksheet (Figure IV) has been developed to assist the analyst in organizing data and in ultimately extracting conclusions and research questions. In using the Worksheet, the analyst can record all of the data concerning each P.V.M. conflict. The Worksheet can be appropriately annotated to reflect the conflict, Basic Question, factor of description/analysis or sub-factor being considered. In the columns for Rebel and Authorities' Activities and Functions, the analyst can note firm or tentative data and conclusions/research questions and can in a separate column note miscellaneous comments or source data. It is significant that, in line with the symmetrical nature of the model, the perspectives of both the rebels and the authorities are to be employed in reflecting data and conclusions/research questions.

The analyst should first consider the three What Factors: [1] Status, [2] Action Decision, and [3] Broad Objectives. These factors are introductory in nature, and their consideration can elicit a basic understanding of the broad matter being examined. The analyst initially notes that a P.V.M. exists or once existed. On the Worksheet, in terms of Status, he notes whether the P.V.M. is/was rural or urban-oriented, domestic or international, and performs/performed acts associated with the [21] Subversion, [22] Terrorism, [23] Guerrilla Warfare, or [24] Conventional Warfare Phases. At some time, the analyst will note that the P.V.M. made the Action Decision to use armed force to

FIGURE IV

PVM CONFLICTS WORKSHEET

P.V.M.(s) _____ Basic Question Being

Authorities _____ Considered:

____ Single P.V.M. Conflict?

____ Multiple P.V.M. Conflict?

DATA/FINDINGS SECTION:

(a) Factor of Description/ Analysis

(b) Sub-factor of Description/ Analysis

(c) Rebel Activities/ Functions—Data or Conclusions

(d) Authorities' Activities/Functions— Data or Conclusions

(e) Comments/ Sources

achieve some [3] Broad Objectives against the authorities, which may represent a single state, a number of states, or an international entity.

The observer next considers Factors [4]-[20], the Who, Where, Why and How Factors. The model encompasses virtually all of the "factors of success," "strategic variables," "principles," and "input/output factors," which appear in the literature concerning the conduct of P.V.M. conflicts. Many writers have suggested that a rebel campaign may have "failed" or "succeeded" due to the role played or not played by one or more of the various factors. For example, an author might attribute an insurgent P.V.M.'s "failure" to the movement's inadequate [4] Leadership, weak [14] Organization, remote [11] Ideology, narrow [5] Membership base, and inappropriate [7] Domestic Environment.(9)

As the observer considers the associated sub-questions and sub-factors, he attempts to ascertain the degree of applicability of each factor to the particular P.V.M. conflict being examined. He tries to determine the impact of each factor on the final outcome or present status of the conflict. Much description is necessary, but the emphasis should be upon analysis. Each factor is viewed in terms of both the P.V.M. and the authorities. At some time, the analyst will record on the Worksheet conclusions/research questions concerning each factor. These conclusions may never be firm, remaining as predictions or as hypotheses perhaps susceptible to further study.

The purpose of the Who Factors is to determine the identity and the nature of the various [6] Actors in a conflict involving a P.V.M. The analyst is interested in the [4] Leadership of the P.V.M. and assessing such sub-factors as backgrounds, qualities, and functions. The [5] Membership of the P.V.M. may be assessed in terms of the sub-factors of backgrounds, skills, and numbers.

The examination of [6] Actors/Roles in a P.V.M. conflict should not be limited to the P.V.M. and the authorities but should also include any other relevant domestic or international individuals. Remembering that each P.V.M. is part of the larger international P.V.M. System, the analyst should examine an individual conflict as it relates to other P.V.M. conflicts. In many cases the same actors may be involved in more than one conflict. The main actors within the world P.V.M. System are: supranational governmental entities; supranational unofficial organizational entities; governments of states (considered as single Actors); official or government-related state sub factors in, for example, the police, army, judiciary, and legislature; unofficial national sub-actors in, for example, a political party, labor union, and insurgent P.V.M.; and individuals. Actors in the last three groups may also operate internationally.

Actors within the international P.V.M. System may play a number of roles, sometimes in multiple and simultaneous fashions. An Actor may perform as a perpetrator of movement political violence (i.e., an active P.V.M. in a combatant status); suppressor of movement political violence (i.e., the authorities, be they domestic or international, in a combatant status); target of movement political violence; victim of movement political violence; ally of a combatant P.V.M. (could be combatant itself, i.e., actually involved in violent activities, or a non-combatant); ally of authorities in combatant or non-combatant status; and uninvolved or neutral individual.

The Where Factors are closely related to the Who Factors. Clearly, the total environment or setting in which a P.V.M. operates has a major impact on the nature and outcome of conflict. The total environment considered here is of course the international P.V.M. System. In considering the Where Factors, the international P.V.M. System may be examined under [7] Domestic Environment, [8] International Environment, and the international [9] Political Violence Movement system/linkages. A Domestic Environment is essentially a state and may be examined in terms of socio-economic, political, and geographic/strategic aspects. It may be viewed as a domestic Political Violence Movement System.

Under [8] International Environment, the broad international socio-economic, political, and geographic/strategic aspects of a particular P.V.M. conflict should be examined. Because of the immense complexity of the world today, examination under [8] of a P.V.M. conflict is initially and primarily a fact-gathering exercise. The international [9] System/Linkages is designed to place in perspective, and to generate conclusions and research questions concerning, facts gathered about the International Environment. Consequently, factor [9] encompasses such matters as neighboring states/sanctuaries/foreign occupations; material resources flows; human resources flows; propaganda/ideology/diplomacy flows; international rivalries/alliances/miscellaneous relationships; international governmental organization activities; and non-governmental international political and other organization activities. The relationships of these various factors to one another are treated in the model as "linkages."(10) Viewing a particular P.V.M. conflict from the perspective of the P.V.M. System/Linkages is especially useful in highlighting the importance of external influences on the outcomes of insurgencies. For example, the outcome of the struggle in Angola and the on-going insurgent struggles in the rest of Southern Africa are especially susceptible to broad spectrum analysis.

The analyst should be familiar with the possible "causes" of conflicts involving P.V.M.s to better understand current movements and to gain insights into future P.V.M. conflicts. The [10] Cause may be assessed in terms of underlying preconditions (socio-economic, political and externally-oriented conditions) as well as precipitants (immediate events which tend to trigger the initiation of violent actions). It is also useful to assess [11] Ideology which P.V.M.s use to characterize and to attain their political aims.

If the analyst has been asking the Basic Questions in sequence and considering the associated factors of analysis/description, the sub-questions, and the sub-factors, he will be familiar with the general nature and broad objectives of a P.V.M. the composition of a P.V.M. and the identity and nature of its opponents and allies, and possible reasons behind the existence of the P.V.M. The analyst will next want to know how the rebels operate. Consequently, he should consider the How Factors or modus operandi, including [12] Strategy, [13] Popular Support, [14] Organization, [15] Propaganda/Communication, [16] Tactics, [17] Domestic Material Support, [18] International Support, [19] Intelligence and [20] Counterintelligence.

Of crucial importance is strategy. Selection and implementation of the appropriate strategies to attain political objectives is perhaps the most important function of both the rebels and authorities. In the case of the P.V.M., strategy or the lack of it dictates to a large degree what the application of such factors as Popular Support, Organization, Propaganda/Communication, and Tactics will be. The authorities also must develop and implement a strategy appropriate to the threat which will counter P.V.M. efforts in Popular Support Organization, etc. Identification of strategies is useful later in describing and analyzing how the participants in a P.V.M. conflict operate. No broad strategies may be apparent, and indeed, none may exist. The P.V.M. may be engaging in limited violence perpetrated solely on behalf of limited tactical-level objectives. On the other hand, the authorities may have no broad strategic plan for combating the rebels but may be merely *reacting* on an incident-by-incident basis to P.V.M. actions.

Popular Support is viewed by most observers and most practitioners like Mao Tse-tung, Vo Nguyen Giap, and Che Guevara as the key to successful insurgency against an incumbent regime. Popular Support may manifest itself in the form of mere sympathy for a P.V.M. or in active support. Active participants may serve as an observer or messenger; provide supplies, weapons, ammunition, medicine and food; treat the wounded and sick; provide funds and intelligence information; participate in strikes, demonstrations, and riots; engage in passive resistance; conduct sabotage; or print and distribute propaganda.

Depending upon the rebels' broad objectives, P.V.M.s may or may not actively seek popular support. If they do, they may obtain it through means related to the factors of [14] Organization, i.e., through diversifying the organization to encompass mass movements; [15] Propaganda/Communication, i.e., by communicating emotional/ideological appeals to the populace; and [16] Tactics, i.e., gaining support through the use of terrorism. In some cases, a P.V.M. that is little interested in obtaining Popular Support within the country where it primarily operates may be less reluctant to engage in acts of terrorism.

The other How Factors are of obvious significance. Organization encompasses those institutional arrangements or mechanisms used to get a job done. Aspects include structure, mass movements, unity/cohesion, recruitment, and training. The methods of propagandizing a P.V.M.'s objectives to its own members, to the state in which it is based or operating, to international entities, and to world public opinion are aspects included within the scope of [16] Propaganda/Communication. Domestic Material Support [17] involves the domestic acquisition of such essentials as clothing, funds, shelter, food, arms, ammunition and medicine. Intelligence [19] is defined to mean gathering information about one's opponent, while [20] Counterintelligence refers essentially to maintaining internal security and loyalty.

The How Factor of [18] International Support is designed to involve the observer in determining the nature, extent, and impacts of the possible types of linkages developed previously in the analysis. At this point, the analyst should be familiar with the international transfer of funds, ammunition, advisors, intelligence, combatants, and with the provision of sanctuaries and international diplomatic support. The analyst should attempt to evaluate as broadly and as innovatively as possible the obvious and the not-so-obvious impacts of both material and political International Support furnished to the major participants in the P.V.M. conflict by external or international entities. Contemporary P.V.M.-related matters that could be considered in regard to particular P.V.M. conflicts and in regard to International Support are the role of the Palestine Liberation Organization (P.L.O.) vis-a-vis the United Nations and the Big Powers; the role of the Soviet Union and Cuba in Angola and elsewhere in Southern Africa; the possibility of action by regular Cuban troops in other Latin American states; the benefits accruing to Rhodesian insurgents by virtue of the diplomatic and other political actions of the United States, Great Britain, and the international community in general; and, the possible dispersal of American weaponry from Hanoi's captured stocks to P.V.M.s all over the world.

The [16] Tracts factor examines the actual acts of political violence in the P.V.M. conflict. It is valuable to view the planning and application of tactics from the perspective of each side because of the symmetrical nature of the struggle. Moreover, such an approach can force the observer to relate participant tactics to other factors like [3] Broad Objectives, [12] Strategy, [13] Popular Support, [15] Propaganda/Communication, and [18] International Support.

As the observer considers each tactic or offensive method used in a P.V.M., he should attempt to ascertain the impacts of that use. How does the practice of kidnapping foreign diplomats relate to an insurgent movement's efforts to obtain and retain Popular Support? How does the assassination of politicians or security force members within an insurgent situation impact on Popular Support? What are the possible effects on International Support of the hijacking of international commercial airliners by rebels furthering Propaganda/Communication? The analyst is encouraged to ask these kinds of questions, taking into consideration the multiple and complex linkages and impacts. As he assesses the various tactics and actions applied by a P.V.M., he can pose similar questions from the perspective of the authorities.

The When Factors are designed to assist the analyst in assessing the past, present, and future activities of P.V.M.s. In general, the Basic Question involves when certain P.V.M. activities occurred in history. The primary interest is how these P.V.M. activities can analytically and sequentially be considered in terms of increasingly violent phases or stages of conflict. In order to assist the analyst in examining P.V.M. activities, an analytical construct called the Political Violence Movement Phases can be used. These phases, [21]-[24] can be used to characterize the activities of a P.V.M. at a particular point in its development. A P.V.M. can be said to pass through the P.V.M. Phases as it moves forward (or backward) along a violence intensity scale. From low to high intensity, a P.V.M. may move through the following Phases, each of which corresponds to one of the model's factors of description/analysis: [21] Subversion/Organization Phase, involving organizational expansion and subversive activity, possibly with limited violence; [22] Terrorism Phase; [23] Guerrilla Warfare; and [24] Conventional Warfare. Use of the P.V.M. Phases to describe and analyze P.V.M.s gives the Political Violence Movement System a time dimension. Hard and fast characterizations of P.V.M.s relative to particular phases at different points in time are not possible. P.V.M. conflict situations vary widely from one another. Nevertheless, use of the P.V.M. Phases as an analytical tool can facilitate comparing P.V.M. conflicts and assessing the past, present, or future actions available to P.V.M.s.

The idea behind the P.V.M. Phases is that virtually any developing P.V.M. will go through certain phases relating to the types of activities in which it engages. Activities associated with the Subversion/Organization phase typically include making the initial [2] Action Decision; developing the movement's initial [14] Organization, including cells and networks; establishing an external [19] Intelligence system to gather tactical information and an internal [20] Counterintelligence system for insuring the loyalty of P.V.M. members; supplying the movement with [17] Domestic Material Support and the material aspects of [18] International Support; and seeking the backing of foreign political groups (the political aspects of International Support). During [21] ,the P.V.M. usually begins to promote its [10] Cause and [11] Ideology through the use of a multifaceted [15] Propaganda/Communication effort. Other activities or methods associated with Subversion/Organization might include legal or clandestine efforts to establish a political party or front groups, protest marches, petitioning, picketing, work stoppages, demonstrations, the distribution of propaganda materials, espionage, general strikes, riots, and looting. Low-level terrorism like arson and sabotage may occur. If the P.V.M. is little interested in acquiring popular support, Subversion/Organization might be of very short duration, and the rebels might move quickly into the next Phase, [22] Terrorism. Activities initiated in one Phase may of course continue into other Phases.

Regardless of the type and extent of generally non-violent activity which preceded it, the Terrorism Phase is representative of the kind of offensive actions that are most prevalent among contemporary P.V.M.s. It involves such [16] Tactics as kidnapping, assassination, hijackings, bombings, arms thefts, and robberies. In insurgency, terrorism is often the first type of violence in which the participants engage. Insurgent terrorism, contrasted to generally more intensively violent activities of a [23] Guerrilla Warfare Phase, is usually resorted to early because of the insurgents' weakness in numbers, weaponry, and [13] Popular Support. Unless the insurgent [10] Cause, fueled by an attractive [11] Ideology, is quickly adopted by the bulk of the population, terrorism is a readily available means for striking at a regime and at citizens unsympathetic to the movement. "International terrorism," in which rebels perpetrate acts of terrorism across international borders, is also usually representative of the inherent weakness of the P.V.M. concerned. A P.V.M. could, like the Palestine Liberation Organization, have substantial military, monetary, and political strength and yet need to employ international terrorism to further its political aims.

There is no clear distinction between the [22] Terrorism and [23] Guerrilla Warfare Phases, and acts of terrorism may continue in the latter phase. The Guerrilla Warfare Phase generally finds rebels engaging in larger-scaled operations, using more and heavier weapons and occasionally engaging government platoons or larger units on a more or less equal basis. The temporary occupation of the Uruguayan town of Pando in 1969 by the Tupamaro insurgents (11) is an example of the Guerrilla Warfare Phase. The traditional Communist insurgency model prescribes that during [23], "liberated" areas are established where rebels maintain control and rebel forces engage the government forces in the contested areas. The [24] Conventional Warfare Phase begins when conventional military operations on the part of the rebels begin to predominate. The rebels can deploy battalion-size or larger units, heavy artillery, tanks, and aircraft.

The last Basic Question relates to significance. The Factors — [25] Incentives, [26] Capabilities, [27] Vulnerabilities, [28] Intentions, and [29] Law build upon, and are designed to place in evaluative perspective, all the previous Factors. Incentives, Capabilities, Vulnerabilities, and Intentions are all inseparably related from an analytical standpoint. These five So What Factors are most applicable to current P.V.M.s and their overall significance, but the analysis of contemporary P.V.M.s can also benefit from the evaluation of past or defunct P.V.M.s. It is possible to view past P.V.M. conflicts in terms of the So What Factors — the analyst can attempt to view the conflict from particular points in past time, from both the P.V.M. and the authorities' points of view. If data are available, the analyst of an historical case might compare what each side thought was going to happen with what actually did happen. Whatever reasons why events did and did not occur can then be applied to contemporary P.V.M. conflicts, and their possible relevance can be considered.

The [25] Incentives Factor relates essentially to what conditions, events, objectives, and motives might lead a P.V.M. to undertake different actions. An analyst interested in predicting P.V.M. behavior might ask what political events, economic conditions, social upheavals, and military measures might serve as incentives for a P.V.M. to change any aspect of its behavior. Of particular interest would likely be such behavior patterns as targeting for different terrorist acts, the application of various levels of force, and the confining of P.V.M. operations to a single state versus international terrorism activities. Incentives for rebels to change their behavior in such areas might result. From promises of increased material or political [18] International Support, rebels might perceive that certain new targets (perhaps nuclear) would provide especially spectacular publicity. They might learn through intelligence information that a particular target was weakly defended or otherwise very vulnerable.

Capabilities[26] are viewed in the military sense. Capabilities of a P.V.M. may involve skills of leaders and members; the number of combatants, supporters, and sympathizers in various locations around the world; training; degree of commitment, motivation, and fanaticism; degree of domestic [13] Popular Support; material or political [18] International Support; organizational unity and cohesion; [19] Intelligence and [20] Counterintelligence; types and members of ammunition and weapons; financial resources; and, other [17] [18] Material Support like vehicles, supplies, explosives, and technical equipment. Capabilities analysis must make allowances for uncertainty and unpredictability, including the possibility that a P.V.M. could rapidly upgrade some of its capabilities through linkages to other movements or governments.

It can be highly misleading to view [25] Incentives and [26] Capabilities without simultaneously taking into account [27] Vulnerabilities characterizing each side in the P.V.M. conflict at any given time. Either side of a conflict has Vulnerabilities. An analysis of Vulnerabilities can involve the strengths and weaknesses of whole societies, of insurgency and counterinsurgency training, of particular tactics employed, and of the physical security given certain targets. The observer of a particular P.V.M. conflict is encouraged to consider both a macro- and a micro-level in assessing the Vulnerabilities of each side. At the micro-level, traditional [22] Terrorism and [23] Guerrilla Warfare targets include bridges, roads, railway lines, airport facilities, telephone and telegraph lines, power nets, vital industrial plants, repair shops and depots, warehouses, headquarters, convoys, and enemy units. Targets associated with today's highly technological and increasingly interdependent world include the large jets and other airliners; supertankers, Middle Eastern pipelines, and related petroleum processing facilities; television and radio stations; telephone and other communications terminals; services like power, water and mail; computer data and control systems; nuclear power plants, nuclear weapons, radioactive materials, and associated transportation processes; chemical, biological and radiological agents; the Suez and Panama Canals; multinational corporations; and highly publicized national and international expositions, conferences.(12) Analysts assessing contemporary Vulnerabilities of P.V.M. activity must think creatively and remember that because of extensive "linkages" in such areas as transportation, communications, weaponry, and computer technology the impacts of terrorist activities may extend beyond particular incidents. Fortunately, most contemporary targets have not yet been significantly attacked by P.V.M.s. A good question for the analyst with a "big-picture" systems perspective is, "Why not?"

In considering [28] Intentions, the observer of current P.V.M.s attempts to combine knowledge of each P.V.M. and its past with knowledge about other movements and their past. Consideration of Intentions must encompass all factors of description and analysis. Thinking about Intentions especially involves close attention to [26] Incentives, [27] Capabilities and [28] Vulnerabilities. Consequently, the rebels' Intentions will likely vary according to the Incentives which they perceive and to their perceptions of their own Capabilities and the enemy's Vulnerabilities. The ability of an outside observer to ascertain Intentions of P.V.M.s or of the authorities opposing them is of course a difficult task; it is more of an intelligence task than an academic one. Nevertheless, it is a valid and necessary function for any outside observer to attempt to determine Intentions.

Intentions may involve broad strategies or the application of specific tactics to particular targets. What are the enemy's long-range Intentions? Do rebels plan to employ tactics of [23] Guerrilla Warfare or [24] Conventional Warfare, or do they plan to confine their offensive actions to [22] Terrorism? Are rebels planning to target diplomats, aircraft, or business facilities? Will terrorists attack a particular target at a particular time?

The last Factor of description and analysis is [29] Law. Conflicts involving P.V.M.s must also be viewed from a legal perspective. Law includes the sub-factors of domestic statutes, international statutes, international organizations, and dangers to civil liberties. Insurgency-type P.V.M. conflicts often involve such legal-related problems as recognition of belligerency, diplomatic recognition, governments in exile, intervention of one state in the affairs of another, international peacekeeping forces, the legality of rebel terrorism, the role of alliances, the legal status of non-uniformed rebels, the use of chemical or biological weapons, legal protections to be afforded non-combatants, suspension of civil liberties to better combat rebels, and the existence of rebel sanctuaries. International terrorism in P.V.M. conflicts may involve problems of extradition treaties, the right of political asylum, diplomatic immunity, state responsibilities for protecting foreign diplomats, difficulties in taking legal action against P.V.M.s operating internationally, and the applicability of domestic or national laws aimed at acts of international terrorism. Also related to [29] Law are areas of international cooperation to hinder the operations of P.V.M.s. These areas include police investigations, discovery of illegal weapons or contraband, border security, contingency planning, studies, airport security, visa and immigration procedures, customs, and intelligence collection and the sharing of intelligence data.

CONCLUSION

Although P.V.M. conflicts can be viewed from both the rebels' and authorities' perspectives, it is recognized that the discussion of the model is almost exclusively concerned with the rebel perspective. Nevertheless, the description of the model offers a different way of explaining phenomena which have been called political terrorism, international terrorism, or insurgency.

The presentation indicates the following: 1. Inquiry concerning political violence by movements can be furthered considerably by using a systems approach. 2. Subject delimitation is vitally needed in all academic-oriented endeavors relating to contemporary political violence. Although conceptual and definitional disarray is common in most social sciences, it appears that the potential of nuclear terrorism and other aspects of contemporary political violence necessitate an organized and conceptually coherent approach to maximize the utility of academic research. 3. An "interrogative approach" using certain Basic Questions and sub-questions, characterized by encouragement for other analysts to develop their own questions and to think innovatively, appears to be a good starting point for bringing order to a disparate body of knowledge. 4. All of the foregoing represents an attempt at pre-quantitative and pre-theoretical organization and conceptualization. The overriding premise inherent in the model is that the matter of "political violence movements" is one worthy of serious study. The study of P.V.M.s will be enhanced to the extent that scholars, the media, government analysts, businessmen and the general public can examine, using a common non-emotional language, the conflicts in which such movements are involved.

NOTES

(1) Harold L. Nieburg, *Political Violence: The Behavioral Process,* New York: St. Martin's, 1969, p. 13.

(2) Harry Eckstein, "On the Etiology of Internal Wars," *History and Theory,* Vol. 4, No. 2, pp. 133-134, 1965; Ted R. Gurr, *Why Men Rebel,* Princeton: Princeton University Press, 1970, p. 11.

(3) Edward Luttwak, *Coup d'Etat: A Practical Handbook,* London: Allen Lane, 1968, p. 24; David Galula, *Counterinsurgency Warfare: Theory and Practice,* New York: Praeger, 1964, pp. 4-5.

(4) Eckstein, supra note 2, p. 134.

(5) Richard L. Kuiper, "Theory and Practice of Insurgency," *Education Journal,* Maxwell Air Force Base, Alabama: Air Force R.O.T.C., Air University, September-October 1974, p. 31.

(6) Galula, p. 5; and, Samuel P. Huntington, "Patterns of Violence in World Politics," *Changing Patterns of Military Politics,* ed. Huntington, New York: Free Press of Glencoe, 1962, p. 20.

(7) William A. Henderson, "The Analysis Mystique," *Air University Review,* Vol. 18, No. 2, pp. 34-37, January-February 1967.

(8) Henderson, supra note 7.

(9) Thomas H. Greene, *Comparative Revolutionary Movements,* Englewood Cliffs, New Jersey: Prentice-Hall, 1974, p. 2.

(10) See, e.g., James N. Rosenau, ed., *Linkage Politics: Essays on the Convergence of National and International Systems,* New York: Free Press, 1969, especially the essays by Rosenau.

(11) Maria Esther Gilio, *The Tupamaro Guerrillas of Uruguay,* trans. Anne Edmondson, New York: Ballantine, 1970, pp. 119-159; James A. Miller, "The Tupamaro Insurgents of Uruguay," *Political Violence and Insurgency: A Comparative Approach,* eds. Bard E. O'Neill, D.J. Alberts and Stephen J. Rossetti, Arvada, Colorado: Phoenix, 1974, p. 227 and passim.

(12) For discussions of some of these targets, see Brian M. Jenkins, "High Technology Terrorism and Surrogate War," passim; Brian M. Jenkins, "International Terrorism: Trends and Potentialiies," Rand Corporation paper, p. 5339, January, 1975, presented at Conference on International Terrorism, U.S. State Department, Washington, D.C., March 25-26, 1976.

APPENDIX: INTEGRATIVE/INTERROGATIVE APPROACH AS IT APPLIES
TO POLITICAL VIOLENCE MOVEMENT CONFLICTS
(Summary of Basic Questions, Factors of
Description/Analysis, Sub-Questions,
and Sub-Factors)

Since the model is designed to be applicable to present, past and future P.V.M.s, the verb tense in the questions may be altered accordingly.

I   WHAT IS THE GENERAL SITUATION INVOLVING A PARTICULAR POLITICAL MOVEMENT VIS-A-VIS THE AUTHORITIES?   (Problem Overview)

[1] *Status:* What kind of political phenomenon is the political grouping, i.e., is it a political violence movement (P.V.M.)? (Sub-factors: rural vs. urban; insurgency vs. international terrorism)

[2] *Action Decision:* What immediate events or general circumstances characterized the initiation of action by the P.V.M.? (Sub-factor: spontaneous vs. planned)

[3] *Broad Objectives:* What are the broad objectives of the P.V.M./authorities vis-a-vis the opponent?

II WHO ARE THE ACTORS IN THE P.V.M. CONFLICT? (Actors)

[4] *Leadership:* Who are the leaders of the P.V.M./the key leaders among the authorities opposing the P.V.M.? (Sub-factors: backgrounds; qualities; functions)

[5] *Membership:* Who comprises the membership of the P.V.M./the relevant subordinates among the authorities opposing the P.V.M.? (Sub-factors: backgrounds; skills; numbers; psychological dimension)

[6] *Actors/Roles:* Who are all of the actors associated with the P.V.M. conflict, and what roles do they play?

III WHERE WITHIN THE INTERNATIONAL P.V.M. SYSTEM DOES THE P.V.M. CONFLICT EXIST OR HAVE RELEVANCE? (Environments/Linkages)

[7] *Domestic Environment:* Where is, and what is the nature of, the domestic environment in the P.V.M. conflict? (Sub-factors: socio-economic; political; geographic/strategic)

[8] *International Environment:* Where is, and what is the nature of, the international environment in the P.V.M. conflict? (Sub-factor: sanctuary)

[9] *Political Violence Movement System/Linkages:* Where does the P.V.M. conflict fit within the Political Violence Movement System? (Sub-factors: Neighboring states/sanctuaries/foreign occupations; material resources flows; human resources flows; propaganda/ideology/diplomacy flows; international rivalries/alliances/miscellaneous relationships; international governmental organization activities; nongovernmental international political and other organization activities)

IV WHY DOES THE P.V.M. CONFLICT EXIST? (Origins/Purposes)

[10] *Cause:* Why did certain preconditions lead to, or combine with, precipitating events to comprise a "cause" sufficiently

compelling to prompt the creation of a P.V.M. and a P.V.M. conflict? (Sub-factors: preconditions; precipitants)

[11] *Ideology:* Which ideologies or "myths" do the P.V.M. and the authorities employ in the P.V.M. onflict?

V   HOW DO THE REBELS AND THE AUTHORITIES OPERATE IN THE P.V.M. CONFLICT? (Modus Operandi)

[12] *Strategy:* How does the P.V.M./authorities plan and implement strategies to attain objectives, and what are these strategies?

[13] *Popular Support:* How does the P.V.M./authorities acquire popular support from the people within the state, if applicable?

[14]*Organization:* How is the P.V.M./authorities organized for the conduct of the P.V.M. conflict? (Sub-factors: structure; mass movements; unity/cohesion; recruitment; training)

[15] *Propaganda/Communication:* How does the P.V.M./authorities employ propaganda/communication techniques? (Sub-factors: propaganda techniques; communication techniques; propaganda of the deed)

[16] *Tactics:* How does the P.V.M./authorities plan and apply tactics to attain objectives, and what are these tactics? (Sub-factors: offensive methods; broad tactical goals; characteristics of operations)

[17] *Domestic Material Support:* How much does the P.V.M./authorities acquire necessary material support for the P.V.M. conflict from within the state?

[18] *International Support:* How does the P.V.M./authorities acquire material and political support from within the international Political Violence Movement System?

[19] *Intelligence:* How does the P.V.M./authorities acquire and make use of intelligence?

[20] *Counterintelligence:* How does the P.V.M./authorities use counterintelligence techniques to promote internal security?

VI   WHEN — IN HISTORY AND IN TERMS OF THE P.V.M. PROCESS — DOES THE P.V.M. CONFLICT TAKE PLACE? (Phases/Authorities' Response)

[21] *Subversion/Organization Phase:* When and to what degree did the P.V.M. conflict generally assume the character

of the subversion/organization phase? (Sub-factors: P.V.M. tactics; authorities' response)

[22] *Terrorism Phase:* When and to what degree did the P.V.M. conflict generally assume the character of the terrorism phase?

[23] *Guerrilla Warfare Phase:* When and to what degree did the P.V.M. conflict generally assume the character of the guerrilla warfare phase? (Sub-factors: P.V.M. tactics; authorities' response)

[24] *Conventional Warfare Phase:* When and to what degree did the P.V.M. conflict generally assume the character of the conventional warfare phase? (Sub-factors: P.V.M. tactics; authorities' response)

VII   SO WHAT? WHAT IS THE SIGNIFICANCE OF THIS P.V.M. CONFLICT IN TERMS OF THE OUT-COME/PRESENT STATUS? (Significance)

[25] *Incentives:* What incentives does the P.V.M./authorities have for intensifying, diminishing, or otherwise altering its objectives, strategies, tactics, targets, etc., in the P.V.M. conflict?

[26] *Capabilities:* What are the capabilities of the P.V.M./authorities in the P.V.M. conflict, and what were they during each phase of the P.V.M. Process?

[27] *Vulnerabilities:* What are the vulnerabilities of the P.V.M./authorities at the present time as well as during each phase of the P.V.M. Process? (Sub-factors: macro-level; micro-level)

[28] *Intentions:* What are the intentions of the P.V.M./authorities?

[29] *Law:* What is the impac of law, to include domestic and international statutes and international organizations, on the P.V.M. conflict? (Sub-factors: domestic statutes; international statutes; international organizations; dangers to civil liberties)

NOTE: Since the model is designed to be applicable to present, past and even future P.V.M.s, the verb tense in the above questions can be altered.

Jay Mallin:
Terrorism as a Military Weapon

It is a dress which is justly supposed to carry no small terror to the enemy, who think every such person a complete marksman.

General George Washington

Terrorism is a disease of modern society. It is a virus growing in an ill body. The effects of the virus can sometimes be ameliorated, but there is no certain cure.

The causes of terrorism are diverse; often one cause overlaps another or several causes. There is the social cause: Uruguayan young people denied their rightful place in a society that was stagnating. There is the racial cause: black and Indian militant groups in the United States. And, of course, there is the political cause: Israelis seeking independence from Great Britain; Cubans seeking freedom from Dictator Batista and then from Dictator Castro; Algerians seeking independence from France; northern Irish Catholics seeking to destroy British rule, and, conversely, Irish Protestants seeking to neutralize the Catholics.

Each instance was or is one of armed conflict—in a word, of war. Whether the cause be social discontent or national aspirations, a larger or smaller segment of a population wars on another segment or on a foreign adversary. The feasible weapon is terrorism. A military observer, Colonel William D. Neale, noted, "Terror, it is obvious, is a legitimate instrument of national policy."(2)

The complexity of causes of terrorism, the diverse ideologies that have employed terrorism, the multitudinous arms and tactics available to terrorists—all these factors have made terrorism one of the most complicated problems of the times. Certainly the scope of the problem defies understanding by any single discipline. Terrorism is a tangled skein of varied human motivations, actions, hopes, emotions, and goals.

A conference on terrorism and political crimes held in 1973 made the following conclusion, among others:

> The problem of the prevention and suppression of "terrorism" arises in part because there is no clear understanding of the causes leading to conduct constituting "terrorism." The International Community has been unable to arrive at a universally accepted definition of "terrorism" and has so far failed to control such activity.(3)

Terrorism cannot be explained by psychologists who construct facile theories. It cannot be countered by police who view terrorism as simply one more type of criminal activity: identify the criminals, arrest them, throw them in prison or perhaps shoot them, and the problem is solved. Terrorism cannot be handled by conventional military men who scoff at it as being beneath their notice.

The academician who wishes to study terrorism with academic dispassionateness finds theories, explanations, and chronological statistics but little else. Penetrating interviews with genuine terrorists, for example, are of minimal availability.

Terrorism *is* a tangled skein, and any observer attempting to unravel and separate one thread leaves himself open to criticism, justified criticism. "You say terrorism is a military weapon. What about kidnappings solely for financial gain in Italy and the brigandage in Argentina motivated by monetary profit?"

Precisely. The skein is a mess of threads; it may not be possible to separate any one of them cleanly. Nevertheless, the effort is worth attempting if it contributes a pinpoint of light in what is certainly a long, dark tunnel. This article will attempt to focus on one thread: terrorism as a military weapon.

In September 1972 the world was stunned to learn that the Twentieth Olympic Games, a symbol of international harmony, had been attacked by political terrorists. A group of urban guerrillas belonging to the Palestinian Black September movement had forced their way into the Israeli quarters at the Olympic Village and seized nine hostages. The guerrillas issued a number of demands, including one for the release of 200 Palestinian prisoners in Israel. Day-long negotiations took place between the guerrillas and the West German government, and eventually the government appeared to accede to the Palestinian demands. An accord was reached whereby the terrorists, together with their hostages, were to be taken to an airport and there provided with air transportation to Egypt. At Furstenfeldbruck Airport, however, German snipers opened fire on the terrorists, and in the resulting battle all Israeli hostages died, as did four guerrillas, a police officer, and a helicopter pilot.

Thanks to the sophistication of modern communication systems, people in many lands were kept abreast of developments minute by minute. Americans watched television in fascination as events unfolded before their eyes. When the final holocaust occurred at the German airport, shock, horror, and revulsion swept the civilized world.

The question was repeatedly asked, what did the Palestinians hope to gain by their action? Did not the kidnappings—and the resulting killings—do their cause far more harm than good? The actions of terrorists, however, cannot be measured in the way other acts of war or revolution are appraised. Urban guerrillas do not march to the same drum that regular soldiers or even rural querrillas march to. Colonel Neale stated:

> Terroristic violence must be totally ruthless, for moral scruples and terror do not mix and one or the other must be rejected. There can be no such thing as a weak dose of terror. The hand that controls the whip must be firm and inplacable.(4)

Although not generally viewed as such, the Olympic action was nevertheless fundamentally a military move. Having failed in three conventional wars to defeat the Israelis, the Arabs and Palestinians resorted to unconventional tactics: specifically, terrorism in the border zones and against Israeli installations in foreign lands. If the Arab leaders had not themselves been conventional, they might have utilized unconventional tactics much earlier—perhaps more successfully than were their efforts to defeat the Israelis in "regular" warfare.

Basically, terrorism is a form of psychological warfare (frighten your enemy; publicize your cause). Seen within this context, the Olympic attack achieved its purpose. Kidnapping the Israeli athletes did no military harm to Israel. As a psychological blow, however, it probably boosted Palestinian morale, and it certainly spotlighted worldwide the Palestinian cause. It encouraged future moves by Palestinian terrorists—the historical record attests to this. As a psychological blow the Olympic attack demonstrated that wherever Israeli figures of prominence went abroad, whether they be diplomats or athletes or whatever, they were susceptible to terrorist attack.

War is armed conflict, and armed conflict is the province of the military. Terrorism is a form of armed conflict; it is therefore within the military sphere. When diplomats fail, soldiers take over. When soldiers fail, terrorists take over. The political terrorist, however, is a soldier, too. He wears no uniform, he may have received little or no training, he may accept minimal discipline, his organization may be ephemeral—but he is a soldier. He engages in armed conflict in pursuit of a cause. His weapons are the gun and the explosive. His battlefield is the city street, and his targets are the vulnerable points of modern society.

Certainly not all terrorists are soldiers. Not all terrorism is military. For purposes of this article, it is postulated that terrorism is military when: 1. It is utilized as a substitute for "regular" warfare, as in the case of the Palestinians against the Israelis. 2. It is used in conjunction with other military activities, as in the cases of Cuba (against Batista) and Vietnam (against the Saigon administrations). 3. It is used as the chosen weapon of conflict by a population segment against another segment and/or a foreign power, as in Northern Ireland.

Terrorism is sometimes believed to be synonymous with urban guerrilla warfare. Urban guerrilla warfare, however, is a broader term: it encompasses urban terrorism but other actions as well, i.e., ambushes, street skirmishes, assaults on official installations, and other types of hit-and-run urban combat. Also, it may be noted that terrorism is not confined to urban zones: it can be conducted in rural areas as well, as was notably the case in South Vietnam.

Thus, terrorism in certain circumstances is conducted as a military tactic. The purpose of military action is often to achieve political goals. "For political aims are the end and war is the means. . . " stated Clausewitz.(5) In some instances terrorism is a part of the means, or is *the* means.

Terrorism as a tactic can be traced back to ancient times. Today's terrorists take human hostages; Incas of old seized the idols of the people they had conquered and held these as hostages to ensure that the defeated would not rebel. Terrorism as a tactic of urban guerrilla warfare dates back to the struggles in the past century and in this century to Russian revolutionaries against the czars. The concept of terrorism as a military instrument, however, is comparatively new. One of the papers developed at the first National Security Affairs Conference, held at the National War College in 1974, noted:

> Despite Mao's emphasis on the relationship between guerrilla warfare and the rural peasant, despite the doctrinaire vision of armed, revolutionary conflict culminating on the open battlefield, and despite the role of rural warfare in the most important revolutions of the past half-century, the rapid urbanization of much of the world now suggests new opportunities, and hence new strategies for revolutionary warfare, and, in particular, a new attitude toward the role of the city as the ultimate revolutionary battlefield.(6)

For the political militant, urban guerrilla warfare offers clear advantages over rural guerrilla warfare. If he is a city youth, he can remain in the cities and need not meet the rugged demands of rural and hill fighting. In the cities there is an abundance of potential targets. The countryside offers few targets. In the cities there are opportunities for militant actions (such as the placing of bombs) that do not necessarily entail direct personal conflict with the police. In the countryside guerrillas must eventually prove themselves by combat with units of the regular army. Rural guerrilla warfare requires a great deal of physical exertion with few gratifying results over a long period. In urban areas guerrillas can commit spectacular acts that garner great publicity and, then, if they have not been identified by the authorities, can return to "normal" lives until the time comes for their next violent action.

The growing technological complexity of our times increases the vulnerability of modern life. Not only does technology engender vulnerability, it also develops more sophisticated weapons that can kill or endanger more people and do more damage. Professor Zbigniew Brzezinski aptly referred to "the global nervous system";(7) Swedish Premier Olof Palme, at the United Nations, discussed "technology's multiplication of the power to destroy."(8)

One has but to look about a modern city and he will see a plethora of targets. Aqueduct pumping stations and conduits, power stations and lines, telephone exchanges, post offices, airport control towers, radio and television stations—all these form part of a city's nervous system. Terrorists can shoot at policemen, rob banks, sabotage industrial machinery, kill government officials, incapacitate vehicles, and set bombs in theaters and other public localities. Destruction of an enemy's cities is an accepted strategy of modern warfare; whether it be accomplished by aerial bombers or by land-bound terrorists is merely a matter of means. The National War College paper previously noted also pointed out:

> The destruction of a hydroelectric system, the crippling of a central computer bank, the acceleration of a social disorder by racist and counterracist assassination, the undermining of an economy by the pollution of an entire wheat crop . . . all these are but mere samples of the kind of violence which would lend itself to strategic manipulation. Although disguised in the name of revolution or rebellion, such violence could be decisive in terms of distracting a nation, or isolating it, or even paralyzing it. It would be, in effect, a new form of war.(9)

As postulated, terrorism could be used in conjunction with "regular" military activities. Or it could be used as a substitute. Colonel Seale R. Doss sets forth in the aforementioned paper that, "with the rapidly shifting alliances and animosities of the modern world, no nation could be quite sure in any case just which foreign power had (or even *if* some foreign power had) sponsored its disasters, for such violence would lend itself, like underworld money, to political laundering."(10)

Because terrorism as an instrument of war is a relatively new concept, there has been little doctrinal categorization or interpretation of, or doctrinal direction for, this type of warfare specifically. The three foremost warrior-theoreticians of guerrilla warfare, Mao Tse-tung, Vo Nguyen Giap, and Ernesto "Che" Guevara, virtually ignored this method of combat. Giap has said only that *"to the counter-revolutionary violence of the enemy, our people must definitely oppose [place in opposition] revolutionary violence,"* and that *"the most correct path to be followed by the peoples to liberate themselves is revolutionary violence and revolutionary war."(11)* (Emphasis is Giap's.) By "revolutionary violence" Giap probably meant all available means of warfare, including terrorism.

Guevara alone approached the subject of urban guerrilla warfare as a specific type of combat, and then he did so only in brief. In his book *La Guerra de Guerrillas* he provided limited recognition to what he called "sub-urban warfare." The sub-urban guerrilla group, he stated, should not carry out "independent actions" but rather should "second the action of the larger groups in another area." As for terrorism itself, Guevara said, "We sincerely believe that that is a negative weapon, that it does not produce in any way the effects desired, that it can turn a people against a determinate revolutionary movement and that it brings with it a loss of life among those who carry it out far greater than the benefits it renders." Guevara separated terrorism from assassination, which he felt was "licit' although only in "very selective circumstances," namely, against "a leader of the oppression."(12)

La Guerra de Guerrillas has served as a basic instructional book for Latin American guerrillas. It has, however, no instructions for urban guerrilla warfare. This is especially interesting in view of the fact that the urban guerrilla movement played as important a role, perhaps a more decisive role, than did the rural guerrillas in the 1956-1958 Cuban civil war. Fidel Castro and Guevara preferred, however, to promote the mystique of the rural guerrilla. They had been rural guerrilla captains, and it did not suit the historic position they envisioned for themselves to grant recognition to the urban clandestine movement that participated so significantly in the conflict.(13)

There was a practical consideration as well in the Castro-Guevara effort to develop the mystique of the rural guerrilla. Almost as soon as Castro came to power in Cuba, that small country launched an extensive program of subversion, with most of the effort concentrated on creating *fidelista* guerrilla movements in rural areas of Latin America. Castro and Guevara sought to duplicate their own guerrilla operation: launched from abroad, it had functioned in isolated rural areas. Guerrilla warfare, declared Guevara, is "the central axis of the stuggle" in Latin America.(14) So deeply did Guevara believe in the guerrilla mystique that eventually it led him to his death in Bolivia. It was only after repeated failures. including Guevara's death, that Castro turned his attention to urban movements.

A perusal of other military instructional literature reveals a similar dearth of attention to urban guerrilla warfare. North Vietnamese Lieutenant General Hoang Van Thai's *Some Aspects of Guerrilla Warfare in Vietnam*(15) deals entirely with rural combat. The *Handbook for Volunteers of the Irish Republican Army*(16) is a fine basic book on rural guerrilla warfare, and much that it says is applicable to urban guerrilla combat, but it does not touch on this specifically despite the long utilization of urban terrorist tactics by the Irish Republican Army (IRA). Bert "Yank" Levy's *Guerrilla Warfare*(17) has a brief chapter on "the city guerrilla," but the book is primarily about rural guerrilla warfare. Spanish General Alberto Bayo's *One Hundred and Fifty Questions to a Guerrilla*(18) and Swiss Major H. von Dach Bern's *Total Resistance*(19) also have material useful to an urban guerrilla particularly in regard to sabotage activities, but again the books are concerned mainly with rural guerrillas.

The only document specifically dealing with urban guerrilla warfare that has received international recognition was written by a Brazilian politician-turned-terrorist, Carlos Marighella. Marighella wrote the *Minimanual of the Urban Guerrilla* for use by Brazilian terrorists, but its instructional contents are valid for guerrillas in any city in the world. Marighella stated:

> The urban guerrilla is an implacable enemy of the government and systematically inflicts damage on the authorities and on the men who dominate the country and exercise power. The principal task of the urban guerrilla is to distract, to wear out, to demoralize the militarists, the military dictatorship and its repressive forces, and also to attack and destroy the wealth and property of the North Americans, the foreign managers, and the Brazilian upperclass.(20)

Marighella declared: "The urban guerrilla is a man who fights the military dictatorship with arms, using unconventional methods. . . . The urban guerrilla follows a political goal . . ."(21)

It is interesting to note that just as Mao, prophet of rural guerrilla warfare, believed that type of combat was secondary to "regular" warfare,(22) Marighella, prophet of urban guerrilla warfare, envisioned urban combat as supplementary to rural guerrilla combat. He stated that the function of urban guerrilla warfare was "to wear out, demoralize, and distract the enemy forces, permitting the emergence and survival of rural guerrilla warfare which is destined to play the decisive role in the revolutionary war."(23)

As for terrorism specifically, Marighella said, "Terrorism is an arm the revolutionary can never relinquish."(24) It is also a weapon the military cannot ignore.

Anyone writing about terrorism labors under the difficulty that it has not been possible for anyone to develop an entirely satisfactory definition of terrorism. Mainly this is due to the fact that there is no precise understanding of what the term "terrorism" encompasses. There are too many grey areas of violence and of intimidation that may or may not be labeled as terroristic. Whether any particular area of activity or specific act is indeed terroristic largely depends on the circumstances within which this is undertaken. Example: Is sabotage a form of terrorism? Seeking an answer, we go full circle, for whether sabotage is terroristic depends on the definition of terrorism.

Therefore, in this article the following working definition is offered: Political terrorism is the threat of violence or an act or series of acts of violence effected through surreptitious means by an individual, an organization, or a people to further his or their political goals. Under this definition sabotage committed for political purposes is indeed a form of terrorism.

Perhaps there is no such thing as "military terrorism." Or perhaps this is merely a semantic lack. At any rate, terrorism is one form of military activity that can be utilized by an organization or a people in pursuit of their political goals. Terrorism is a military weapon.

(Most often, terrorism consists of a series of acts of violence. All terrorism is criminal in the eyes of the government that is assailed. But there may be "criminal terrorism" in which the violence is committed purely for monetary, not political gain. Frequently this type of terrorism will disguise itself as political terrorism, especially in situations wherein genuine political terrorism is rampant, e.g., the Argentine situation.)

Terrorism as a military arm is a weapon of psychological warfare. The purpose, as the very word indicates, is to engender terror in the foe. The terror thrust encompasses the following ingredients: 1. Terrorism publicizes the terrorists' political cause. 2. Terrorism demonstrates the capability of the terrorists to strike blows. 3. Terrorism heartens sympathizers of the terrorists' cause. 4. Terrorism disconcerts the enemy. 5. Terrorism eventually—the ultimate goal—demoralizes the enemy and paralyzes him. 6. Conceivably, in certain circumstances, terrorism could deter potential allies of the terrorists' target country from assisting that country. ("If you provide aid to our enemy, we will unleash our terror tactics against you, too.") 7. Sabotage causes material damage to an enemy's vital installations; the damage, in turn, has a psychological effect on the foe and on the populace. It frightens the foe and emboldens the ally.

Terrorists function within an area controlled by the enemy whether it be a metropolis or an airliner in flight. The terrorists either: represent a significant portion of the population (as in the case of a struggle against an unpopular dictator), and their actions are applauded, even when they cause discomfort to the population (as when rebels knocked out a substantial portion of Havana's electric and water systems during the Cuban civil war(25); do not receive any significant amount of popular support and are generally condemned as outlaws (the minuscule ethnic militant groups in the United States are an example); or, are foreign or foreign-supported and are seeking to destroy the enemy's control structure or to achieve some other political result (as in the case of the I.R.A. bombs in restaurants and othe public places in London).

Whereas in Case One the terrorist may try to minimize civilian casualties in order not to turn the population against him, in Case Three the more casualties there are the better the terrorist feels his goals are served: he is applying ruthless pressure against his enemy, and the number of casualties is a measure of his success. In Case Two, whether the terrorist concerns himself over civilian casualties is largely determined by whether his fanaticism is tempered by mercy.

At what point does terrorism become the concern of the "regular" military? For a military establishment that is *attacking,* terrorism can be used as a substitute for conventional warfare or in conjunction with conventional warfare and/or rural guerrilla warfare. For a military establishment that is responsible for *defending* an area or a country, the military role in the handling of a terrorist problem is determined by local circumstances: Is the government of the country under attack run by civilians or by the military? What constitutional and other legal responsibilities and restrictions are placed on the military? What useful capabilities do the military have that the police do not have?

The level of intensity of terrorist activity appears to be a determinant of military response more than any other factor. In most national cases military activity has been largely limited to guard and military intelligence duties in support of the police authorities. In other cases, however—notably in pre-Israel Palestine, Cyprus, Algeria, Uruguay, Argentina, and Northern Ireland—the military took over primary responsibility for combating terrorists because the police were overwhelmed.(26) In those cases cited where the military sought to maintain foreign control over populations, it is significant that the independence struggles were nevertheless successful (except in Ireland, where the conflict continues). In the two countries where indigenous military have sought to suppress major terrorist movements, the military were successful in one instance (Uraguay), and the outcome is as yet inconclusive in the other (Argentina). One may reasonably gather from this that terrorism is an effective weapon when used by a substantial portion of a population against foreign occupation troops. As a weapon against indigenous authorities supported by a military establishment, its efficacy is open to question. Terrorism appears to have succeeded only in such cases wherein it was used in conjunction with other military tactics (Cuba, South Vietnam).

There appear to be three fundamental functions of terrorism as a military weapon: 1. psychological warfare—demoralize the enemy (his government, armed forces, police, even the civilian population) through assassinations, bomb explosions, agitation, and so on. The Viet Cong utilized the entire arsenal of violence in their campaign in South Vietnam. 2. material destruction—destroy or damage the enemy's utilities, communications, and industries. Destruction by sabotage, particularly against specific targets limited in size, can be as effective as destruction by air raid. 3. economic damage—engender a state of psychological unease and uncertainty in a city or a country and commerce dries vs, investment funds vanish. The deterioration of the Cuban economy during the 1956-58 revolution was a major factor in the downfall of the Batista regime.

Terrorism utilized as a military weapon, whether by a foreign power or by domestic insurgents, is somewhat akin to air raids: it is warfare conducted in the enemy's rear. In both cases the tactic aims at destroying the foe's installations, killing his officials, and battering his morale. Lamentably, in both cases the deaths of civilians are an additional result, unacknowledged as a goal but nevertheless often deliberately sought.

If, then, terrorism is a military weapon—a weapon to be used for a military goal: the defeat of an enemy—how much recognition of this weapon has been extended by "regular" military establishments? Traditionally the regular military have looked askance at any type of unconventional warfare. This remains true today even though the line of differentiation between conventional and unconventional warfare grows increasingly blurred. In the cases of the British, Israeli, Argentine, and Uruguayan armies, the military have been forced by circumstances to recognize their responsibility in dealing with terrorism. Reality has legitimatized the bastard, military terrorism, in fact if not in name. The daring Israeli commando rescue of 102 airline-hijack hostages at Entebbe, Uganda, in July 1976 was a dramatic example of the utilization of military power in a counterterror endeavor.

In South Vietnam terrorism was a major problem facing the American and South Vietnamese forces. Nevertheless the main responsibility for combating it was turned over to civilian intelligence organizations, such as the Central Intelligence Agency. In general, of the military branches only the U.S. Marines recognized the military importance of Viet Cong terrorism and sought not only to conquer territory but to hold it and to provide security for its inhabitants.(27) It is interesting to note that the U.S. Joint Chiefs of Staff's *Dictionary of Military and Associated Terms* finds no place for the words "terror" or "terrorism."(28)

U.S. military interest in terrorism appears to be minimal. The fact that one of the panels at the National War College's National Security Affairs Conference dealt with "New" Forms of Violence in the International Milieu" was encouraging. There have been lectures and panels at the Institute for Military Assistance at Fort Bragg, North Carolina, and a protection-against-terrorism manual for U.S. military personnel being sent overseas has been written there. The *Air University Review* has published a number of relevant articles. This attention, however, must be considered inadequate in view of the enormity of the problem. Major General Edward G. Lansdale, U.S.A.F. (Ret) has warned:

We live in a revolutionary era. My hunch is that history is waiting to play a deadly joke on us. It did so on recent graduates of the Imperial Defence College in London, who now find themselves facing the savagery of revolutionary warfare in Northern Ireland. It did so on Pakistani officers under General Niazi, who undoubtedly wish now that they had learned better ways of coping with the Mukti Bahini guerrillas. It is starting to do so on Argentine graduates of the Escuela Nacional de Guerra in Buenos Aires, who are waking up to the fact that Marxist E.R.P. guerrillas intend to win themselves a country with the methods of the Tupamaros next door.(29)

There are existing situations and possible situations which counsel greater understanding of terrorism by the U.S. military. American military personnel have already been subjected to terrorist attacks in countries as diverse and far apart as Iran and Guatemala. It is not inconceivable that an international terrorist organization might decide, for tactical and ideological reasons, to strike at U.S. military personnel and even installations in a number of countries. N.A.T.O., concerned over the spread of terrorism, conducted through the intelligence agencies of its member states a study of an international terrorist organization that is believed to operate globally.(30)

The United States provides military equipment and guidance to a substantial number of friendly countries. Of what use is tank warfare doctrine to an army confronted with a major terrorist problem? Are U.S. Military Advisory Groups prepared to provide the assistance needed? Another scenario: U.S. forces are stationed in a foreign country, perhaps as part of an international peacekeeping force, and the local rebels resort to terror tactics. Are the U.S. military prepared to cope with such a situation?

There are additional scenarios that might require military involvement in terror situations within the United States itself, much as troops were required at critical moments during the civil rights struggle of the sixties. Recognizing the constitutional and historical limitations on the military and recognizing that a terror level akin to those in Argentina and Northern Ireland is not likely to develop in the United States within the foreseeable future, one can, nevertheless, postulate situations in which the military would have to exercise counterterror capabilities. Two possibilities exist: 1. Terrorists seize the Capitol in Washington while Congress is in session. Or they take another major edifice in an American city. Handling the crisis is beyond the means of the police. 2. Terrorists have a nuclear weapon or a major bacterial weapon. They hold the weapon in a heavily guarded building in the center of a city, and they threaten to devastate the city if their demands are not met. Again the situation is beyond the capability of the police.

Hypothetical situations, yes. But terrorists have seized buildings in other countries, and the U.S. government is concerned over the possibility of terrorists obtaining a nuclear bomb. These situations could occur within the United States. The U.S. military would do well to prepare to assist if they are called upon to do so.

Beyond that is the necessity of recognizing that in today's world terrorism is often a military weapon. General Robert E. Lee said of the Confederacy's own guerrillas, "I regard the whole system as an un-mixed evil."(31) Evil or not, guerrilla warfare has been employed by in-numerable combatants down through the ages, always bedeviling the regulars. Disdaining it will not make it go away. Disdaining terrorism will not make it go away, either. Unhappy though it may make the graduate of the Imperial Defence College, or of the Escuela Nacional de Guerra, or of the U.S. Military Academy, it is a tactic that must be dealt with. Far better that the U.S. military be prepared than that they, too, be caught by surprise. Tactics must be studied, doctrines must be developed, defenses must be constructed. For, as one writer stated, "Step by step, almost imperceptibly, without anyone being aware that a fatal watershed has been crossed, mankind has descended into the age of terror."(32)

NOTES

(1) Richard M. Ketchum, *The Winter Soldiers,* New York, 1973. Washington prescribed the "rifle dress" for his troops because it was associated in the minds of the British with the apparel worn by skilled riflemen.

(2) Colonel William D. Neale, USA (Ret), "Terror—Oldest Weapon in the Arsenal," *Army,* August 1973.

(3) M. Cherif Bassiouni, editor, *International Terrorism and Political Crimes,* Springfield, Illinois, 1975.

(4) Neale, supra note 2.

(5) H. Rothfels in *Makers of Modern Strategy,* Edward Mead Earle, editor, New York, 1970.

(6) Colonel Seale R. Doss in *Defense Planning for the 1980s & the Changing International Environment,* Washington, D.C., 1975.

(7) "The U.S. and the Skyjackers: Where Power is Vulnerable," *Time,* 21 September 1971.

(8) "The City as Battlefield: A Global Concern," *Time,* 2 November 1970.

(9) Doss, supra note 6.

(10) Ibid.

(11) Vo Nguyen Giap, *The South Vietnam People Will Win*, Hanoi, 1965.

(12) Ernesto Guevara, *La Guerra de Guerrillas*, Havana, 1960.

(13) See: Jaime Suchlicki's *University Students and Revolution in Cuba, 1920-1968*, Coral Gables, Florida, 1969; Ruby Hart Phillip's *Cuba, Island of Paradox*, New York, 1959; Jay Mallin's *Fortress Cuba*, Chicago, 1965.

(14) Guevara, "Guerrilla Warfare: A Method," *Cuba Socialista*, September 1962.

(15) Foreign Languages Publishing House, Hanoi, 1965.

(16) Issued by General Headquarters, 1965.

(17) Panther Publications, Boulder, Colorado, 1964.

(18) Twenty-eighth edition, Havana, 1961.

(19) Panther Publications, Boulder, 1965.

(20) Carlos Marighella, *Minimanual of the Urban Guerrilla*, Tricontinental, Havana, November 1970.

(21) Ibid.

(22) "When we say that in the entire war [against Japan] mobile warfare is primary and guerrilla warfare supplementary, we mean that the outcome of the war depends mainly on regular warfare, especially in its mobile form, and that guerrilla warfare cannot shoulder the main responsibility in deciding the outcome." From "On Protracted War" in *Selected Military Writings of Mao Tse-tung*, Peking, 1963.

(23) Marighella, supra note 20.

(24) Ibid.

(25) Mallin, supra note 13.

(26) Robert Taber, *The War of the Flea*, New York, *1965; Challenge and Response in Internal Conflict*, three volumes, Washington, D.C., 1967, 1968.

(27) William R. Corson, *The Betrayal*, New York, 1968.

(28) Washington, D.C., 1972.

(29) Major General Edward G. Lansdale, USAF (Ret), "The Opposite Number," *Air University Review*, July-August 1972.

(30) "Radical Nations Aid, Finance Global Terror, N.A.T.O. Thinks," *Miami Herald*, 6 February 1976.

(31) Bruce Catton, *A Stillness at Appomattox*, New York, 1953.

(32) Paul Johnson, quoted in David Fromkin's "The Strategy of Terrorism," *Foreign Affairs*, July 1975.

Ernest Evans:
American Policy Response to International Terrorism: Problems of Deterrence

In the late 1960s, the United States government began to build a structure of deterrence against acts of transnational terrorism. Alexander George and Richard Smoke generally define deterrence as the art of convincing an adversary not to undertake a given course of action by persuading the adversary that the costs and risks of that course of action outweigh the benefits. Deterrence is achieved when C (costs) + R (benefits) are greater than B (benefits). There are basically two ways of attaining deterrence: 1. The value of the C + R part of the formula can be increased by threatening retribution which is deterrence by punishment or what Thomas Schelling called "coercive diplomacy." 2. The value of the other B (benefits) part of the formula can be decreased by not allowing the adversary to obtain any rewards from his actions. The adversary is deterred by denial. (1)

International terrorism became a problem for the United States in the late 1960s with the beginnings of widespread attacks on American diplomats, on American airliners, and on American citizens overseas. Efforts to deter these acts of terrorism followed two policies: One policy was established for "two-step" terrorist incidents, including kidnapping — ransom demand and hostage-taking — negotiation. A second policy was established for "one-step" terrorist incidents in which an act of violence did not involve hostages.

In the late 1960s when diplomatic kidnappings first became common, the United States pursued a much softer approach to terrorism than it has recently. When Charles Elbrick, U.S. Ambassador to Brazil, was kidnapped by Brazilian terrorists in September 1969, Secretary of State William Rogers and other officials in the Department of State urged the Brazilian government to accede to the terrorists' demands that Brazil release a group of political prisoners. When the Brazilians released the prisoners and when the Ambassador was found alive, the Department of State thanked Brazil.(2) However, with the kidnapping of Daniel Mitrione in Uruguay in August, 1970 the U.S. government began to follow a harder line by refusing to make concessions to terrorists or to bargain with them. This hard-line policy was forcefully reiterated in response to the kidnapping of a Dutch student and three Americans in Tanzania in May of 1975. The students were taken to Zaire, where they were held for ransom. The parents of the students raised the ransom, and the four students were released. It was soon learned that Ambassador Beverly Carter of Tanzania had acted as an intermediary between the terrorists and the parents; Carter had consequently violated Department of State's policy of "no negotiations, no concessions" in dealing with terrorist demands. Carter was reprimanded and denied an expected apointment as Ambassador to Demark. At a press conference, Secretary Henry Kissinger explained the rationale for refusing to negotiate with or make concessions to terrorists holding Americans as hostages:

> On the other hand, if terrorist groups get the impression that they can force a negotiation with the United States and an acquiescence in their demands, then we may save lives in one place at the risk of hundreds of lives everywhere else.
> Therefore it is our policy — in order to save lives and in order to avoid undue pressure on Ambassadors all over the world, it is our policy that American Ambassadors and American officials not participate in negotiations on the release of hostages and that terrorists know that the United States will not participate in the payment of ransom and in the negotiation for it.(3)

Under Kissinger's leadership, the American policy towards political kidnappings explicitly indicated that kidnappings could be prevented, or at least reduced, only by eliminating the values of prisoners and ransoms in the right side of the George-Smoke formula. The policy sought to achieve deterrence by denial.

Did the American deterrence policy really deter and was Kissinger correct when he claimed that to negotiate with terrorists and to grant their demands would lead to a greatly increased number of kid-nappings? A comparison between the United States with its hard-line policy and other countries with soft-line policies indicates that the American policy did not deter terrorism.

The Federal Republic of Germany pursued a very different policy from that of the United States towards political kidnappings between 1970 and 1975. In March 1970, the West German Am-bassador to Guatemala was kidnapped by a group of terrorists who demanded that the Guatemalan government release a number of prisoners and pay a monetary ransom. The West Germans put con-siderable pressure on the Guatemalan government to meet the terrorists' demands, but the Guatemalans refused. The Ambassador was killed, and consequently the Federal Republic of Germany vir-tually broke diplomatic relations with Guatemala.(4) The West Ger-mans pursued their soft-line policy of negotiating with terrorists during the next five years. Because the United States pursued a much more intransigent policy than West Germany during this period, one would expect that there should have been significantly more kid napping incidents involving West Germans than Americans. If money and prisoners are what terrorists want from a kidnapping, then a terrorist would more likely kidnap a West German than an American because the West Germans would make great efforts to accede to demands while the Americans would not. However, as Table I in dicates, significantly more kidnapping incidents involving American than West Germans occurred between 1970 and 1975.

In a political kidnapping, however, terrorists have a number o goals, only one of which is money and the release of prisoners Although terrorists may be denied the release of prisoners and money they will attempt kidnappings to obtain at least four other benefits o goals:

Publicity. Sir Geoffrey Jackson, the former British Ambassador t Uruguay, was kidnapped by the Tupamaro guerrillas and held fo eight months. After his release, Sir Geoffrey said he had discusse with his captors why they had seized him. He mentioned that a majo factor in his kidnapping was the guerrillas' desire for publicity. H said that the Tupamaros called their act "armed propaganda." T them, the kidnapping would show that they were powerful enough t kidnap an important foreign amba⁵ .dor without the Uruguaya government being able to do anythin bout it.(5)

Harassment: A number of Tupamaro manifestos and undergroun interviews indicated that very often their abductions of prominer figures were meant to harass and demoralize the Uruguayan politic elite and its military and police establishments.(6)

TABLE I

THE NUMBER OF POLITICAL KIDNAPPINGS INVOLVING THE
UNITED STATES AND THE FEDERAL
REPUBLIC OF GERMANY

Instances of political kidnappings involving demands on the governments of the United States and the Federal Republic of Germany over 5-year periods (1970-1975):

	No. of incidents
West Germany	9
United States	21

Instances of political kidnappings involving demands on private West German and American companies over 5-year periods (1970-1975):

	No. of incidents
West Germany	2
United States	13

Source: Brian Jenkins and Janera Johnson, *A Chronology of International Terrorism*, Santa Monica: The RAND Corporation, 1975.

Polarization of Society: Carlos Marighella, the Brazilian theorist of urban guerrilla warfare, has written that a major goal of terrorist acts, including kidnappings, must be to force authorities to be repressive, thereby polarizing society.(7) Marighella assumed that the guerrillas would effect polarization, but his assumption for Brazil has been a dubious one.

Aggravation of State-to-State Relations. A number of terrorist incidents have been staged to aggravate relations between states or to prevent relations from developing a political outcome unfavorable to the terrorist group. For example, the Ma'alot incident in May 1974 was largely motivated by a desire of the Palestinians to sabotage the Israeli-Syrian disengagement talks.(8)

American efforts to deter "one-step" terrorist incidents in which no attenpt is made to take a hostage have centered around efforts to negotiate multilateral conventions against terrorism. However, the United States had not had much success with international agreements about "one-step" terrorism. The U.S.-backed anti-hijacking conventions in Tokyo in 1963, in the Hague in 1971 and in Montreal in 1971 have won broad international backing, but American efforts to strengthen these accords by suspending air service to countries that harbor hijackers have failed. The conventions against diplomatic kidnappings — the Inter-American Treaty of 1971 and the United Nations Treaty of 1973 — have not yet received enough ratifications to come into effect. Finally, the United States needs a major effort to negotiate a general treaty against international terrorism, but the U.N. Draft Convention on International Terrorism was decisively defeated in the General Assembly in the fall of 1972.

Some of the reasons for the failure of these American-supported conventions can be demonstrated by examining the history of on major American effort, the 1972 Draft Treaty on International Terrorism. This draft treaty was introduced in the U.N. General Assembly in September of 1972 by Secretary of State William Rogers. The treaty pledged its signatories to either extradite or punish any individuals on their territory who had committed a terrorist act of international significance. An act of terrorism was judged to be of international significance if four conditions were met: 1. the act had to take place or have effects outside the territory of the state in which the offender was a national; 2. the victims of the attack had to be citizens of a state other than that state where the attack took place; 3. the attack had to be committed neither by nor against a member of the armed forces in the course of military hostilities; 4. the attack had to be intended to damage the interests or obtain concessions from a state or international organization.(9) Although these are fairly precise guidelines, exactly what acts the convention would have covered is open to dispute. The drafters specifically noted that wars being waged by indigenous rebels in places like South Africa were not covered by the convention.(10) Those drafting the convention were attempting to achieve "deterrence by punishment" and they hoped to increase the costs and risks of terrorism to the point where it would be deterred.

The U.S. introduced with the draft convention a resolution which urged states to ratify three anti-hijacking conventions and which called for prompt measures against international terrorism. Aware the debates in the legal committee that the American resolution commanded little support, the United States shifted its support to second resolution which had been introduced by some Western European and Latin American states. The second resolution, unlike the American resolution, reaffirmed in one paragraph the right of national self-determination. It was hoped that that paragraph would meet these objections to the original American resolution, concerning wars of liberation that had been raised by Arab, African, Asian and Communist states. However, a coalition of Third World and Communist states refused to accept the second resolution, and instead introduced and passed their own resolution which condemned racist and colonialist regimes as terroristic and called for an *ad hoc* committee to meet in 1973 to consider the problem of international terrorism. The *ad hoc* committee did meet for several weeks in 1973; but nothing resulted from its deliberations. Undoubtedly the coalition of states that voted for the resolution referring the issue to the *ad hoc* committee intended that nothing would result from the committee. American efforts to pass a multilateral convention had been wholly unsuccessful.

The convention was defeated, because those wanting it, above all the United States, had a very different view of terrorism than most members of the United Nations. To understand these different interpretations of terrorism, we should distinguish between a "humanitarian" issue and a "political" issue. A humanitarian issue can be defined as an issue about which there is a very broad consensus that the phenomenon in question is a problem; disagreements about the issue are limited to technical questions of how best to deal with the problem. A political problem, on the other hand, is a problem about which there is no consensus as to what the nature of the phenomenon under discussion is; a political problem involves a basic clash of values. To the United States and the other nations supporting a convention, terrorism was a humanitarian issue. These nations stressed humanitarian themes in the U.N. debates: they often referred to the needs of preserving innocent human lives from terrorist attacks and of preserving international order. These themes were consensual in nature. Unless one is a sadist, one cannot be in favor of killing innocent people; unless one believes in perpetual chaos, one cannot be opposed to the maintenance of international order. Tables II, III, and IV indicate what countries stressed humanitarian themes. The tables also indicate that the issues of the loss of life and of the protection of international order were serious, pressing issues and that "reasonable" wars of liberation did not justify the killing of the innocent.

TABLE II

THE ARGUMENTS OF THE STATES IN FAVOR OF ACTION AGAINST TERRORISM

	Protection of innocent lives	Defense of international order	Immoral use of force	Delay not justified
Australia			X	X
Austria	X	X	X	X
Belgium	X	X		X
Bolivia	X			
Brazil	X			
Canada	X			
Colombia			X	
Costa Rica	X	X		
Denmark	X		X	X
Dominican Republic				
Fiji	X			
Guatemala				
Haiti		X		
Iceland	X	X	X	X
Iran	X	X	X	X
Israel	X			
Italy	X	X		X
Japan	X			
Lestho	X			
Netherlands	X			X
New Zealand			X	X
Nicaragua	X	X	X	
Paraguay	X			X
Philippines				
Portugal				
South Africa	X			
Turkey		X		X
United Kingdom	X	X	X	X
U.S.A.	X	X	X	X
Uruguay	X	X	X	X
30 Countries	21	11	10	14

TABLE III

THE ARGUMENTS OF THE STATES OPPOSED TO ACTION AGAINST TERRORISM

	Definitions unclear	Causes not being studied	Acting in haste	Liberation struggles
Albania				X
Algeria				X
Bulgaria				X
Burundi		X		X
Beylorussian SSR	X			X
Cameroon	X	X		X
Chad				X
China				X
Cuba				X
Cyprus		X		X
Czechoslovakia				X
Dem. Yemen		X		X
Ecuador				X
Egypt	X	X		X
Ghana			X	X
Guinea		X		X
Guyana				X
Hungary				X
India			X	X
Indonesia		X		X
Iraq	X		X	X
Jamaica		X	X	X
Jordan	X		X	
Kuwait			X	
Lebanon		X		X
Liberia		X		X
Libya	X		X	X
Madagascar	X		X	X
Malaysia		X		X
Mali		X		
Mauritania		X		X
Mexico		X		X
Mongolia			X	
		X		X

TABLE III

THE ARGUMENTS OF THE STATES OPPOSED TO
ACTION AGAINST TERRORISM (Cont)

	Definitions unclear	Causes not being studied	Acting in haste	Liberation struggles
Niger	X			X
Nigeria		X		
Oman				X
Pakistan		X		X
Peru			X	X
Poland		X		X
Romania				X
Saudi Arabia		X	X	X
Senegal	X	X	X	X
Sierra Leone				X
Somalia	X	X	X	X
Sri Lanka	X			X
Sudan		X	X	X
Syria		X		X
Tanzania	X	X	X	X
Tunisia		X	X	X
Uganda	X			X
Ukrainian SSR				X
USSR				X
UAE		X		X
Venezuela	X	X		X
Yemen	X	X		X
Yugoslavia				X
Zambia				X
57 Countries	16	29	15	52

TABLE IV: THE VOTE ON THE RESOLUTION REFERRING ACTION ON TERRORISM TO AN *AD HOC* COMMITTEE

In favor: Afghanistan, Albania, Algeria, Bahrain, Botswana, Bulgaria, Burma, Burundi, Beylorussian SSR, Cameroon, Central African Republic, Chad, Chile, China, Congo, Cyprus, Czechoslovakia, Dahomey, Democratic Yemen, Ecuador, Egypt, Equatorial Guinea, Ethiopia, Gabon, Gambia, Ghana, Guinea, Guyana, Hungary, India, Indonesia, Iraq, Jamaica, Jordan, Kenya, Kuwait, Lebanon, Liberia, Libya, Madagascar, Malaysia, Mali, Mauritania, Mexico, Mongolia, Morocco, Niger, Nigeria, Oman, Pakistan, Panama, Peru, Poland, Qatar, Romania, Rwanda, Saudi Arabia, Senegal, Sierra Leone, Somalia, Sri Lanka, Sudan, Syria, Togo, Trinidad and Tobago, Tunisia, Uganda, Ukrainian SSR, USSR, United Arab Emirates, United Republic of Tanzania, Upper Volta, Venezuela, Yemen, Yugoslavia, Zambia.

In opposition: Australia, Austria, Belgium, Bolivia, Brazil, Canada, Colombia, Costa Rica, Cuba*, Denmark, Dominican Republic, Fiji, Guatemala, Haiti, Honduras, Iceland, Iran, Israel, Italy, Japan, Laos, Lestho, Luxemburg, Netherlands, New Zealand, Nicaragua, Paraguay, Philippines, Portugal, South Africa, Turkey, United Kingdom, United States, Uruguay.

Abstaining: Argentina, Barbados, El Salvador, Finland, France, Greece, Ireland, Ivory Coast, Malawi, Nepal, Norway, Singapore, Spain, Sweden, Thailand, Zaire.

*Cuba voted against the resolution not because it opposed it but because it opposed the whole idea of debating terrorism at all; the Cuban representative said the debate was an attempt to stifle wars of national liberation.

Source: Official Records of the General Assembly, 27th Session, 6th Committee, 1390 Meeting, p. 483. Vote on A/C.6/L.880/Rev. 1

To the coalition of Third World and Communist countries that blocked American efforts for a multilateral convention, terrorism was not a humanitarian issue; it was a political issue arising from struggles against what were considered racist and colonialist regimes. Of the 76 countries that voted in favor of the Third World-sponsored resolution referring action on terrorism to an *ad hoc* committee, some 57 made speeches in the 6th Committee. Of these 57, some 52 expressed concern that the issue of international terrorism might be used to repress wars of liberation. Other themes raised by these countries were all related to the concern for "wars of liberation." Unclear definitions were discussed, because it was feared that terrorism and wars of liberation might be confused; demands were made that the causes of terrorism, thought to be colonialism and racism, be studied as well as the phenomenon of terrorism itself; a slow, careful approach to terrorism was urged so that the causes of it could be studied. To most members of the United Nations, terrorism was not a humanitarian problem, but was a political manifestation of the wars of national liberation being waged against racism, colonialism, and apartheid.

The American policy on the deterrence of international terrorism suffered from "depoliticization" and from a failure to take into account the political factors involved in terrorism. If American policy is to be effective, it needs to be repoliticized; policy makers should take political factors into account. They might consider some of the following suggested changes in future U.S. foreign policy:

To deter hostage-taking situations, American policy makers must realize that such kidnappings cannot be deterred simply by refusing to make concessions or to negotiate. If such situations are to be deterred, policy makers will have to consider the other reasons for political kidnappings: publicity, aggravation of state-to-state relations, harassment, and polarization of society. In regard to these reasons, a policy of negotiating and making certain "cosmetic concessions" to those holding hostages might have some definite deterrent impact. Because kidnappings generate publicity regardless of the outcome of the kidnapping, one cannot hope to reduce the overall level of publicity. What one *can* hope to do is make sure that the publicity the terrorist group receives is negative in nature. Therefore, it is crucial in publicity to make clear that the terrorists and the terrorists alone will be responsible should any hostages be killed. A governmental policy of "no negotiations no concessions" enables terrorists to argue to world public opinion, with some apparent success, that the death of any hostage is the fault of the government, because it failed to be reasonable. If a government allows itself to be publicly portrayed as inflexible and rigid, then terrorists can blame that government for any subsequent deaths or disasters. If, however, a government shows that it is willing to talk and to make certain minor concessions, without agreeing to demands for ransoms and prisoners, then the moral responsibility for any destruction will be clearly fixed upon the terrorists. Finally, should terrorists get consistently bad publicity from hostage-taking incidents, they are less likely to stage additional incidents; terrorist groups need favorable publicity to succeed.

The chances of negotiating multilateral conventions are dependent on the policies that the U.S. adopts towards the various wars of liberation being waged around the globe. If the U.S. is to negotiate multilateral convention against terrorism successfully, some concessions must be made to the feelings of Third World nations about colonialism and racism. The precise form of these concessions may vary, but a few possible areas of negotiation can be defined. In the Middle East, the U.S. may be able to get Arab support for action against terrorism by promising to urge Israel to agree to a Palestinian state on land seized during the 1967 war. In black Africa, the U.S. may be able to get cooperation against international terrorism by agreeing to taking a strong stand against Rhodesia and South Africa; the U.S. might, for example, repeal the Byrd amendment. The U.S. could seek a multilateral convention against terrorism by strong political bargaining with Third World nations. American policy makers probably will not get a multilateral convention by continuing to argue that terrorism is a humanitarian issue and that all states have an interest in combating terrorism.

NOTES

(1) Alexander George and Richard Smoke, *Deterrence in American Foreign Policy: Theory and Practice.* New York: Columbia University Press, 1974, pp. 48, 59-60.

(2) New York *Times,* September 6, 8, 1969.

(3) "Secretary Kissinger's News Conference at Vail, August 17, 1975," *Department of State Bulletin,* September 15, 1975, p. 408.

(4) Carol Baumann, *The Diplomatic Kidnappings,* The Hague: Martinus Nijhoff, 1973, pp. 99-100.

(5) Author's interview with Sir Geoffrey Jackson, November 3, 1975.

(6) "Interview with 'Urbano' (Tupamaro Leader) by Leopoldo Madruga," in *Urban Guerrilla Warfare in Latin America,* ed. James Kohl and John Litt, Cambridge, Massachusetts: The M.I.T. Press, 1974, p. 281.

(7) Carlos Marighella, "The Minimanual of the Urban Guerrilla," in *Urban Guerrilla Warfare* by Robert Moss, London: I.I.S.S., 1971, p. 40.

(8) New York *Times,* May 17, 1974.

(9) "American Draft Convention on Terrorism," *Survival,* Vol. XV, No. 1, January/February, 1973, p. 32.

(10) John R. Stevenson, "International Law and the Export of Terrorism," *Department of State Bulletin,* Dec. 4, 1972, p. 651.

III.
LEGAL
PERSPECTIVES

Alfred P. Rubin:
International Terrorism and International Law

In discussing a problem of non-state behavior with serious implications on the international legal order, definitions of "terrorism" or "international terrorism" always seem to become so narrow or so broad that they are not useful for policy discussions. There are reasons why definitions must be narrow or broad. ⟨An examination of acts commonly referred to as "terrorism" quickly reveals that there is no common factor to distinguish all of them from common crime.⟩

Is "violence" required? If so, a definition would seem to exclude disrupting a telecommunications system by electronic means, flooding a country with counterfeit currency, or spreading anthrax or typhoid bacilli through the normal mails. Is a political motive required? If so, a definition would seem to exclude the bombing of the parcel storage area of La Guardia Airport for which no organization has yet taken "credit" and the December, 1975 kidnapping of O.P.E.C. Ministers in Vienna. Definitional problems are also raised in regard to the self-proclaimed motives of the most sordid criminals, like the members of the Manson family.

Is a "conspiracy" required? If it is, a definition must exclude political assassinations in the United States, like the murders of the Kennedy brothers and Martin Luther King and the attempted assassination of Governor Wallace. "Conspiracy" cannot be considered until it is shown to have existed, probably a long time after the assassination and after the time for appropriate national or international reaction. Is a "terror-outcome" required?

If it is, a definition must exclude at least the King and second
Kennedy assassinations, and the attempt against George Wallace,
and the 1972 Munich Olympic Massacre, where outrage rather
than terror was the dominant result.

It may be that for some useful purposes "terrorism" can be
defined by referring to one or more of these four factors —
violence, political motive, conspiracy, and terror-outcome. If so, it
must be conceded that the discussion relates to a particular
subset of what many people consider to be "terrorism" and not
to "terrorism" as a generic whole. Using only the four limited
factors, it is confusing and misleading to refer at all to
"terrorism." What is being discussed is not "terrorism" but some
specific acts which an author, legislator, or parties to a treaty
seek to define for a specific purpose. Those acts may deserve to
be called "aircraft hijacking" or "piracy" but not "terrorism."

One factor is recognized in all acts commonly labeled
"terrorism." The act of terrorism constitutes a common crime
under the municipal law of the territory (or of the flag-state of
the aircraft or vessel) where it occurs. What however distinguishes
the common crime of murder, arson, burglary or kidnapping
from the identical crimes enacted and labelled "terrorism"? Why
are the bank robberies of the Symbionese Liberation Army called
"terrorism" and the murders by the Manson family labelled,
"crime"? The distinguishing factor is the attempt by law-
enforcement officials to apply extraordinary procedures to the
activities labeled, "terrorism," while denying the need for
extraordinary procedures in regard to the identical acts not
labelled, "terrorism." The reasons for applying the label in one
case and not in another seem to have little to do with the
nature of the acts. The definitions of terrorism were determined
by the response of officialdom to the crimes. The definition was
not determined by motive or direct effect, but by whether or
not a political or general systemic significance is perceived in the
act by law enforcement officials.

During the nineteenth-century non-European political societies
were occasionally labeled, "piratical," when international cooperation in their suppression was sought or when the bounties
appropriate to pirate-hunters in municipal law were to be
collected. A leading British case (1) was that of the Magellan
Pirates (1853). Insurgents in Chile were labelled, "pirates,"
allowing the Royal Navy personnel to collect a public bounty
supplied by the British Parliament to encourage the suppression
of piracy. (2) The labeling occurred despite the fact that the
political object of the "pirates" was never questioned, and the

traditional, international law regarding piracy permitted attaching the label "piracy" only when depredations were committed for private gain. (3) Nowadays, when bounties are not generally given to public officials for the capture of "terrorists" or of any other criminals, the reasons for attaching the label, "terrorism," seem to relate primarily to the concepts of law enforcement officials regarding the threat posed by particular fugitives or accused criminals to the perceived legal order. Indeed, it would be an error to suppose that the Royal Navy in the mid-nineteenth century was more activated by hope of pecuniary gain than by a concept of the needs of society for untrammeled trade opportunities. Questions of motivation, however, need not be resolved.

For purposes of legislation and international agreement, there would seem to be little point in attempting to define "terrorism" as a set of acts. A more useful definition would include a direct specification of various types of activity for which policy makers, not law enforcement officials, conclude that extraordinary measures are appropriate. Law enforcement officials are excluded, because as a group they have a less balanced view of the total interests of society, law enforcement being only one important interest of society.

It is presumed that the normal law of any society is able to maintain order in that society, that restraints on law enforcement authorities include those made by social traditions including the constitution of the society, and that a compelling case for departure from those traditions must be made before such a departure should be authorized. Reasonable people may differ as to whether the threat to society posed by some acts, like a conspiracy to cross state lines to raise a riot, is enough to justify the kind of enforcement activity that would be necessary to suppress that threat. An evaluation of the threat and the depth of the traditions that might have to be disrupted to limit that threat should be evaluated by a legislature. It is not made simply by applying the label, "terrorism," to the acts that need to be suppressed. Similarly, bank robbery for ostensibly political purposes may pose a kind of threat significantly different from that of bank robbery for purposes of romantic adventure or personal gain. Whether a difference in police authority ought to flow from the difference in threat is a matter to be carefully considered by the guardians of social traditions, legislatures and judges, not by the police authorities. Given the strong interest in the United States in suppressing all kinds of riots and bank robberies, it is difficult to understand why police would treat a "routine" robbery differently than a politically motivated robbery. It is hoped that the full power of the law is brought to bear to apprehend "routine" bank robbers and that the reasons for limiting police authority to pursue and apprehend them apply as well to the pursuit and apprehension of "political" bank robbers. If the full power of the law under existing restraints is not strong enough in the one case, it would seem proper to consider increasing that power for both cases. Briefly, the definition of "terrorism" for purposes of municipal law seems to be irrelevant to any real problems of municipal law.

In an act that affects more than one state, a malefactor fleeing across a national boundary cannot be pursued by law enforcement authorities without the cooperation of the authorities of the state of refuge. The usual way of assuring necessary cooperation is through an extradition treaty. However, due to a 150 year old tradition by which many states offer refuge to the downtrodden without regard to the criminal law formulations of the state from which one has escaped, there is a "political offense exception" to the rules that usually require extradition. Whether that exception should be applied to cases of common, politically motivated crimes has consequently become a matter of treaty interpretation among states. Attempts to achieve international agreement to limit the scope of the "political offense exception" or to create an "exception to the exception" arouse deep apprehensions in those states where traditions make them likely states of refuge. A revolutionary government of a self-proclaimed Communist state may regard the laws on kidnapping in the United States as political expressions of a hated, ruling class, just as in the United States people regard the laws of some revolutionary governments in self-proclaimed Communist states as inherently suppressive and subject to a degree of political manipulation that makes supposed offenses against them inherently political. From these points of view, if there can be found some acts which all states can agree are so disruptive of the international legal order that cooperation in their suppression is politically and ideologically acceptable, there may be room for a useful concept of "terrorism."

Some international agreement, coupled with various municipal law regulations, has been reached to help suppress aerial hijacking. It is possible that similar agreements can be reached to protect nuclear materials, if national and existing international safeguards can be shown to be inadequate. Surely there is a common state interest in restricting the means to spread dangerous biological or poisonous substances and to apprehend individuals or private groups who are not direct agents of state authority and who possess such substances. Other areas for cooperation may well exist. The key seems to be whether the acts sought to be suppressed are so dangerous to the common interest of all states that questions of ideology can be overcome.

This discussion does not identify any acts that are not already criminal in the laws of all states, unless mere private possession of substances with potentially disastrous uses is not illegal. The United States probably has as much difficulty as any country in controlling private possession of dangerous substances. The history of attempts to restrict the private possession of small arms in the United States illustrates this difficulty, although special cultural and traditional considerations affect gun control in the United States. Of course, small arms are not weapons with the potentially disastrous effects and transnational reach required before the cooperation of ideological enemies in their suppression would be feasible. In fact, the United States does legally prohibit the unauthorized private possession of many substances, like those given various labels under the Atomic Energy Act of 1954, as amended, (4) and strictly regulates the import and export of "implements of war" (5) as defined further in the Traffic in Arms Regulations. (6) There may well be a basis for agreement with states not sharing the American view of the value of strategic arms control and the need to implement those regulations and others to keep tactical weapons out of the hands of private parties.

Another legal approach to "terrorism," which avoids definitional problems, seems to reach an important area of agreement by which states might be able to cooperate in the suppression of various municipal law crimes. Part of the consensus definition of "Aggression" adopted by the General Assembly of the United Nations on December 14, 1974 labels an "act of aggression" and defines its legal consequences as flowing from "the sending by or on behalf of a State of armed bands, groups, irregulars or mercenaries, which carry out acts of armed force against another State of such gravity as to amount to the acts listed above, or its substantial involvement therein." The "acts listed above" include the usual forms of military action and "the action of a State in allowing its territory, which it has placed at the disposal of another State, to be used by that other State for perpetrating an act of aggression against a third State." (7) This formulation by the U.N. has a very long history; its ambiguities are deliberate. (8)

Other pertinent documents include the U.N. General

Assembly's Declaration on Principles of International Law Concerning Friendly Relations and Co-Operations among States in Accordance with the Charter of the United Nations, adopted without a vote on October 24, 1970. Among several provisions that might be considered pertinent to questions arising from failures of states to cooperate in the suppression of politically significant violations of the municipal law of second states are the following:

> Every State has the duty to refrain from organizing or encouraging the organization of irregular forces or armed bands, including mercenaries, for incursion into the territory of another State.
> Every State has the duty to refrain from organizing, instigating, assisting or participating in acts of civil strife or terrorist acts in another State or acquiescing in organized activities within its territory directed towards the commission of such acts, when the acts referred to in the present paragraph involve a threat or use of force. (9)

These provisions undoubtedly reflected accepted international practice in 1970. The leading modern precedent is the claim presented by the Secretary General of the United Nations with the approval of the General Assembly (10) against Israel in 1949 for the failure of Israel to control or punish the irregular armed band within its territory that killed the U.N. Mediator, Count Bernadotte. Israel's reply to the claim admitted some degree of laxness, denied legal culpability, but Israel paid as reparation $54,628, the total amount requested by the United Nations. Because the reparation was paid, Israel's denial of legal liability seems unconvincing. It is abundantly clear that the rest of the international community did attach some legal responsibility to Israel for the depredations of irregular forces within its territory. (11) Later developments, including Israeli protests and military actions against Lebanon for failure to control the Palestinian irregulars encamped in Lebanese territory along Israel's border, would seem to strengthen the precedent. The presence on Syrian soil "of the organization responsible for many of the recent incidents" was termed "illegal" and a violation by Syria of its international obligations in a speech before the Security Council by the United States Representative on October 28, 1966. (12)

The defenses against allegations of illegality based on failures to help suppress politically motivated crimes in neighboring states' territory have, in the main, focused on denying the facts (which seems to imply an admission of the existence of the legal rule which seems to have been violated by the accuser's version of the facts) or attempting to classify the armed bands in such a way as to bring into consideration the rules regarding armed conflict between states (which seems to admit a legal obligation to help suppress the bands to the extent of not participating in such an armed conflict). Why legal arguments have not been made when facts and classifications can hardly be credibly denied, as in the case of Libya granting haven to kidnappers of the ministers of the Organization of Petroleum Exporting Countries in December 1975, is unclear, but it may be doubted that any state would suppose the rules codified in the General Assembly Resolutions or practice have changed.

NOTES

(1) Spink Ecc. and Ad. 81, 164 E.R. 47.

(2) 13 and 14 Vic. c. 26 (1850).

(3) See: works cited in Rubin, "Is Piracy Illegal?," *American Journal of International Law*, Vol. 70, No. 92, 1976, note 11.

(4) See, for example: the provisions forbidding unlicensed possession of "special nuclear material" (42 U.S.C. 2073), "source material" (42 U.S.C. 2092), and "byproduct material" (42 U.S.C. 2111).

(5) See: 22 U.S.C. 1934.

(6) The "Munitions List" containing the specifications is in 22 C.F.R. 121.01.

(7) G.A.O.R., 29th Sess., Supplement No. 31, Res. 3314 (XXIX), article 3 (f) and (g).

(8) See: L. Ferencz, *Defining International Aggression*, Dobbs Ferry: 1975, 27-53.

(9) U.N.G.A. Res. 2625 (XXV), Part II, Annes, paragraph 1.

(10) G.A. Res. 365 (IV) of December 1, 1949.

(11) A good summary of the facts is in Sohn, *Cases on United Nations Law*, second edition, rev'd, Brooklyn: 1967, 47-50.

(12) *U.S. Department of State Bulletin*, December 26, 1966, pp. 970-972.

Alona E. Evans:
The Realities
of Extradition and Prosecution

"Extradition or submission of the accused to prosecution" is the legal formula which appears in several recent multilateral conventions and bilateral agreements which attempt to deter terrorist attacks upon aircraft or upon internationally protected individuals. The resolution is central to the 1970 Convention for the Suppression of Unlawful Seizure of Aircraft (Hague Convention, Art. 7) (1) the 1971 Convention for the Suppression of Unlawful Acts against the Safety of Aircraft (Sabotage Montreal Convention Art. 7), (2) and the 1971 Convention to Prevent and Punish the Acts of Terrorism Taking the Form of Crimes against Persons and Related Extortion That Are of International Significance (O.A.S. Convention Art. 5), (3) The formula is used in the United Nations Convention on the Prevention and Punishment of Crimes against Internationally Protected Persons, including Diplomatic Agents (U.N. Convention Art. 7) (4) which is not yet in force. It is implicit in the 1963 Convention on Offenses and Certain Other Acts Committed on Board Aircraft (Tokyo Convention Art. 15). (5) The formula has also been incorporated into the 1973 Memorandum of Understanding between the United States and Cuba Regarding the Hijacking of Aircraft and Vessels and other Offenses (Art. First) and in the agreement concluded by Canada and Cuba on the same day which has substantially the same text. (6)

The wording of the Hague Convention is typical: "The Contracting State in the territory of which the alleged offender is found shall, if it does not extradite him, be obliged, without exception whatsoever ... to submit the case to its competent authorities for the purpose of prosecution" (Art. 7). The O.A.S. Convention qualifies the provision for extradition with an exception for nationality of "other legal or constitutional impediment" (Art. 5) and reserves the right of asylum (Art. 6). The U.N. Convention urges prosecution "without undue delay" (Art. 7) and reserves treaties on asylum by which the parties were bound when the Convention came into force (Art. 12). Both the O.A.S. Convention (Art. 4) and the U.N. Convention (Art. 9) provide for "fair treatment" of the accused. (7) The United States and Canadian agreements with Cuba speak of "returning" the accused rather than extraditing him (Art. First; Art. 1). Both make an exception to return or prosecution" ... in those cases in which the persons responsible for the acts were being sought for strictly political reasons and were in real and imminent danger of death without a viable alternative for leaving the country, providing there was no financial extortion or physical injury to the members of the crew, passengers, or other persons in connection with the hijacking" (Art. Fourth; Art. 4).

Several questions arise in connection with the application of these agreements, in particular, the Hague and Montreal Conventions which have the widest acceptance of the punitive agreements. How is custody of the offender to be obtained? Is extradition preferable to deportation? Is deportation preferable to extradition? What is meant by "prosecution"? Should the emphasis be on prosecution by the state in which the offender is found? Should the defense of the political offense be barred?

OBTAINING CUSTODY OF THE OFFENDER

The Hague Formula seems to emphasize extradition as an end in itself, with prosecution by the territorial state as an alternative. The discussions of the conventions at the drafting conferences had this emphasis. Some countries like the Soviet Union have put great emphasis on mandatory extradition, as was evidenced in the Soviet proposal draft "sanctions" convention. Their draft with other, rather differently focused drafts came to naught at the 20th Session (Extraordinary) of the International Civil Aviation Organization Assembly and International Conference on Air Law held in 1973 in Rome. (8)

Extradition is the formal method of acquiring custody of a fugitive offender. Other methods include, in a declining order of legality, deportation (exclusion and expulsion), induced "voluntary" return, use of physical force, and kidnapping. (9) Extradition has developed over a century and a half into a strict process which is formulated in common terms in extradition treaties, extradition statutes, or in extradition provisions within codes of criminal procedure. (10) Extradition is a criminal proceeding in which the interests of the concerned states in a regularized process are assured and the rights of the accused are protected to the extent that he can question identification, existence of the charge in the laws of both states, political character of the charge (i.e., raise the political defense), and the length of time of his detention during the extradition process.

Deportation, on the other hand, is a civil proceeding designed to prevent the admission of an undesirable alien into a country (exclusion) or to remove an undesirable alien from a country (expulsion). Even with the fairly strict administrative proceedings followed in the United States in regard to exclusion and the stricter ones in regard to expulsion, an individual is not protected to the same extent as he would be under extradition. Extradition is subject to delays in official communications and to procedural complications emanating from both requesting and requested states, as in cases in which the quality of evidence in support of a request does not meet the alleged standards of the requested state or when appellate review in the courts or by the Executive Branch of the requested state may hamper or terminate the process. Deportation, taking place wholly under the authority of and within the discretion of the state in which the accused has been found, tends to be simple and often quite speedy. It is not surprising, then, to find that deportation is the more common method of acquiring custody of international terrorists as well as other international offenders like violators of narcotics laws.

In cases of aircraft hijacking for which statistics are most readily available, 970 individuals between January 1, 1960 and June 1, 1976 successfully hijacked or attempted to hijack 468 aircraft around the world. (11) Approximately thirty-five percent of these individuals have been apprehended and submitted to prosecution. This percentage includes a few individuals who have been charged with aircraft sabotage and attacks upon aviation facilities. Concerning the recovery of offenders, an examination of the practice of forty states shows that twenty states requested the extradition of seventy-eight offenders. Extradition was granted in five cases. Twenty-two requests for sixty-six offenders were denied; however, forty-two of these offenders were prosecuted by the requesting state, an action which conforms to the Hague Formula. (12) In the same period, eighty-eight persons were returned by deportation to the states in which their offenses had been committed. Among the states which have used deportation as a form of "disguised extradition" are Canada, Cuba, Greece, Malawi, Saudi Arabia, the United Kingdom, and Yugoslavia. Cuba has returned twenty-four hijackers to the United States, eleven of them since the conclusion of the 1973 Agreement. (13) Interestingly, only one hijacking of a United States registered aircraft to Cuba has occurred since the Agreement was concluded; that hijacker has not been returned, nor has Canada been able to recover custody of the only person to hijack a Canadian registered aircraft to Cuba.

The emergence of the *Toscanino-Lujan-Lira* (14) Addenda to the *Ker-Frisbie* (15) Rule suggests that acquisition of custody over fugitive offenders by informal procedures has the sanction of United States courts, provided that the offender is not subjected to overt pressure by officials of the United States. Given the increasing substitution of deportation for extradition and, for example, the language of the United States and Canadian Agreements with Cuba, it can be argued that "lawful return" should be substituted for "extradition" in returning international terrorists. On the other hand, assuming that the degree of civilization of a state can be measured by its criminal justice system, the route of "disguised extradition" leaves something to be desired in terms of orderly criminal procedure. If officials are using deportation for extradition, we need to determine the reasons behind their actions. It should be observed that the process of extradition could be made more effective by the development and use of *inter alia* procedures for judicial assistance in such matters as interrogation of witnesses, service of documents, assumption of prosecution, and enforcement of foreign criminal judgments. (16) The Council of Europe has begun to develop some of these procedures by concluding the European Convention on the International Validity of Criminal Judgments in 1970 and the European Convention on the Transfer of Proceedings in Criminal Matters in 1972. Ample historic and jurisprudential reasons exist as obstacles to such developments, especially when common law states are involved, but if legal control of international terrorism is the aim, then such obstacles to improved procedures must be reconsidered.

PROSECUTION

The emphasis in anti-terrorism conventions is on extradition, with prosecution presumably the objective. The conventions indicate that the accused shall be submitted to competent authorities — who are not defined — "for the purpose of prosecution" — which is not defined. Clearly, peculiarities of local criminal justice systems may frustrate the execution of prosecution. In the United States from the moment that a perpetrator is arrested, the factor of discretion — prosecutorial, defense, and judicial — can inhibit prosecution. A district attorney may decide not to submit information to a grand jury or may decide not to bring in an indictment because of the mental condition of the accused or because of inadequate evidence.

The accused may turn state's evidence in return for immunity from prosecution. Plea bargaining, endorsed by the Supreme Court in *North Carolina v. Alford*, (17) may result in an accused pleading guilty to interference with a flight crew (49 U.S.C. Section 1472(j)) which carries a penalty of a term of years or life, rather than to aircraft piracy (49 U.S.C. Section 1472(i)) which carries a penalty from twenty years to death. After sentencing, there is the possibility of appeal; after incarceration, there is the possibility of parole.

In the United States since January 1, 1961, 249 individuals have participated in the hijacking of registered aircraft, and 134 of these people have been apprehended. Of this number, eighty have been convicted, five acquitted, and thirteen cases are pending. Twenty-six accused individuals did not stand trial, or charges against them were dismissed because of their mental condition.

The eighty convictions demonstrate something about the factor of discretion. Of these, thirty-one were convicted of aircraft piracy, seventeen were convicted of interference with a flight crew, and twelve were convicted of kidnapping (18 U.S.C. Section 1201). The other twenty were convicted on various federal and state charges, ranging from interruption of air commerce by extortion (18 U.S.C. Section 1951) to custodial interference (a state charge).

Judicial discretion has also been evident in the sentencing of aircraft hijackers. Although the death penalty has not been sought in any case to date, six hijackers have been sentenced to life imprisonment. The average sentence on a charge of aircraft piracy is twenty-eight years; for interference with a flight crew, thirteen years. The average sentence for the federal charge of kidnapping is ten years.

It is difficult to establish reliable information about

prosecutions for hijacking in foreign countries. The practice in 41 states involves the trials of 226 persons and various charges, including treason, aircraft hijacking, murder, attempted murder, damaging aircraft, extortion, illegal possession of firearms, and illegal coercion. Sentences have ranged from five months to fifteen years. Life imprisonment has been imposed once in Canada and Egypt and three times in Israel. The death sentence has been handed down once in the Philippines, twice in Iraq, Jordan, and the Soviet Union, and three times in Cuba. In three cases in the Soviet Union, death sentences were commuted to fifteen years; in one case in Yemen, the death sentence was commuted to life imprisonment. Ten hijackers convicted in Canada, Lebanon, Malawi, Spain, Sweden, and Yugoslavia were deported after they served part of their sentences or were pardoned with deportation as a consideration. The record indicates that the Hague Formula, to "submit the case to [the state's] ... competent authorities for the purpose of prosecution," may produce substantial variation in charges and sentences for the same offense.

If prosecution is the real objective of the conventions — and prosecution is the only purpose of extradition — then the emphasis should be placed on *prosecution*, not only in the state in which the offense was committed, but in any state in which the offender is found. The Hague, Montreal, and U.S. Conventions do provide for limited universal jurisdiction, i.e., universal jurisdiction effective among the parties to these conventions. Moreover, those states like Sweden and Israel which subscribe to the passive personality theory of criminal jurisdiction have added scope for prosecution. With attention directed to prosecution, the establishment of international minimum standards of criminal process becomes a matter of state concern. Discrepancies in the criminal justice process, the use of military courts or ad hoc tribunals, cavalier attitudes toward elementary principles of due-process of law, marked variations in penalties contribute to the reluctance of states to extradite offenders to some countries. At the same time, difficulties in establishing an adequate basis for a criminal proceeding against the accused in the state in which he has been found, together with crowded dockets or other concomitants of local criminal justice, contribute to reluctance to give more than lip-service to "submit to prosecution." Certainly, attention by states to the establishment of uniform measures of judicial assistance would help to alleviate these barriers to carrying out the Hague Formula. Prototypes of conventions on judicial assistance exist. A convention establishing international standards of criminal justice would be worth considering, especially if the application of the concept of universal jurisdiction to international criminal law is going to be encouraged.

When is the defense of the political offense to be considered? The defense of the political offense is implicit in the Hague Formula in that the alternative of prosecution in the state in which the accused is found may have to be resorted to, because extradition has been denied on the ground that the accused is a political offender. The defense of the political offense is recognized in the O.A.S. Convention and in the U.N. Convention. In the fifteen reported instances in which extradition was denied and prosecution followed in states requesting extradition, the political factor was undoubtedly present between West Germany and Czechoslovakia, France and the United States, Denmark and Poland, and Sweden and Greece, although in the West German cases the territorial state had jurisdiction over the offenders under its extradition law and would prosecute them. (18) Yugoslavia also claimed jurisdiction over three hijackers *vis à vis* a request from Algeria; however, after convicting the three hijackers, Yugoslavia deported them to Algeria where they were tried on charges arising from the same incident. (19)

There is an increasing trend toward circumscribing the political defense in terms of certain offenses. For example, the 1971 Extradition Treaty between the United States and Canada which became effective in March 1976 denies political defense to a person charged with "kidnapping, murder or other assault" against an internationally protected person or in aircraft hijacking. (Art. 4(2)(i)(ii)) (20) Although a hijacking for political reasons can be dismissed under the theories of self-defense or the defense of necessity, submission to prosecution, as has been done in *inter alia* the Federal Republic of Germany, Denmark, Austria, and Turkey, meets the objective of the hijacking and sabotage conventions. What happens *after* the criminal justice process has been completed (whether deportation elsewhere is ordered, a decision that may necessitate consideration of the strictures on deportation in the Convention on the Status of Refugees or political asylum is granted) (21) is a separate matter and should be so regarded.

What if a state fails to prosecute or grants political asylum in violation of the conventions? Violations of this kind on the part of one state affords a ready excuse for another state's failure to extradite or prosecute, thereby undermining the ultimate objective of developing a system of legal control over international terrorism. In this situation a choice of actions should be available. For example, under the 1974 Antihijacking Act, the United States can suspend air services between it and another country which is found to be " . . . acting in a manner inconsistent with the Convention for the Suppression of Unlawful Seizure of Aircraft [Hague Convention], or . . . [which] permits the use of territory under its jurisdiction as a base of operations or training or as a sanctuary for, or in any way arms, aids, or abets, any terrorist organization which knowingly uses the illegal seizure of aircraft or the threat thereof as an instrument of policy." (22) This unilateral measure, albeit considering the amount of foreign air traffic in and out of the United States, could be a drastic, if temporary, international remedy.

However, a sanctions remedy to be fully effective should be multilateral. The failure of the International Civil Aviation Organization to reach any conclusion in 1973 regarding an agreement designed to enforce the Tokyo, Hague, and Montreal Conventions, whether an independent convention or an amendment to the 1944 Convention on International Civil Aviation (Chicago Convention), (23) should not deter concerned states from pursuing a sanctions remedy. Another approach to enforcement would be to invoke strict liability or liability-without-fault against a state for failure to meet its international obligations to implement the conventions and to extradite or prosecute offenders thereunder. The delinquent state would be liable for damages to the victims for personal injuries, both physical and mental, (24) and for loss of property. The notion is hardly novel, because it emerges from the established concept in international law of state responsibility for the protection of aliens.

Control of international terrorism by apprehension and prosecution of offenders has been supplemented by prevention, including the institution and rigorous enforcement of security programs at airports. Prevention techniques have resulted in the present decline of aircraft hijacking and other attacks upon aircraft. Concern for successful security programs, however, should not deflect international interest from the prosecution of terrorists. The punitive aviation conventions and the prospective punitive convention on internationally protected persons are the prototypes for further international criminal legislation which will include other kinds of offenses as well. Legislative development should include a wide range of measures for judicial assistance as well as the establishment of international minimum standards for the criminal justice process. These measures and standards would encourage states to participate more freely in the operation of an international system of criminal justice. For those states unwilling to cooperate, international agreements establishing the principle of strict liability or liability-without-fault and providing for the enforcement of the Tokyo, Hague, and Montreal Conventions, would supply necessary punitive controls. None of these suggestions is utopian, but all of them can be achieved in the near future with patience and persistence.

NOTES

(1) 22 UST 1641, TIAS 7192. This Convention is in force for 76 states.

(2) 24 UST 564, TIAS 7570. This Convention is in force for 66 states.

(3) AG/doc. 88 rev. 1, February 2, 1971. O.A.S./Official Records/Ser.P. This Convention is in force for four states.

(4) A/Res./3166 (XVIII) February 2, 1974.

(5) 20 UST 2941, TIAS 6768, 704 UNTS 219. This Convention is in force for 82 states.

(6) 24 UST 737, TIAS 7579. Canada, Treaty Series 1973 No. 11. Art. 2 of the Canadian Agreement does not contain a clause relative to punishing the preparation of hostile expeditions directed from one state against the other. Bilateral agreements relative to the control of aircraft hijacking have been reported between Afghanistan and the Soviet Union, 1971; Colombia and Cuba, 1974; Finland and the Soviet Union, 1973; Iran and the Soviet Union, 1973; Mexico and Cuba, 1973; and Venezuela and Cuba, 1973. Twelve of the thirteen extradition treaties which have been concluded or revised by the United States since 1961 have included aircraft hijacking as an extraditable offense.

(7) See: Declan Costello, "International Terrorism and the Development of the Principle *aut dedere aut judicare*," World Peace through Law Center, Seventh Conference on the Law of the World, Washington: 1975.

(8) International Civil Aviation Organization, Legal Committee, Soviet Proposal, LC Working Draft No. 826, 9/1/73. See *Report*, United States Delegation to the 20th Session (Extraordinary) of the I.C.A.O. Assembly and International Conference on Air Law, Rome, Italy, August 28-September 21 1973, published Jan. 22, 1974.

(9) See: A. E. Evans, "Acquisition of Custody over the International Fugitive Offender — Alternatives to Extradition: A Survey of United States Practice," *British Year Book o*

International Law 1964, Vol. 40, p. 77, 1966.

(10) See, for example: Whiteman, *Digest of International Law*, Vol. 6, p. 727, 1968; M. C. Bassiouni, *International Extradition and World Public Order*, 1974; I. A. Shearer, *Extradition in International Law* 1971.

(11) The statistics used in this paper are based upon the compilation made by the Office of Air Transportation Security, Federal Aviation Administration, issued as of Jan. 1, 1976, with additional information drawn from *inter alia* Federal Aviation Administration, Civil Aviation Security Service, "Chronology of Hijackings of U.S. Registered Aircraft and Current Legal Status of Hijackers," Jan. 1, 1976; International Federation of Air Line Pilots Associations, "1974 Hijacking Statistics and Summary of Statistics 1969-74," Jan. 22, 1975; Transport Canada, Civil Aviation Security, "Hijacking Incidents Involving Canada, March 1, 1976;" "Attentats contre la navigation aerienne," Numéro Spécial, *Revue de Droit Pénal et de Criminologie*, Vol. 52 Nos. 3-4, Dec. 1971-Jan. 1972; P.-G. Pötz, "Die strafrechtliche Ahndung von Flugzeugentführungen," *Zeitschrift für die gesamte Strafrechtswissenschaft*, 489, Jahrgang 24, Heft 2, 1974; *Current Digest of the Soviet Press*, New York *Times*, Chicago *Tribune*, Boston *Globe*, *Christian Science Monitor*, London *Times*, *Facts on File*, *Keesings Contemporary Archives*.

(12) For example, a French national who hijacked a Trans World Airlines aircraft to Lebanon in 1970 was prosecuted in Lebanon on minor criminal charges, deported to France, and prosecuted there on charges related to the hijacking. *La Semaine Juridique*, Vol. 46, No. 7, p. 1699, Feb. 16, 1972. An American national and a Guatemalan national who hijacked a Braniff aircraft from Mexico to Argentina in 1971 were prosecuted in Argentina on a charge of hijacking and sentenced to five and three years imprisonment, respectively. Following an amnesty decree, they were extradited to Mexico in 1974. *Re Jackson and Sánchez Archila*, Federal Court, La Plata, Dec. 15, 1971 (unreported); Re: *Jackson*, Supreme Court 1972, *Jurisprudencia Argentina*, Vol. 19, p. 454, July-Sept. 1973.

(13) Five hijackers were returned directly to the United States; the others came via Barbados, Bermuda, Canada, and Jamaica. Cuba has deported three hijackers to Mexico.

(14) *United States v. Toscanino*, 500 F.2d 267 (2d Cir. 1974); *United States ex rel. Lujan v. Gengler*, 510 F.2d 62 (2d Cir. 1975); *United States v. Lira*, 515 F.2d 68 (2d Cir. 1975).

(15) *Ker v. Illinois*, 119 U.S. 436 (1886); *Frisbie v. Collins*, 342 U.S. 519 (1952).

(16) See: Heinrich Grützner, "International Judicial Assistance and Cooperation in Criminal Matters, Appendix II, Bassiouni and Nanda, *A Treatise on International Criminal Law*, Vol. 2, p. 189, 1973.

(17) 400 U.S. 25, (1970).

(18) Pötz, 493, supra note 11.

(19) T. Vasiljevic, "Mesures a l'Egard de la Piraterie Aerienne en Yougoslavie (Etat actual)," *Revue de Droit Pénal et de Criminologie*, Vol. 52, Numéro Spécial, Nos. 3-4, Dec. 1971 - Jan. 1972 p. 463 at 465.

(20) TIAS 8237.

(21) 189 UNTS 150. The 1967 Protocol on the Status of Refugees, to which the United States is party, incorporates Arts. 2-34 of the Convention. 19 UST 6223, TIAS 6577, 606 UNTS 267.

(22) Sec. 1114(a), 88 *Stat.* 409 (1974).

(23) 61 *Stat.* 1180, TIAS 1591, 15 UNTS 295. The Chicago Convention is in force for 134 states. See: supra note 8.

(24) See, for example: *Husserl v. Swiss Air Transport Co., Ltd.*, 388 F.Supp. 1238 (S.D.N.Y. 1975).

IV.
MEDIA
PERSPECTIVES

H.H.A. Cooper:
Terrorism and the Media

It has become far more alluring for the frantic few to
appear on the world stage of television than remain
obscure guerrillas of the bush.

— J. Bowyer Bell (1)

By its very nature, a terrorist act is meant to be
impressive. It is calculated to be an attention-getting activity.
The watchers are those whom the terrorist wishes to impress;
the very horror of all terroristic behavior lies in the incidental
role assigned to the instant victim and the callous indifference
towards his fate displayed by the perpetrator. These objects,
or they can be classified no higher, of the terrorists'
attentions are mere pawns in a larger power play. The
quintessence of terrorism is captured by Roland Gaucher where
he writes:

The goal of terrorism is not to kill or destroy property
but to break the spirit of the opposition. A minister is
assassinated; his successor takes warning. A policeman is
killed; ten others tremble. High tension lines are sabo-
taged; the news sweeps over the country. Terrorism
seeks above all to create a sensation — within the ranks
of the enemy, in the public opinion and abroad. (2)

The basic theory of terrorism is strikingly akin to that o
general deterrence. Both require the aid of extensive publicit
to reach their ulterior targets. While the role of the media i
clearly, in the one case, legitimate by association, it is th
association itself which is called in question when the media i
used by the terrorist to attain his objective.

ROLE OF THE MEDIA

The power of the Fourth Estate for good or evil
unquestionable. A free press is the first target of dictators, an
it is no mere sentiment that makes the First Amendment c
the United States Constitution perhaps the most strenuousl
defended fundamental precept of all. The political potency c
the modern, mass media scarcely needs exemplification. Ofter
times, the media has proved itself capable of resolving situ
tions with which the conventional political machinery h
shown itself unable to cope. Its dynamic value in penetratir
the defenses of obdurate power in defense of a reprehensib
interest has been demonstrated over and over again in sur
classic cases as the Profumo scandal in the United Kingdor
the Watergate affair in the United States, and the case of *D*
Spiegel in the Federal Republic of Germany. Since the 195
an even more potent medium than the press, the television, h
reached into even the humblest living rooms across the face
the world bringing drama, entertainment and a real li
immediacy to events, personalities, and life situations to whi
the viewer can relate only through the lambent filter of t
television screen. Television cameras have reached far out in
space, beneath the oceans, deep into the bowels of the earth
and into the hearts and minds of men and women. In o
times, a political campaign would be unthinkable without t
active participation of the media. Overnight, the most obscu
characters can, through some newsworthy event, become hou
hold names. This is heady stuff indeed, and its implicatic
were clearly perceived long ago by that distinguished Canadi
Marshall McLuhan. All this power now stands ready to
harnessed in the service of world terrorism. It is small won(
that those who control these dangerous forces should pon(
both their power and their own responsibilities in this matt
If both terrorist intentions and the power of the media a
thus abundantly clear, the same cannot, unfortunately, be s
for the attitude of the media towards its role in these matt(
There can be no doubt as to that role and its importance

it is perceived through the terrorists' eyes. The media is the indispensable carrier of the Message. The transmission of that message in the form and manner dictated by the terrorist is a purpose scarcely less important to him than the accomplishment of the act which he desires to publicize. This aim has not escaped the notice of responsible journalists. Writing in the Washington *Post*, Steven S. Rosenfeld declared:

> We of the Western Press have yet to come to terms with international terror. If we thought about it more and understood its essence, we would probably stop writing about it, or we would write about it with a great deal more restraint. (3)

Yet these very words have about them the ring of heresy for many others. There are those who would claim not merely a sacred right to publish anything remotely newsworthy, but a veritable duty of no lesser magnitude to that end. Leaving aside all considerations of a purely mercenary or self-serving nature, can such extensive license be appropriately claimed where a countervailing public interest of such importance as that suggested by Rosenfeld and others is at stake? If the freedom to publish rests, as indeed it must, upon a general public interest expressed in terms of "the need to know," is this not most sensibly limited by that other public interest in denying to those who would damage the common weal the use of this potent, near irresistable force of the media? There is a real competition of interests here which must be resolved on a philosophical plane before the practical issues can be tackled. The terrorist is an urgent suitor; if he cannot get what he seeks by seductive means, he will not hesitate to attempt rape. The real problem seems to be uncertainty on the part of the media whether to play coy handmaiden or harlot.

PURPOSES OF TERRORISM

Many have pondered upon the distinctive characteristics which modern terrorism appears to present. Although terrorism has an extremely lengthy history and certain constant features throughout the course of its employment as a coercive modality there are, in our age, discernible elements which mark it out from the phenomenon of earlier times. What have certainly not changed are the fundamental coercive purposes of terrorism nor the practical premises upon which the technique

is based. Such changes as have come about are a consequence
of modern technology, the vastly increased power which this
has generated for the individual, and the enormous increment
in vulnerability for society that it has brought in its train.
Terroristic activity is now perfectly feasible which but a decade
or so ago would have rested in the realm of science fiction. (4)
In a sense, what has been altered is the balance of power. An
individual holding a whole city to ransom with a remote-
control nuclear device can realistically talk on terms of parity
to the representatives of the most powerful nation state. This
is an uncomfortable reversal of fortune that many are still, as
yet, unwilling to admit in all its implications. The interesting
philosophical and practical questions it raises cannot be so
lightly shrugged off. The very fact that such an awful thing
can now be done at all, once admitted, puts an entirely new
face upon terrorism. What we have seen emerging in the last
few years, by way of curtain raisers, is something quite
different from what we have traditionally understood; it is
nothing less than an entirely new set of power-politics, with
new rules and new players. The game itself remains the same;
only the value of the pieces and the stakes have changed.

The other distinctive characteristic of present-day terrorism
is a direct consequence of modern, mass communications. The
terrorist, like many of the criminal classes, has always been
publicity hungry. Lucheni, the anarchist killer of the Empress
Elizabeth, was an avid collector of newspaper clippings and
longed to kill somebody,

> but it must be someone important so it gets into the
> papers. (5)

Some seventy odd years later, Arthur Bremer, the individual
who attempted to assassinate presidential candidate George
Wallace, could only think to say:

> Well, I was on Cronkite's program today.

The prospect of standing alone for a moment upon the stage
of world history is fatally attractive to many tormented minds
and will be ever so. But organized terrorism has truly made
the television its own and, in consequence, as a manifestation
of our times it has become larger than life, more real and
more dreadful than would even have been possible without the
medium. The Baader-Meinhof gang in West Germany have

shown themselves the true masters of media exploitation. In March, 1975 the spectacular kidnapping took place in West Berlin of the mayoral candidate, Peter Lorenz. Writing in *Encounter*, Melvin J. Lasky observed:

> Not the least historic aspect of this unprecedented Berlin incident was the impressment of the nation's television screens to serve the master plan of the terrorist kidnappers. "For 72 hours," one T.V. editor told me, "we just lost control of the medium, it was theirs, not ours... We shifted shows in order to meet their time-table. Our cameras had to be in position to record each of the released prisoners as they boarded the plane to freedom, and our news coverage had to include prepared statements at their dictate... It's never happened before! There is plenty of underworld crime on our screens but up to now Kojak and Columbo were always in charge... Now it was the real thing, and it was the gangsters who wrote the script and programmed the mass media. We preferred to think that we were being "flexible," but actually we were just helpless, as helpless as the police and the Bonn government... Surely it must be the first recorded case of how to hijack a national T.V. network! ...." (6)

This, of course, is a classic case of media rape. But one cannot help but feel from the sentiments expressed that the media enjoyed it just the same.

This ability to capture the media, and through it national and international attention, has not only changed terrorist tactics but also the terrorist's perception of his role and potentialities. Brian Jenkins has said:

> Terrorist attacks are often carefully choreographed to attract the attention of the electronic media and the international press. Taking and holding hostages increases the drama. If certain demands are not satisfied, the hostages may be killed. The hostages themselves often mean nothing to the terrorists. Terrorism is aimed at the people watching not at the actual victims. Terrorism is theater. (7)

These theatrics have only become possible because the wider stage is now set and a large captive audience is waiting. The television camera crew and hordes of press reporters and camera men are nowadays a standard part of the event. Indeed, it is difficult to imagine any important terrorist action now taking place without them. Not unnaturally, the media travels to where the action is and we should probably be highly critical of those who undertake this difficult and sometimes dangerous job if they deliberately ignored such happenings. It is not the presentation of news, as such, which gives rise to concern, but rather the manner of its presentation. A well-known British authority on terrorism who has personal media experience, Brian Crozier, has opined:

> Media publicity tends, very often to favor the terrorist side because of the drama they represent. And also — and I apologize to the professional people here present who may not agree with me — but it is in the nature of television as a medium that it tends to favor the revolutionary side. This is not a reflection on the people who are involved in television. It is the character of the medium itself. (8)

Television is indeed, itself a powerful and dramatic force. When focused upon that side of the emerging story which seems, for a moment, to be the more dramatic, it is not surprising then that a somewhat distorted presentation of the matter is created.

While there may be understandable sympathy for the media as victim of such irresistible terrorist rape as that described in the Lorenz case, there can surely be none where the media itself rushes headlong into the arms of the terrorist not merely to embrace the cause, but to make readily available all the many advantages that our free and highly protected media can offer. The media then becomes an active participant in the event itself and no mere detached recorder of it, and no defense of brainwashing can sound even remotely plausible. There is an interesting analogy here with the case of Patricia Hearst who was kidnapped and apparently participated in the criminal activities of her kidnappers after some sort of conversion to their cause. But the mass media has patently not been carried off like Patricia Hearst or the Sabine Women. Whether skillful seduction or innate lust may have been the operative cause, there have certainly been some remarkable incidents in which the press, film producers, and television have cooperated in publicizing the terrorists' activities. A reporter and photographer from *Der Spiegel* actually accompanied members of the Baader-Meinhof gang in an attack and sacking of a house in Hamburg. There were clearly mutual advantages to this arrangement, but the idea of representatives of the media being in collusion in this way with dangerous criminals is one which must give pause to even the most ardent defender of the liberty of the press. This is no isolated case. There has been similar collusion between British and American media representatives and the Irish Republican Army. Indeed, the clandestine press conference has now become an accepted part of terrorist underground activity. While members of the Weather Underground remain on the F.B.I.'s most-wanted list, film-makers have met secretly with them and have produced a documentary designed to publicize the organization's activities and cause. Bernardine Dohrn, while a much sought fugitive from justice, was nevertheless able to publish a long article in the New York *Times* concerning the end of the Viet Nam war. It may well be argued that there are two sides to every story and that the media would be failing in its job were it not to afford facilities for the publication of the non-official side. Yet how is one to regard a television interview with the Chief of Staff of the Provisional Wing of the Irish Republican Army by both the British Broadcasting Corporation and Independent Television in which he was allowed to announce the stepping-up of a bombing campaign in England — one week before the cowardly attack upon the bars in Birmingham in which twenty-one innocent lives were taken? It has been said by a distinguished American psychiatrist that:

> Terrorism has unfortunately become a form of mass entertainment. (9)

The quality of that entertainment is a matter of perspective and the announcement by O'Connell carried by the B.B.C. must have been about as entertaining as the war-time broadcasts of William Joyce, the infamous Lord Haw Haw, announcing the departure of German bombers for their nightly raids on British cities. The media must surely question its role in such an activist intervention.

PUBLIC OPINION AND THE MEDIA

The role of the media is by no means confined, of course, to the simple reporting of newsworthy events. The media plays a most influential part in the formation of public opinion through analysis and comment upon news and other matters of interest. Raw news forms, indeed, but a minor part of its copious production and it is, rather, this processed and somewhat synthetic content which is offered for consumption by the public at large. Objectivity in not a characteristic of this process. Indeed, the very interest in this, for the public, lies in the subjectivity of the presentation, the color or patina which these events take on as seen and interpreted by the more influential media figures. Here, presentation is of the essence, for it is in this process that the truly skillful exercise their art so as to make of the event something distinctive and captivating. After all, why do we read one newspaper rather than another, or allow ourselves to be entertained by one radio or television network in preference to its competitors? Surely it is not because the factual events themselves which we regard as news are inherently variable or markedly different according to the source which engages our attention? We should expect to find that all news had more or less the same ring to it, and when we do find that one sector of the press is more diligent, more up-to-date perhaps, or even less selective in its presentations than another, we are inclined to extend our preferences in that direction on the grounds that we are that much better informed as a result. Yet what really commands our allegiance is the way that these relatively standard matters are served up to us, the distinctive slant that they are given by the editorial filter through which they have passed. Thus we can talk of a liberal approach, or a conservative approach, of a radical press, a reactionary press, and even, deprecatingly, of a yellow press. Each of these, in its own distinctive way, gives us entertainment, intellectual stimulation, and a significantly different way of looking at many of the same things. Here is the true power of the media: the ability to convey not news, but the true sense of our life and times through the eyes of those who have the ability to see and report on events after their own distinctive fashion.

It is not difficult to see how this unique faculty should come to be so esteemed and jealously guarded. Nor is it difficult to see how it might come to be feared by those resentful of the influence generated by it. The fabric of modern social life is woven in large part by these purveyors of news and opinion. Their influence upon our daily existence is truly enormous. It is a resolute individual indeed, in civilized countries today, who can abstain from even glancing at newspaper, listening subconsciously to the radio or watching, albeit intermittently, television. It is no accident that the outbreak of guerrilla warfare in the remote highlands of central Peru in the early 1960s should coincide with the sudden, massive appearance in that area of the small, transistor radio, a modern electronic marvel, among a bitterly poor and age-old people. These radios beamed powerful propaganda into the most miserable hovels in Quechua and Aymara, autochthonous tongues rarely used or heard in official circles, carrying an extraordinary message of hope and insurgency to those who dwell in those bleak, inhospitable parts. That Chile did not succumb, entirely, before the titanic surge of left-wing propaganda and the emotions generated by it is due in no small measure to the dogged persistence of the right-wing media which even during the darkest days of the Allende regime maintained its vigorous and, at times, strident opposition. It is no exaggeration to aver that he who controls the media is most powerfully equipped in the struggle to win the hearts and minds of the people.

To speak of an act of terrorism that failed, somehow, to command the attention of the media is to give utterance to a thought as incongruous as that of giving a war to which nobody came. It would be irresponsible as well as impracticable of the media to ignore those events. In any case, as we have seen by inference, it is inappropriate to regard the media in this, or indeed any other matter, as monolithic. Were one sector of the media to ignore something newsworthy, it is certain that another would be only too eager to pay the proper amount of attention. Dramatic events, particularly on television, command a premium for the audience reaction they are able to generate. Who can afford to be so ostrich-like in so competitive a world? The act of terrorism by its very nature gains the attention of the media. The media then stands, in a sense, as a bulwark of sorts between the terrorist and the true audience which he wishes to reach, the audience to which his message of fear must be carried if his ulterior objective is to be attained. Herein lies the dilemma for governments and for the media: what to do with the news once it has broken. It would be tempting, if unrealistic, to state simply that the message might not be carried. Some governments have, indeed, tried just that, imposing a partial or total news blackout on terroristic happenings. Under a headline *Censor's Hand Hides Violence In Argentina*, Robert Cox wrote in the Washington *Post* of May 6, 1976:

Allied with an official policy of silence over major issues, it has had the effect of masking from the people — and perhaps even from the government — the grim reality of the problems that the country faces. Since April 22, the media has been prohibited from reporting, mentioning or commenting on political violence unless the events published are issued by the government or security services.

Such action, of course, carries a message of its own; and this, too, is the message that the terrorist is trying to get across. There is a Catch 22-like quality about this problem. If the message is conveyed at the terrorist's dictate, then victory to the terrorist; if it is suppressed, he has still won a victory of sorts just the same. Is there a solution to this dilemma?

PROPAGANDIZING OF TERRORISM

Clearly, any practical solution, in a free society is almost entirely dependent upon the cooperation of the media or a substantial segment of it. Without a reasonable measure of agreement on what needs to be done and how to go about doing it, no progress at all is likely. The representatives of the media must first perceive that there is a problem and, secondly, that they are part of it. Only in this way can they begin to move positively towards becoming a part of the solution. The propaganda of the deed is at least as old as nineteenth century anarchism. While the deed itself is the peculiar work of the terrorist, the propaganda needs the help and encouragement of the media. The terrorist needs the media as a fish needs water. It is an essential element in his very existence as a terrorist. It is not that publicity makes terrorists, as some feel that pornography breeds prurience. While the glorification of violence and prospect of making the front cover of *Time* or *Newsweek* may attract some, this is not the life-blood of the true terrorist; it is merely an incidental benefit. (10) The serious terrorist is not, primarily, on an ego-trip; his thirst for publicity has another thrust altogether. His message is symbolic, a representation of his cause, and a manifestation of his potency. It is not a personal message as such, at all; it is the message of terrorism everywhere.

It is this propagandizing of terrorism rather than the straightforward, objective reporting of terrorist incidents which gives rise to the greatest concern. If a proper distinction can be made between these two media activities, an important advance towards an acceptable solution can be found. The problem lies in the channels through which news must pass before it can be disseminated. Can it ever be presented so purely as to be free from all subjective bias and, in any event, would such a presentation be so very much better in terms of denying the terrorist his goal? Much of the drama lies in the presentation. The peculiar appeal of television is to be found in the immediacy, the sense of being there while history is being made, the delicious thrill of being a participant in some highly dangerous spectacle — from a safe distance. The film documentary while it could capture the latter emotion could never pretend to convey the audience to the very scene of an on-going event. The television camera can now do contemporaneously with the action what, under other circumstances, the voice, the bated breath, the pregnant pause of the radio announcer earlier achieved, namely the building of suspense and the transformation of the event as it unfolds into a new art form. This is certainly what the public wants.

The real question is whether what the public wants is good for it. An associated question is whether some antiseptic, artless form of instruction, were it even possible, might be better. What is certain is that the way the story is told, whether by voice or camera, not only holds or loses the interest of the audience; it is most material in forming a lasting impression of the event. If a story is dramatic, in itself, what purpose is served by telling it as though it were not? Is this not the greatest deception of all? It is this rather than any formal restraint on the exercise of reportorial art that concerns the serious media professional. On balance, so far as the event itself is concerned, there seems to be little alternative to telling it like it is or, perhaps more correctly, as it appears to be to the person who has assumed the responsibility of telling it.

Such a policy, tempered with proper professional discretion, would certainly seem to be the lesser of two evils. Granted, the primary objective of the terrorist is gained in that the event, in all its stark horror as manufactured, is exposed to a wider audience which it is intended to strike. Yet suppression of the event, which could hardly be attained in its entirety, might well, through partial revelations, half-truths, and frightening speculations, be a greater mischief. Confidence in the media would certainly be lost and authority itself called into question. The terrorist would have succeeded, incidentally, in causing that very crisis of creditibility that is an important secondary objective of his war on society. (11) For much the same reasons, the media ought not to be denied the profession-al edge of the breaking story; after all, yesterday's news is about as interesting as day-old fried eggs. The legitimately-acquired scoop can only in the rarest of instances prejudice the security and effectiveness of on-going operations against terror-ists, and interference with publication of the event or even its postponement can scarcely be justified on other grounds. For its part, the media ought not to exaggerate the story for dramatic purposes, but should rather be content with the inherent drama it provides. This ought not, in most cases, represent anything of a professional sacrifice.

ROLE OF ANALYST AND SOCIAL COMMENTATOR

Different again is the media role of analyst and as social commentator. This aspect necessarily involves a conscious at-tempt to mold public opinion in this forum; the terrorist can be cast as hero or villain according to the viewpoint of the expositor. Such comment, in slant and extension is usually dictated by what is considered topical. There can be no doubt about the topicality of terrorism in our times, and the question arises not whether the attention devoted to it is justified on these grounds, but rather whether such attention is counterproductive in terms of the realization of the objectives the terrorist seeks to obtain. Here, there is much more room for maneuver and the need for a more questioning attitude on the part of media professionals as to their proper place in the scheme of things. Those who live in countries where the freedom of the press is cherished can hardly complain when that freedom is held to extend to even those who have declared themselves enemies of society as it is presently constituted. Unquestionably, legitimate public curiosity exists about the terrorists. Who are they? What is their background? How do they think? How are they different from the rest of us? All of these and a host of other questions can be answered by the media professional only by in-depth interviews and a more intimate contact with the terrorist than would ordinarily be enjoyed by the lay public to which this information is eventually purveyed. The relationship is, obvious-ly, one of mutual benefit. The media is using the terrorist just as the terrorist is using the media. Under such circumstances, something in the nature of a symbiotic relationship develops. It would be surprising, indeed, were those who are particularly sought out by the terrorist for their known sympathies not to be partisan in their approach. Yet even the most objective of media representatives is liable to be affected by the empathy which can develop in these circumstances. It is difficult not to allow these feelings to creep into reportage or commentary. Yet is the public curiosity to go unsatisfied on that account? How far can the public interest in knowing about these matters override the public interest in not knowing about them? It should not for a moment be thought that all media opinion is favorable to the terrorist, far from it. There are many whose lack of detachment is such as to cause fear or concern on other grounds. What is unrealistic is to claim that the media has no educational role at all in these matters. (12) All good teachers inject something of themselves into the subject they expound and it would be odd indeed if the representatives of the media were exceptions to the rule. The public expects not only to be informed but also to be instructed. Media responsibility in this area is confined to not allowing such instruction to masquerade as news pure and simple.

INVESTIGATIVE REPORTING

A more pregnant question is how far the media might go in search of the story-behind-the-story so as to be able to perform this educational assignment adequately. Every good teacher spends a lot of time on research of an original nature so as to be able to extend the frontiers of knowledge in his subject area and his students benefit, incidentally, from this enlargement of his capabilities. The last few years have seen an enormous growth of what is known as investigative reporting, and this has come, almost, to be a social function in itself. The story of Watergate as told by Woodward and Bernstein is educational; it is also influential upon the course of events, both shaping and conveying them by the same instrumentality. It is almost a philosophical impossibility for the media professional to extricate himself or herself from the event which is being analyzed and reported. Most would agree that making news is wrong both morally and functionally. But what of those situations where the media is called upon by the terrorist to play a more active role, not simply as reporter but as advocate or mouthpiece? At times, the event only seems to begin with the arrival of the television cameras and their crews.

Hostage negotiations not only take place under the glare of the arc lights; media people are demanded as negotiators and witnesses to secure the keeping of promises and good faith negotiations. These are not roles the conscientious professional can refuse, for they are clearly in the nature of the job. Yet how does this assumption of a more active participation affect objectivity in reporting? How far can the representatives of the media go without being *used* by the terrorist for his own purposes, for the transmission of the message of terror? Again, the indispensable thing seems to be a true sense of identity on the part of the media professional, not an easy thing to develop or retain in a crisis. It is certainly not a task for government in a country where interference with the freedom of the press is socially and politically unacceptable.

CONCLUSIONS

What conclusions might be reached from this brief examination? The media certainly does not create the terrorist, but like a skillful make-up artist, can assuredly make of him either a Saint or a Frankenstein's monster. It might be thought both simple and satisfactory just to show the terrorist as he really is. In a world where the very nature of terrorism is in dispute such a course is neither simple nor satisfactory. With or without media help, the exigencies of domestic and world politics have deemed that one man's terrorist is another man's hero. The media only reflects that reality. If the media indeed contributes to the terrorist problem, it is not too much to hope that it can also contribute to its solution. It cannot do so if its own attitude is that *the news is the news is the news*, nor can it do so if the attitude of those, in either the public or private sector, who would become media managers, is one of hysterical distrust bordering on paranoia. The terrorist has simply seen the chink in modern society's armor and is seeking, not unnaturally, to exploit that knowledge; but he has not been able to deal society a fatal blow by these means nor has he found our Achilles heel. What the media needs is a sense of proportion, and this cannot be acquired by government fiat anymore than an individual can do so by such means. There is no panacea, fortunately, against seduction, and the appropriate defense against rape is not to speak softly and carry a big stick. Protection comes best through alertness against danger. If the media can truly see itself as a part of the problem it is well on the way to becoming an important part of the solution.

NOTES

(1) Transnational Terror, Washington, D.C.: American Enterprise Institute for Public Policy Research, 1975, p. 89.

(2) The Terrorists, London: Secker and Warburg, 1968, p. 298.

(3) November 21, 1975.

(4) See, for example, Analysis of the Terrorist Threat to the Commercial Nuclear Industry, Vienna, Virginia, B.D.M. Corporation, 1975.

(5) Cited by Barbara Tuchman, The Proud Tower, New York: Bantam Books, 1972, p. 118.

(6) Ulrike Neinhof and the Baader-Meinhof Gang, *Encounter*, Vol. 44, June, 1975 pages 9-23 at pages 15-16.

(7) International Terrorism: A New Mode of Conflict, California Arms Control and Foreign Policy Seminar, December 1975, p.4.

(8) *Terroristic Activity: International Terrorism*, Hearings before the Sub-Committee to Investigate the Administration of the Security Act and Other Internal Security Laws of the Commission on the Judiciary, United States Senate, Washington, D.C.: United States Government Printing Office, 1975, at 189.

(9) Dr. Frederick J. Hacker in *Terrorism, Part 1*. Hearings before the Committee on Internal Security House of Representatives. Washington, D.C.: United States Government Printing Office, 1974, at 3021.

(10) These questions received extensive consideration in the United States news media following the attempts on President Ford's life in 1975. See, for example, *Assassination Attempts Spark Controversy over News Media*, by Martin Arnold, New York *Times*, September 28, 1975.

(11) Under the headline *Muting The Messenger*, the New York *Post* of September 29, 1975, observed, "No society can improve its health by concealing or minimizing the sickness within it, and no remedies will be advanced by maintaining a pretense of general well-being. Once the media become partners in that form of cover-up they abdicate a basic reason for their existence."

(12) Such a position was indeed taken by a media representative at the Seminar on International Terrorism: National, Regional and Global Ramifications, held under the auspices of the Ralph Bunche Institute on the United Nations at the City University of New York and the State University of New York, June 9-11, 1976. This strange abdication of

functions was greeted with a howl of protest by the academics in attendance and met with little support from other media representatives.

Bernard Johnpoll:
Terrorism and the Mass Media in the United States

Readers of major American newspapers during the mid and late 1960s and the early 1970s could have assumed that terrorism had become a way of life on American college campuses. Listeners to radio news broadcasts or viewers of the Walter Cronkite or Huntley-Brinkley shows on television could make the same assumption. Actually there was little terrorist activity on American college campuses; the majority of American students were bitterly opposed to acts of violence. Only a small minority of students was involved in these activities. However, the media reported an inordinant amount of "news" about the activities of small, volatile groups and ignored the actions of the majority of students. (1)

Yet there is no evidence that the media in the United States or in most of the Western democratic nations overplayed terrorist activities. A careful perusal of American newspapers and radio wire-service logs would indicate that such coverage was kept to a minimum — possibly underplayed at times. An explosion in New York City's financial district is certainly worthy of first page newspaper coverage and lead story play on radio and television. Yet, except in New York City, such explosions have, except in rare cases, been given secondary coverage.

The media were not involved in the violence, and their overlords did not favor involvement. The mass media were merely doing their jobs in transmitting news. Unfortunately, the lack of actions of the non-violent majority was not news. The actions of the violence prone minority, however, did make news, because news, by its very nature, is made more easily by a violent minority than by a passive minority. The actions of terrorists, no matter how insignificant their number, is more exciting and entertaining than any non-violent activity.

Unfortunately, acts of terrorism cannot be ignored and are newsworthy because they deviate from the norm, they affect the lives of large segments of the population, and they have considerable value as adventurous entertainment. In reporting terrorism the media must consider five key ingredients of news.

First, news must be timely. It must have occurred within a short time of the date of publication or broadcast, or it must antedate an event by a reasonable amount of time. The Battle of Bunker Hill, for example, was news in mid-June 1775, but a year later it was no longer news; it was ancient history. Likewise, the results of primaries are interesting one day, but will be of little newsworthiness after the national election. News must be understood as current history, with emphasis on current.

Second, to be newsworthy an event must be unique; it must deviate from the routine monotony of simple everyday existence. Seven million New Yorkers riding on subways every day without incident is hardly worth reporting (although, I might concede, that the very fact that there was no incident on the subways during any given day might be so unique as to be newsworthy). However, an exceedingly long delay of several hours, which caused the riders to escape on foot through a darkened tunnel, would be sufficiently unusual to be worth publishing or broadcasting.

Third, an adventure would be newsworthy. One individual crossing the Atlantic in a sailboat is an adventure that would interest an audience. An act of violence, especially one in which the perpetrator might face danger, has an element of adventure. When violence has the added attraction of being ostensibly politically motivated, news interest is heightened, because of popular assumption that the event may affect the lives of the audience. Heroes and villains participate in most adventures — especially in terrorist actions — and the public, no matter how sophisticated it appears to be, loves to cheer the hero and hiss the villain.

Fourth — and this ingredient is essentially a generalization from the third point — a news event must have some entertainment value. At times it may have only entertainment value. Much of what the public reads in a newspaper — or at least what a large part of the public reads or hears most avidly — is little more than entertainment in the guise of news. Comprehensive reporting of the private lives of show business or political personalities in the media is news only because of its entertainment value. The offer of a million-dollar annual salary by the American Broadcasting Company to Barbara Walters is essentially a private matter between the newscaster and the network, but the news of the offer is entertaining and is therefore considered worthy of reporting. The actions of avenging vigilantes, anarcho-communist bomb-throwers, Klansmen, Weathermen, or members of the Symbionese Liberation Army, are also entertainment. They are as diverting as the adventures of the Scarlet Pimpernel, Zorro, or the Lone Ranger and Tonto. Derring-do is entertaining and adventurous, and the public assumes that there is some derring-do about the pecadillos of the terrorist.

Fifth, news may require that an event somehow affects the lives of those being informed of it. A tax rise, an incipient war, or a crime wave are newsworthy. Each event either affects the reader or listener directly or has the potential for impact on the life of each member of the audience. A tax rise has an economic impact; incipient war or a crime wave might result in loss of life or property. A terrorist campaign might result in both economic and physical loss for the news audience. (2)

Terrorist activities are by their very nature newsworthy, because they affect our lives. Everyone or anyone is a potential victim: a superintendent of schools in Oakland, a President of the United States, or a graduate student at the University of Wisconsin. In a perverse manner, terrorist activities can be entertaining. As the public is entertained by movies of horror, terror, and catastrophe it is entertained by the reports of acts of violence and terror. When adventure is added to those reports there is little that appears to be more entertaining than a revolutionary act, no matter how repulsive it may appear to us rationally. Moreover, a bombing or an assassination is universally accepted as a unique event of universal interest. Finally, the immediacy of a terrorist action cannot be denied, as we realized from the announcements that moviemakers were rushing to prepare films on the Israeli raid at Entebbe.

What caused some movements to turn to violence; how do they each employ terror, and to what avail? It is useless to discuss what the media can do about terror. The media are not judicial institutions; their sole role in modern society is to transmit information. How to erase terror is a juridical and ethical question, not a question of the media.

Although terrorists may use their tactics to win publicity, they have in only rare cases led to totally unethical actions on the part of a small segment of the press. Such actions occurred occasionally during the last century, particularly in the South. There the press invariably sided covertly or overtly with the Klan, except when the media were owned by transplanted pro-Union Northerners. A careful perusal of the newspapers in North Carolina, Tennessee, South Carolina, Mississippi, and Texas of 1866-1880 indicates a pro-Klan bias. In California the press was, in one case, directly involved in unethical actions. The case, involving James King of William and his vigilantes in San Francisco of 1856, concerns one of the most hideous crimes perpetrated in the name of justice in the United States. It also was the most outrageous misuse of freedom of the press in American journalistic history. King owned the *Daily Evening Bulletin*, one of the most virulently personal newspapers ever published. A gambler named Charles Cora, accused of killing a United States marshal, was in the city jail after a jury was unable to decide on his guilt. At this time, a city supervisor, Jim Casey, attempted to kill King after the latter had exposed him as an ex-convict. Casey sneaked into Cora's jail cell to avoid vengeance by King's cohorts. Both men were Roman Catholics, and King's newspaper had been violently anti-Catholic. At the instigation of King's newspaper, a band of vigilantes was formed, and the jail was raided, Cora and Casey were placed on trial before a kangaroo court, and both were hanged. (3)

During the development of the famous Haymarket case the Anarcho-Communist newspapers were directly involved in the instigation of terror. These dailies and weeklies, published in English and German, screamed at the top of their type, "Death to the Oppressors" and "*Truth* is two cents a copy, dynamite is forty cents a pound. Buy them both, read one, use the other." These papers did not have mass circulations, although no accurate figures exist. The equipment used by these newspapers leaves little doubt that their national circulation surpassed two or three thousand copies. (4) Newspapers with mass circulation ignored the rantings of the terrorists. The anarchists continued their own operations. They distributed a booklet by Johan Most which outlined ways to make bombs, and they called for an *Attentat*. Only after the bomb had been thrown at Haymarket was there much of an outcry in the mass media. Adequate coverage of these terrorists would probably have averted the horrors of Haymarket Square in May of 1886.

During the twentieth century the press played a significant role in the use of terror in only one case involving the near-lynching in San Diego of Emma Goldman and her manager, Ben Reitman, in 1912. At least three San Diego newspapers used their columns to call upon the public to ride Miss Goldman and Mr. Reitman out of San Diego on a rail — with some inferences that the world might be better off if they were given "one-way tickets to h--l."

A few other instances of the use of terror by the press, particularly where lynchings have occurred in the South or Southwest, may be uncovered. It is, however, exceedingly rare for the mass media to be directly involved in mob violence or terrorist activities or to condone them. In fact, newspapers have occasionally themselves been victims of terrorism when, for example, the offices of the Los Angeles *Times* were bombed in 1910.

Nevertheless, the press does play a major role in the terrorist movement; it has acted as a disseminator of publicity about, for example, the Puerto Rican F.A.L.N., the S.L.A., and especially, the Weathermen faction of the Students for a Democratic Society. The S.D.S. was, at its largest, a tiny organization of less than 7,500 members. Of these, fewer than ten percent paid dues regularly. Moreover, S.D.S. was a basically transient organization whose membership rarely remained in the group more than a few weeks or months at most. Its ideology, never rigorous, kept shifting, and its members found themselves invariably in one or another of a large number of factions ranging from social democratic to philosophical anarchist to Maoist, Trotskyite, Stalinite, and official Communist. On the periphery of the S.D.S. was a small group from the drug sub-culture and some even smaller organizations of ultra-revolutionary followers of the nineteenth-century anarcho-terrorist, Johannes Most; these groups — the Crazies of New York and the Molotov Cocktail Brigade of Berkeley, California — were purely peripheral.

Almost all members of the S.D.S. came from the upper-middle class, and the vast majority was white. The leading S.D.S. chapters were at prestigeous universities — Harvard, Yale, Princeton, Chicago, Berkeley, Columbia, Stanford, Wisconsin, Michigan, and Buffalo. Most chapter members had been attracted to the S.D.S. by its anti-war and anti-racism activities. A few were interested in the S.D.S. as an agency for educational reform. Few were genuinely revolutionary. (5) However, the S.D.S. — or at least a major faction of the S.D.S. — became a notoriously violent revolutionary movement for four years between 1967 and its demise after a dynamite blast in Greenwich Village in 1971.

During its early years the S.D.S. was a basically social-democratic organization sponsored by the Socialist-oriented League for Industrial Democracy. Between 1959 and 1962 the S.D.S. accepted the views of the League with only a few minor disagreements and it was absolutely non-violent. In 1962 the S.D.S. made a major shift in its emphasis, not toward violence and revolution but toward a form of individualist anarchism and Socialism in the now famous Port Huron statement. The S.D.S. saw itself almost as the normal offspring of the old Intercollegiate Socialist Society and attempted to win to its membership all left-wing Liberals and Socialists who also believed in democracy. It was a basically constructive, Socialist student organization which was generally ignored in the mass media. Its actions were not adventurous, entertaining, or unique, and the average American would never surmise that it would have a major impact on the country. S.D.S. was only one of many Socialist organizations which have lived and died anonymously in the United States.

By 1963, the S.D.S. appeared to recognize its own obscurity. Its members recognized their inability to fashion the group into a major organization, and some blamed their failure on the refusal of the media to take S.D.S. seriously. Their recognition created a disenchantment with the organization's non-violence. In June, 1963 a small group of leaders issued a revised statement of principles. The new statement, which is sometimes too obscure to follow, called for local insurgency — which did not mean terror but rather organized resistance by members of the local communities. Moreover, because S.D.S. members had found it difficult to win working people to their point of view, the leaders decided it was necessary to win over the *lumpenprolétariat*; a class of semi-criminals, permanent relief and welfare clients, members of gangs, and motorcycle groups. Their decision was based on several major assumptions: first, most of the *lumpen* were young like the members of S.D.S.; second, the *lumpen* were already organized into street and motorcycle gangs; third, these young people were already alienated from both their families and from the society that their elders ruled.

Attempts to organize the young and alienated *lumpen-proletariat* had minimal success. The youngsters showed little interest, but another audience did hear and follow the S.D.S. Young students who opposed the then raging war in Vietnam were ready to follow any leader who would keep them out of the conflict. Some opposed the war on ethical bases; others opposed it for purely personal reasons. Most feared being drafted into the military to fight the war.

In 1964-65 when the S.D.S. had a membership of 1,200 on twenty-seven campuses, the organization's leaders began to direct the struggle to stop the war. First, they organized a sit-down in New York's financial district, which paralyzed banking operations. Then they organized a mass rally which was less than passive. (6) It soon became apparent that these spectacular actions won attention in the media. Subsequently, an acceleration of violence occurred. By mid-1966 some of S.D.S. leaders had decided to turn the group into an urban guerrilla army and to turn protest into rebellion. (7) The violent, terror-prone S.D.S., and its latter-day incarnation, the Weathermen, had been born. The results of rebellion were spectacular. News coverage in the press and on television and radio rose sharply. During the twenty-one year period, 1937-1957, acts of terrorist violence in the United States were given a total of 315 inches of column space in the New York *Times*, or over fifteen inches a year. During 1967-1971, the *Times* devoted to terrorist activities more than 3,350 inches of column-space, an average of more than 840 inches of news space a year. (8)

The Weathermen did not recruit many members with their spectacular activities. The petty bombings of policemen's statues were total failures. The bombing of a draft registration office in California was a failure, although news of it appeared in the national press and on television. The four "Days of Rage" in Chicago — a violent romp through the city's business district reminiscent of *Kristalnacht* in Nazi Germany of 1938 — ended in nearly destroying the organization. Finally, an explosion of the Weathermen's bomb factory in a New York City town house fatally wounded S.D.S.

Publicity is one of the major drives that leads to terroristic activity. The Metlotsky "Mad Bomber" case in New York is one of the most famous of these, but because his case did not involve any political, social, or economic issue, it is only relevant peripherally. Of far more interest are the various nationalist and "revolutionary" groups like the National Front Army of Puerto Rico (F.A.L.N.) and the Symbionese Liberation Army (S.L.A.). Unlike the S.D.S., these two groups never had a period of relative calm during which they might develop an ideology. Both began as avowedly terrorist organizations. Although the F.A.L.N. spoke in terms of an independent Socialist Puerto Rico and the S.L.A. asserted that it would replace capitalism with some form of socialism, neither developed any hard theoretical base. Consequently, members of, for example, the S.L.A. never had time for frustration because the group's constructive revolutionary work was being ignored. In fact, the S.L.A. appears to have considered its violence and terrorism to be a kind of ideology unto itself. Its ideology seems to have been a half-baked combination of the worst of Fanon and Sorel.

The F.A.L.N. developed from a number of other nationalistic, quasi-Socialist terrorist groups who have existed among Puerto Ricans since the last two decades of the nineteenth century. F.A.L.N. appeared under different names during the 1950s, and during the 1970s became very effective with a number of senseless bombings of banks and Fraunces Tavern in New York. The F.A.L.N. hoped to arouse the people of Puerto Rico — and people of Puerto Rican descent — by publicity. It assumed that bombings and other violent actions would assure publicity. (9) Its assumption that violent action would assure publicity proved to be correct, but the myth that publicity would win it support proved to be delusory. The Puerto Rican independence movement remains small, noisy, and militant; it appears to have more support in New York than in Puerto Rico.

The media has justifiably publicized other terrorist tendencies. The antics of criminal radicals like Susan Saxe receive great press coverage nationally and regionally by committing admittedly insane acts of murder and terror which are by their very nature newsworthy. The publicity has not, however, led to a sudden upsurge of followers for Ms. Saxe. For a day or two, a Susan Saxe Brigade was formed at one of the Albany high schools, but it was more theater than revolution and lasted only long enough for the teen-agers to have some fun. A small Molly Maguire Band of supposedly pro-I.R.A. youths was formed in Scranton in 1975. It was more prank than crank; the Band got some limited publicity: the youngsters had a lark, and then both were never heard of again.

Publicity and terrorist activities do not follow the chicken and egg syndrome. Publicity does not spawn terror in the same way that terror leads to publicity. The media cover acts of violence and terror because those acts are newsworthy. The suppression of news — any news — requires an authoritarian regime, and although authoritarianism may make life safer for some, it is stifling and is eventually as terrifying as any Molly Maguire, Weatherman, or Klansman. Little or no evidence indicates that publicity spawns terrorism. If it did, there is no way the media in a free society could be prevented from printing news about terrorism, nor should there be any restraint.

NOTES

(1) Data relating to the number of persons involved in terrorist activities on campus can be obtained from *Hearings before the Subcommittee to Investigate the Administration of the Internal Security Act and Other Internal Security Laws*, United States Senate, Committee on the Judiciary, June 10, 1970, part 4, Washington: U.S. Government Printing Office, 1970, 443-506.

(2) The analysis is based on my own seventeen years of news editing with Pittsburgh, Boston, and New York newspapers. There is little published matter on the basis of news.

(3) Arnold Madison, *Vigilantism in America*, New York: Seabury Press, 1973, 48-50.

(4) The newspapers were *Alarm, Vorbate, Arbeiter Zweitang* (all Chicago), *Freiheit* (New York), *Truth* (San Francisco), San Francisco *Alta*, June 14, 1851; San Francisco *Herald*, August 16, 1851; July 11, 1851; September 28, 1851. See also: George R. Stewart, *Committee of Vigilance: Revolution in San Francisco, 1851*, Boston: Houghton Mifflin Company, 1964 and particularly letters signed "Ciudado," "Pacifica," and "Justice" in the newspapers.

(5) See: *New Left Notes*, 1969-1971.

(6) San Francisco *Chronicle*, April 18, 1965.

(7) *National Guardian*, March 25, 1967 and April 8, 1967; *New Left Notes*, June 24, 1968; *Hearings*, supra note 1, 533-548.

(8) Measurements were made by myself.

(9) Interviews 1968-76 with Puerto Rican nationalists on Independentistas, New York, Ponce. See also: *Claridad*, 1975-1976.

Yonah Alexander:
Terrorism and the Media in the Middle East

There is nothing novel about terrorism (1) in the history of man's inhumanity to man. Indeed, from time immemorial violence in the name of higher political and ideological principles — taking the form of random and systematic intimidation, coercion, repression, and destruction of lives and property — was not unnatural. It has been used continuously and intentionally by both legitimate regimes and opposition bodies to create a climate of extreme and unmanageable fear in the target groups in order to achieve avowed realistic or imaginary goals. (2)

Despite this long history as a symbol, tool, method, and process of force, terrorism has evaded a universally common and satisfactory definition. (3) Now, as we enter the last quarter of the twentieth century, the controversy lingers over the permissibility or impermissibility of political and ideological violence, principally, but not exclusively, as part of a parochial or transnational revolutionary strategy. Some feel that the validity of their cause, such as the right of self-determination, justifies the resort to violence against colonialism and imperialism. (4) To others, terrorism, regardless of motivation, is considered a criminal act that therefore necessarily must be punished in accordance with the relevant laws applicable. (5)

The disagreement over the acceptability or unacceptability of this particular mode of power is confusing and destabilizing to the international system. In fact, the prevailing morally mixed-up climate of indecision and even sympathy for and tolerance of political and ideological violence has provided terrorists with a more hospitable environment in which they can function with impunity and sanctity. (6)

What is most disturbing and frightening about this climate is the realization that there are special characteristics of modern times which make present and future forms of terrorism a potential threat to the very existence of civilization itself. In contradistinction to older precedents, contemporary terrorism has introduced a new breed of warfare in terms of technology. Today, terrorists possess or have access to highly sophisticated and offensive weapons of destruction and death, like computer-guided missiles, the effects of which are immeasurbly harmful to lives and property. Rapid air transport provides terrorists with new mobility, and modern communications enable terror groups to communicate quickly with one another within and across national boundaries. The nature of the industrialized society, which includes *inter alia* urban centers and complicated infrastructures, provides soft and vulnerable targets for unexpected disruptions with far-reaching consequences.

Finally, modern technology has provided terror groups with a critical communications instrument — the mass media — which willingly or unwillingly serves their specific or general needs for propaganda and psychological warfare. (7) More specifically, the strategy of terrorism followed by sub-national groups does not prescribe instant victories over established regimes or states. On the contrary, their struggle for intended ends is seen as complicated and protected. Terror groups, by their very nature, are too small and too weak to achieve a victory in hand-to-hand confrontation on the battlefield. Because sheer violence can accomplish little or nothing in terms of ultimate goals, an extension of the duration and impact of the violent deed is therefore mandatory in the terrorist strategy. As Walter Laqueur put it: "The media are the terrorist's best friend. The terrorist's act by itself is nothing, publicity is all." (8)

Because terrorists realize the importance of publicity, terrorist operations have been broadly symbolic rather than physically oriented. In relying on immediate and extensive coverage by television, radio, and press reporters for the maximum amount of propagandizing and publicizing, terrorists can rapidly and effectively reach a watching, listening, and reading audience at home and abroad. They hope to attain essentially one or two of the following communications purposes. First, they want to enhance the effectiveness of their violence by creating an emotional state of extreme fear in target groups, ultimately altering their behavior and dispositions, or to bring about a general or particular change in the structure of government or society. Second, they hope to draw forcibly and instantaneously the attention of the "whole world" to themselves in the expectation that this audience will be prepared to act or, in some cases, to refrain from acting in ways that will promote the causes the terrorists presumably represent.

Terrorism is like advertising; it increases the effectiveness of its messages by focusing on spectacular violent deeds and by keeping particular issues alive through repetition. Carlos Marighella in his much publicized *Minimanual of the Urban Guerrilla* provides insight into this strategy:

> The coordination of urban guerrilla action, including each armed action, is the principal way of making armed propaganda.
>
> These actions, carried out with specific and determined objectives, inevitably become propaganda material for the mass communications system.
>
> Bank assaults, ambushes, desertions and diverting of arms, the rescue of prisoners, executives, kidnappings, sabotage, terrorism, and the war of nerves, are all cases in point.
>
> Airplanes diverted in flight by revolutionary action, moving ships and trains assaulted and seized by guerrillas, can also be solely for propaganda effects.

He further elaborates:

> The war of nerves or psychological war is an aggressive technique, based on the direct or indirect use of mass means of communication and news transmitted orally in order to demoralize the government.
>
> In psychological warfare, the government is always at a disadvantage since it imposes censorship on the mass media and winds up in a defensive position by not allowing anything against it to filter through.
>
> At this point it becomes desperate, is involved in greater contradictions and loss of prestige, and loses time and energy in an exhausting effort at control which is subject to being broken at any moment. (9)

The utilization and manipulation of the mass media, as

directed by Marighella and other proponents of political and ideological violence, have been tried by practically all terrorist movements. They have sought not only to spread fear among the primary targets but have also publicized their discontent as well as their ideologies to make their violent deeds appear heroic. For example, the kidnapping of Patricia Hearst in February 1974 was used as a form of propaganda for the revolution of the S.L.A. To ensure their prisoner's safety, the terrorists insisted that the media carry in full their messages from both tapes and printed material. Two years later, the media were continuing with renewed vigor to magnify the case out of proportion to its real significance, thus providing sensational mass entertainment and serving the publicity needs of the S.L.A. as well. (10) Similarly, in November 1975, the Montoneros kidnapped the industrial director of Germany's Mercedes-Benz plant in Buenos Aires and released him after the company *inter alia* published advertisements in newspapers in Europe, Washington, D.C., and Mexico, denouncing the "economic imperialism" of multinational corporations in developing countries. (11)

The communications purposes that revolutionary terror groups seek through the media are attention, recognition, and legitimacy. As Weisband and Roguly succinctly observed:

> For the terrorist, the path to legitimacy is through one's reputation for resilience, for self-sacrifice and daring, for brutality, and, above all, for effective discipline over words and actions. The terrorist is his own torch and bomb; he ignites the flames of national passion and, if possible, of political sympathy, and he does it by violating universal human sensibilities. It is the credibility that violence produces whenever it appalls that renders terrorism horrifying yet powerful and, if successful, self-legitimating. (12)

Can the validity of this observation be tested in light of the Middle East experience, particularly as related to the Arab-Israeli problem? What are the psychological warfare and propaganda aims of the Arab states and the Palestinian movements? What role do the mass media play in propaganda, and what impact do communications efforts have on the outcome of the confrontation?

The question of terrorism in the context of the Middle East conflict is complicated essentially because of the absence of a standard definition of terrorism. One may justify political and ideological violence in the region or reject it, according to the measure of one's identification with the causes involved. For the purposes of this paper, terms like "terrorists" and "guerrillas" will be used interchangeably without any moral judgment on their merits.

The root of the Middle East conflict — involving the Arab states, the Palestinians, Israel, and other interested parties — grew from the territorial rift over Palestine. Concern for the fate of the area as part of the Arab world began to be articulated as soon as the Arab press, including *Al-Manor* (Cairo) and *Al-Carmel* (Haifa), published reports on the emergence of Zionism as a national ideology in the 1880s. (13) It was, however, with the establishment of Israel in "Arab Palestine" in 1948 that the Jewish State became an Irredentist entity, because it was viewed as a foreign malignancy in the heart of the Arab world. Its presence was ideologically alien, morally and legally indefensible, diplomatically an affront, politically an injustice, and militarily a constant threat to Arab security and Arab hopes for unity and economic and social advancement. (14)

The psychological trauma of being humiliated, victimized, and threatened inevitably fomented among the Arabs an intense antipathy toward, and an extreme intolerance of, Zionism and the State of Israel. (15) The avowed aim of Arab nationalism became unmistakably clear: to reoccupy Palestine as well as other occupied territories, thereby erasing the consequences of Zionist aggression in the Middle East. (16)

To be sure, the strategic and tactical approaches to achieve this aim have been a source of intra-Arab controversy and conflict. The most dramatic example of Arab divisiveness is related to the role of the Palestinians themselves. (17) Although the Palestinians constituted the main force resisting the pre-1948 Jewish community, their active role was greatly diminished by the intervention of the Arab states after the establishment of Israel. Moreover, despite their existence as a distinct group with a common national origin, shared experience, and a united purpose, Palestinians were unable to voice their grievances and demands effectively until after the Six-Day War, because the Arab states were unwilling to solicit, let alone follow, their views. Yet the "Fidayun," those Palestinians who sacrifice themselves for the cause, were not totally ignored. (18 In fact, some of the more radical Arab states like Iraq and Syria, for ideological as well as tactical reasons within intra

Arab rivalries, have molded their own Palestinian groups to be the vanguard of a way of national liberation. It is not surprising, therefore, that other Arab states, each having its particular policy needs, have joined in supporting the activities of various emerging resistance units. (19)

As a consequence of these developments, the "Palestinian Revolution," regarded by the Arabs as an integral part of the International Liberation Movement, is not a monolithic body in terms of its ideological disposition. Although the defeat of Egypt, Jordan, and Syria in the Six-Day War has made the loosely organized guerrilla groups realize that the success of their revolution will finally depend on their own efforts, they have been unable to form a common ideological base for a confrontation with the Jewish State. On the contrary, with the involvement of a younger, predominantly leftist, Palestinian leadership, ideological differences among the resistance movements have deepened, contributing to further misunderstanding and conflict. Fatah, the Palestine National Liberation Movement, has no political ideology except the recovery of Palestine through an armed struggle, while the Popular Democratic Front for the Liberation of Palestine (P.D.F.) is a Trotskyist group committed to total revolution aimed at Zionism, imperialism, and "Arab reaction." (20) These differences have resulted in bitter internal rivalries between the two major guerrilla groups and have generally weakened the growth and effectiveness of Palestinian movements. (21)

Moreover, the insistence by the guerrillas that the Arab states on the border of Israel provide sanctuary and logistical support (22) has "Vietnamized" the area, leading to a series of bloody civil wars like the Lebanese episode in 1976 and the "massacres" in Jordan in September 1970 and during the summer of 1971. (23) It is not surprising that the Arab countries reject the Palestinian notion of "state-within-a-state" and are reluctant to compromise their sovereignty even for the sake of Palestine. (24) Consequently, any agreement between the Arab state and the Palestinians, as well as among the Arab countries themselves, reflects a particular balance of forces and specific political circumstances that surround and affect the situation.

While these antagonistic relationships have had obvious psychological repercussions on the Arab world, the setbacks suffered have not altered two facts: the Arab states regard Palestine as a major Arab cause, and the Arab states have, to a larger or smaller extent, provided political, financial, material,

172 TERRORISM: INTERDISCIPLINARY PERSPECTIVES

and military aid to guerrilla groups, because they constitute practical and unequivocal expression of the Arab desires vis-a-vis Palestine.

Moreover, the Arab states as well as the Palestinian movements have resorted through the mass media to psychological warfare and propaganda as adjuncts and supplements to armed action and terrorism to form, control, or alter the dispositions of individuals and groups in and outside the region. They have sought to promote a spirit of dedication to the cause of Palestine and to incite hatred, violence, acts of terror, and war against Israel; to persuade Israeli Arabs, who are subject to the strains between the demands of loyalty to the Jewish State and ties of family and culture with fellow Arabs in neighboring states, to show solidarity with their kinfolk and disloyalty to their adopted country; to encourage Arabs living in the occupied territories — the West Bank, Gaza Strip, Sinai, and the Golan Heights — to resist collaboration with the Zionist enemy and to join the resistance forces; to impress upon Israeli Jews that their ideology has placed them in an untenable position that may eventually produce their ultimate destruction; to demoralize Israel's military establishment and to foment disunity, dissension, and confusion in its political leadership; to clarify for diaspora Jews the damaging effect of helping Israel because this aid creates a "dual loyalty" and antagonizes non-Jewish communities; to discredit and deprive Israel of extensive political, military, and economic support abroad; to maintain as consistently as possible a posture of injured party before world public opinion by stressing the plight of the Arab refugees and the conquest of Arab lands and to obtain the sympathy and commitment of large powerful countries and other states and their populations to the cause of Arab Palestine.

Although the purposes of psychological warfare and propaganda are generally held in common by the Arab countries and the Palestinian movements, it is clear that each party also has its distinct self-interests that inevitably dictate separate policies and actions. These trends for solidarity and parochialism are clearly reflected in the generally controlled and conformist mass media of the Arab states and in the communications network of the resistance movements. (25) An examination is useful of the post-June, 1967 experiences of Egypt, the leading Arab state in the Middle East conflict and of the Palestine Liberation Organization (P.L.O.), because it is the umbrella th covers most of the Palestinian groups, including Fatah, the main constituent body of the P.L.O.

EGYPT AND THE MEDIA

After its defeat in 1967, Egypt was frustrated by military weakness and political stalemate. (26) In its quest for lost leadership, it has sought to conduct war by other means. A detailed explanation of Egypt's open support and encouragement of Palestinian terrorism as part of its overall strategy was given by Beirut's *Al-Hayat*:

> The maturity of Arab public opinion in general and Palestinian public opinion in particular after the June defeat, created a situation exposing Cairo in two limitations: on the one hand, it could not start a war of retaliation against the enemy to restore its honour; on the other, it was afraid to take the initiative for any peace solution, be it even by supporting the Security Council Resolution in the form of King Hussein's proposal, so as not to lose that public which it had held captive for twenty years when it actually represented the line of solving the Palestine problem by military action. As a result of this double complication — inability to reach a military solution and doubts about proclaiming a peace solution — Egyptian policy, together with Egypt's diplomacy and press, finds itself in a crisis of hesitation. In this crisis, which has sunk Cairo into oblivion more and more, it started to look for a 'wave' by which it could reach the coast of 'renewed leadership,' trying several times to ride on the crest of the fedayun, which it could not do before, in view of the maturity produced by defeat among the Palestine people. (27)

From the defeat of 1967 to the death of Nasser in September 1970, Egypt's support for the Palestinian movements became more pronounced and comprehensive. For example, Radio Cairo on April 18, 1968, broadcasted President Nasser's speech at El-Mansura in which he said, "We recognize the terrorist movement ... we will support and give aid to this movement ... the activities of the Asifa commandos and the Fatah are a positive element in our campaign." Speaking before the Arab Socialist Union (A.S.U.), Egypt's only political party,

Nasser stated,

> Brothers! The renaissance of the Palestine people is an incredible phenomenon. It is clear that the Arab people support their resistance. On our part, we give all we have, in the military, political and technical spheres. We are ready to do so without accounting, unreservedly. (28)

In an interview on the Algerian radio, Ali Sabri, a member of the A.S.U. executive group, was asked, "What aid, material and otherwise, does the A.S.U. give Fatah?" Sabri responded,

> Talk about the details of such aid is not for publicity purposes. It is known to and witnessed by those who are near. The whole world has come to know that the U.A.R. is one of the progressive Arab regimes which gives all it has in support of the resistance organizations, and especially Fatah, which is leading fida'i action at this stage. (29)

Additional details on the nature of this aid were provided by Abdul Majid Farid, Cairo's A.S.U. Secretary, as reported by the government-controlled Middle East News Agency: "Egypt supplied seventy percent of all military and financial aid to fedayun as well as training; Israel well realized that rockets fired at Beit Shean and other Israeli settlements are Egyptian produced." (30)

Clearly, the Egyptians realized that their support for terrorist activities alone would not liquidate Israel but might help to exhaust it. As *Al-Mussawar*, Cairo's government influenced weekly, elaborated:

> Our war with Israel is waged on two fronts: the regular military front and that of the popular guerrilla war. Our victory depends on coordination between these two, neither of which we may renounce. The belief that the terrorist forces can defeat and liquidate Israel without the assistance of the regular forces is wrong. It ignores the basic facts.
>
> It is also wrong to underrate the value of terrorist operations in the battle because they wear out Israel economically and psychologically. (31)

To maximize the impact of the fedayun, the Egyptian

writer, Hatem Sadeq, suggested that the Israeli Arabs should participate in the liberation struggle. In an article published in the government-operated daily *Al-Ahram*, he wrote:

> The resistance organizations should make use of the thousands of Arabs living within Israel. . . . They must be organized politically and a selected group chosen for military-fedayun operations. Arabs who live in Israel are nearer to its strategic points and even if Israel adopts methods of retaliation and punishment against them, this will only hurt Israel's economy, because these Arabs represent its main man-power in agriculture and construction work. (32)

During 1969 the Egyptian media were also supporting Palestinian terrorist operations outside of the Middle East. Commenting on the failure of the attack at Zurich on an Israeli El-Al airliner in which one terrorist was killed and his three partners, all members of the Popular Front for the Liberation of Palestine (P.F.L.P.), were captured, *Al Ahram* on February 20, 1969, stated that the attack "proved that the will of the resistance will not falter despite the enemy's counterblows." The newspaper also disclosed that the Egyptian government would provide health insurance for the commandos and their families; under the plan, wounded and sick Palestinians would be flown without charge to Egyptian hospitals "if they are unable to obtain treatment in Jordanian medical institutions."

After the inception of the Middle East cease-fire, arranged through the mediation of the United States in the summer of 1970 and ending the war of attrition along the Suez Canal Zone, Egypt continued to provide its traditional support to the Palestinian cause. On August 7, 1970, the following appeared in *Al-Mussawar*:

> Neither the U.S. initiative nor any response to it affects their [the Palestinians'] position; the contrary, in fact, is true: Egypt's answer reserves for them the freedom to continue in their struggle and to achieve their goals. . . . The eradication of the results of the aggression and the liberation of Palestine may be regarded as complementary goals. The Palestine resistance movement will remain one of the most important phenomena of modern Arab life.

Al-Ahram agreed and asserted: "The Palestinian nation is not a party to the current efforts to reach a peace settlement. The results of these efforts, therefore, do not bind them in any way, and they retain complete freedom of action." (33)

Recalling these words some years later, Heykal in his weekly editorial in *Al-Ahram* wrote

> I remember a meeting I attended with them [the leaders of the Palestine Resistance]. Among those present were Yasser Arafat, Abu Ayad and Abu Lutf. Gamal Abd an-Nasser was speaking at the meeting. That was in the days which followed the acceptance of the Rogers' initiative in 1970. There was at the time the suggestion of the possibility of a solution based on the Security Council Resolution.
>
> Gamal Abd an-Nasser said: 'There is a slim chance, not more than one-half per cent, that we may achieve a solution based on the Security Council Resolution. I cannot but try because our position is one thing and yours something else. As far as you are concerned, if you want my opinion, I say: 1. Intensify your activity against the Israeli occupation as much as possible. 2. This is your means of linking yourselves with the Palestinian masses under the occupation. 3. Do not expose yourself to the danger of liquidation by any Arab country you now operate in. 4. Do not be a party to any political settlement of the present Middle East crisis. 5. Should the countries involved in the present crisis arrive at a solution, you must make a long withdrawal like Mao Tse-tung did in the Long March to Yenan to rebuild his forces and await developments.' (34)

At the same time, the Egyptian media during this period were also critical of the Palestinian movements. The attempt by the "freedom fighters" to present to world opinion the image of a "resistance movement" similar to the Vietnam guerrillas or the Algerian rebels was seen as irrelevant. In an *Al-Ahram* editorial Heykal explained:

> What is most dangerous to the 'Palestine Resistance' today is that part of its elements sit atop a pile of Western sympathizing newspapers, believing that from the crest of this mountain they can observe and dictate

the turn of events in the Arab world.

Vietnam is different from Palestine and even Algeria was different from Palestine. While there a popular war of liberation was possible, it is impossible here.

The ratio between Algerians and French was one to eight, while the ratio between Israelis and Arabs in Palestine is one to two. (35)

Al-Ahram on September 8, 1970 criticized the Popular Front for the Liberation of Palestine (P.F.L.P.) for the hijacking and destruction of Swiss, Pan-Am, TWA, and BOAC airplanes. It asserted that "one of the main goals of the battle is to gain public opinion on the side of the Palestinian struggle and not to lose it . . . the attack on international civil aviation, does not encourage world feeling of solidarity with the Palestinian cause." Another Cairo newspaper, *Al Akhbar*, stated on the following day that "international reaction reflects the denunciation and disgust of people against those who carry out such acts."

After President Anwar Sadat had entered office as Nasser's successor, Egyptian policy continued to give strong support to the Palestinian movements. One dramatic example of this support was the media's reaction to the terrorist attack at Lod airport. At 10:30 p.m. on the night of May 30, 1972, three Japanese terrorists, members of the "Red Army" who were recruited by the Popular Front for the Liberation, killed twenty-six individuals and wounded seventy-six more at the Israeli International Airport near Tel Aviv. On the next day a Radio Cairo broadcast observed, "The heroes proved they can penetrate the conquered territories to avenge the blood of others. Now Israel has no alternative but to close down Lydda [Lod] Airport and to prevent tourist visits if she wishes to protect her borders." The broadcast continued with its analysis of the operation:

The participation of three Japanese in the suicide action at Lod proves that the P.F.L.P. succeeded in obtaining international support as a true revolutionary movement. Strong bonds exist between the Palestinian resistance organizations and other liberation movements in Africa, the I.R.A., and the Vietnamese revolutionaries. The Palestinian uprising is part of a world movement and its victory is not only the responsibility of the Palestinians but a universal responsibility, towards the struggling nations.

Another commentary in *Al Ahram*, on the same day, characterized the operation "as the peak of success," because it was "carried out with such speed, surprise, and accuracy that the Israeli authorities were thrown into shock." The Cairo newspaper further remarked that the incident showed "that Israel could not immune herself against the renewal of commando operations. Every Israeli action aimed at undermining the resistance movement will be met with vengeance with whatever available means to prove that blind force and tyranny can be checked." On June 1, Egyptian Premier Aziz Sidky speaking on Radio Cairo stated:

I want to speak about what the fedayeen did at Lod Airport. I want to refer to the implications of the fact that three men with three submachine guns could succeed in accomplishing what occurred at Lod Airport. This action reveals the truth about Israel. Where is the talent, the genius, the organization, and the supreme capability which are unequalled in the whole world?

The Imperialists, after the June War, repeatedly referred to these qualities, when they said that we are not capable of fighting against Israel because, it is claimed, they are a force which we cannot crush. I want to say, that what happened at Lod proves that we can, with Allah's help, achieve victory in our battle with Israel. This is the only reaction I have to this matter.

The Egyptian press, on the same day, echoed the Premier. *Al Akhbar* predicted that "as long as Israel exults in her military power and her ability to stand up to violent action, there will always be someone capable of taking revenge and returning an extra dose."

After the October War, Egypt continued through the mass media to support the Palestinian movement. At a news conference with the Moroccan press in Rabat on October 30, 1974, President Sadat declared, "A Palestine state will arise; in fact, a new state does exist already and its name is Palestine.... Five states now stand ready on the confrontation front — Egypt, Syria, Palestine, Jordan, and Lebanon. All the world must take this into account, and first of all Israel." (36)

Praise for terrorist attacks has also appeared in the media. On June 15, 1975, a P.L.O. group including a Palestinian, an Iraqi, a Turk, and a Moroccan, was killed in an attack on

Kf'ar Yuval, an Israeli village. In the attack three Jewish settlers were fatally wounded. In a broadcast on that day, Radio Cairo called the operation "a daring act," and in a Hebrew commentary directed to Israeli Jews, the radio praised the "humane attitude of Arafat" and added that the Palestinians "do not have to pay off the still outstanding bills left by the Nazis. Israel as a state is an illegal entity which resembles a foreign limb that has not been accepted by the body." Credit for the attack was also claimed by the Arab Liberation Front, a group supported by the Iraqi government. (37)

When Egypt was criticized for abandoning Arab unity vis-a-vis Palestine during the interim negotiations with Israel, Lufti al-Kuli, a senior editor of *Al-Ahram*, explained on August 6, 1975, his government's motivation: "The Palestinian revolution is . . . militarily incapable in its present and expected strength, even with all possible Arab and international assistance, of liberating Palestine by itself in the foreseeable future. The only possible Palestinian achievement in the foreseeable future would be the establishment of a Palestinian homeland in Palestinian territory occupied during the 1967 war." To al-Kuli, a step-by-step approach was better than "an all-out protracted popular war of liberation."

After the Interim Agreement with Israel was signed in September 1975, Egypt was accused by Libya, Iraq, and Syria and several Palestinian groups of a "sell-out," and Sadat was branded as a traitor to the Arab cause. In Madrid, Palestinian terrorists stormed the Egyptian embassy in September and took the ambassador and two aides hostage, threatening to kill them unless Egypt renounced the Interim Agreement. When Egypt repudiated their demand, the terrorists flew to Algeria with their hostages and with the Iraqi and Algerian ambassadors to Madrid. In response, Sadat stated in a nationally-televised speech that "they thought they could terrorize us or compel us to a path that is not ours. We say no. I repeat: Never will anything of this sort take place." (38)

Notwithstanding this incident and the mounting criticism of Egypt's policy, Sadat continued to stress his government's dedication to the Palestinian cause. On October 18, 1975, in a speech to the Egyptian People's Assembly, he said, "Our commitment to the Palestine issue still exists in spite of everything; in fact, in our calculations the year 1976 will be the 'Palestine Year.' " He stressed that Egypt's primary objective "is the liberation of all the occupied territories, the recovery of the Palestinian people's rights, and enabling them to master their own affairs and to determine their fate freely." (39)

Recently, President Sadat held Syria responsible for failing to support the Palestinian cause. In an interview with the Saudi newspaper, *Akhath*, on February 20, 1976, he stated,

> More than a hundred (countries) would recognize a [Palestinian] Government and the Palestinians' task could be easier, but they are subject to the will of their Syrian patron, who is opposed to the establishment of a Palestinian Government. Syria and not the Palestinians.

Egypt, in a recent move designed to frustrate Syria, strengthened its ties with the P.L.O. by promising to return control to Arafat of the P.L.O.-operated "Voice of Palestine" radio program in Cairo, which suspended broadcasting in 1975 as a consequence of the Interim Agreement between Egypt and Israel. (40)

THE P.L.O., FATAH, AND THE MEDIA

The Arab guerilla movements (41) were initiated in the early 1950s when Palestinian university students in Arab countries, particularly in Syria and Lebanon, formed paramilitary youth movements and became active in Arab refugee camps. Although they sought to "eliminate the Zionist existence" and restore "Arab Palestine" to its "rightful owners," they failed to translate their theories into action. The proliferation of some fifty organizations in the next decade demonstrated their inability to unite against the common enemy.

In 1964 the Palestine Liberation Organization and it military arm, the Palestine Liberation Army (P.L.A.), emerged with headquarters in Cairo. Ahmed Shukairy, who headed the group, believed in a long-term build-up of a regular "Liberation" force that would when it was properly prepared attack Israel. His political mentor was President Nasser, and his base of operations against the Jewish State was the Egyptian ruled Gaza strip. (42)

On June 10, 1967, several days after the defeat in the Six-Day War, he stated on Radio Cairo, "The devoted campaign which our Arab nation conducted is not yet finished. It wi go on until the final victory." On another broadcast he asserted, "The duty of the Arab nation is not only to liquidate the results of the aggression but to eradicate the basic danger. We hope the entire Arab nation will develop a fighting stand: the struggle for the liberation of Palestine." (43) In one of his last statements on the P.L.O. Radio, delivered on August 26, 1967, Shukairy said:

> The liberation of Palestine will continue to be the most important national target for the Arab nation, and above all for the people of Palestine. The last Israeli-imperialistic aggression did not change our standpoint. On the contrary, it has strengthened and bolstered our determination to continue our struggle and to use all our moral and material resources to liberate our occupied homeland. The political solutions, which are mentioned by news agencies and are based on the recognition of Israel, making peace with her and co-existence, are categorically rejected by us.

Several months after this broadcast, Shukairy, who was bitterly accused by other Palestinian groups of failure, was forced to resign from his position of Secretary General. With his departure, the P.L.O. was plagued by internal strife and lost much of its earlier power.

Since Shukairy's resignation the history of the Palestinian movements has been characterized by an endless process of separatism and amalgamation. (44) The most important guerrilla organization that survived the test of time and has provided considerable leadership for unifying forces is "Harakat Tahrir Falastin" (Movement for the Liberation of Palestine), better known as "Fatah" (Conquest). Formed in 1957 under Egyptian sponsorship, this group is led by Yasir Arafat, who developed the ideology and strategy of the movement and later became head of the P.L.O. Under his leadership Fatah was able to appeal to the majority of the Palestinians and has become since 1970 the central, dominant group within the P.L.O.

Fatah's aims are articulated in the P.L.O.'s "Palestine National Covenant," originally promulgated by a Palestinian Congress held in Jerusalem in May, 1964, and later reaffirmed and amended in Cairo in June, 1968. (45) It demands "the liberation of Palestine" and asserts the "national duty to repulse the Zionist, imperialist invasion . . . and to push the Zionist presence from Palestine" (Article 15). It declares that "the existence of Israel is fundamentally null and void, whatever time has elapsed" (Article 19). It "rejects every solution that is a substitute for a complete liberation of Palestine and rejects all plans that aim for the settlement of the Palestine issue or its internationalization."

The P.L.O. and Fatah have always therefore opposed any deviation from the "Covenant." On Cairo's "Voice of Palestine" on June 12, 1970, the following statement of the Central Committee of the P.L.O. was read:

> The fida'i action, which deserves the main credit for foiling the Zionist-imperialist plan to split the East and West Banks and to set up an agent Palestinian entity in the West Bank and in the Gaza Strip, is determined to continue the armed struggle until complete liberation by crushing the Zionist State in Palestine, liquidating Zionist establishments, and restoring Palestine to the Arab nation and the Arab homeland. This fida'i action denounces all attempts to distort its holy struggle and condemns all overt and covert statements about the establishment of a State in the East Bank and certain parts of the West Bank or about a State to include Palestinians and Jordanians under a new cloak. (46)

In another broadcast on the "Voice of Palestine," the Central Committee elaborated on the policy of the P.L.O.:

> Our struggling masses, the imperialist-Zionist aim in establishing the State of Israel was to create a consolidated and lasting colonialist manpower base in the heart of the Arab homeland in order physically to obstruct the unity, progress and development of the Arab nation and to guarantee and protect imperialist interests in the Arab homeland.
>
> In contrast, the aim of the Palestinian masses in particular and the Arab masses in general since the British occupation of Palestine has been to repel the imperialist-Zionist invasion, prevent the establishment of the Jewish state, and liberate Palestine, which is an Arab region and inseparable from the Arab homeland.
>
> The policies of the Arab Governments in 1948 were in line with the imperialist and Zionist plotting, and the result was the comedy of the first Palestine war of 1948. In that year, the Arab armies entered Palestine

not to prevent the establishment of the Zionist State in Palestine but to secure its establishment by preventing the Palestinian and all the Arab masses from taking up arms to defend the soil of the homeland.

Ever since the establishment of the State of Israel, the Arab nation has been paying dearly to build the Arab armies to liberate Palestine. However, the Arab regimes, while pretending to support the slogans of liberation of Palestine, were in fact preventing the Palestinian people and all the Arab masses from effective participation in the battle against Zionism, which is originally connected with world imperialism — particular with the United States and Britain.

This situation continued until the Arab armies were defeated in the 5th June 1967 war.

The Arab Governments met in Khartoum after the June 1967 defeat and adopted a number of resolutions. These resolutions basically meant the final abandonment by these Governments of the aim of liberation of Palestine, since the resolutions introduced the slogan of the so-called political action method to eliminate the consequences of the Zionist aggression of 1967. The Governments thereby disregarded the consequences of the Zionist aggression of 1948 and attempted to take refuge behind the deceptive curtain of their resolutions which declared: No negotiations, recognition, or peace with Israel, and no compromise on the Palestine issue.

Arab Governments accepted the U.N. Security Council resolution of November 1967 which calls for recognition of Israel. As a further concession, the so-called U.S. initiative included in the message of the U.S. Secretary of State William Rogers to the Foreign Ministers of the U.A.R., Jordan and Israel, has been accepted.

The P.L.O. Central Committee, speaking for the Palestinian Arab people and expressing the aims of this people's struggle, declares the Palestinian people's rejection of the U.S. Security Council Resolution and all formulas and forms of its implementation, including the Rogers plan.

The Palestinian people will continue the armed struggle until total liberation is achieved. The Palestinian people will not observe the cease-fire. (47)

In an interview published in the Moroccan newspaper,

Al-Anba, on August 19, 1969, Arafat defined Fatah's aim:

> The objective of our war at this stage of the struggle is to do away with the social, economic and political fortress of Israel in a long and protracted war which must of necessity end in success. The Tartars have ruled this country for seventy years and the Crusaders for nearly 200; but in the end they were defeated and nothing was left of them.

The media available to the P.L.O. and Fatah persistently communicate Fatah's objective. Cairo's "Voice of Palestine" on February 23, 1970, broadcasted:

> Our great masses! From the Voice of Palestine in Cairo we greet you and promise to continue our armed struggle and fulfill our blood-drenched duty — the duty to Jerusalem. We shall put an end to Zionist existence on the land of Palestine; we shall liberate all of Palestine by popular armed revolution.

Interestingly, Fatah spokesmen also declared, particularly in communications outside of the Middle East, that the P.L.O.'s goal is the establishment of "a democratic, secular, Palestinian state" in which Moslems, Christians, and Jews would live harmoniously. In an interview with the editors of the *Arab Bulletin*, published in London, Arafat stated,

> The establishment of a democratic and progressive State in Palestine does not conflict with the interest that this State be Arab.
> The Zionist State has not succeeded in becoming accepted, because it is an artificial State and foreign to the Arab world.
> We proposed our solution, that is, the establishment of a democratic Palestinian State for anybody who wants to live in peace on the land of peace.
> We hope to deliver the Jews from the Zionists. (48

However, another interpretation of the "democratic Palestinian slogan" was reported by Beirut's *An-Anwar* on March 8 and 15, 1970. The following quotations are excerpts from what the spokesmen for the leaders of the Palestinian movements discussed in an "informal chat":

Farid Al-Kahtib [for the Palestine Liberation Movement]: 'It is useless to enter into details on the subject of the Democratic State since the goal in proposing the slogan at this stage is to allow the Israeli enemy a small opening, so that if his military, economic and political powers are exhausted and Israel is in dire need — then it will have no choice but to turn to that small opening in order to find a way out. Then the Palestinian revolution will be able to dispel the obscurity so that the enemy may see things in their true light. Therefore, it is useless to dispel the obscurity at present. In the end, when the Israeli enemy or the Zionist State comes out of this opening — it will only happen according to the wishes of the Palestinian victory.'

Shafiq Al-Hut [Beirut representative of Fatah]: 'There is no merit in talking at length about the slogan of a "democratic State." It is not possible for such a State, devoid of affiliation to come into being. If the slogan of a Democratic State is only intended as an answer to the charge that we aim at throwing the Jews into the sea, then it is a successful slogan and an effective political and propaganda act. But if we regard it as a matter of ultimate strategy of the national Palestinian and Arab liberation movements, then I think that it calls for thorough examination.'

According to these spokesmen, Fatah is prepared to fight as long as it is necessary to liquidate the Zionist enemy, liberate all usurped land, and achieve a victory. (49) To sanctify this struggle, Fatah, which is a secular organization, appealed to religious authorities to proclaim guerrilla operations as a holy war. (50) Arafat in an interview with the Beirut newspaper *Al Hayat*, on December 20, 1968 emphasized the religious aspect of guerrilla warfare: "The liberation of Palestine is one of the aims of the Moslem world. We wage a Jihad against the Zionist enemy."

Another example of Islamic-based communications (51) relates to the "blood" allegations against Jews and Israel. Fatah's Palestine Liberation Radio, based in Cairo, claimed on April 24, 1970 that "according to reports from the occupied homeland, the Zionists began to kidnap small Arab children off the streets. The occupying authorities bleed the children and then throw away their bodies all over the place. Gaza residents saw this with their own eyes." On April 1, 1971, the "Voice of Palestine" of Damascus Radio reported that Arab children had "been kidnapped and bled by a gang of the Zionist enemy intelligence." Fatah revealed that the purpose of the kidnappings was not limited to Passover rituals. Algier's "Voice of the Storm," in its broadcast of April 1, 1971, asserted that the blood of kidnapped children was used for "medical purposes."

Perceiving revolutionary violence as a sanctified strategy, Fatah's military aim, "Al-Assifah" (Storm), was to engage in guerrilla activities during the pre-1967 period, including border raids aimed at escalating Arab-Israeli tension in order to force war on the Arab countries. After Israel's June victory, Fatah was reorganized and intensified its terrorist activities inside Israel, insisting that these attacks were military operations.

Fatah claimed responsibility for the August 18, 1968, "night of the grenades" in Jerusalem where nine civilians were injured; the Mahaneh Yehuda market explosion later that month during which twelve civilians were killed and fifty-two injured; and recently the attack on Nahariya on the Israeli coast in which two children and a woman were killed and six soldiers were injured. (52)

Numerous communiques on Al-Assifah's exploits were reported on Cairo's "Voice of Faith." A broadcast of June 28, 1970 reported,

> Assifah attacked with heavy rockets Kiryat Shemona, Dan and Shear Yashuv, Upper Galilee, inflicting damage and casualities. The 'Clouds of Hell' Group attacked with heavy rockets Beit Shean, Ma'oz Haim, Hamidiya, Neve Or and Neve Eytan, Upper Galilee, inflicting damage and casualties. (53)

Many reports of these activities were fictional, exaggerated solely for psychological warfare and propaganda purposes. In response to a Lebanese correspondent in Amman to the question, "How do you evaluate the resistance movement at present?" Ibrahim Bakr, Deputy Chairman of the P.L.O. responded,

> I think, the Palestinian resistance movement is in its infancy, despite all the heroic acts so far. I must state that the Arab propaganda machine generally exaggerates fedayun activity much beyond its real extent. This

exaggeration, whether knowingly or not, is liable to damage fedayun actions in future. (54)

Another Fatah leader told a correspondent of Beirut's *Al-Hawadeh* that Fatah's publicity has created a credibility gap:

We face a strange stream of journalists coming from all over the world. Each one has a different request. Some wish to speak to fedayun, others to spend some days with the fighters, again others who wish to join them on operations in the conquered land. As a result, our information offices work incessantly, day and night, and the information which we meant to hand out objectively has become publicity.

On the other hand this has had great success in the world, but on the other it has created an abyss between the faith of the masses and the actual ability and effectiveness of fedayun activity.

The Press in general and the Arab Press in particular have credited us with more potentialities than we have. They have created an aura of legendary power which is a very serious matter, as the masses have begun to expect more from us than we are capable of. They have, therefore, begun to doubt our words. (55)

On another occasion, *Al-Hawadeth* elaborated on Fatah's exaggerated publicity:

The multitude of announcements and the competition in boasting about operations, some of which were indeed carried out while others were — regrettably — only imaginary, have a dangerous effect. This can be easily observed anywhere in Jordanian towns, in every hotel or cafe. Announcements, too numerous to count, are pasted [on walls] or distributed by one hand while the other is stretched out for a contribution. People wonder, puzzled: Should they pay? They read the announcements, but do they believe their contents?

One of the Fatah leaders told me: People have begun to joke and say that if they add up the Israeli losses in half-tracks alone, according to the figures given in the various announcements, Israel will not have one half-track left. (56)

Faced with two decisive defeats in Jordan in September, 1970 and July, 1971, Fatah established the Black September terrorist group to demonstrate to the Palestinians and the Arab States that it was still the major force within the resistance. (57) The Black September, which began its activities in November, 1971, has been responsible for a number of operations, including the assassination of the Prime Minister of Jordan, Wasfi Al-Tall, in Cairo; the injuring of Zeid Rifai, Jordanian ambassador to London; the sabotage of a Dutch gas plant; the abortive attempt to hijack a Belgian Sabena airliner at Lod International Airport; the attack at the Munich Olympics; the attack on the Israeli embassies in Bangkok and Nicosia; and the killing of two American and one Belgian diplomats at the Saudi Arabian Embassy in Khartoum. (58)

To preserve its image as a "moderate" organization, Fatah has not officially admitted its connection with the Black September and has publicly disassociated itself from the foregoing deeds. On March 5, 1973, the Palestine News Agency quoted a Fatah spokesman as saying, "Certain information media have tried to link the recent Khartoum operation and Fatah elements by accusing these elements of taking part in the operation. The Fatah movement affirms that it has no connection at all with this operation." Confronted several days later with a public denunciation from Sudan which charged that Fatah was indeed involved in the Khartoum action, Arafat justified the operation. In Beirut's *The Daily Star* of March 15, 1973, Arafat asserted that the acts of Black September "were loud expressions of despair" driving them "increasingly toward the adoption of a policy of consuming the world's tranquility." He suggested in the report that it was virtually impossible to stop revolutionary activities. (59)

The connection between Fatah and the Black September was unexpectedly revealed by Abu Daob, a leader of a Fatah mission planning to assassinate King Hussein. After he was arrested by Jordanian security police, he confessed on Amman's television and radio, as well as in an interview on British commercial television, that "Black September is not an organization separate from Fatah, it is a group of people from Fatah itself." (60) This revelation led to Fatah's decision to stop the Black September activities. On June 16, 1973, Khalaf, or Abu Iyad, the second ranking official in Fatah, announced, "We understand the meaning of Black September as a phenomenon. We understand the motives which prompt these youths to carry out such acts ... but this does not mean that we are the planners or the financiers." (61)

After Fatah's shift in policy, the organization returned to its earlier policy of both praising violence in "Arab Palestine" and disclaiming or denouncing terrorism elsewhere. Subsequently, the P.L.O., in a statement issued by the W.A.F.A. news agency from Damascus, claimed responsibility for the planting of a time bomb in Jerusalem's Zion Square on July 4, 1975, where fourteen people died and more than seventy were injured by the blast. Commenting on the P.F.L.P.-G.C. attack on Qiryat Shemona in Israel, during which eight children, eight civilians, and two soldiers were killed, (62) a P.L.O. broadcast from Sana on April 13, 1975, stated, "The action proves that the guerrillas can continue the armed struggle to defend their right of representation. International recognition of the P.L.O. will increase only by means of armed struggle, which must expand daily so that it may attain various revolutionary forms in the land of battle." Contrarily, in December, 1975 the P.L.O. denied any responsibility for the terrorist raid on O.P.E.C. (Organization of Petroleum Exporting Countries) headquarters in Vienna by the "Arm of Arab Liberation," during which three persons were killed, nine wounded, and several taken hostage, including eleven oil ministers of O.P.E.C. nations, most of them Arab. The demands of the terrorists included the negation of the Egypt-Israel interim agreement and a call to the Arab world for a "total liberation war" against Israel. (63)

THE IMPACT OF THE MEDIA

Although it is difficult to ascertain the exact impact of the foregoing Arab efforts in the media on the outcome of the Middle East conflict, particularly because the Arab-Israeli struggle is not yet over, it is possible to reach some tentative conclusions. The most striking phenomenon is the fact that the Palestinian cause is unquestionably more widely known in the Middle East and elsewhere as a result of the publicity the cause has received in the media. Publicity was certainly one of the major propaganda goals of the Arab states and the Palestinian movements.

On the diplomatic level the recognition of the P.L.O. as deserving an international legal status is gaining momentum. On October 28, 1974, the twenty Arab heads of government meeting at Rabat recognized the P.L.O. as "the sole legitimate representative of the Palestinian people." They also endowed the P.L.O with the right to assert "national authority" and committed the Arab states to support this authority "in all respects and at all levels." (64)

The significance of the Rabat decisions was summarized by Yasser Abed Rabbo, the chief spokesman of the P.L.O., at a news conference held in Beirut on November 2, 1974:

> The establishment of a Palestinian entity on the West Bank and in the Gaza Strip, under the leadership of the P.L.O., is an interim step, because the Palestinian Revolution will not abandon the national aspirations of the Palestinian masses for the complete liberation of the plundered homeland and for establishment of the secular, democratic state [in all of pre-1948 Palestine]. (65)

The international community endorsed this interim step when, eleven days later, it gave Arafat a reception at the United Nations reserved for a chief of state. (66) Since that event the P.L.O. voice in the U.N. has been heard repeatedly. The P.L.O. has as a prominent and active national liberation movement acquired an international status that has not been accorded to any other terrorist or guerrilla group in the world organization or its specialized agencies.

Moreover, a series of diplomatic moves was undertaken by the Arab states, the P.L.O., and their supporters, particularly in the "Third World Nations," to isolate Israel and reject it from international organizations. The reasons for these efforts was articulated by the Lebanese representative at the U.N.E.S.C.O. General Conference meeting in Paris on November 14, 1974. He said, "Israel is a state which belongs nowhere because it comes from nowhere." His move to isolate Israel led the built-in majority of nations at the meeting to pass several resolutions discriminating against Israel. (67)

In July, 1975, the International Women's Year World Conference in Mexico, held under the auspices of the United Nations, included "Zionism" in the Conference's final declaration as one of the ideologies — the others being colonialism, neo-colonialism, foreign occupation, Apartheid, and racial discrimination — which must be "eliminated." (68) In August, a conference of forty Moslem countries, meeting in Jeddah, adopted a resolution which called for the expulsion of Israel from the U.N. and urged that states participating in the meeting sever relations with Israel. Another anti-Israel resolution was passed at the Kampala meeting of the Organization for

African Unity Summit. (69)

On October 17, 1975, the Third Committee of the U.N. decided by a vote of 70 to 29, with 29 abstentions, to recommend the full General Assembly passage of a resolution describing Israel as "the racist regime in occupied Palestine," stigmatizing Zionism as "a form of racialism and racial discrimination," asserting that "Zionism is a threat to world peace and security," and calling upon "all countries to oppose this racist and imperialist ideology." (70)

On November 10, 1975, some twenty-eight years after voting to establish a Jewish State, the U.N. General Assembly endorsed this resolution. The General Assembly also passed two other resolutions which greatly strengthened the legitimacy of the P.L.O. The first called for the participation of the P.L.O. in the Geneva Conference for Peace in the Middle East. The second established a committee, modeled on the U.N. Committee against Apartheid, for "the exercise of the inalienable rights of the Palestinian people." To fulfill its mandate, this committee is authorized "to receive and consider suggestions and proposals from any State and intergovernmental regional organization and the Palestine Liberation Organization." (71)

New efforts to equate Zionism with racism continue to be made. On April 21, 1976, the fifty-nine-nation gathering of Arab and African ministers in Dakar, Senegal, adopted a resolution condemning "imperialism, colonialism, neo-colonialism, Zionism, Apartheid and all other forms of racial and religious segregation and discrimination, notably in Africa, Palestine and the occupied Arab territories." (72) Similar efforts were made at the U.N. Economic and Social Council debate on the Decade for Action to Combat Racism and Racial Discrimination, and at the international anti-Apartheid seminar, sponsored by the U.N. Special Committee against Apartheid, in collaboration with the Organization of African Unity. (73) At the seventh annual meeting of the Islamic Conference of Foreign Ministers from forty-two countries, which met at Istanbul in May, 1976, demands were reiterated that Israel withdraw from all occupied Arab land and that the Palestinians be allowed to establish an independent state. The conference also called for the expulsion of Israel from the U.N. (74)

The United States, which has long refused to recognize the P.L.O., is expected eventually to negotiate with the Palestinians. President Sadat, in interviews in Cairo's *Al-Ahram* (75) and Beirut's *Al-Hawadess*, (76) asserted that he had reached an agreement with Secretary of State Henry Kissinger that the

U.S. Department of State would begin a dialogue with the P.L.O. President Gerald Ford, in an interview with Dallas newspaper editors on April 19, 1976, apparently implied a shift in foreign policy from opposition to the P.L.O. and toward actively seeking to move Israel and the P.L.O. toward mutual recognition and eventual negotiations. (77) Many believe that President Jimmy Carter will disclose and begin implementing a comprehensive Middle East plan, calling for Israel to retreat to its pre-June, 1967 boundaries and for the establishment of a Palestinian state on the West Bank. (78)

Congress is also slowly changing its attitude toward the P.L.O. Senator James Abourezk (D-S. Dak.) stated recently, "Today, more and more Senators are asking for meetings with Yassir Arafat, and the half dozen Senators who recently returned from the Mideast are softening their statements about the Mideast." (79) Senator Adlai E. Stevenson (D-Ill.), who met Arafat during a recent trip to the Middle East, stated that the P.L.O. "may be distrusted, disowned and despised, but it is a reality, if for no other reason than that it has no rival organization among Palestinians. As long as this reality persists, it will have to be reckoned with in any future multilateral negotiating process." (80) Senator Stevenson also asserted that Arab utterances are distorted by the "exaggeration and hyperbole which mark Arab cultures" but which also strengthen Israeli "hardliners." The United States, he said, cannot expect Arafat to say in public what he tells visiting officials in private, because he has to be careful of the reactions of extremists in his organization. (81)

Although the utilization and manipulation of mass media in the Middle East and elsewhere are major forces in raising the level of awareness of the Palestinian problem, it is debatable whether the present and possible future successes of the P.L.O. can be attributed to communications alone. The actions taken by the Arab oil-producing countries since the October War have publicized the Palestinian cause.

In terms of the psychological warfare and propaganda achievements of Palestinian terrorism in the Middle East itself, the communications efforts by the Arab states and the Palestinian movements were not lost on the Moslem and Christian communities in the area. On August 18, 1974, the Israeli police arrested Archbishop Hilarion Capucci, a Syrian national and the head of the Greek Catholic Church in Jerusalem and the West Bank, on suspicion of "subversive" activities, particularly of smuggling arms and explosives on behalf of Fatah. As a church official who held a Vatican passport and a *visa de Service* which

Jerusalem's Foreign Ministry had issued him in deference to his religious status, the prelate was allowed to cross the Lebanese-Israeli border at Rosh Hanikra without inspection. Taking advantage of his privileged position, Archbishop Capucci had repeatedly smuggled various weapons and sabotage material from Lebanon to the West Bank. Arafat, speaking at a Palestinian guerrilla training school in Damascus on September 16, 1974, declared that "Archbishop Capucci provides evidence of the fact that this revolution has extended to the clergymen." He also asserted that Capucci told the Israeli authorities, "If I could turn the Vatican into a base for the Palestine Revolution, I would have done it." (82) Several days later, the P.L.O. invited all spiritual and secular organizations to take urgent steps to get the Archbishop released.

Meanwhile, Archbishop Capucci was indicted by the Israeli State Attorney for carriage and possession of illegal weapons, maintenance of contact with foreign agents, and performance of a service for an unlawful association. The trial of Capucci on these three-count charges lasted for several months. On December 9, 1974, the Jerusalem District Court sentenced the Archbishop to twelve years in prison. (83)

Another clergyman, the Rev. Elia Khoury, head of the Anglican Church in Ramallah, was arrested in April, 1969, and was subsequently deported to Jordan for aiding Palestinian terrorists who had planted explosives in Jerusalem earlier that year. Later, he was elected a member of the Executive Committee of the P.L.O. during the National Council meeting in Cairo. The Rev. Khoury said, "The pulpit of the Church carries influence especially in the Western World. We want to tell the West that the Palestine Question is not only a Muslim question, but a Christian-Muslim cause." (84)

The most dramatic illustration of the impact of the Arab media can be seen in the recent events on the West Bank. The nearly nine-year, conspicuously benign Israeli administration of the West Bank (85) was shattered as P.L.O. agitation urging civil disorder increased among the population. Arab demonstrators, most of them young, threw stones at Israeli soldiers, set fire to automobile tires, and erected roadblocks and barricades. The protesters waved Palestinian flags and chanted, "Palestine is Arab" in opposition to Israeli occupation. The Israeli reaction was swift. Troops and border police stormed schools, killed nine and wounded dozens of Arabs, and caused extensive property damage. The military governors of West Bank towns imposed curfews on residents. The Arab mayors protested these strong measures to quell the demonstrations which had occurred almost daily. (86)

One cause of the Arab rioting was a dispute over Jewish prayer rights in Jerusalem. On May 14, 1975, a Jewish group of nationalist-religious members of the right-wing Betar began a prayer service at the Temple Mount, the site of the First and Second Temples and, therefore, the most sacred place in Jewish tradition. (87) Moslem youths objected to the service, because the area ranks third as a holy place for Islam (88); they clashed with Jewish youths. Police expelled the young Jewish worshippers who were later brought to a Jerusalem magistrate's court on charges of disturbing the peace. They were acquitted on January 28, 1976 by the court which ruled that Jewish prayer — forbidden on the site of *sanctum sanctorum* since 1967 — was now permitted. Although the Israeli government and Jewish religious leaders supported the policy of prohibiting Jewish prayer there, and although the lower court decision was overturned by Israel's high court, the dispute angered the Moslem Arab community. (89) To incite disturbances on the West Bank, agitators charged that Jewish prayers were conducted "in the El-Akza Mosque." The East Jerusalem pro-Palestinian daily *Al-Quds* claimed in an article by a former Jordanian judge that Israel is systematically usurping Moslem religious shrines. (90)

It is unclear as to what degree the media reports of the West Bank "uprising" are complete and accurate. The Israeli military censors briefly closed an East Jerusalem Arabic newspaper, *Al-Shaab*, that had disregarded warnings about publishing censored material. (91) There were also reports that Arabs in the region had offered to stage, in exchange for payment from foreign newsmen, fire-burning demonstrations and road-blocks. (92) One American reporter related that students at the Bir Zeit School "confessed to him that they had smashed windows at the school and then called in reporters to show them Israeli violence." (93)

In view of these events Israel restricted the news coverage on the West Bank. According to one report, "Television crewmen have been roughed up by soldiers, film has been confiscated and exposed and reporters have repeatedly been refused entry to . . . volatile areas." (94) At a meeting with members of the Foreign Press Association, Shimon Peres, Defense Minister, defended new restrictions: "TV adds fuel to an extremely hot situation and we must find a way to avoid adding fuel without curtailing press freedom." (95)

Notwithstanding the restrictions on the media in the area, the impact of Arab communications cannot be underestimated. Arab effectiveness is clearly illustrated by the results of twenty-two municipal elections held on April 12, 1976. The National Bloc candidates, who represent a younger, more outspoken leadership that endorses the P.L.O., won all or most council seats in many towns. The greatest change occurred in Hebron, which had been ruled by traditionalist Sheik Jabari, where all ten positions contested were swept by P.L.O. supporters.

Following his victory, the new Hebron Mayor Kawasme said, "Why shouldn't the people of the West Bank accept the P.L.O. as our representatives? The rest of the Arab world does. Most of the nations of the world do. Why should we be different?" (96) The reelected Ramallah Mayor Karim Khalaf, who endorsed the P.L.O. during his campaign, said, "The vote shows the whole world that the West Bankers are Palestinians who want to establish their own national entity and put an end to the Israeli occupation." (97)

On another occasion Mr. Khalaf reported that the new West Bank municipal leadership decided to act collectively to "foil any attempt by the Israel authorities to involve them in political deliberations." He added that the population in the area is part of the Palestinian people "whose political representative is the P.L.O. and not us." (98)

A less obvious ramification of the impact of the Arab media relates to the Arab community in Israel. This community which, in 1949, included some 170,000 naturalized Israeli citizens, has since almost tripled that number. The Israeli Arabs have always been torn between demands of loyalty to their adopted Jewish state and their national ties to and identification with the Arab people. As Abdul Aziz Zuabi, the late Arab member of the Knesset, said, "The problem of Israeli-Arabs, in one sense, was that while being an integral part of the State of Israel, they were at the same time an integral part of the Arabs of Palestine. Their state was engaged in a war with their people." (99) The pressure of divided loyalty was increased by the ceaseless psychological campaigns mounted by the neighboring Arab media which urged their kinfolk to reject Israeli citizenship and to cooperate with them in the struggle for Palestine.

As a result of these campaigns, many Israeli Arabs have been developing dormant nationalistic sentiments as well as guilt feelings for not having participated actively in the efforts to liberate their homeland. Recent bloody protests against the government expropriation plans for Arab land in the Galilee left six demonstrators dead and scores wounded. The subsequent

General Strike, proclaimed as a "Land Day," as well as the increased acts of terrorism within Israel are not in themselves sufficient evidence to conclude that the majority of the community associates itself with the P.L.O. These events have, nevertheless, placed the Israeli Arabs under a cloud of suspicion as far as the Israeli Jews are concerned.

Finally, the communications efforts of the Arab media to achieve some kind of Israeli recognition of "Palestinian rights" appear to have been partially successful. In December, 1975 Professor Shlomo Avineri on the Israeli state radio criticized Prime Minister Rabin's policies in the Palestinian question. He said that the government should not reject the possibility of negotiations with any group of Palestinians who want a Palestinian state on the West Bank and the Gaza Strip with some link with Jordan. Despite considerable criticism of these views and of the state radio which aired them, Professor Avineri, with the approval of the Israeli cabinet, was appointed Director General of the Israeli Foreign Ministry. (100)

The Israeli media also reflect a growing public debate on the Palestinian issue. David Shalam, in his article "Faits Accomplis," published in *Al-Hamishmar* (Labor's Mapam daily) on December 19, 1975, criticizes the Government's policy vis-a-vis the Palestinians. A week later an editorial in the same left-wing newspaper stated:

> Ignoring the [Palestinian] problem is tantamount to assisting the P.L.O. and others who seek to isolate Israel. While world opinion is opposed to terrorist methods and murder, it supports the demands of the Palestinian public for its own identity. Nor is there an absolute freeze within the Palestinian camp itself, as the P.L.O delegate to the U.N.E.S.C.O. conference indicated when he referred to readiness to sign a non-aggression pact with Israel, and to recognize the Israeli nation. While this recognition is not official, it amounts, no doubt, to a feeler we cannot afford to ignore.

On December 26, 1975, *Ha'aretz*, the independent Israeli daily, also commented on the proposals of the P.L.O. delegate to the U.N.E.S.C.O. conference:

> While the Palestinian organizations aspire to recognition of their own national identity, they rule out the national identity of Israeli Jews. They do this by claiming that the

TERRORISM: INTERDISCIPLINARY PERSPECTIVES *197*

State of Israel constitutes merely a framework for an 'Israeli society' — which is divorced from Diaspora Jewry and can therefore readily amalgamate with the proposed Palestinian State. . . . It may indeed be true that the Arabs of Palestine, who until the end of the British Mandate regarded themselves primarily as members of the overall Arab nation, are now crystallizing as a national entity in their own right and within this larger framework. Yet it is very surprising to hear those who aspire to recognition of their national identity trying in the same breath to deny the national identity of the Jewish population of Israel. The 'Israeliness' of this population does not detract one iota from its Jewishness. Anyone claiming that that 'Israeli nation' is a new national identity divorced from the Jewish People and its history is propounding not a new sociological theory, but a lie for purposes of political propaganda.

Interestingly, Farouk al-Kaddoumi, the head of P.L.O.'s political department, disavowed the remarks made by Ibrahim Souss, the P.L.O.'s delagate to U.N.E.S.C.O., in an interview with *Le Monde* alluding to eventual Israeli-Palestinian coexistence. In a statement sent on December 27, 1975 to the Paris newspaper, Kaddoumi asserted that Souss was not authorized to make political declarations in the name of P.L.O. Peace in the Middle East, said Kaddoumi, could only be achieved by "the installation of a democratic state over the whole of Palestine." Subsequently, Souss clarified his statement in a letter to *Le Monde*. He wrote, "When I spoke of a future without borders or barbed wire, I obviously meant a sole democratic state over the whole of Palestine."

In reaction, *Ma'ariv*, the non-party Tel Aviv newspaper, commented on December 28, 1975, "One more illusion has been shattered. However, this will not prevent the birth of some new illusion every time a P.L.O. leader makes some inconsequential remark which will be eagerly welcomed by the doves in Israel. Yet the aim of the P.L.O. continues to be to annihilate the State of Israel."

Israeli doves have continued with their campaign of recognizing "Palestinian rights." *Ha'aretz* of March 3, 1976 carried in a paid advertisement the Israeli Rakah (Communist) Party outline of a peace plan. It included, *inter alia*, a call for the "recognition of the just national rights of the Palestinian people" and the invitation of the P.L.O. to the Geneva

Conference. On March 4, 1976, the Israeli state radio reported that the leadership of the Independent Liberal Party approved a resolution which calls for self-determination for the West Bank Palestinian Arabs.

More importantly, members of the Israeli government in an apparent shift of policy decided to sit at the same table for the first time with the P.L.O. representatives on March 22, 1976 at the U.N. Security Council debate on the West Bank situation. (101) Israel insisted that participation in the debate "in no way" constituted a change in its policy since Israelis had on various occasions sat in the same hall as the P.L.O. and had taken part in the same deliberations. Nevertheless, that Israeli representatives met face to face with their P.L.O. counterparts around the same table is very significant. Israel has always asserted that the only place it is prepared to meet the P.L.O. is the battlefield. As Moshe Dayan, the former Defense Minister, said, "The aim is that whenever they fight against us we have to fight back, simply that. It is not an educational program. If someone shoots at us, all that we can do is to shoot back." (102)

No one can assert with certainty whether Israel will be willing to negotiate with the P.L.O. at Geneva or elsewhere. However, it is not farfetched to predict that continued Palestinian terrorism and guerrilla activities may elevate the already dangerous collision course in the region into another confrontation on the battlefield. As Zuheir Mohsein, head of the military department of the P.L.O. and chairman of the Syrian-sponsored A-Saika fidayun group, stated in an interview in the West German weekly *Die Zeit* on December 14, 1975, "A Palestinian State limited to the West Bank and Gaza will not satisfy our demands. We want every piece of earth, every field, every village and every house that belonged to us." Asked whether "it can be expected that the Israelis will agree to national suicide," Mohsein replied, "They must recognize that; otherwise, they will recognize it only when they change their way of thinking. And this will happen only when they bend their knees before us, after we have beaten them hip and thigh — beaten them militarily."

Because it is extremely unlikely that Israel will destroy itself, it can be concluded that the alternatives for the Middle East are either coexistence or nonexistence. If the former alternative is chosen, then it is imperative that all concerned take the following concrete steps: reverse the endorsement of terrorism as an approved value; register a sense of revulsion at all acts of violence; cease financial support, stop flow of weapons, and deny all facilities and sanctuaries to any group insisting on terrorism as a mode of politics; eliminate government-sponsored propaganda and psychological-warfare activities of terror groups; cooperate with national and international bodies in the suppression of transnational terrorism; and determine to accept mutually the rights of self determination of all national movements in the Middle East.

Whether these steps, which would lead eventually to reconciliation and peace, will be taken will depend on many factors, including a great deal of humanity, wisdom, and courage on the parts of Arabs, Israelis, and other interested parties.

NOTES

(1) For recent studies on terrorism, see: Yonah Alexander, ed., *International Terrorism: National, Regional and Global Perspectives*, New York: Praeger Publishers, 1976; James A. Arey, *The Sky Pirates*, New York: Charles Scribner's Sons, 1972; *Assassination and Political Violence*, New York: Bantam, 1970; M. Cherif Bassiouni, ed. *International Terrorism and Political Crimes*, Springfield, Ill.: Charles C. Thomas, 1975; Carol Elder Baumann, *The Diplomatic Kidnappings: A Revolutionary Tactic of Urban Terrorism*, The Hague: Martinus Nijhoff, 1973; J. Bowyer Bell, *The Myth of the Guerrilla: Revolutionary Theory and Malpractice*, New York: Knopf, 1971, and *Transnational Terror*, Washington, D.C.: American Enterprise Institute for Foreign Policy; Stanford, Cal.: Hoover Institution on War, Revolution and Peace, 1975; *Civil Violence and the International System*, London: The International Institute for Strategic Studies, 1971, Adelphi Papers 82 and 83; Peter Clyde, *A Anatomy of Skyjacking*, London: Abelard-Shuman, 1973; Ted Robert Gurr, *Why Men Revolt*, Princeton: Princeton University Press, 1969; Edward Hyams, *Terrorists and Terrorism*, New York: St. Martin's Press, 1974; H. T. Lambrick, *The Terrorist*, London: Rowman, 1972; Jay Mallin, ed. *Terror and Urban Guerrillas: A Study of Tactics and Documents*, Coral Gables, Fla.: University of Miami Press, 1971; Robert Moss, *Urban Guerrillas*, London: Temple Smith, 1972; David C. Rapoport, *Assassination and Terrorism*, Toronto: Canadian Broadcasting System, 1971; Sam C. Sarkesian, ec. *Revolutionary Guerrilla Warfare*, Chicago, Ill.: Precedent Publishing, 1975; *Terrorism*, Washington, D.C.: U.S. Government Printing Office, 1974, a four volume Staff Study prepared by the Committee on Internal Security of the

U.S. House of Representatives, 93rd Congress, Second Session. For discussions related to terrorism and the media, see: William J. Drummond and Augustine Zycher, "Arafat's Press Agents," *Harper's* Vol. 252, No. 1510, March 1976, pp. 24-30; F. Salomone, "Terrorism and the Mass Media" in Bassiouni, supra, pp. 43-46; R. L. Tobin, "More Violent Than Ever: Preoccupation with Bad News in the Mass Media," *Saturday Review*, Vol. 51, November 9, 1968, pp. 79-80; *Time*, September 18, 1972, p. 50; and *Newsweek*, September 18, 1972, pp. 67-68.

(2) For an historic-comparative discussion of the ideology, theory and practice of revolutionary terrorism and its use against various forms of government, see: Paul Wilkinson, *Political Terrorism*, New York: Halsted Press, 1975 and also Roland Gaucher, *The Terrorists: From Tsarist Russia to the O.A.S.*, London: Secker and Warburg, 1968. For a contemporary survey, see: Lester A. Sobel, ed., *Political Terrorism*, New York: Facts on File, 1975; Brian M. Jenkins and Janera Johnson, *International Terrorism: A Chronology, 1968-1974*, Santa Monica, Cal.: Rand, March, 1975.

(3) For a definitional focus on terrorism, see: Jordan J. Paust, "Some Thoughts on Preliminary Thoughts on Terrorism," *American Society of International Law*, Vol. 68, July 1974, pp. 502-3 and John Dugard, "An Ideal Definition of Terrorism" in "International Terrorism: Problems of Definition," *International Affairs*, January 1974, pp. 74-75.

(4) See, for example: "The Official Transcript of Sirhan's Testimony" in *The Lost Significance of Sirhan's Case*, Los Angeles: Organization of Arab Students, 1969; Yiftah Yahalom, *Arab Terror*, Tel Aviv, World Labor Zionist Organization, n.d.; J. Bowyer Bell, "Assassination in International Politics: Lord Moyne, Count Bernadotte, and the Lehi," *International Studies Quarterly*, pp. 59-82.

(5) See: Canadian Council of International Law, *International Terrorism*, Proceedings of the Third Annual Conference held at the University of Ottawa, October 18-19, 1974. For a strong plea against terrorism, see: Brian Crozier, *A Theory of Conflict*, London: Hamish Hamilton, 1974. Burton Zewiebach, *Civility and Disobedience*, New York: Cambridge University Press, 1975 provides a general discussion of the problem of political obligation: when are we obligated to obey the laws?

(6) See: Seymour Maxwell Finger, "International Terrorism and the United Nations" in Alexander, *International Terrorism* supra note 1, pp. 323-349.

(7) For studies on the role of communications in politics, see: Yonah Alexander, *The Role of Communications in the Middle East Conflict: Ideological and Religious Perspectives*, New York: Praeger Publishers, 1973; Bernard C. Cohen, *The Press and Foreign Policy*, Princeton: Princeton University Press, 1963; W. Phillips Davison, *International Political Communications*, New York: Praeger Publishers, 1965; *Mass Communications and Conflict Resolution: The Role of Information Media in the Advancement of International Understanding*, New York: Praeger Publishers, 1974.

(8) "The Futility of Terrorism," *Harper's* Vol. 252, No. 1510, March 1976, p. 104.

(9) Carlos Marighella, *Minimanual of the Urban Guerrilla*, Havana: Tricontinental, n.d., p. 103. For a similar discussion, see: Jerry Rubin, *Do It!* New York: Simon and Schuster, 1970.

(10) See, for example: Joseph M. Russin, "The Transformation of Patricia Hearst," The Washington *Post*, Outlook Section, June 23, 1974, pp. 1 and 5.

(11) For a discussion of terrorism in Argentina, see: Sobel, *Political Terrorism*, supra note 2, pp. 83-106.

(12) Edward Weisband and Damir Roguly, "Palestinian Terrorism: Violence, Verbal Strategy, and Legitimacy," in Alexander, *International Terrorism*, supra note 1, pp. 278-279.

(13) See: Anis Sayegh, *Palestine and Arab Nationalism*, Beirut: Palestine Liberation Organization Research Center, n.d., which reports that during this period the first articles attempting to expose the "Zionist plot" appeared. For an anthology of readings of the history of Zionism and Palestine from 1897 until the establishment of Isreal, see: Walif Khalidi, *From Haven to Conquest*, Beirut: Institute for Palestine Studies, 1971.

(14) See, for example: Henry Cattan, *To Whom Does Palestine Belong?* Beirut: Institute for Palestine Studies, 1959, for a strong statement on the Arab character of Palestine and George J. Tomeh, *Israel and South Africa*, New York: New World Press, 1973.

(15) Quoted in *Al-Ahram* (Cairo), October 15, 1955. See also: address of Abdel Khaleh Hassouna, Secretary General of Arab States before Overseas Writers Association, Washington, D.C.: November 3, 1953, mimeographed; Fayez A. Sayegh, "The Palestinians' Response to Zionism: From Resistance to Liberation," *Arab Journal*, Vol. 3, No. 1, Winter 1965-66, 12-15 and Ahmad Shukairy, *Liberation — Not Negotiation*, Beirut: Palestine Liberation Organization Research Center, 1966.

(16) For a classic deterministic interpretation of history in

the Middle East which dictates that Israel's existence cannot be accepted under any circumstances, see: *Al-Ahram*, May 14, 1971.

(17) For a brief but comprehensive study of the present state of the Palestine movement, its political attitudes, and its future prospects, see: Hisham Sharabi, *Palestine Guerrillas: Their Credibility and Effectiveness*, Beirut: Institute for Palestine Studies, 1970, and *The Arab World*, Vol. 15, No. 5, May 1969 for a special issue containing several articles on the Palestinian groups; Gerard G. Chaliand, *The Palestinian Resistance*, Baltimore, Md.: Penguin Books, 1972.

(18) Arab solidarity is illustrated, for example, in the statement "each one of us is a fedayin" *Al-Nahar*, Beirut: March 1: 1969.

(19) For specific examples of Palestinian support by individual Arab states, see: *Al-Muharir*, Beirut: February 17, 1969; *Al-Gumhuriya*, Baghdad: March 13, 1969; *Al-Ahram*, Cairo, March 16, 1969; *Al-Ba'ath*, Damascus: June 16, 1969; and Jerusalem *Post*, March 6, 1969.

(20) For a description of the organizational development of the Palestinian movements together with an examination of the political ideologies of the various groups, see: Leila S. Kadi, *Basic Political Documents of the Armed Palestinian Resistance Movement*, Beirut: Fifth of June Society, n.d. This report, by Gerard Chaliand, was originally published in *Le Monde Diplomatique* March, 1969. For a briefer discussion of the subject, see: *Al-Nahar*, Beirut: March 18, 1969.

(21) For sampling of reciprocal recrimination, see: *As Siyad*, Kuwait, March 11, 1969; *Nida al Watan*, Beirut: July 24, 1969; *Free Palestine* London: June, 1970; *Akher Sa'a*, Cairo: December 16, 1970; and *An-Nahar*, Beirut: September 23, 1971.

(22) Iraqi News Agency, July 27, 1969.

(23) For details see: *As-Safa*, Beirut, April 26, 1969; *As-Sayad*, Beirut, July 31, 1969; the *Times*, September 24, 1970; *Free Palestine*, London: Vol. 4, No. 9, September, 1971; and the New York *Times*, November 5, 1971.

(24) See: *Fateh*, Beirut, Vol. 3, No. 2, April 12, 1971. In Jordan the government has imposed limitations on the movement of the Feduyeen and on arms supplies to commando bases. In effect, the Palestinian resistance activities in Jordan are virtually liquidated.

(25) The Palestinian guerrillas maintain a communications network on a scale unequalled in the history of subnational groups. For example, the official mouthpiece of the P.L.O. is "The Voice of the Palestinian Revolution" radio station, which

broadcasts daily from Derá in South Syria, and morning, noon, and evening from Damascus, Cairo, Baghdad, Algiers, and Tripoli. The Saudi Arabian and Sudanese radio stations broadcast regular programs in cooperation with the P.L.O.

(26) For a brief discussion of the causes and effects of the 1967 War by an Arab official, see: *The Arab-Israeli Conflict*, Beirut: Palestine Liberation Organization, 1967 and also Robert J. Donovan, *Six Days in June: Israel's Fight for Survival*, New York: New American Library, 1967 and Walter Laqueur, *The Road to Jerusalem: The Arab-Israeli Conflict, 1967*, New York: Macmillan, 1968.

(27) *Al-Hayat*, April 19, 1969.

(28) Radio Cairo, July 23, 1969.

(29) Radio Algiers, February 3, 1969.

(30) M.E.N.A., March 20, 1969.

(31) *Al-Mussawar*, Cairo, January 8, 1969.

(32) *Al-Ahram*, Cairo, May 5, *1969*.

(33) *Ibid.*, August 22, 1970.

(34) Reported by Cairo Radio, November 17, 1972.

(35) Reported by M.E.N.A., August 6, 1970.

(36) Quoted in *Brief*, No. 93, November 1-15, 1974, p.1.

(37) *Brief*, No. 108, June 16-30, 1975, p.2.

(38) Quoted in *Near East Report*, Vol. XIX, No. 38, September 17, 1975. For an Egyptian perspective, see: Ihsan Abdulgudus, "Pros and Cons of the Second Israeli Withdrawal," *Al-Ahram*, August 29, 1975.

(39) Reported by the B.B.C., October 21, 1975.

(40) Following repeated criticism of the interim agreement by Cairo's "Voice of Palestine," Egypt closed the V.O.P. broadcasting operations in September 1975. The V.O.P. in Algiers announced in the following month that it "will resume transmission from another location . . . and will cover Palestine, Trans-Jordan, Syria, Lebanon and Northern Egypt." The station was subsequently located in Lebanon until it resumed broadcasting in Egypt in May, 1976. For details, see: *Near East Report*, Vol. XIX, No. 38, September 17, 1975, and *Southwest Asia*, Vol. II, No. 46, November 21, 1975.

(41) See, for example: H. Sharabi, *Palestine Guerrillas: Their Credibility and Effectiveness*, Beirut: Institute for Palestine Studies, 1970, for a general survey and also John Laffin, *Fedayeen*, New York: Macmillan, 1973, and Mosely Lesch, *The Politics of Palestinian Nationalism*, Los Angeles, University of California Press, 1973.

(42) For an excellent survey, see: Y. Harkabi, *Fedayeen*

Action and Arab Strategy, London: Institute for Stretegic Studies, December 1968.

(43) Radio Cairo, July 31, 1967.

(44) See: Fouad M. Moughrabi, "The Palestine Resistance Movement: Evolution of a Strategy," a paper delivered at the XVII Annual Convention of the International Studies Association, Toronto, Canada, February 25-29, 1976.

(45) For a discussion, see: Y. Harkabi, *Palestinians and Israel*, Jerusalem: Keter Publishing House, 1974, pp. 49-70.

(46) For more recent developments on this matter, see: *Brief*, No. 93, November 1-15, 1974.

(47) "Voice of Palestine," Cairo, July 26, 1970.

(48) Reported in *An-Nahar*, Beirut, April 8, 1969.

(49) "Voice of Fatah," June 26, 1970.

(50) *Majlat Al-Azhar*, October 1968.

(51) For a detailed discussion of the religionization of the conflict, see: Alexander, *The Role of Communications in the Middle East Conflict*, supra note 7.

(52) For a survey of terrorist attacks, see: Ben Moshe, ed. *Issues and Analysis (Arab Terror vs. Pioneering)*, Jerusalem: World Zionist Organization, n.d.

(53) "Voice of Fatah," June 28, 1970.

(54) *Al-Huriya*, Beirut, March 3, 1969.

(55) *Al-Hawadeth*, Beirut, April 11, 1969.

(56) *Al-Hawadeth*, Beirut, April 7, 1969.

(57) For an account of Black September, see: Christopher Dobson, *Black September: Its Short Violent History*, New York: Macmillan Publishing Co., 1974.

(58) See, for example: Marie Syrkin, "Political Terrorism," *Midstream*, Vol. 18, No. 9, 1972, pp. 3-11.

(59) See Dobson, supra note 57.

(60) *Arab Report and Record*, February 15-28, 1973, p. 83.

(61) *Ibid.*, March 16-31, 1973, p. 145.

(62) Ben Moshe, supra note 52, pp. 4-5.

(63) *Near East Report*, Vol. XIX, No. 52, December 25, 1975.

(64) *Arab Report and Record*, No. 20, 1974, p. 465.

(65) Quoted in *Brief*, No. 93, November 1-15, 1974.

(66) See: Hatem I. Hussaini, ed. *Toward Peace in Palestine*, Washington, D.C.: The Arab Information Center, n.d.

(67) *Palestine and Zionism: The Palestinian Perspective at the U.N.*, New York: Office of the Permanent Observer of the Palestine Liberation Organization to the U.N., 1975.

(68) "P.L.O.'s International Victories," *Palestine*, Beirut

Vol. II, No. 10, March 1976, pp. 28-32.
(69) *Ibid.*
(70) See: Jerusalem *Post*, October 24, 1975 and *Brief*, No. 116, October 16-31, 1975.
(71) "P.L.O.'s International Victories," *Palestine*, Beirut, supra note 68.
(72) Jerusalem *Post*, April 23, 1976.
(73) *Free Palestine*, London: Vol. IX, No. 5, May 1976.
(74) New York *Times*, May 16, 1976.
(75) Reported by Washington *Post*, April 2, 1976.
(76) Reported by the B.B.C., January 17, 1976.
(77) Jerusalem *Post*, April 22, 1976.
(78) Jerusalem *Post*, April 29, 1976.
(79) Quoted in *Near East Report*, Vol. XX, No. 19, May 12, 1976.
(80) Quoted in *Near East Report*, Vol. XX, No. 18, May 5, 1976.
(81) *Near East Report*, Vol. XX, No. 21, May 26, 1976.
(82) Quoted by the Palestine News Agency, W.A.F.A.
(83) Jerusalem *Post*, December 10, 1974.
(84) Quoted in *Free Palestine*, London: Vol. VII, No. 7, July, 1974.
(85) Immediately following the 1948 War, the Kingdom of Jordan annexed the West Bank and granted citizenship to its Palestinian population. This area was conquered by Israel in June 1967. Since 1967 Israel has been pursuing a policy of encouraging closer Jordan-West Bank ties in order to dilute the influence of the P.L.O. and pave the way for some sort of agreement with Jordan. This policy included plans to involve Jordan in the selection of West Bank civil servants, relax restrictions on movement of goods and people across the Jordan River bridges, and increase the participation of West Bank residents in Jordanian affairs.
(86) See, for example: *Palestine*, New York: Vol. I, No. 1, April 1, 1976; *Free Palestine*, London: Vol. IX, No. 3, March 1976, Vol. IX, No. 4, April 1976, and Vol. IX, No. 5, May 1976.
(87) For a detailed discussion of the significance of Temple Mount, see: Alexander, *The Role of Communications in the Middle East Conflict*, supra note 7, and "What Future Jerusalem," *International Problems*, Vol. XIII, No. 4, September 1974, 50-55.
(88) *Ibid.*
(89) Jerusalem *Post*, January 29, 1976.

(90) Reported in *Southwest Asia*, No. 8, February 27, 1976.
(91) Washington *Post*, February 20, 1976.
(92) New York *Times*, May 18, 1976.
(93) Leonard Davis, "West Bank Unrest: Putting It in Perspective," *Near East Report*, Vol. XX, No. 12, March 24, 1976, p. 3.
(94) New York *Times*, May 4, 1976.
(95) New York *Times*, May 9, 1976.
(96) New York *Times*, April 15, 1976.
(97) *Ibid.*
(98) Jerusalem *Post*, April 16, 1976.
(99) An interview with Abdul Aziz Zuabi, July 15, 1968.
(100) New York *Times*, February 16, 1976. For further details regarding Shlomo Avineri's views, see his volume: *Israel and the Palestinians: Reflections on the Clash of Two National Movements*, New York: St. Martin's Press, 1971.
(101) New York *Times*.
(102) *Ha'aretz*, Tel Aviv, March 19, 1968.

V.
CURRENT
CHALLENGES
AND
FUTURE
IMPLICATIONS

Edward F. Mickolus:
Statistical Approaches to the Study of Terrorism

> Political terrorism can be characterized as a plethora of random attacks by groups who are not subject to the norms of human behavior in a law-abiding society. Their great strength is their unpredictability, and the totally indiscriminate nature of their actions. Whereas the methods of social science have proven useful in a number of areas, the activities of terrorists follow no patterns which can be systematically analyzed. In addition to eluding police authorities, terrorists have successfully eluded rigorous investigation by talented academic researchers.

The myth of terrorist randomness quoted above has generally been accepted by political scientists, but it is in fact fallacious. Definitions of terrorism vary tremendously among governments, think tanks, and academic researchers, but while hot debates over the inclusion of certain kinds of unconventional violence or certain groups of participants may be ego-satisfying and intellectually entertaining, studies of political violence have for too long remained noncumulative, because we are unable to define terrorism. Although we may disagree on definitions of terrorism, transnational terrorism can be defined as:

> the use, or threat of use, of anxiety-inducing extranormal violence for political purposes by any individual or group,

whether acting for or in opposition to established governmental authority, when such action is intended to influence the attitudes and behavior of a target group wider than the immediate victims and when, through the nationality or foreign ties of its perpetrators, its location, the nature of its institutional or human victims, or the mechanics of its resolution its ramifications transcend national boundaries.(1)

The concept can be refined, by identifying types of terrorism, using location and the nature of the perpetrators as a guide (Figure I).

Figure I: Types of Political Terrorism

		Direct Involvement of Nationals of More than One State?	
		Yes	No
Government Controlled or Directed?	Yes	Interstate	State
	No	Transnational	Domestic

Interstate terrorism is an action (as described above) carried out by individuals or groups controlled by the governmental authority of a sovereign state. Examples include the anti-Basque campaign conducted by Spanish authorities in France and attacks against Palestinian groups in Europe and the Middle East by Israeli intelligence agents.

Transnational terrorism, the subject of our inquiry, is an action carried out by basically autonomous non-state participants, whether or not they enjoy some degree of moral and/or material support from sympathetic governments. Examples include the kidnappings of diplomats and businessmen overseas, the skyjacking of international flights, and embassy barricade-and-hostage episodes.

Domestic Terrorism is behavior characterized by extranorma violence but which is confined to the nationals of only one state. The domestic parallel to transnational terrorism, it is carried on by basically autonomous non-state participants but only affects citizens of one state. Examples include bombings by the I.R.A. and U.D.A. within the borders of Northern Ireland, Weathermen underground bombings in New York, and assassination attempts of governmental leaders by nationals of the officials' country.

State terrorism includes terrorist actions conducted by a national government within its borders; it is the domestic equivalent of interstate terrorism. Examples include the Holocaust in Nazi Germany, the Ukraine's pogroms, and police state tortures.

I.T.E.R.A.T.E. METHODOLOGY

Several approaches have been made to empirically investigate transnational terrorist behavior. We could review the literature of terrorism, including books on the art of guerrilla warfare by those whom we can consider practitioners.(2) We could ask terrorists about their behavior, interviewing either those imprisoned or still in the field.(3) However, terrorists might attempt to propagandize their cause, using an interviewer as another medium for the dissemination of their views. A terrorist might also be unaware of constraints on his behavior, and interviewing could become a futile exercise in mutual illusion.

As a check on data from literature and interviews, we could observe terrorist behavior itself. Observation is the approach taken by the I.T.E.R.A.T.E. (International Terrorism: Attributes of Terrorist Events) project, which focuses on individual incidents. In the pilot version of the dataset, 107 distinct descriptors of an incident were used to give a composite of approximately five hundred terrorist incidents reported in the initial Rand chronology.(4) Terms used to describe incidents verbally were coded into machine-readable numeric forms. Characteristics of an incident like the type of attack,(5) the location, the identity and nationality of the perpetrators, the nationality and identity of the victims, the targets of the demands of the terrorists, the types and extent of demands made, and the outcomes (damage, casualties, governmental responses) of the incident can consequently be quickly summarized in a centrally-available data pool. (See Appendix C for a listing of I.T.E.R.A.T.E.-1 variables and values.) Work is now underway to include other chronologies into the computer files as well as to create a textual description of each incident (tentatively entitled, LITERATE: ITERATE Listing.)

An appreciation of I.T.E.R.A.T.E. as a source of research is afforded by its uses in summarizing trends, comparing terrorist campaigns cross-nationally and longitudinally, evaluating policy prescriptions for crisis management, and incident negotiation support.

TRENDS IN TRANSNATIONAL TERRORISM

Table I and Figure II sketch annual trends in the type of transnational attacks which have occurred worldwide.(6) Once we have corrected them for letterbombing,(7) we note a disturbing rise in terrorist attacks over the past few years (a drop in 1975 is probably due to poor data rather than to restraint by terrorists.) The taking of hostages (i.e. barricade-and-hostage, kidnappings, non-air takeovers, and skyjackings) has become a popular tactic among terrorists, although purely destructive actions like bombings of facilities and assassinations,(8) are also becoming increasingly frequent. Moreover, the probability of a terrorist's success in taking a hostage has grown dramatically since the early 1970s. Despite the publicity given to recent attacks in the Philippines,(9) improvements made in security procedures in 1973, bilateral extradition-or-prosecution treaties (typified by the U.S.-Cuba accord), and the unwillingness of governments to grant asylum have led to a dramatic decrease in aerial hijackings.(9) Purely destructive acts, rather than mere dramaturgical annoyances, are unfortunately increasing.

Figure III shows steady increases in injuries and total casualties, with deaths due to terrorist actions showing in 1974 a more erratic increase. Indiscriminate selection of victims appears to have added greatly to the casualty totals, although most attacks appear to be aimed at individuals or institutions with a symbolic value. In general, methods like letterbombing and skyjacking which have proven too difficult to use or which are relatively ineffective have been replaced by other methods, e.g., barricade-and hostage scenarios, which appear (to the terrorists) to satisfy their goals. Adaptation, rather than throwing in the towel, appears to be the rule.

CROSS-NATIONAL COMPARISONS

Most of the world has become easily accessible with the advent of high-speed methods of transportation. With an increase in potential transnational ties among people has come greater operational possibilities for terrorists. Has the capability of terrorists to strike virtually anywhere in the world been used? What have been their sites of operations? Table III indicates some major patterns.(10)

Most domestic terrorism occurs in the emerging nations of the Third World, but in transnational actions, nearly half of the incidents reported in the past eight years have occurred in Westernized, highly affluent nations. Forty-two percent of all incidents occurred in Atlantic community nations or forty-six percent if letterbomb incidents are

TABLE I

TRANSNATIONAL TERRORIST INCIDENTS, 1968-1975

Incident type	1968	1969	1970	1971	1972	1973	1974	1975	Total
Kidnapping	1	4	31	17	11	34	31	32	161
Barricade & Hostage	0	0	2	1	4	8	12	17	44
Skyjacking	33	80	70	37	38	19	11	6	294
Takeover of Non-Air Transportation	0	0	3	0	1	0	1	1	6
Bombing	38	82	83	71	74	93	147	78	666
Letterbomb	2	2	2	2	222	50	6	3	289
Armed Attack	2	7	8	12	4	10	12	10	65
Murder or Assassination	7	5	12	8	7	14	11	19	83
Arson or Molotov Cocktail	0	14	21	10	1	15	13	6	80
Theft or Break-in	3	7	13	2	1	1	2	3	32
Sabotage	0	0	0	1	3	0	1	0	5
Total	86	201	245	161	366	244	247	175	1,725
Total without letter-bomb	84	199	243	159	144	194	241	172	1,436

Figure II: Annual Frequencies of Selected Types of Transnational Terrorist Incidents

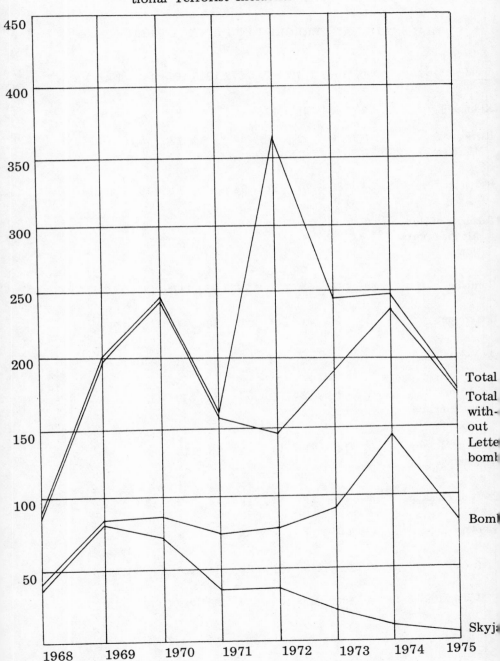

Figure III: Annual Casualties from Transnational Terrorist Attacks, 1969-1975

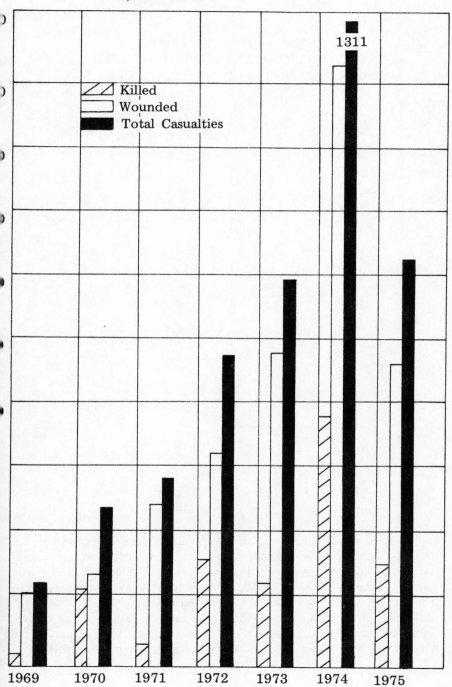

TABLE II

ANNUAL CASUALTIES FROM
TRANSNATIONAL TERRORIST ACTIONS
AND DOMESTIC NON-COMBATANTS.)

Year	Killed	Wounded	Total
1968	12	36	48
1969	16	98	114
1970	104	135	239
1971	39	242	281
1972	154	321+	475+
1973	119+	477	596+
1974	375	936	1,311
1975	155	469	624
Total	974	2,714	3,688

excluded. Eastern European nations appear to have been relatively immune to attacks, suffering only sporadic skyjackings from dissidents.
Latin America and the Middle East rank second to Western nations as
sites of attacks. Asia and Africa infrequently experience such incidents. Terrorist groups in Middle Eastern nations have not
developed undergrounds necessary to attack certain types of targets
(Israel has there established few diplomatic or military installations at
which terrorists could attempt kidnappings), and consequently they

TABLE III

LOCATION OF INCIDENT, BY COUNTRY, REGION, AND TYPE.

Location	B&H	Skyjack	Kidnap	Murder	Armed Attack	Bombs	Letter Bombs	Arson
ATLANTIC COMMUNITY								
Austria	2	1	—	1	—	3	—	1
Belgium	—	—	—	1	—	12	3	2
Canada	—	2	2	1	—	4	3	—
Cyprus	—	—	—	2	2	1	—	—
Denmark	—	—	1	1	—	4	—	—
France	4	5	4	8	4	29	3	2
Gibraltar	—	—	—	—	—	—	1	—
Greece	2	5	—	1	2	38	—	—
Ireland	—	2	2	2	—	8	1	1
Italy	—	5	2	4	—	24	1	10
Netherlands	4	1	—	—	—	6	—	2
Northern Ireland	—	—	2	1	5	8	—	1
Norway	—	—	—	1	—	1	—	—
Portugal	—	1	—	—	—	2	1	—
Spain	1	2	3	4	—	3	—	3
Sweden	2	1	—	1	—	6	—	—
Switzerland	—	3	—	—	1	4	7	—
W. Germany	1	6	1	4	3	21	1	10
UK	3	2	1	4	1	81	34+	3
US	—	98	—	6	5	114	11	10

TABLE III

LOCATION OF INCIDENT, BY COUNTRY, REGION, AND TYPE (Cont)

Location	B&H	Skyjack	Kidnap	Murder	Armed Attack	Bombs	Letter Bombs	Arson
MIDDLE EAST								
Algeria	1	1	—	—	—	—	1	—
Bahrain	—	1	—	—	—	—	—	—
Dubai	—	2	—	—	—	—	—	—
Egypt	—	5	—	1	1	—	4	—
Iran	—	2	1	4	—	4	—	—
Iraq	—	1	—	—	—	—	—	—
Israel	6	1	1	1	10	28	2	3
Jordan	1	2	3	4	1	7	4	1
Kuwait	1	—	—	1	—	—	—	—
Lebanon	1	10	11	4	10	25	7	2
Libya	—	1	—	—	—	—	1	—
Morocco	—	—	—	—	—	2	—	—
Saudi Arabia	—	—	—	—	—	1	—	—
Sudan	1	—	—	—	—	1	—	—
Syria	—	—	—	1	—	3	—	—
Tunisia	1	—	—	—	—	—	—	—
Turkey	—	3	4	—	1	25	1	4
Yemen	—	2	—	—	—	—	—	—
LATIN AMERICA								
Argentina	1	8	44	5	5	119	1	3
Bahamas	—	1	—	1	—	—	—	—
Bolivia	—	1	4	—	—	4	—	2
Brazil	—	8	8	5	—	3	1	4

TABLE III

LOCATION OF INCIDENT, BY COUNTRY, REGION, AND TYPE (Cont)

Location	B&H	Skyjack	Kidnap	Murder	Armed Attack	Bombs	Letter Bombs	Arson
LATIN AMERICA (Cont)								
British Honduras	—	1	—	—	—	—	—	—
Chile	—	2	—	—	—	5	1	—
Colombia	—	24	5	2	1	2	—	—
Costa Rica	—	2	—	—	—	—	—	—
Cuba	—	1	—	—	1	—	1	—
Dominican Republic	1	2	2	—	—	2	—	—
Ecuador	—	6	—	—	—	5	1	—
El Salvador	—	—	—	—	—	3	—	—
Guatemala	—	—	5	3	—	1	—	—
Haiti	1	—	—	—	—	1	—	—
Honduras	—	1	—	—	—	1	—	—
Jamaica	—	1	—	—	—	2	—	—
Mexico	1	11	6	—	1	19	—	—
Netherlands Antilles	—	1	—	—	—	—	—	—
Nicaragua	1	1	—	—	—	—	—	—
Panama	—	1	—	—	—	—	—	1
Paraguay	—	—	1	1	—	—	—	—
Peru	—	1	—	—	—	5	1	1
Puerto Rico	—	3	—	—	—	6	—	—
Uruguay	—	1	10	—	2	3	—	—
Venezuela	—	6	2	—	1	1	—	1

TABLE III

LOCATION OF INCIDENT, BY COUNTRY, REGION, AND TYPE (Cont)

Location	B&H	Skyjack	Kidnap	Murder	Armed Attack	Bombs	Letter Bombs	Arson
AFRICA								
Angola	—	2	3	—	—	—	—	—
Botswana	—	—	—	—	—	—	1	—
Chad	—	—	1	—	—	—	—	—
Ethiopia	—	4	13	2	1	1	—	—
Kenya	—	1	—	—	—	—	—	—
Mozambique	—	—	2	—	—	—	—	—
Rhodesia	—	—	—	—	—	—	1	—
Somalia	—	—	1	—	—	—	—	—
South Africa	1	1	1	—	—	—	2	—
Spanish Sahara	—	—	1	—	—	—	—	—
Tanzania	—	—	1	1	—	—	1	—
Uganda	—	—	1	—	—	—	—	—
Zaire	—	—	—	—	—	—	2	—
Zambia	—	—	—	—	—	1	2	—
ASIA								
Afghanistan	—	—	—	1	—	—	—	—
Australia	—	2	—	—	—	7	—	2
Bangladesh	1	—	—	1	—	1	—	—
Burma	—	—	1	—	—	—	—	—
Cambodia	—	—	—	—	—	3	—	—
India	—	3	—	—	—	4	55	—
Japan	—	2	—	1	1	3	—	6
Malaysia	1	—	—	—	—	—	35	—
Nepal	—	1	—	—	—	—	—	1

TABLE III

LOCATION OF INCIDENT, BY COUNTRY, REGION, AND TYPE (Cont)

Location	B&H	Skyjack	Kidnap	Murder	Armed Attack	Bombs	Letter Bombs	Arson
ASIA (Cont)								
New Zealand	—	—	—	—	—	1	—	1
Pakistan	1	—	—	1	1	2	—	—
Philippines	1	4	2	2	—	8	—	—
Singapore	—	—	—	—	—	—	—	1
South Korea	—	2	—	1	—	—	—	—
S. Vietnam	—	3	—	—	—	—	—	—
Thailand	1	1	1	1	—	—	—	—
EAST EUROPE								
Czechoslo-vakia	—	6	—	—	—	—	—	—
Finland	—	1	—	—	—	—	—	—
Poland	—	4	—	—	—	—	—	—
Romania	—	2	—	—	—	—	—	—
USSR	—	5	—	—	—	—	—	—
Yugoslavia	—	—	—	—	—	—	—	1

Other Actions

Takeover of Non-Air Means of Transportation: Poland 2
Cuba, Lebanon, Thailand, US 1

Theft or Break-in of Facilities: Uruguay 10; Argentina 8; US 3; Lebanon 2;
Brazil, Dominican Republic, Ireland, Japan, Jordan, Portugal,
Sweden, United Kingdom 1

Sabotage not involving bombs: Italy, Jordan, Kuwait, Netherlands, UK,
West Germany

do not engage in certain types of incidents in the Middle East to the extent one might expect. Rather, they have gone abroad to resort to a barricade-and-hostage action. Latin groups with undergrounds have engaged in other types of incidents. Consequently, logistic constraints at times prevent some terrorists from imitating the tactics of other groups.

Transnational terrorism as a threat to Western security appears greater when the nationality of the victims of attack (Table IV), rather than the location of the incident is considered. Although no nation can consider itself completely safe and many nations have suffered from transnational threats and incidents, the overwhelming majority of assaults are aimed at citizens of the Western, industrial nations. Atlantic community citizens suffered in 63% of all incidents, while United States citizens were victimized in a high 36% of all cases. Transnational terrorism is an oddity rather than a serious problem for Africans and Asians, and Eastern Europeans suffered only occasional assaults. In the Middle East, Israelis are the most harassed, with nationals of the moderate Arab nations also being attacked. Latin American guerrillas frequently select non-Latins as victims, particularly those perceived to be rich capitalist exploiters. In general, nationals of the Third World who are victimized are most often their nation's ambassador or a manager of a multinational corporation's local subsidiary. Although all countries *can* be subject to the occasional terrorist incident abroad, Western citizens face the highest probability of being terrorized. Further cross-tabulation of the I.T.E.R.A.T.E. data to show victimization by location may aid the offices of security in various foreign affairs ministries in determining budget priorities for their overseas protection.

POLICY PRESCRIPTIONS—SHORT TERM

In recent years, a debate has raged among members of the Cabinet Committee to Combat Terrorism, police negotiations experts, think-tank researchers, and interested academics over the question of granting concessions to terrorists during hostage situations.(11) Will terrorists be deterred from future attacks if they are unable to obtain what they are demanding? Will other groups copy the successful tactics of terrorists who obtain concessions? What are the terrorists seeking? How should negotiations be conducted even if a no-concessions policy is to be followed? Are there any constraints or patterns of behavior for individuals faced with bargaining with a no-concessions policy?

The U.S. State Department holds that negotiators should be willing to talk with terrorists holding hostages but should never agree

TABLE IV

VICTIMS OF TERRORIST ACTIONS, BY NATIONALITY AND REGION

Nation	Number of incidents	Nation	Number of incidents
NORTH ATLANTIC		**ASIA (Cont)**	
Austria	7	Japan	12
Belgium	7	Malaysia	1
Canada	13	Nepal	1
Cyprus	1	New Zealand	1
Denmark	3	North Korea	1
France	39	Pakistan	1
Greece	20	P. R. China	1
Holy See	2	Philippines	8
Ireland	15	Singapore	2
Italy	54	South Korea	4
Netherlands	17	South Vietnam	4
Portugal	9	Taiwan	1
Spain	54	Thailand	1
Sweden	5		
Switzerland	15	**AFRICA**	
West Germany	40	Angola	1
United Kingdom	173	Ethiopia	14
United States	616	Gabon	1
		Ivory Coast	1
ASIA		Kenya	1
Australia	6	Liberia	1
Bangladesh	1	Malawi	1
Hong Kong	1	Mozambique	4
India	11	Nigeria	1
Indonesia	4	Rhodesia	2

TABLE IV

VICTIMS OF TERRORIST ACTIONS, BY NATIONALITY AND REGION (Cont)

Nation	Number of incidents	Nation	Number of incidents
AFRICA (Cont)		**LATIN AMERICA (Cont)**	
Senegal	1	Panama	4
South Africa	9	Paraguay	3
Tanzania	1	Peru	5
Zaire	1	Puerto Rico	9
		Uruguay	11
LATIN AMERICA		Venezuela	13
Argentina	28		
Bahamas	5	**MIDDLE EAST**	
Bolivia	5	Algeria	8
Brazil	16	Dubai	1
British Honduras	1	Egypt	16
British West Indies	1	Iran	9
Chile	15	Iraq	5
Colombia	30	Israel	119
Costa Rica	3	Jordan	26
Cuba	21	Kuwait	3
Dominican Republic	7	Lebanon	27
Ecuador	9	Libya	2
Guatemala	1	Morocco	1
Haiti	3	Palestinians	24
Honduras	2	Qatar	1
Jamaica	1	Saudi Arabia	10
Mexico	25	South Yemen	1
Netherlands Antilles	2	Syria	4
Nicaragua	3	Turkey	12

TABLE IV

VICTIMS OF TERRORIST ACTIONS, BY NATIONALITY
AND REGION (Cont)

Nation	Number of incidents	Nation	Number of incidents
MIDDLE EAST (Cont)		OTHER	
United Arab		C.E.N.T.O.	3
Emirates	1	N.A.T.O.	1
Yemen	2	O.A.S.	2
		U.N.	1
EAST EUROPE		Foreigners	31
Albania	1	(i.e., source	
Czechoslovakia	8	inspecific about	
East Germany	1	nationality of	
Finland	1	victim)	
Poland	9		
Romania	2		
U.S.S.R.	33		
Yugoslavia	26		

to extortionate demands for the release of U.S. citizens. Has this policy been successful in deterring future attacks? The answer is unclear. Table V indicates that the United States is very rarely the target of explicit demands for monetary ransom or the release of prisoners and consequently may have been somewhat successful in not becoming the target of future demands. However, American citizens are the most popular kidnap victims. American citizens may be chosen as victims for other reasons than as pawns in negotiations with the U.S. government. Terrorists may believe, for example, that they can negotiate directly with the corporation employing a victim. They may also believe that a target government may be more willing to grant concessions for an American citizen than for one of its own. They may also believe that the United States might apply great pressure upon a target government to obtain the safe release of an American.

TABLE V

NATIONALITY OF TARGETS OF DEMANDS,
BY NATION, REGION, AND MULTIPLICITY
OF TARGETS

Target of demands	Number of incidents involving only one target	Number of incidents involving more than one target	Total
ATLANTIC COMMUNITY			
Austria	1	0	1
Canada	2	0	2
France	3	2	5
Greece	5	0	5
Ireland	1	0	1
Italy	1	0	1
Netherlands	0	2	2
Spain	1	0	1
Sweden	1	1	2
Switzerland	0	4	4
Turkey	4	0	4
United Kingdom	1	5	6
United States	2	2	4
West Germany	4	8	12
LATIN AMERICA			
Argentina	2	1	3
Bolivia	1	1	2
Brazil	4	0	4
Colombia	1	0	1
Dominican Republic	3	0	3
Guatemala	4	0	4
Haiti	1	0	1

TABLE V

NATIONALITY OF TARGETS OF DEMANDS, BY NATION, REGION, AND MULTIPLICITY OF TARGETS (Cont)

Target of demands	Number of incidents involving only one target	Number of incidents involving more than one target	Total
LATIN AMERICA (Cont)			
Mexico	3	0	3
Nicaragua	2	0	2
Uruguay	4	0	4
Venezuela	1	0	1
MIDDLE EAST			
Algeria	0	1	1
Egypt	1	2	3
Israel	7	2	9
Jordan	2	2	4
Kuwait	0	1	1
Lebanon	0	1	1
Saudi Arabia	0	1	1
ASIA			
Burma	1	0	1
India	2	0	2
Japan	1	2	3
Philippines	3	0	3
Singapore	1	0	1
Thailand	0	1	1

TABLE V

NATIONALITY OF TARGETS OF DEMANDS,
BY NATION, REGION, AND MULTIPLICITY
OF TARGETS (Cont)

Target of demands	Number of incidents involving only one target	Number of incidents involving more than one target	Total
OTHER			
South Africa	1	0	1
Tanzania	0	1	1
Yugoslavia	1	0	1
PFLP terrorists	1	0	1
Corporations	25	5	31
Target not specified	28	0	28

One may also question whether the terrorists take hostages solely out of the expectation that their stated demands will be satisfied. Not all of the incidents can be characterized as aiming for the securing of money or prisoner release (Table VI). Many other publicly-stated motivations have been given, and more can be suggested if we view terrorism as a general strategy, rather than focusing on an isolated incident. A group may be trying to obtain great publicity for their cause and may consider a government's concessions to their demands as merely a bonus. They may hope that the government does not agree to their demands, pointing later for example to the lack of charity of the government or corporation in not distributing food to people or to the government's inability to release prisoners who were killed secretly. I may well be, to paraphrase Ernest Evans of M.I.T., that the relationship of the no-concessions position to deterrence is not one of success or effectiveness, but rather of irrelevance.(12)

I.T.E.R.A.T.E. may also prove useful in suggesting how talks with terrorists should be conducted during an incident. Characteristics of the situation — the nationality and rank of the hostages, the nationality and other characteristics of the mediators selected, the views of the terrorists on the sanctity of life (measured by their giving warnings in bombing incidents, sequential release of hostages during an attack, and types of other incidents staged), as well as the group'

TABLE VI

TERRORISTS' PUBLICLY STATED MOTIVATIONS FOR ACTIONS

Stated demands or motivations	Barricade & hostage	Kidnapping	Aerial hijacking
Release Political Prisoners (only)	13	25	16
Monetary Ransom (only)	1	47	7
Release prisoners and monetary ransom	3	9	5
Publish manifesto	0	10	1
No demands mentioned	0	18	1
Questioning and/or instruction of hostages	0	6	0
Retaliation	0	2	4
Other (including free passage from scene of incident, specific political changes)	14	15	9

previous history of tergiversation or trustworthiness in other bargaining situations — are aids in determining negotiation tactics during a current crisis.

INTERMEDIATE AND LONG-RANGE PLANNING

One often hears that governments should attempt to get at the root causes of terrorism rather than fight its symptoms; cures for the ills of the nation are what is needed, rather than tighter security measures. What are the root causes of terrorism? Do they lie with an individual, a group, or characteristics of a nation? Why are some nations selected as victims while others become targets of demands? Why do some nations breed terrorist groups while other apparently similar nations have been relatively free from nurturing violence? Why have some nations been chosen as sites for attacks? Systematic cross-national research on the characteristics of nations, comparing them on national wealth, political institutions and political participation, feelings of relative deprivation on the part of the populace and legal systems and using I.T.E.R.A.T.E. as a partial index of levels of transnational terrorism, may aid us in answering these questions, and developing preventive measures.

I.T.E.R.A.T.E. may also help us to plan for kinds of incidents which have not occurred. Terrorist groups may be able to steal nuclear material to either make a bomb or somehow disperse the radioactive substances into a populated area. What are the characteristics of a group wanting to engage nuclear terrorism? What would they want? Would a group want to kill thousands of people? What are the characteristics of that group, and is it similar to other groups who have the technical capabilities to engage in nuclear blackmail? By comparing historical incidents involving many hostages as well as cases of mass murder, we may come to understand future terrorist behavior and plan ahead.

CRISIS MANAGEMENT SUPPORT

In Ruritania, an American citizen is kidnapped by unknown persons. Our Embassy receives a message from a group purporting to hold our national hostage, demanding ransom and prisoner releases to secure the hostage's safety. How do we know this demand is not a hoax? Once we have established its reliability, how do we deal with the incident? What do we know about the behavior of the kidnapper's group wanting to engage in nuclear terrorism? What do they want? Will our hostage be killed during negotiations? Can we get the group to extend their deadline? What are their relations to the government, other groups, and to the population?

I.T.E.R.A.T.E. can serve as a tool for policy analysis. By comparing its large files of cases of actual kidnappings with historical instances of hoaxes, we can note systematic differences between the two and make a better decision about the credibility of the present kidnapper's demand. In Table VII, some types of incidents previously engaged in by transnational terrorist groups are listed.(13) Is the present group claiming responsibility for past incidents that have been recorded? Is the name of the present group being used as a "cover" for another group which wishes to maintain "plausible deniability" in the event of public revulsion at the outcome of the latest outrage? Has the group claiming responsibility for a past incident engaged in that kind of action historically? If not, are there any reasons to believe that the group would have added this tactic to its repertoire? Further analysis of the group's profile via use of other I.T.E.R.A.T.E. descriptive variables can lead to tentative answers to our other questions. Work is now under way to develop a C.A.S.C.O.N.-like(14) interactive version of I.T.E.R.A.T.E.; it allows an analyst to query the system in standard English, with answers in the form of sentences, rather than tables and graphs. Expansion of the I.T.E.R.A.T.E. data base could also be accomplished in a similar manner.

TABLE VII

GROUP CLAIMING RESPONSIBILITY FOR INCIDENT, BY COUNTRY OF MEMBERS' NATIONALITY, REGION, AND INCIDENT TYPE

Country	Group	Kidnap	B&H	Skyjack	Bomb	Armed Attack	Murder
AFRICA							
Angola	Popular Movement for the Liberation of Angola (M.P.L.A.)	3	—	—	—	—	—
Chad	Toubou rebels	1	—	—	—	—	—
Ethiopia	Eritrean Liberation Front (E.L.F.)	13	—	7	2	1	2
French Somaliland	Liberation Front for the Somali Coast	1	—	—	—	—	—
Mozambique	C.O.R.E.M.O.	1	—	—	—	—	—
	F.R.E.L.I.M.O.	1	—	—	—	—	—
Spanish Sahara	Saharan nationalists	1	—	—	—	—	—
Zaire	People's Revolutionary Army	1	—	—	—	—	—

TABLE VII

GROUP CLAIMING RESPONSIBILITY FOR INCIDENT, BY COUNTRY OF MEMBERS' NATIONALITY, REGION, AND INCIDENT TYPE (Cont)

Country	Group	Kidnap	B&H	Skyjack	Bomb	Armed Attack	Murder
ASIA							
Bangladesh	Bengali guerrillas	—	1	—	—	—	—
Burma	Shan insurgents	1	—	—	—	—	—
India	Kashmiri nationalists	—	—	1	—	—	—
Japan	Korean Youth League	—	4	1	—	1	1
	United Red Army	—	—	1	—	—	—
Nepal	Nepalese Communist Party	—	—	1	—	—	—
Pakistan	Black December	—	1	—	—	—	1
Philippines	Kabataang Makabayan	—	—	1	—	—	—
	Moro National Liberation Front	—	1	—	—	—	—
	Philippine nationalists	2	—	—	—	—	1
	Philippine People's Revolutionary Front	—	—	—	2	—	—
South Molucca	South Moluccans	—	3	—	—	—	—
Thailand	Pattani Liberation Front	1	—	—	—	—	—

TABLE VII

GROUP CLAIMING RESPONSIBILITY FOR INCIDENT, BY COUNTRY OF MEMBERS' NATIONALITY, REGION, AND INCIDENT TYPE (Cont)

Country	Group	Kidnap	B&H	Skyjack	Bomb	Armed Attack	Murder
NORTH AMERICA							
Canada	Canadian-Hungarian Freedom Fighters Federation	—	—	—	—	—	1
	Quebec Liberation Front	2	—	—	—	—	—
Puerto Rico	Armed Commandos of Liberation	—	—	—	1	—	—
	F.A.L.N.	—	—	—	17	—	—
	Latin American Anti-Communist Army	—	—	—	4	—	—
United States	Puerto Rican Resistance Movement	—	—	—	1	—	—
	Black Panthers	—	—	5	—	—	—
	Black Revolutionary Assault Team	—	—	—	3	—	—
	Jewish Armed Resistance	—	—	—	1	—	—
	Jewish Defence League	1	—	—	8	—	—
	Republic of New Africa	—	—	—	2	2	—
	Revolutionary Action Party	—	—	—	2	—	1
	Revolutionary Affinity Group 6	—	—	—	1	—	—

TABLE VII

GROUP CLAIMING RESPONSIBILITY FOR INCIDENT, BY COUNTRY OF MEMBERS' NATIONALITY, REGION, AND INCIDENT TYPE (Cont)

Country	Group	Kidnap	B&H	Skyjack	Bomb	Armed Attack	Murder
EUROPE							
indeterminate	National Youth Resistance Org.	—	—	—	2	—	—
Cyprus	EOKA-B	—	—	—	—	—	1
France	Action for the Rebirth of Corsica	—	1	—	—	—	—
	Committee of Coordination	—	—	—	2	—	—
	Group for the Defense of Europe	—	—	—	1	—	—
	Youth Action Group	—	—	—	3	—	—
Greece	E.A.N. – Greek Anti-Dictatorial Youth	—	—	—	1	—	—
	Free Greeks	—	—	—	1	—	—
	Greek Militant Resistance	—	—	—	1	—	—
	Greek People	—	—	—	7	—	—
	L.A.O.S.-1	—	—	—	7	—	—
	L.A.O.S.-13	—	—	—	1	—	—
	Popular Revolutionary Resistance Group	—	—	—	—	—	—

TABLE VII

GROUP CLAIMING RESPONSIBILITY FOR INCIDENT, BY COUNTRY OF MEMBERS' NATIONALITY, REGION, AND INCIDENT TYPE (Cont)

Country	Group	Kidnap	B&H	Skyjack	Bomb	Armed Attack	Murder
EUROPE (Cont)							
Greece	Resistance, Liberation, Independence (A.A.A.)	—	—	—	4	—	—
Italy	Ordine Nero (Black Order)	—	—	—	1	—	—
	Red Brigade	1	—	—	—	—	—
Portugal	A.R.A.	—	—	—	1	—	—
Spain	E.T.A.—Basque Nation and Homeland	4	—	—	—	—	1
	G.A.R.I.	2	—	—	9	—	—
	Hammer and Sickle Cooperative	—	1	—	1	—	—
Switzerland	Les Beliers-Jura	—	1	—	—	—	—
United Kingdom	Black Liberation Front	1	2	—	—	—	—
	I.R.A.—Provisional Wing	—	—	4	66	5	2
	Red Flag 74	—	—	—	3	—	—
	Young Militants Org. (Northern Ireland)	—	—	—	4	—	—

TABLE VII

GROUP CLAIMING RESPONSIBILITY FOR INCIDENT, BY COUNTRY OF MEMBERS' NATIONALITY, REGION, AND INCIDENT TYPE (Cont)

Country	Group	Kidnap	B&H	Skyjack	Bomb	Armed Attack	Murder
EUROPE (Cont)							
West Germany	Baader-Meinhof Group	—	—	—	3	—	—
	Holger Meins Commando	—	1	—	—	—	—
	Meinhof-Antich Group	—	—	—	1	—	—
	Second of June Movement	1	—	—	—	—	—
Yugoslavia	Ustasha and other Croatians	—	1	1	19	—	2
MIDDLE EAST AND NORTHERN AFRICA							
Algeria	Soldiers of the Algerian Opposition	—	—	—	2	—	1
Iran	Iranian Peoples' Strugglers	—	—	—	—	—	2
	Iranian terrorists	—	—	1	1	—	2
Israel	Masada-Action and Defence Movement	—	—	—	1	—	—

TABLE VII

GROUP CLAIMING RESPONSIBILITY FOR INCIDENT, BY COUNTRY OF MEMBERS' NATIONALITY, REGION, AND INCIDENT TYPE (Cont)

Country	Group	Kidnap	B&H	Skyjack	Bomb	Armed Attack	Murder
MIDDLE EAST AND NORTHERN AFRICA (Cont)							
Jordan	Jordanian Free Officers Movement	—	—	1	—	—	—
	Jordanian National Liberation Movement	—	—	1	—	—	—
Lebanon	Lebanese Revolutionary Guard	—	—	—	1	—	—
	Lebanese Revolutionary Socialist Movement	—	—	—	1	—	—
	Lebanese Revolutionary Socialist Org. (Shibbu Gang)	—	—	—	—	—	1
	Revolutionary Socialist Action Organization	1	—	—	—	—	—
Palestine	Action Organization for the Liberation of Palestine	—	—	—	—	1	—
	Al Saiqa	—	1	—	—	—	—
	Arab Liberation Arm	—	1	—	—	—	—
	Arab Liberation Front	—	1	—	—	—	—

238 TERRORISM: INTERDISCIPLINARY PERSPECTIVES

TABLE VII

GROUP CLAIMING RESPONSIBILITY FOR INCIDENT, BY COUNTRY OF MEMBERS' NATIONALITY, REGION, AND INCIDENT TYPE (Cont)

Country	Group	Kidnap	B&H	Skyjack	Bomb	Armed Attack	Murder
MIDDLE EAST AND NORTHERN AFRICA (Cont)							
Palestine	Arab Nationalist Youth for the Liberation of Palestine	—	—	2	—	—	—
	Arab Nationalist Youth Organization for the Liberation of Palestine	—	—	1	—	—	—
	Black September	—	3	2	11	3	7
	Eagles of National Unity	—	1	1	—	—	—
	Eagles of the Palestine Revolution	—	2	—	5	1	2
	El Fatah	1	—	3	—	1	—
	Islamic Liberation Org.	—	1	—	—	—	—
	Moslem International Guerrillas	—	—	—	4	1	—
	Muhammad Boudia Commando	—	—	—	—	2	—
	Nationalist Organization of Arab Youth	—	—	—	1	—	—
	Nationalist Youth Group for the Liberation of Palestine	—	—	—	—	—	—
	Organization for the Victims of Zionist Occupation	—	—	1	—	—	—

TABLE VII

GROUP CLAIMING RESPONSIBILITY FOR INCIDENT, BY COUNTRY OF MEMBERS'
NATIONALITY, REGION, AND INCIDENT TYPE (Cont)

Country	Group	Kidnap	B&H	Skyjack	Bomb	Armed Attack	Murder
MIDDLE EAST AND NORTHERN AFRICA (Cont)							
Palestine	Organization of Arab Nationalist Youth for the Liberation of Palestine	—	—	—	1	—	—
	Organization of Sons of Occupied Territories	—	—	1	—	—	—
	Organization of Victims of Occupied Territories	—	1	—	—	—	—
	Palestine Liberation Army	1	—	—	—	—	—
	Palestine Liberation Organization (P.L.O.)	—	—	—	1	1	—
	Palestine Popular Struggle Front	—	—	1	2	1	—
	Palestine Revolutionary Forces	—	—	—	1	—	—
	Palestinian guerrillas	1	1	3	14	11	7
	Popular Democratic Front for the Liberation of Palestine (P.D.F.L.P.)	—	1	—	1	4	—

TABLE VII

GROUP CLAIMING RESPONSIBILITY FOR INCIDENT, BY COUNTRY OF MEMBERS' NATIONALITY, REGION, AND INCIDENT TYPE (Cont)

Country	Group	Kidnap	B&H	Skyjack	Bomb	Armed Attack	Murder
MIDDLE EAST AND NORTHERN AFRICA (Cont)							
Palestine	Popular Front for the Liberation of Palestine (P.F.L.P.)	3	4	15	36	4	2
	P.F.L.P.-General Command	—	1	—	—	1	—
	Punishment Squad	—	1	—	—	—	—
	Seventh Suicide Squad	—	1	—	—	—	—
	Squad of the Martyr Patrick Arguello	—	—	—	—	1	—
Syria	Arab Communist Org.	—	—	—	5	—	—
Turkey	Turkish People's Liberation Army (T.P.L.A.)	4	—	1	1	—	—
LATIN AMERICA							
Argentina	Argentine rightists	—	—	—	—	—	1
	Comite Argentino de Lucha Anti-Imperialisto	—	—	—	5	—	—

TABLE VII

GROUP CLAIMING RESPONSIBILITY FOR INCIDENT, BY COUNTRY OF MEMBERS' NATIONALITY, REGION, AND INCIDENT TYPE (Cont)

Country	Group	Kidnap	B&H	Skyjack	Bomb	Armed Attack	Murder
LATIN AMERICA (Cont)							
Argentina	E.R.P. – People's Revolutionary Army	15	—	3	25	2	1
	F.A.L.–Argentine Liberation Front	1	—	—	—	1	—
	F.A.P.–Peronist Armed Forces	—	—	—	15	—	3
	M.A.N.O.–Argentine National Organization Movement	1	—	—	—	—	—
	Montoneros	4	—	—	17	—	—
	Peronist guerrillas	—	—	—	1	—	—
Bolivia	Bolivian peasants	1	—	—	—	—	—
	E.L.N.–National Liberation Army	1	—	—	1	—	—
Brazil	A.L.N.–Action for National Liberation	4	—	1	1	—	—
	Aurora Maria Nacimiento Furtado Command	—	—	—	—	—	1
	M.R.-8–Revolutionary Movement of the 8th	1	—	—	—	—	—
	V.A.R.-Palmares–Armed Revolutionary Vanguard-Palmares	—	—	1	—	—	—

TABLE VII

GROUP CLAIMING RESPONSIBILITY FOR INCIDENT, BY COUNTRY OF MEMBERS' NATIONALITY, REGION, AND INCIDENT TYPE (Cont)

Country	Group	Kidnap	B&H	Skyjack	Bomb	Armed Attack	Murder
LATIN AMERICA (Cont)							
Chile	Chilean refugees	—	1	—	—	—	—
	Leftist Revolutionary Movement	—	—	1	—	—	—
Colombia	E.L.N.–National Liberation Army	1	—	2	—	—	—
	F.A.R.C.	1	—	—	—	—	—
	Invisible Ones	1	—	—	1	—	—
	United Front for Guerrilla Action	—	—	—	—	1	—
Cuba	Anti-Castro Cubans	—	—	—	14	—	—
	Cuban Liberation Front	—	—	—	1	1	—
	Cuba Movement 4	—	—	—	1	—	—
	Cuban Power 76	—	—	—	1	—	—
	Cuban Scorpion	—	—	—	4	—	—
	Cuban Secret Government	—	—	—	7	—	—
	Cuban Youth Group	—	—	—	20	—	—
	El Poder Cubano	—	—	—	6	1	1
	F.L.N.C.	—	—	—	—	—	—

TABLE VII

GROUP CLAIMING RESPONSIBILITY FOR INCIDENT, BY COUNTRY OF MEMBERS' NATIONALITY, REGION, AND INCIDENT TYPE (Cont)

Country	Group	Kidnap	B&H	Skyjack	Bomb	Armed Attack	Murder
LATIN AMERICA (Cont)							
Cuba	M-7	—	—	—	3	—	—
	Secret Organization Zero	—	—	—	1	—	1
	Young Cubans	—	—	—	1	—	—
	Youths of the Star	—	—	—	1	—	—
Dominican Republic	Dominican guerrillas	1	—	—	1	—	—
	United Anti-Reelection Command	—	—	—	—	—	1
Ecuador	dissidents	—	—	—	1	—	—
Guatemala	F.A.R.—Revolutionary Armed Forces	3	—	—	—	—	—
	M.R.-13	—	—	—	—	1	1
Haiti	Coalition of National Brigades	—	1	—	—	—	—
	Haitian Coalition	—	—	—	—	—	—
Mexico	Armed Communist League	—	—	1	—	—	1
	Mexican guerrillas	1	—	—	—	—	—
	People's Revolutionary Armed Forces (F.R.A.P.)	2	—	—	—	—	—

TABLE VII

GROUP CLAIMING RESPONSIBILITY FOR INCIDENT, BY COUNTRY OF MEMBERS' NATIONALITY, REGION, AND INCIDENT TYPE (Cont)

Country	Group	Kidnap	B&H	Skyjack	Bomb	Armed Attack	Murder
LATIN AMERICA (Cont)							
Mexico	23rd of September Communist League	1	1	—	2	—	—
	United Popular Liberation Army of America	1	—	—	—	—	—
Nicaragua	F.S.L.N.–Sandinist Front of National Liberation	—	1	1	—	—	—
	MoPoCo	1	—	—	—	—	—
Peru	Condor	—	—	—	1	—	—
Uruguay	O.P.R.-33—Organization of the Popular Revolution-33	1	1	—	—	—	—
	Raul Sendic International Brigade	—	—	—	—	—	—
	Tupamaros	7	—	—	1	2	1
Venezuela	People's Revolutionary Army-Zero Point	—	—	1	—	—	—
	Red Flag	1	—	—	—	—	—

TABLE VII

GROUP CLAIMING RESPONSIBILITY FOR INCIDENT, BY COUNTRY OF MEMBERS' NATIONALITY, REGION, AND INCIDENT TYPE (Cont)

Country	Group	Kidnap	B&H	Skyjack	Bomb	Armed Attack	Murder
OTHER							
	Unknown	5	—	3	287	21	31
	Individuals or Groups who engaged in incidents as a one-time event, and were not involved in a campaign of terrorism	4	3	230	5	4	6

246 TERRORISM: INTERDISCIPLINARY PERSPECTIVES

A FINAL WORD

I.T.E.R.A.T.E. has been shown to have interesting possibilities when used by capable government analysts. However, we must remember that statistical analysis alone cannot answer everything. All disciplines and methods of analysis are useful, including contributions from international law, sociology, psychology, psychiatry, police, intelligence, political science, as well as statistics and mathematics. Students and observers of terrorism have quibbled over definitions of the field and over the "real nature" of the terrorist problem. It is argued, inter alia, that "we can only understand terrorists by noting their cultural heritage," and others note the "breakdown of society" or the "individual's identity crisis" or any other intellectual fad currently in fashion. We must recognize that all of us can be useful in the explanation and response to terrorism, and we must transcend our territorial bickering. We owe cooperation among ourselves to the 3,688 past victims of transnational terrorism as well as to the future victims of attack. We may well be the next targets. To paraphrase Keynes, we owe it to ourselves.

NOTES

(1)Compare this formulation of the problem of transnational terrorism with that of, inter alia, Brian M. Jenkins and Janera Johnson, "International Terrorism: A Chronology, 1968-1974," Santa Monica, The Rand Corporation, R-1597-DOS/ARPA, March, 1975; David L. Milbank "International and Transnational Terrorism Diagnosis and Prognosis," paper prepared for delivery to the State Department Conference on International Terrorism, Washington D.C., March 25-26, 1976, with appendices; and Jordan J. Paust "Terrorism and the International Law of War," *Military Law Review* Vol. 64, 1974, pp. 1-36.

(2)For those wishing to engage in this research strategy, th following works may prove helpful: Tariq Ali, ed., *The New Revolutionaries: A Handbook of the International Radical Left*, New York, Morrow, 1969; Anthony M. Burton, *Urban Terrorism: Theory Practice and Response*, London, Leo Cooper, 1975; Regis Debray "Revolution in the Revolution?" *Monthly Review*, July-August, 1967; John D. Elliott, "Writer-Theoreticians of Urban Guerrilla Warfare, *Short Essays in Political Science*, Washington, D.C., America Political Science Association, March, 1975; Frantz Fanon, *The Wre ched of the Earth*, New York, Grove Press; Harmondsworth, Penguir 1967; John Gerassi, ed., *Venceremos: The Speeches and Writing of Ch*

Guevara, London Panther, 1968; Ernesto Che Guerva, *Episodes of the Revolutionary War*, New York, International Publishers, 1968; Ernesto Che Guevara, *Guerrilla Warfare*, New York, Random House, 1969; Abraham Guillen, *Philosophy of the Urban Guerrilla*, translated and edited with Introduction by Donald C. Hodges, New York, Morrow, 1973; Sidney Hook, "The Ideology of Violence," *Encounter*, April, 1970, pp. 26-38; Leo Huberman and Paul M. Sweezy, eds., *Regis Debray and the Latin American Revolution*, New York, Monthly Review Press, 1968; Daniel James, ed., *The Complete Bolivian Diaries of Che Guevara (and other captured documents)*, New York, Stein and Day, 1968; Leila Khaled, *My People Shall Live: The Autobiography of a Revolutionary*, London, Hodder and Stoughton, 1973; New York, Bantam, 1974; Jay Mallin, ed., *Terror and Urban Guerrillas: A Study of Tactics and Documents*, Coral Gables, University of Miami Press, 1971; Carlos Marighella, "Minimanual of the Urban Guerrilla," *Tricontinental (Havana)*, Jan.-Feb., 1970, pp. 15-56; Sergey Nechayev, "Cathechism of the Revolutionist" in Michael Confino, ed., *Daughter of a Revolutionary*, London, Alcove, 1974, pp. 221-230; J. Niezing, *Urban Guerrilla: Studies on the Theory, Strategy, and Practice of Political Violence in Modern Societies*, Rotterdam University Press, 1974; B.V. Savinkov, *Memoirs of a Terrorist*, New York, Kraus, 1970; D.V. Segre and J.H. Adler, "The Ecology of Terrorism," *Encounter*, Feb., 1973, pp. 17-24, reprinted in *Survival*, Summer, 1973; Andrew Sinclair, *Guevara*, London, Fontana/Collins, 1970; Max Stirner, *Der Einzige and sein Eigentum (The Ego and Its Own)*, Berlin, 1845, translated by Steven T. Byington, London, Fifield, 1907; New York, Boni and Liveright, n.d.; "Terrorism and Marxism," *Monthly Review*, Nov., 1972, pp. 1-6; Leon Trotsky, *Terrorism and Communism*, Ann Arbor, University of Michigan Press, 1963; Pierre Valliers, *White Niggers of America: The Precocious Autobiography of a Quebec Terrorist*, New York: Monthly Review Press, 1971; Ehud Yaari, "Al Fatah's Political Thinking," *New Outlook*, Nov.-Dec., 1968, pp. 20-33.

(3)The pioneering work of J. Bowyer Bell immediately comes to mind, as well as that of Gerald McKnight in a slightly different context. Unfortunately, due to the clandestine nature of terrorist groups, as well as the institutional affiliations and personal predispositions of most reseachers, such areas of inquiry shall remain the domain of a courageous handful.

(4)See Jenkins and Johnson, supra note 1.

(5)For definitions of these types of incidents, see: Edward F. Mickolus, "Trends in Transnational Terrorism" in Marius Livingston, ed., *Terrorism in the Contemporary World*, Greenwood Press, 1976; Edward F. Mickolus, "Transnational Terrorism," in Michael Stohl, ed., *The Politics of Terror: A Reader in Theory and Practice*, Marcel Dekker, forthcoming.

(6)In the tables and figures, only incidents of transnational terrorism, as defined, are included. Events related to the Vietnam conflict are not included, nor are the numerous cross-border raids between Arabs and Israelis against military targets. Plots to engage in actions classified as terrorist, but which were discovered before the carrying out of the operation, are not included, nor are threats to engage in such actions (although such events may be included in I.T.E.R.A.T.E.-2). Although the present computerized version of I.T.E.R.A.T.E. includes only the Rand chronology, statistics for the tables presented herein were hand-calculated from the data sources listed in Appendix A.

(7)Due to oddities in the reporting on letterbombs, totals have been calculated including and excluding each incident reported. A shift in our definition of a letterbomb incident from one which counts each letterbomb as an incident to one which counts the number of times a perpetrator mailed letterbombs would also drastically alter the total number of incidents, and give a false impression overall of the number of attacks due to all types of incidents.

(8)A score of definitions have been offered for the term, "assassination." Rather than attempt to distinguish between the political murder of a low-level official and a high-level official (if such an arbitrary cut-off point could be established with any meaning), determine the motivations of the killer, etc., and become a part of a definitional debate as unproductive as that on "terrorism," a general category of political murder and assassination is employed. To qualify for inclusion, such acts must satisfy the conditions of the definition of transnational terrorism.

(9)Skyjackings were much more frequent than herein reported, due to the large number of attempts which were thwarted on the ground. To qualify for inclusion in the present study, such attacks must have the attributes of our definition of transnational terrorism. Incidents which did not involve a crossing of a border (such as events involving the payment of ransom and parachuting of the hijacker from the plane within the territorial confines of the nation of embarkation), domestic attempts to hijack a plane to another country which involved no injuries in the resolution of the incident, and incidents which involved only one nationality of passengers, crew, perpetrator, destination, and embarkation point of the flight are thus not included. While skyjackings and non-air takeovers can become barricade-and-hostage situations, these incidents are not treated as B&H if they occurred in transit. Hence, the multiple skyjackings of the Popular Front for the Liberation of Palestine in September, 1970 are treated as skyjackings, although negotiations were conducted on the ground.

(10)The location of an incident is considered to be the place in which the incident began. Its year is that date on which it became known to individuals other than the terrorists that a terrorist incident was taking place. In the case of skyjacking, the location is the nation in which the plane had last touched ground before the hijackers made their presence as hijackers known. In cases in which the embarkation point is not known, the location is considered to be that nation in which the plane landed and the negotiations took place, where appropriate. If both of the above do not apply, the nation of registry is used.

The location of an incident need not be a nation-state. Protectorates, colonies, and mandated territories may also experience terrorism, and are considered by the government to be different types of security and administrative environments, not comparable to the metropole. Hence, areas such as Puerto Rico and Gibraltar are included as locations, despite the legal citizenship of their residents.

(11)For a more complete cataloguing of the arguments involved, see Edward F. Mickolus, "Negotiating for Hostages: A Policy Dilemma," *Orbis*, Winter, 1976, 1309-1325.

(12)See: Ernest Evans, "American Policy Response to International Terrorism," paper presented to the Conference on Terrorism in the Contemporary World, held at Glassboro State College, April 26-28, 1976. Note also Evans' dissertation for the M.I.T. Department of Political Science.

(13)The name of the group claiming responsibility for the incident is what is reported, rather than the identity of the group which police, intelligence services, or the press speculate as having been involved. Often groups give "cover" names to be able to deny responsibility of their umbrella organization for particularly hideous crimes, or for operations which failed to achieve the objectives of their perpetrators, or to commemorate the names of their fallen comrades, now perceived as martyrs. Actions which are less frequent than those mentioned in Table VIII, and the groups responsible for such incidents (with nationality in parentheses), include:

Theft:
4	Jewish Defense League (U.S.), 7 unknown
3	F.A.L. (Argentina), F.A.P. (Argentina), Palestinians, Tupamaros (Uruguay)
2	E.R.P. (Argentina), I.R.A. (U.K.)
1	Armed Popular Front (Uruguay), Ethiopian students, Japanese students
7	Unknown

Arson:	61	Unknown
	5	Revolutionary Force 7 (U.S.)
	2	Marxist Youth League (Japan), Palestinians
	1	Black September, I.R.A., J.D.L., Movement of Youthward Brothers in War of the Palestinian People, Popular Front for the Liberation of Palestine, Proletarian Revolutionary Action Group (Chile or Italy), Puerto Rican Liberation Front, Bandera Roja (Venezuela), National Liberation Armed Forces (Venezuela), We Must Do Something (France), groups or individuals who engaged in incident as a one-time event
Sabotage:	3	Unknown
	2	Black September
	1	P.F.L.P.
Letterbomb:	100	Palestinians
	67	Black September, 48 unknown
	42	I.R.A.
	35	Malay-Arab group (Malaysia)
	3	El Poder Cubano
	1	M.A.N.O. (Peru), Yanikian Commandos (Turkey)
	48	Unknown
Non-air Takeover:	5	one-timers
	1	Palestinians

When the nationality of the perpetrators is known, but no organization name is available, it is so noted, e.g. "Palestinians" or "Iranian guerrillas."

(14)For a fuller discussion of the capabilities of C.A.S.C.O.N., see: Lincoln P. Bloomfield, Robert R. Beattie, and G. Allen Moulton, with Robert M. Mandel and John J. Spear, "C.A.S.C.O.N. II: Computer-Aided System for Handling Information on Local Conflicts: User's Manual" (Cambridge, Mass.: Arms Control Project, Center for International Studies, M.I.T., C/72-14, Sept., 1972), 83 pp.

APPENDIX A: I.T.E.R.A.T.E. DATA SOURCES

I.T.E.R.A.T.E. collects descriptions from a multiplicity of governmental, academic, and journalistic reports on incidents of terrorism. At present, it includes the sources listed below. Further work on the project will extend the coverage of incidents, including reporting from the F.A.A. on skyjacking, the U.S.I.A. · on attacks on U.S. installations, and embassy reports, both U.S. and foreign.

James A. Arey, *The Sky Pirates*, New York, Scribner's, 1972.

Carol Edler Baumann, *The Diplomatic Kidnappings: A Revolutionary Tactic of Urban Terrorism*, The Hague, Nijhoff, 1973.

J. Bowyer Bell, *The Myth of the Guerrilla: Revolutionary Theory and Malpractice*, New York, Alfred A. Knopf, 1971.

Yaroslav Bilinsky, "The Background of Contemporary Politics in the Baltic Republics and the Ukraine: Comparisons and Contrasts," in Arvids Ziedonis, Jr, Rein Taagepera, and Mardi Valgemae, *Problems of Mininations: Baltic Perspectives*, California State University, San Jose, Association for the Advancement of Baltic Studies, Inc., 1973

"Bombing Incidents, Mob Action and Harassment against U.S. Installations Overseas, July 1, 1969—June 30, 1970," Washington, D.C.: U.S. Information Agency, Sept. 4, 1970.

"Briefing Packet," Washington, D.C., U.S. Information Agency, Seminar on International Terrorism, August 11, 1975.

"Chronology of Attacks upon Non-Official American Citizens, 1971-1975" Washington, D.C., U.S. Department of State, Jan. 20, 1976.

"Chronology of Hijackings - 1968 through 1975," Washington, D.C., U.S. Department of State, 1976.

"Chronology of Significant Terrorist Incidents Involving U.S. Diplomatic/Official Personnel, 1963-1975," Washington, D.C.: U.S. Department of State, Jan. 20, 1976.

Peter Clyne, *An Anatomy of Skyjacking*, London, Abelard-Schuman, 1973.

John K. Cooley, *Green March, Black September: The Story of the Palestinian Arabs*, London, Frank Cass, 1973.

Brian Crozier, *Annual of Power and Conflict, 1974-1975*, London, Institute for the Study of Conflict, 1975.

Curtis Cutter, interview conducted by the author, Feb., 1976.

Christopher Dobson, *Black September: Its Short, Violent History*, New York, Macmillan, 1974.

Karl and Debbie Dortzbach, *Kidnapped*, New York, Harper and Row, 1975.

John D. Elliott, "Action and Reaction: West Germany and the Baader-Meinhof Guerrillas," *Strategic Review*, Winter, 1976, pp. 60-67.

Claude Fly, *No Hope But God*, New York, Hawthorne, 1973.

Brian Michael Jenkins, "Hostage Survival: Some Preliminary Observations," Santa Monica, The Rand Corporation, draft, April, 1975, presented to the U.S. Information Agency's International Terrorism Seminar, Washington, D.C., August 11, 1975.

Brian Michael Jenkins, "International Terrorism: A New Mode of Conflict," Santa Monica: California Arms Control and Foreign Policy Seminar Research Paper 48, published by Los Angeles: Crescent Publications, Jan., 1975.

Brian Michael Jenkins, "International Terrorism: A New Mode of Conflict," in David Carlton and Carlo Schaerf, eds., *International Terrorism and World Security*, London, Croom Helm, 1975, pp. 13-49.

Brian Michael Jenkins and Janera Johnson, "International Terrorism: A Chronology, 1968-1974," Santa Monica, The Rand Corporation, R-1597-DOS/ARPA, March, 1975.

Brian Michael Jenkins and Janera Johnson, "International Terrorism: A Chronology, 1968-1974 (Supplement)," Santa Monica, The Rand Corporation, October, 1975, advance copy.

James Kohl and John Litt, *Urban Guerrilla Warfare in Latin America*, Cambridge, Mass., M.I.T. Press, 1974.

Jay Mallin, ed., *Terror and Urban Guerrillas: A Study of Tactics and Documents*, Coral Gables, Florida, University of Miami Press, 1971.

"Meir Kahane: A Candid Conversation with the Militant Leader of the Jewish Defense League," *Playboy*, Oct., 1972, pp. 69ff.

Robert Moss, *The War for the Cities*, New York, Coward, McCann and Geoghegan, 1972, published in England as *Urban Guerrillas: The New Face of Political Violence*, London, Temple Smith, 1971.

David Phillips, *Skyjack: The Story of Air Piracy*, London, Harrap, 1973.

Lester A. Sobel, ed., *Political Terrorism*, New York, Facts on File, 1975.

Peter Snow and David Phillips, *The Arab Hijack War*, New York, Ballantine, 1970.

The Terrorist and Sabotage Threat to U.S. Nuclear Programs: Phase One Final Report, prepared for Sandia Laboratories under Contract No. 82-9139 by the Historical Evaluation and Research Organization, Dunn Loring, Virginia, August, 1974.

U.S. House of Representatives "Political Kidnappings, 1968-73," a staff study prepared by the Committee on Internal Security, 93rd

Congress, 1st session, Washington, D.C., U.S. Government Printing Office, August 1, 1973.

U.S. Senate, Committee on the Judiciary, Subcommittee to Investigate the Administration of the Internal Security Act and Other Internal Security Laws, "Terroristic Activity: International Terrorism, Part 4, Hearings," 94th Congress, 1st session, Washington, D.C., U.S. Government Printing Office, May 14th, 1975.

United Nations, document A/C.1/L.872, 20 November 1972.

Paul Wilkinson, *Political Terrorism*, New York, Wiley, 1975.

The aforementioned data sources have been supplemented by accounts given by the Associated Press ticker, A.B.C. FM Radio News, A.B.C. Evening News, C.B.S. Evening News, N.B.C. Evening News, the Detroit Free *Press,* New Haven *Register,* New York *Times,* and Washington *Post.* Chronologies from journalistic sources which have proven helpful include:

A.B.C. News Olympic Special, 8 p.m., Jan. 5, 1976.

Chicago *Tribune,* June 18, 1974.

Chronologies provided the author by Carol Edler Baumann.

The Economist, August 9, 1975.

New York *Times,* Dec. 20, 1973 and May 16, 1974.

"One Act of Guerrilla Violence after Another: Major Arab Terrorist Attacks in the Last 3½ Years," *U.S. News and World Report,* May 27, 1974.

"Terrorists: Where Are They Now?" The Economist, March 9, 1974.

U.S. News and World Report, May 27, 1974.

Washington *Post-Parade,* March 16, 1975, p. 7.

APPENDIX B: STATISTICAL AND MATHEMATICAL APPROACHES TO THE STUDY OF TERRORISM: A SURVEY OF CURRENT WORK

I.T.E.R.A.T.E. is part of a small but growing "invisible college" attempting to apply the tools of systematic empirical inquiry to the analysis of terrorist behavior. This appendix briefly describes some of the ongoing projects on terrorism which employ mathematical and/or statistical techniques to supplement their description, explanation, and prediction.

Brian Jenkins, et. al., Project on International Terrorism, The Rand Corporation. Jenkins and his associates have conducted the most useful basic research on terrorism which has been published. Their bibliographies, chronologies of incidents of international terrorism, and attempts to create systematic typologies of groups and events form the foundation for future studies. Their most recent chronology supplement presents one-way frequency distributions which illustrate recent trends in types of attacks, as well as geographical differences. Such work will eventually lead to profiles of the major groups, with qualitative and quantitative analyses of their modus operandi.

R.H. Anderson and J.J. Gillogly, "Rand Intelligent Terminal Agent (R.I.T.A.): Design Philosophy," Santa Monica, The Rand Corporation, R-1809-ARPA, Feb., 1976. The authors, in conjunction with Jenkins' project, are attempting to create an artificial intelligence model which would serve as an aid in the analysis of terrorist incidents. The computerized system uses information on previous incidents (e.g. I.T.E.R.A.T.E.-type data) as well as a series of conditional rules about the interpretation of incidents. Based upon data fed into it regarding a current incident, the computer is then able to derive conclusions about the perpetrators' identity and probable behavior during the incident. While predictive power is a future goal of the system, its present advantage is that it forces the analyst to make explicit his unstated assumptions about terrorist behavior. The computer is then able to demonstrate how these assumptions logically interact, pointing out inconsistencies. The analyst is then able to further refine the system's logic by changing the probabilities assigned to the conditional statements, adding new rules, modifying or deleting existing rules, changing or adding incidents to the data base, and teaching the system new inference rules through examples.

Ric Blacksten, "Appendix: Hostage Games," in Ric Blacksten and Richard Engler, "Ketron Concept Paper: Hostage Studies, Arlington, Virginia, Ketron, Inc., Jan 8, 1974. Blacksten uses decision trees, payoff matrices, and game theoretic propositions to analyze common kidnapping and skyjackings. Utilities to terrorists and governments of various suggested policy options are discussed, with rational solutions suggested for each. Hypothetical values are filled in the payoff matrix for illustrative purposes.

Henry B. McFarland and Edward Mickolus, "An Economic Theory of Terrorist Activity," in preparation. McFarland, in Northwestern's Department of Economics, suggests viewing terrorists as a sort of business with resource constraints. One then assumes that a given group maximizes the weighted sum of expected changes in confidence in the government, confidence in the group, membership of the group, and equipment. There are N possible activities the group may engage in, each with resource costs. The damage or gain to the confidence parameters changes in absolute value as the "crime" is committed more often. Were these constant the group would specialize in only one activity (e.g. bombings), unless costs rose. The group is faced with maximizing the payoffs yielded by an equation which arises from the above considerations (requiring solving first and second order differentiations). Attempts to test such a theory will come partly from Mickolus' I.T.E.R.A.T.E. dataset on the resources of the group at the beginning of the year, number of terrorists in the attack force for a given incident, and utility yield of any incident engaged in during the year.

Ted Robert Gurr, *"Some Characteristics of Contemporary Political Terrorism," paper delivered to the Conference on International Terrorism held by the U.S. Department of State, Washington, D.C. March 25-26, 1976.* Gurr surveys episodes and campaigns of domestic terrorism in 87 countries during the decade from 1961 to 1970. For Gurr's study, terrorism involves destructive violence via stealth rather than open combat against political targets conducted by groups operating clandestinely and sporadically. Despite most of the conventional wisdom on terrorism, his statistics show that "the typical terrorist campaign was conducted by tiny groups and was short-lived. Their public motives were not notably different from those of groups using other unconventional methods of political action. More specifically, the perpetrators of terrorist activities were more often motivated by hostility toward particular policies and political figures than by revolutionary aspirations. Their actions were more often a social nuisance than a serious threat to life and property, more often a security problem than an immanent revolution."

Shahron Williams, *"Doctoral Dissertation in Political Science," Queens College, City University of New York, in preparation.* Williams will be attempting to establish linkages between the magnitude, duration, and intensity of insurgency terrorism and international intervention, using multiple regression and time series analysis. Her prospectus envisages dealing with the following questions: "Given the linkages between terrorism as a technique for influencing behavior and the use of insurgency warfare as an instrument of change, how does terrorism affect the internationalization of internal war? Does terrorism initiate or hasten outside intervention, and if so, at what point? Does intervention take place when terrorism reaches a specific intensity and is employed over a specific period of time? Do the targets of terrorist activities promote intervention?" Another series of questions notes terrorism outside of the conflict arena's borders: "If terrorist activities are employed across the borders of two or more states, how does the intensity and duration of these activities affect the relationship between the host state(s)? Will the 'transnationalization' of terrorism lead to attitude changes on the part of the target state toward the insurgents as the intensity and duration of terrorism increases? By nature of their transnational behavior, do the insurgents maintain their independence as actors challenging the authority of the target government, or do they merely become pawns to the national interest of the host state(s)? What is the relationship between the intensity, duration, and goals of the insurgents and their ability to become and/or remain significant transnational actors?" Williams' last series of concerns focuses on measures taken to counter terrorism: "Given the transnational character of terrorism, does counterterrorism as employed by the target state initiate further intervention? If so, at what point? How does the transnational character of terrorism inhibit/promote counterterrorist measures? Does counterterrorism, out of necessity, acquire a transnational character in order to effectively combat terrorism?"

James P. Needham, "M.A. Thesis in Police Science and Administration," Institute of Contemporary Corrections and the Behavioral Sciences, Sam Houston State University, in preparation. Needham is striving to create a model of management considerations that will allow prison administrators to develop their own hostage plans. He believes that there is a viable hostage negotiations model currently being used by law enforcement authorities which could be modified for use in prison situations. To obtain data for the model, he has conducted a survey of the police departments in fifty of the largest American cities and the State Departments of Corrections of the fifty states. The model may well be of use to national governments in dealing with diplomatic kidnappings and barricade-and-hostage situations.

Ernest Evans, "American Policy Response to International Terrorism," paper delivered to the Conference on Terrorism in the Contemporary World, held at Glassboro State College, April 26-28, 1976. Evans, both in the paper and in his dissertation for the Political Science Department of M.I.T., is interested in how the United States has responded, unilaterally, bilaterally, and in multilateral negotiations, to the problem of international terrorism. As a part of his general survey, the debates of the Legal Committee of the United Nations General Assembly regarding the U.S.-sponsored proposed convention on international terrorism of 1972 were content-analyzed for recurring themes. He was able to isolate four basic orientations of the delegations which spoke, finding concerns for the rights of belligerents in colonial conflicts, differing definitions of what constitutes terrorism, and great selectivity in the perceptions of delegations. Comparison of policy statements with voting behavior is forthcoming.

Lawrence C. Hamilton, "Doctoral Dissertation in Mathematical Sociology," Conflict and Peace Studies Program, University of Colorado, in preparation. Hamilton is concerned about terrorist extortion, and is attempting to collate files on a thousand terrorist incidents from a number of sources, including F.A.A., State, I.C.A.O., Rand, and about ten others. After this data has been transformed to a computer file, it shall provide a basis for various types of analysis, such as statistical evaluation of policy effectiveness, trends, and innovation-diffusion behavior. Results may also be compared with a set of game-theoretical predictions.

Appendix C: I.T.E.R.A.T.E.-1 INCIDENT CODING SHEET

Each incident noted by the dataset's sources was entered on a coding sheet before being keypunched and becoming part of the computer files. Approximately 150 variables were abstracted from this coding sheet, which lists 107 descriptors, e.g. the descriptor DATE was broken down into three variables: month, day, and year for the start of the incident. I.T.E.R.A.T.E.-2 will use a revised version of the coding sheet.

Descriptor Number	Descriptor Name
1	DATE OF START OF INCIDENT month day year
2	CODE NUMBER a four digit code number to be used for quick access to each discrete incident
3	TYPE OF EVENT
	1 kidnapping
	2 seizure—barricade and hostage
	3 seizure—occupation without hostages
	4 bombing—letter/parcel bombs
	5 bombing—arson/Molotov cocktail
	6 planted bombs—single detonation
	7 planted bombs—booby-trap detonation after initial explosion
	8 armed attack—missiles
	9 armed attack—other (including sniping, machine-gun attacks)
	10 skyjacking
	11 takeover of non-air means of transportation
	12 assassination/murder
	13 sabotage—not involving bombing
	14 exotic pollution, including C.B.W.
	15 nuclear-related

16   extortionate threat with no subsequent terrorist action

17   other actions

18   hoax

4   TARGET SELECTION

1   indiscriminate selection of targets

2   discriminate selection—selective attack on specific targets of symbolic value

5   WARNING—Did group sending a warning of attack?

1   yes

2   no

6   LOCATION OF ACTION—NATION

A 3-digit code for each nation or territory, somewhat modified from that developed by Bruce M. Russett, J. David Singer, and Melvin Small, "National Political Units in the Twentieth Century: A Standardized List," *American Political Science Review*, Sept., 1968, pp. 935-950.

7   LOCATION OF ACTION—ENVIRON

1   urban

2   rural

3   in transit in air or water

8   LOCATION OF ACTION—SCENE OF THE CRIME

1   home of victim; base or installation of victim

2   office

3   motor vehicle, train, aircraft, boat, embarkation area

4   street

5   other

9   GROUP INITIATING ACTION

A four-digit code unique to each group. Up to four groups may be listed in the I.T.E.R.A.T.E.-1 file. The name of the major initiator of the action is the first group listed.

10   ORGANIZATION CLAIMING RESPONSIBILITY FOR ACTION

Same procedure as descriptor 9.

11   ORGANIZATION ACTUALLY RESPONSIBLE FOR ACTION
Same procedure as descriptor 9. Descriptor 9 lists group who was popularly believed responsible, whereas 11 notes group who was responsible according to the most reliable sources available.

12   VITA—terrorist groups who denied responsibility for event
Same procedure as descriptor 9.

13   NUMBER OF TERRORIST GROUPS INVOLVED IN INCIDENT

14   NATIONALITY OR HOME COUNTRY OF TERRORISTS DIRECTLY INVOLVED
Up to four nationalities may be included.

15   NUMBER OF NATIONALITIES. OF TERRORISTS INVOLVED

16   FEDAYEEN Was terrorist group considered fedayeen?
1   Yes
2   No

17   NUMBER OF INDIVIDUAL TERRORISTS INVOLVED IN INCIDENT

18   NUMBER OF MALE TERRORISTS INVOLVED IN INCIDENT

19   NUMBER OF FEMALE TERRORISTS INVOLVED IN INCIDENT

20   LEADER—Did group have an obvious leader?
1   Yes
2   No

21   AGE OF GROUP MEMBERS
Mean age of group members, 2 digits

22   AGE RANGE OF GROUP MEMBERS
Difference between age of oldest and youngest group members

23   EDUCATION OF GROUP MEMBERS (MODE)
1   illiterate
2   grade school
3   high school
4   some college
5   college graduate
6   higher degree

24	**HOME COUNTRY OF VICTIMS NOT CITIZENS OF HOST COUNTRY** Same 3-digit coding as descriptor 6. Up to four possible nationalities may be included.
25	**NUMBER OF NATIONALITIES OF VICTIMS**
26	**NUMBER OF HOSTAGES**
27	**TYPE OF U.S. VICTIM**

1   diplomatic
2   military
3   other U.S. government
4   commercial, business
5   other nonofficial, e.g. tourist, missionary, student
6   no U.S. involvement as victims

28	**HIGHEST RANK OF ANY HOSTAGE**

1   ambassador or chief of mission
2   high-ranking military
3   corporate head
4   low-level diplomat
5   low-ranking military
6   citizen

29	**TYPE OF TARGET-IMMEDIATE VICTIMS**

1   host government officials
2   foreign diplomats or official nonmilitary
3   host government military
4   foreign military
5   corporation officials
6   prominent opinion leaders
7   private parties, e.g. tourists, missionaries, students

30	**TARGET TYPE**

1   people
2   installations
3   both

31	**NUMBER OF GOVERNMENTS UPON WHOM DEMANDS WERE MADE**
32	**NUMBER OF SEPARATE ENTITIES UPON WHOM DEMANDS WERE MADE** In addition to governments, include corporations, private individuals, international organizations.

33   **IDENTITY OF GOVERNMENTS UPON WHOM DEMANDS WERE MADE**
Same 3-digit coding as descriptor 9. Up to four governments.

34   **IDENTITY OF ENTITIES UPON WHOM DEMANDS WERE MADE**
A unique 4-digit number is assigned to nongovernmental entities. Up to four entities can be listed.

35   **DEMANDS ON HOST**—Were demands made upon the host government?
1   yes
2   no

36   **ATTRIBUTED PURPOSES OF INCIDENT**
1   wringing of specific concessions, e.g. ransom, prisoner release, publication of message
2   causing widespread disorder, demoralizing society, breaking down the existing social order
3   deliberately provoking repression, reprisals and counterterrorism, which may ultimately lead to the collapse of an unpopular government
4   enforce obedience and cooperative behavior
5   punishment of an individual or symbol judged "guilty"

37   **DEMANDS—MONETARY RANSOM**
1   demand was made
2   demand was not made

38   **DEMANDS—ARMAMENTS**
1   demand was made
2   demand was not made

39   **DEMANDS—RELEASE OF MEMBERS OF OWN GROUP IMPRISONED**
1   demand was made
2   demand was not made

40   **DEMANDS—RELEASE OF PRISONERS NOT OF OWN GROUP**
1   demand was made
2   demand was not made

41   DEMANDS—INDEPENDENCE; SELF-RULE OF TERRITORY; IDENTIFIED BY GROUP
1   demand was made
2   demand was not made

42   DEMANDS—SPECIFIC POLITICAL CHANGES
1   demand was made
2   demand was not made

43   DEMANDS—AMNESTY OR SAFE PASSAGE FOR INITIATORS OR FLY TERRORISTS TO SAFE HAVEN
1   demand was made
2   demand was not made

44   DEMANDS—PUBLISH OR BROADCAST A STATEMENT BY GROUP
1   demand was made
2   demand was not made

45   DEMANDS—CHANGE SENTENCES OF (BUT STILL IMPRISON) PRISONERS
1   demand was made
2   demand was not made

46   DEMANDS—OTHER
Includes release of all Arab women detained in Israel; audience with Indira Gandhi; allow relative to leave country; close Sehonau Castle
1   demand was made
2   demand was not made

47   DEMANDS—TERRORISTS ABLE TO MAKE DEMANDS KNOWN
1   terrorists unable to make demands known
2   terrorists unable to make demands known during incident; authorities able to determine demands a posteriori
3   terrorist made demands known.

48   DEMANDS—NONE
1   no demands were made
2   demands were made

49   TERRORIST NEGOTIATION BEHAVIOR
1   terrorists lessened demands during negotiations
2   terrorists increased demands during negotiations
3   terrorists did not change demands

4   terrorists substituted demands during negotiations (unable to state whether the change was an increase or decrease)

5   up-the-ante doublecross, e.g. more demands were made after other side fulfilled their part of the bargain

6   other side agreed to comply, terrorists broke contact

7   no contact for negotiations was ever established

50   TYPE OF TARGET UPON WHOM DEMANDS WERE MADE

1   host government
2   victim's government
3   other foreign government
4   corporate officials
5   international organizations
6   individuals
7   other non-state actors
8   other
9   combination of targets

51   TYPE OF NEGOTIATOR FOR TARGETS

1   police
2   high-ranking host government official
3   lower-level host government official
4   high-ranking victim government official
5   lower-level victim government official
6   high-ranking foreign government official
7   lower-level foreign government official
8   corporate official
9   private parties, family
10   prominent opinion leaders
11   other

52   RESPONSE OF TARGET

1   capitulation
2   stalling, with compromise on demands
3   Bangkok solution—terrorists drop all demands, granted safe passage out of country
4   no compromise, no shoot-out with terrorists
5   shoot-out with terrorists, or attempt to arrest terrorists, or nationwide search for terrorists with no compromise or capitulation by target regarding demands

53	OBJECTIVES OF PRESSURE BY VICTIM'S GOVERNMENT ON HOST COUNTRY

    1   Become firmer in negotiations, do not capitulate nor compromise on granting of terrorists' demands

    2   stall for time, and be willing to compromise

    3   capitulate

    4   no pressure was exerted by the victim's government upon the host government

54	NUMBER WOUNDED—DOMESTIC NONCOMBATANT VICTIMS
55	NUMBER WOUNDED—FOREIGN COUNTRY NONCOMBATANT VICTIMS
56	NUMBER WOUNDED—POLICE OR MILITARY COMBATANTS
57	NUMBER WOUNDED—TERRORISTS
58	NUMBER KILLED—DOMESTIC NONCOMBATANT VICTIMS
59	NUMBER KILLED-FOREIGN COUNTRY NONCOMBATANT VICTIMS
60	NUMBER KILLED—POLICE OR MILITARY COMBATANTS
61	NUMBER KILLED—TERRORISTS
62	DOLLAR VALUE OF OTHER LOSSES
63	NUMBER OF PRISONERS RELEASED
64	NUMBER OF PRISONERS WHOSE RELEASE WAS DEMANDED
65	AMOUNT OF RANSOM PAID In thousands, 6 digits
66	AMOUNT OF RANSOM DEMANDED In thousands, 6 digits
67	RANSOM TYPE

    1   Robin Hood—ransom does not go directly to terrorists, but is paid to a group selected by the initiators of the action as worthy of financing, e.g. poor, children, workers' groups

    2   organizational coffers—ransom is paid to the group

    3   both Robin Hood and organizational coffers

    4   no ransom was demanded

68   AMOUNT OF ROBIN HOOD RANSOM DEMANDED
In thousands, 6 digits

69   AMOUNT OF ROBIN HOOD RANSOM PAID
In thousands, 6 digits

70   AMOUNT OF ORGANIZATIONAL COFFERS RANSOM DEMANDED
In thousands, 6 digits

71   AMOUNT OF ORGANIZATIONAL COFFERS RANSOM PAID
In thousands, 6 digits

72   SOURCE OF RANSOM PAYMENT

      1   governmental
      2   corporation
      3   family
      4   other, e.g. public collection, other private sources
      5   no ransom paid

73   FATE OF VICTIMS

      1   no damage nor casualties, hostages released, no capitulation by targets
      2   no damage nor casualties, hostages released, capitulation or compromise by targets
      3   victims killed, no capitulation by targets
      4   victims killed, capitulation or compromise by targets
      5   damaged material, no capitulation by targets
      6   damaged material, capitulation or compromise by targets
      7   victim killed when attempting escape, had been captured
      8   victim successfully escaped, had been captured
      9   victim killed attempting to avoid capture
      10   victim successfully avoided capture
      11   hostages killed in shootout
      12   hostages killed, no provocation, during negotiations
      13   hostages killed during negotiations, terrorist-imposed deadline had expired

	14 damaged material, hostages released, no capitulation
74	NUMBER OF NATIONS PUBLICLY DENYING THAT SAFE HAVEN WOULD BE GRANTED IF REQUEST WERE MADE
75	NUMBER OF NATIONS DENYING SAFE HAVEN AFTER REQUEST WAS MADE
76	IDENTITY OF NATIONS SPON-TANEOUSLY DENYING SAFE HAVEN Same 3-digit coding as descriptor 9. Up to four nations may be included.
77	IDENTITY OF NATIONS DENYING SAFE HAVEN REQUEST Same 3-digit coding as descriptor 9. Up to four nations may be included.
78	NUMBER OF NATIONS SPON-TANEOUSLY GRANTING SAFE HAVEN
79	NUMBER OF NATIONS GRANTING SAFE HAVEN UPON REQUEST
80	IDENTITY OF NATIONS SPON-TANEOUSLY GRANTING SAFE HAVEN Same 3-digit coding as descriptor 9. Up to four nations may be included.
81	IDENTITY OF NATIONS GRANTING SAFE HAVEN UPON REQUEST Same 3-digit coding as descriptor 9. Up to four nations may be included.
82	ULTIMATE DESTINATION OF GROUP E.g. if skyjackers, where did they disembark and accept sanctuary?
83	GROUP VIEWS TOWARD OWN DEATH Attributed via observation of group behavior during event 1 suicidal 2 willing to die, prefer not to 3 elaborate getaway plans and execution of plans 4 dropping of demands for safe passage from scene
84	TERRORIST FATE—NUMBER DEAD AT SCENE IN SHOOT-OUT
85	TERRORIST FATE—NUMBER DEAD BLEW SELVES UP AT SCENE

86   TERRORIST FATE—NUMBER DEAD VIA DEATH PENALTY

87   TERRORIST FATE—NUMBER RECEIVING LONG JAIL TERM
Long jail term = five years or more

88   TERRORIST FATE—NUMBER RECEIVING LONG JAIL TERM, BECOMING DEMAND IN SUBSEQUENT INCIDENT

89   TERRORIST FATE—NUMBER RECEIVING LONG JAIL TERM, BECOMING DEMAND IN SUBSEQUENT INCIDENT, RELEASED DURING NEGOTIATIONS

90   TERRORIST FATE—NUMBER RECEIVING SHORT JAIL TERM

91   TERRORIST FATE—NUMBER RECEIVING SHORT JAIL TERM, BECOMING DEMAND IN SUBSEQUENT INCIDENT

92   TERRORIST FATE—NUMBER RECEIVING SHORT JAIL TERM, BECOMING DEMAND IN SUBSEQUENT INCIDENT, RELEASED DURING NEGOTIATIONS

93   TERRORIST FATE—NUMBER FREED BY COURT VERDICT

94   TERRORIST FATE—NUMBER WHO ESCAPED CAPTORS, EITHER EN ROUTE TO PRISON OR IN PRISON

95   TERRORIST FATE—GRANTED SAFE HAVEN, ALLOWED TO GO FREE IN BANGKOK SOLUTION OR MODIFIED BANGKOK SOLUTION

96   TERRORIST FATE—ARRESTED, NOT BROUGHT TO TRIAL, FREEDOM OBTAINED BY OTHER THAN COURT VERDICT OR ESCAPE, "SURRENDERED" TO FRIENDLY GOVERNMENT

97   WAS REQUEST FOR EXTRADITION MADE?
1   yes
2   no

98   IDENTITY OF NATION REQUESTING EXTRADITION
3-digit coding from descriptor 9.

99	WAS EXTRADITION REQUEST GRANTED?
	1 yes
	2 no
	3 extradition request not made
100	IDENTITY OF NATION RECEIVING EXTRADITION REQUEST
101	DATE OF ENDING OF INCIDENT month day year
102	LENGTH, IN DAYS, OF INCIDENT
103	IMPACT ON U.S. INTERESTS—U.S. CITIZENS WERE VICTIMS
	1 yes
	2 no
104	IMPACT ON U.S. INTERESTS—U.S. SHIPS OR AIRCRAFT WERE INVOLVED
	1 yes
	2 no
105	IMPACT ON U.S. INTERESTS—U.S. OFFICIAL INSTALLATIONS INVOLVED, e.g. military bases, embassies, consulates
	1 yes
	2 no
106	IMPACT ON U.S. INTERESTS—U.S. CORPORATIONS INVOLVED
	1 yes
	2 no
107	IMPACT ON U.S. INTERESTS—U.S. GOVERNMENT WAS A TARGET OF DEMANDS
	1 yes
	2 no

Missing Data is divided into values which are unknown (coded as a multiple of 9, e.g. 9, 99, 999, etc.), and those which are in principle irrelevant to the incident (e.g. if no demands for ransom were made, the amount of organizational coffers ransom demanded is in principle irrelevant), which are coded with an 8 at the end of the string of 9's. This allows real 0 values to occur for ratio data.

APPENDIX D: A GLANCE AT 1976

A quick tally of transnational terrorist incidents for the first five months of 1976 appears below. If we were to simple-mindedly assume that these trends are linear, we would expect the totals mentioned in the second column:

	Jan.-May	Yearly Projection*
Theft	2	5
Armed Attack	12	29
Arson	9	22
Bombing	47	113
Skyjack	7	17
Murder	13	31
Barricade & Hostage	2	5
Kidnap	7	17

Casualty figures continue their depressing climb: 77 dead, 248 wounded in all incidents for which we have data.

*It would be absurd to place absolute faith in these projections. It would mean, inter alia, that types of incidents which have not occurred historically cannot occur, as the yearly projection would be 0.

Joseph Margolin:
Psychological Perspectives in Terrorism

The behavioral approach to terrorism has usually been preempted to a narrow, parochial and highly questionable effort to apply conventional psychiatric methods to the personality of skyjackers. Much effort has been directed to the pathology of the terrorist on the unproven assumption that the terrorist is "sick." It is a common assumption of our society that people who do not think as we do are disturbed. The effort to prove this assumption leads to searching only in the places where it is likely to be confirmed.

Constituting a sharp divergence in emphasis from other presentations, the behavioral approach presented here emerges logically from the prior work of psychology, psychiatry, and other disciplines. It is intended as an integral part of the total response to terrorism. Some examples of a more scientific approach will be offered to measure its consistency with other approaches and its value in the total effort. The approach is based on the premise that the behavioral sciences which contribute greatly in other sectors can make a practical contribution to work in terrorism. It is certainly a less expensive approach than some, and it is clearly essential to the success of current efforts.

Two levels must be considered. The macro-level includes the psychological and sociological bases of the large international and transnational issues. These issues relate within the society to the state of public opinion, the cultural patterns, and the characteristics and role of leaders. The relevance of the behavioral issues is also important to the carrying through of large economic and political programs or national or international agendas.

The micro-level is responsive to the study of specific terrorists and terrorist acts. These individual events or case studies can sometimes be assembled into larger units which may extend our understanding of events at the macro-level and at times permit some explanation of policy of programs at the international level. During this discussion we will concentrate on the micro-level and its extensions.

ASSUMPTIONS ABOUT THE TERRORIST

Research in terrorism has been characterized by a series of contradictory assumptions about the terrorist. We are at one moment led to the belief that the terrorist is a psychotic, at others a fanatic, and at still other times that he is a highly rational individual governed by good planning and armed not only with modern weapons but with a firm ideology and sound information about his objective. Other discussions introduce the concept of the itinerant terrorist for hire, whose rewards may, however, be psychological or ideological rather than solely financial.

Probably all these assumptions are valid at one time or another. However, whichever may be valid, it must be assumed that the terrorist is human. Whether rational or irrational, he is governed as we all are by the same laws of behavior. It is a respected warning in psychology that "although you may know the laws of behavior, no one is exempt from them."

No area in the study of terrorism is receiving adequate attention today. Despite the apparent significance and pervasiveness of behavioral factors in terrorism, the behavioral sciences have been neglected more than other relevant disciplines. Much of the behavioral intervention currently undertaken is intuitive. Clearly, what is needed is a handbook of instructions that can provide support to a broad circle of potential crisis managers. However, the preparation of such a document would require a broad level of effort and skill accompanied by adequate training for readers, to assure that a handbook would not be used mechanically and without sensitivity.

A handbook based purely on the behavioral sciences may not be the best approach to terrorism, because the behavioral scientist cannot be isolated from other disciplines. Each discipline must take account of the truths, opportunities, and limits provided by other disciplines. No one terrorist or hostage is governed by purely behavioral principles A need exists for a holistic approach that integrates political science, economics, the military, and the technological. Some other areas of research are using or preparing effective interdisciplinary strategies. However, before seeking ideal solutions, we should be immediately concerned with the absence of sufficient behavioral research or methodology to make the required contribution to an interdisciplinary effort in terrorism. Although reference is made to research and methodology, a great deal of good clinical sensitivity is available and perhaps in use. However, sensitivity alone does not provide the badly needed systematic approach to terrorism.

EMPHASIS ON THE ABNORMAL

Much of the behavioral approach in the study of terrorism has been derived from abnormal psychology and psychoanalysis. Indeed, it is only fitting that the deep anger and fear associated with terrorism should be initially explained by abnormal psychology. However, the almost exclusive emphasis on psychopathology has resulted in a paucity of attention to the many elements of psychology and sociology that operate in daily behavior and play. These psychological and sociological elements can explain a significant part of almost every phase of the terrorist act. The emphasis on pathology is not unlike the emphasis in the development of the mental health field in which for many years the greatest focus was on diagnosis. When it was realized that diagnosis was insufficient, emphasis shifted to dynamics, and approaches were redirected and corrected.

An approach through abnormal psychology may at times be counterproductive. Support for the belief that the terrorist is psychotic is likely to increase the general public's perceived threat and the consequent effectiveness of the terrorist act. People have a prevailing fear of the irrational that must be considered. However, whether a terrorist is irrational or not is probably less important than identifying the objectives, fears, the relationships, and the style of thinking and decision-making of the terrorist. We need to have the kinds of information that will provide a basis for prediction and control of terrorist behavior. If a terrorist is seeking a psychological effect, how can it be frustrated? How can we immunize against it, or counter the effects of it? How can we understand and assess the counter forces or ambivalence present within the terrorist to use them most effectively in the deterrence of terrorism? Ambivalence is present in all men; it is to decision-making what the use of the antagonistic muscles is in motor behavior. An understanding of ambivalent forces and processes can provide considerable leverage toward producing a desired effect.

NORMAL PSYCHOLOGY

An examination of the normal psychology of the terrorist should obviously include both the terrorist and the public, including those who will have to deal with terrorism. Everyone has strengths and weaknesses, and the ability to deploy one's own resources is an important skill. Understanding our own characteristics can be as useful as knowing those of the terrorist or his hostage.

An implication is not being made that the behavioral scientist has a unique skill with which to direct anti-terrorist operation. However, behavioral science must not be overlooked in selecting those who can make the best use of the entire range of skills and instruments to be employed.

What skills do we already have? As we know, a great deal of behavioral science skill has been employed by individuals working in related fields. Much of the insight into terrorism is intuitive, while the rest derives from education or experience. New concepts about terrorism can be introduced to make what is an ill-distributed capability more broadly available to those dealing with the problem. Important caveats should be restated concerning ethical regulation and procedures in research and program development. Research with human subjects is closely regulated both by the behavioral professions and by the government, and these regulations have been considered in the material that follows.

A few writers on terrorism have dipped into the behavioral sciences to provide support for positions or theories. Fischman has effectively extracted the relevance of the hundred-year-old concept of anomie by Durkheim and its significant role in understanding much terrorist behavior. Frustration-aggression theory has been mentioned by some writers; it is a theory that psychology professors like, because at least superficially it is easily understandable.

FRUSTRATION-AGGRESSION THEORY

Much terrorist behavior is a response to the frustration of

various political, economic, and personal needs or objectives. A terrorist act is frequently intended to elicit a response that will demonstrate that a government will continue to frustrate the terrorist's "legitimate aspirations." A government's response establishes a context within which the terrorist activity is explained and normalized. The terrorist's prophecy is fulfilled and becomes truth to the terrorist and to some of the public.

How can we make use of an assumption that terrorism is self-fulfilling? 1. The principle that terrorist aggression is "lawful" (and it is scientifically lawful) provides the terrorist with responsibility without guilt. This belief in "lawfulness," conveyed to a victim, may result in the victim's feeling guilty and mentally accepting and justifying further aggression by the terrorist. Consider the value of understanding the terrorist and victim when we wonder why hostages often come away with considerable respect or admiration for their kidnappers. 2. The terrorist's motivation is strengthened, because his political objectives mesh with his personal and psychological needs.

The value of examining these points is that we may find a weakness in a situation of terrorism and thereby disrupt it. 1. A potential hostage can be prepared for or immunized against the "logic of lawfulness," and 2. if other frustrations or objectives can be introduced, the strength of the terrorists' decisions can be undermined or their effect altered. Therefore, any theory that is applied must be more than explanatory or diagnostic; it must be capable of becoming the basis either for a policy or an intervention. What is suggested is a systems approach involving the search for critical points in the terrorist act and in the response to it. What is further suggested is an examination of those critical points for valuable clues to the regular or normal psychological processes and values and the unspoken personal objectives of the terrorist.

THE GOAL GRADIENT

The goal gradient is an interesting psychological analogue to the law of gravitation. It states that the closer the individual approaches a desired objective, the stronger is the individual's need for satisfaction. Penologists felt that the number of escapes attempted by inmates close to the time for their release was illogical, but were proved to be lawful, human behavior. When the curve of intensity of need increases sharply as an individual approaches a *positive* goal, the curve of avoidant feelings increases even more sharply as one approaches a *negative* goal, or a situation that is feared or disliked. One need only experiment with the possibilities of such curves to find many ways in which tension, motivation, even direction of the activity of the terrorist can be altered by controlling the psychological distance from positive and negative goals. Control is likely to be possible in a hijacking or a situation in which hostages are held.

ZEIGARNIK EFFECT

Another relatively well-known psychological principle is the *Zeigarnik* effect of the interrupted-task phenomenon. Simplified, it suggests that the interruption of tasks, which the individual has begun, will have profound effect on what he remembers to be important as well as on his level of tension and on the establishment of new motives and values. An individual's need to complete a process that has been interrupted may be greater than the original motivation to do it. A full development of the *Zeigarnik* effect would suggest a wide range of applications in negotiation settings and in other crises.

UNCERTAINTY PRINCIPLE

A pattern of principles can be developed employing past and current research on the conditions of uncertainty and how they effect behavior, including uncertainty about the task or the objective, information received, the characteristics of the information source, or the competence of the decision-maker.

COGNITIVE STYLE

Greater comprehension of the cognitive style of terrorists would be useful. What are their thought processes particularly as they relate to cultural or other definable and generalizable differences? The Office of Naval Research has funded some research associated with field dependence and independence which could be usefully transferred to work in terrorism.

THREAT

A primary aspect of terrorism is threat; it is used more often in terrorism than in conventional · warfare. Relatively little research and funding have been directed to the problem.

STIMULUS DEPRIVATION

Significant effects have been achieved on individuals and small groups through isolation and stimulus deprivation. The treated individual suffers loss of confidence, uncertainty, and some disorientation. Deprivation can be best employed with marginal individuals or groups who are uncertain of their place in their movement and generally lack the approval of the larger terrorist apparatus. This strategem probably accounted for the strange willingness of a group of hijackers of a KLM plane to surrender to the Christian President of Cyprus. They had been ignored or rejected by almost all nations that they had tried to terrorize or impress. Whether the response to the terrorism was deliberate or inadvertent, it appears that the right strategy was applied with the right group.

CURRENT RESEARCH

A.R.P.A. has funded some research, and a considerable amount of relevant research findings could be extracted from the behavioral literature. The direct application of such research to terrorism has been rare.

The nature of crisis situations is being examined by several A.R.P.A. and O.N.R. projects. Most, however, have not used data bases adequate to the problem of terrorism. Intercultural comparisons should be extended as well as other variables like resource availability and social and cultural distance between actors.

The Behavioral Studies Group has also been engaged in some of the developing countries in research that may be transferable to the terrorist situation. The research of the Group relates to the "credibility of information" referred to above. Media sources, although moderately credible, are rendered more credible when peer groups of individuals validate the media source of information and values. Basically, the media provide information which is processed and validated or rendered invalid by peer groups of terrorists. Whether dealing with large populations or with specific terrorists in a crisis situation, one should know how information is understood and believed or how decisions are made in order to deal with terrorism.

Another critical variable that has apparently not been considered is the area of heuristics or the problem-solving readiness of the actors — law enforcement officers, terrorists, or hostages — in a crisis. The Behavioral Studies Group has been engaged in research on heuristics at George Washington University for several years and are readying it for application to a number of areas.

These research studies are but a few of the resources already available or requiring further examination from the behavioral sciences. However, the selection of areas for study and subsequent research require their own methodology.

RESEARCH NEEDS

We should devise research that will provide valuable clues to which regular or normal psychological processes and values are significant and most useful to those trying to deal with the control of terrorism. Several tentative research projects may prove useful.

Research could be devised which is directly applicable to the need to know as much as possible about the terrorist. One study might seek as much information as possible about the eventual rehabilitation of terrorists. Initially, this study may sound irrelevant, presumptuous, or both. All wars end eventually, and recently there is reason to believe that the relationship of supply to demand of terrorists is leading toward chronic unemployment for some. Senator Jacob Javits has pointed out that today fewer countries require liberation. Furthermore, it is not reasonable to expect that trained and experienced terrorists will want to become tillers of the soil or administrators. Cuba has absorbed some terrorists, but former revolutionaries and terrorists still wander the earth, or worse, interfere with peace-time operations in their countries. A study might investigate the past rehabilitation of members of groups like the F.L.Q. in Quebec and some Cubans. It might explore the possible needs of current groups like the Palestinians or some Latin American terrorist groups. Possibly some of the wealthy segments of the population in affluent middle-eastern countries might wish to do something about the oversupply of terrorists in the Middle East.

However, without exploring the possibility of actual short-range rehabilitation, research might uncover benefits that would be derived from a greater understanding of the goals and motivational processes of the terrorist. Political, tactical and strategic values should be clearly evident.

Certainly additional research is needed into the sociological structure of terrorist groups, their roles, and how they develop from the structure of a group and the nature of society.

The ecology of terrorism has not been studied intensively. We need to understand the matrix in which the process operates; we need to know what its active and its passive elements are.

Terrorists are frequently seen as unrestricted by anything but loyalty to their own group and to some political or millenarian ideals. However, it is unlikely that any individual or group is without pressures from family or from the views of the general public or a specific segment of it. Terrorists probably respond to the attitudes of those whom they presume to ignore, because their inability to stimulate a sufficient response can be very provoking. We know that terrorists expected assistance from the families of some of the more affluent, socially well-placed Latin American terrorists. That terrorists had easy access to private funds made public control of terrorism difficult in some Latin American nations.

It would be useful to understand what conditions exist when terrorists as a minority are in control. The struggle in Lebanon in 1976 could reveal a great deal. Although insights might need to be adjusted for specific cultures and specific situations, worthwhile generalizations could be derived. In the Lebanon situation, one can ask such concrete questions as, "Do the people of the West Bank of the Jordan want to be ruled by the P.L.O., or do they merely sympathize with their objectives?"

A totally different area of investigation might involve sex role differences in terrorist organizations. Is there a process of stereotyping men and women within terrorist groups and in different cultures? In regard to stereotyping, does an hierarchy exist among the several transnational terrorist groups? Are there particular cultural or national groups, or particular individuals who assume high status and others who receive less favored treatment? What are the dynamics or the causes that form hierarchical organization?

Some questions can be addressed to the people whom terrorists want to affect. Is there a difference in the people's perception of the effects of terrorism when raw atrocities are committed and when ordinary kidnapping and negotiating for a ransom occur?

A study of the selection of targets would probably be productive. An examination of the way in which demands are developed and made, how long they persist, and whether they vary and change over time would be useful. An understanding might be reached about the effects of the passage of time, and the intervening action or inaction by the participants in an act of terrorism.

Probably much data exist for the study of the forms and

identities of terrorist organizations within different cultures. How is it being processed and for what objectives? Is there an identification norm, internationally or regionally? Who are the effective behavioral and ideological models? Is there an overlap of style, terminology, developmental patterns? Do patterns vary depending on major events in the terrorist world, or do they remain fairly constant?

One of the key purposes of terrorists and a primary source of their effectiveness is their ability to produce fear or disturbance without actually engaging in acts of terror. While remaining silent for varying periods of time after a terrorist act, terrorists engage in the intermittent reinforcement of fear, distraction, and tension to reduce productivity and confidence in governments and economic conditions. Is there an antidote to passive terrorism? What does a defending group or nation do during the periods of silence while they wait for the "next shoe to drop"? Can the media help, or do they remain an unwitting accomplice by response or non-response to a terrorist who seems to control a fuse? What is the benefit of reporting to the public that the media is being manipulated by terrorists who may or may not act?

A wide range of possible behavioral research, essentially observational, but partially quite rigorous, would, it is hoped, produce a body of knowledge that could be applied to an understanding and improved control of terrorist behavior. It would also strengthen governments and populations against the onslaughts of terrorism.

How do we use information from research? Part of it can and should simply be incorporated into the general knowledge of people dealing with terrorism. Much material can be drawn together into "strategies" which are responsive to general terrorism or to specific difficulties posed by terrorists. Strategies are complex formulations comprised of the application of behavioral, economic, or political principles organized into a comprehensive whole. Strategies are used in a wide range of sectors like transportation and public health. A strategy can be prepared to meet a number of different conditions and to confront alternative turns of events. Strategies are frequently achieved by clever negotiators on an ad hoc basis, and many strategies are currently in operation. Many have been incorporated into existing policy. It is however far more efficient to have a body of knowledge concerning what can be done and what is available, than relying on chance, memory, or intuition to achieve the right behavioral action or reaction. Alternative strategies also provide other models for ways to deal with given terrorist situations. They will probably work effectively if they are not followed inflexibly.

Some simple examples of a strategy would include the following. 1. The reduction of frustration does tend to lower the need for aggression on the part of the terrorist. Reducing frustration can be achieved in ways other than satisfying the direct demands of a terrorist. It is possible for a negotiator to yield to a series of needed comforts or benefits that are requested after the basic demands have been made. Satisfaction of the secondary requests may diminish the terrorist's need for violent action and weaken one source of motivation.

However, the satisfaction derived from the meeting of minor needs, a variable, can be increased by manipulating that variable. By withholding the satisfaction of minor demands for a brief period and then yielding to them as tension begins to build, a negotiator will enhance their value. By successively withholding and yielding to requests, a negotiator may begin to displace the terrorist's attention from his basic demands and to divert potential aggression from his hostages to a different target.

There are caveats to these strategies. Frustration, especially when produced by or coupled with punishment, may produce extremely rigid, non-adaptive behavior that may endure after secondary requests are met, thereby making the goal directly accessible. A negotiator must know as much about the terrorist as possible in order to assess whether or not the terrorist's rigid, non-adaptive process will lead to the killing of prisoners or destruction of property after concessions are made. The negotiator should assess the flexibility of a terrorist's behavior by probing or testing early in their encounter.

Sometimes prolonged or intense frustration produces flight rather than further struggle for demands, particularly when survival is not threatened by flight. After fleeing an encounter, the terrorist and the negotiator may physically or psychologically leave the situation.

If it is possible to create a sufficiently frustrating situation without jeopardizing the prisoners or property and to suggest that achievement of the terrorist's objectives is an increasingly unlikely possibility, it may be possible to create conditions in which flight or withdrawal are preferred by the terrorist. If it is possible, the introduction of an avenue for escape, even with the concession that hostages be released, may prove of great value to the terrorist. With a change in the value of alternatives, a terrorist may be willing to barter hostages for his escape. It appears that this strategy has succeeded in several operations over the past five years.

The development of conflict situations provides some interesting approaches for negotiators and law enforcement personnel. There are at least three kinds of conflict situations: 1. approach-approach, 2. approach-avoidance, and 3. avoidance-avoidance conflicts. The approach-approach conflict may occasionally be used to create conflict among members of a group of terrorists, confronting them with a choice of priorities of demands to satisfy or change.

Approach-avoidance, in which both promise and danger exist in a single goal area, may be more useful. Unfortunately, what is frequently considered as an approach-avoidance situation by law enforcement personnel may result in a doubly reinforcing situation for terrorists. If, for example, terrorists come to believe they will not achieve their objective of ransom or some political objective such as release of prisoners, they know they can gain some secondary objections: notoriety, attention, and demonstrated bravery. The terrorists' perception of the value of secondary alternatives should be fully appreciated by law enforcement personnel.

In an approach-avoidance situation, an important comparison has been noted between the goal gradient or the approach gradient when it is positive and when it is negative. Consequently, the pull toward the positive goal increases with proximity to it, but it increases less powerfully than the tendency to retreat from a negative goal. The tendency to retreat from a negative goal increases very steeply as it is approached. Vacillation on the part of the terrorist can be moved toward either goal by increasing the approach gradient, or by decreasing the avoidance gradient. In a like manner, the point of vacillation can be moved away from the goal by decreasing the approach gradient and increasing the avoidant forces. Consequently, the value of a ransom or the possibility of political success can be synchronized with increased threat or danger of unpleasant consequences for the act of terrorism, thereby maximizing the effect and the timing sought. Having control of timing can be exceedingly valuable to law enforcement personnel.

The last group of principles discussed relate to micro-levels but may have implications for broader international or macro-levels. However the impact of the removal of sanctuary in Cuba has demonstrated how an avoidance-avoidance situation can be produced.

These are only a few of the strategies that can be developed.

They are designed only to be illustrative not demonstrative. Our greatest obstacle to success may be response by rote, and it is too easy for terrorists to learn routine procedures and responses. It is through creative and heuristic application of economic, psychological and sociological principles, tailored to meet a specific situation, that we can cope successfully with terrorism. Those principles lead to strategies that we must develop to extend the skill of the craftsman as negotiator or law enforcement officer.

In general we have sought to demonstrate the non-abnormal aspects of behavioral intervention. There are, however, areas of projective theory, new small group methods, and both established and new theories that provide avenues to improved understanding. The best result of research is probably a mix of normal and abnormal psychological and sociological approaches, integrated into various political processes, and combined after a careful assessment of the compatibility and consistency of the several approaches, into strategies.

The research may appear to be complex; it is not without risks. However, the applications of the behavioral sciences in conjunction with other disciplines has been achieved in other sectors, and it is being achieved in an unplanned way in the control of terrorism. It is hoped that a more systematic approach may be achieved.

Irving Louis Horowitz:
Transnational Terrorism,
Civil Liberties, and
Social Science

The polarization of political behavior and the fragmentation of political belief are well illustrated in the current rhetoric concerning terrorism and what to do about it. Attitudes toward the uses of terror and the functions of terrorists range from a gratuitous belief in terror as the only possible means to bring about social change to a view of terror and terrorists as the last refuge of scoundrels. The range of views extends from terrorists as the only authentic heroes in a notably unheroic age to their demotion as petty criminals who coat their venal acts with an ideological gloss.

In such a climate of opinion, the attempt to introduce gradations and shadings of meaning into the problem of terror invites instant rebuke from an impatient Left and retaliation from an outraged Right. Only "reformists" and "bleeding hearts" apparently are willing to challenge the common rhetoric. Despite the rhetoric, communist dictatorships, no less than democracies, no less than capitalist systems, must face the problem of terrorism. Skyjackings, assassinations, bombings, extortions, and sabotage do not stop at any national or regional borders.

The definition of terrorism employed here is the selective use of fear, subjugation, and intimidation to disrupt the normal operations of a society. All social systems seek ethical and legal norms that satisfy the conditions for continued human survival without giving offence to the major ideological premises on which these respective societies have come to rest. Consequently, while different social systems react differently to terror in accordance with their vision of self interest, no surviving society can be indifferent to the problems raised by terrorism.

Special problems in the analysis of terrorism and civil liberties exist for the analysts themselves. Research social scientists, often responsive to a governmental or semi-official agency whose prime concern is political or industrial tranquility, can easily tailor their models to suit the needs of clients, thereby overlooking many alternate possibilities for analyzing terrorism. As the collective repository of empirical, even normative wisdom on the subjects of both terror and liberty, they are charged with the task of arriving at satisfactory formulations of the problem, if not meaningful solutions, while operating within a paradigmatic framework unexamined or uncritically imbibed.

Social scientists who accept a civil libertarian viewpoint must decide how to respond to an attack on civil liberties by those presumably acting in the name of terror. Even more damaging may be the response to terror by the organized society itself. Before we settle the question of what to do about terrorists, we might also try to ask what are the consequences of action and then determine a scale of levels of response in terms of levels of assault on the system. Our effort reflects a pragmatic Deweyian viewpoint. Living in democracy is living experientially; living experientially is living dangerously. To prevent social change in the name of democracy is already to have lost the battle.

An alternative approach of social science to the study of terrorism would be to disaggregate the types of violence perpetrated and thereby defuse the emotionalism surrounding the issue of terror. At this point in time, the emphasis among researchers is to aggregate information on letter-bombings, hijackings, assassinations, and consequently to blur essential distinctions between random terrorist movements and foreign-controlled movements. The need for legal sanctions against the random murder and incarceration of innocent "third party" people is manifest. We also need to emphasize that a place for legitimate dissent remains a steady need, if the world community of nations is not to become frozen into its present political positions, along with the economic and social inequities such a freezing of policies entails.

Social science must first determine whether terrorism is a function of larger ambitions and aims, thereby making it a dependent variable. Second, social science needs to distinguish types of violence and injury perpetrated against persons and/or places in order to help establish some qualitative measures of terrorism and counterterrorism. Third, social science should provide empirical assistance to the legal efforts involved in developing international measures to combat terror of guerrillas and counterterror of the state. These three interrelated tasks will help restore a feeling of the independent and objective role of social science in combating terror and safeguarding civil liberties.

This paper is restricted to one part of this widespread discussion of terror: the question of safeguarding civil liberties when the state invokes counterterror or force to quell disturbances. My aim is to describe the costs and benefits of the control of terror, showing how and why terrorism arises, who the terrorists are, and what the impact is on civil rights and liberties. Only then can appropriate policies and postures be set forth.

THE DANGERS OF TERRORISM

We are in a high-risk situation, not simply with respect to those who are labelled as terrorists, but perhaps more pointedly, with respect to what occurs in the social system as a result of measures to contravene terrorist activities. It would be sheer sophistry to deny the existence of terrorism by the dubious method of asserting that either its complexities or ambiguities somehow eliminate the problem. We must therefore first outline how terrorism affects the civil liberties of all citizens. Then we can turn our attention to how counterterror works and what it all means for our civil liberties.

The first point is that the power to inflict injury is a bargaining power which in its very nature bypasses the due process of law and seeks an outcome by means other than the democratic or consensus problem-solving formula. Within its very nature, the act of terror — whoever performs it — in some sense violates civil liberties. All the cries about redressing injustices cannot disguise this violation.

A second point is that terrorism presumes not simply what is socially valued but what victims can tolerate. That is, a kind of threshhold of pain replaces a sense of shared values and of the rationality that comes with consensus politics. As a result, the act of terrorism, without regard to who performs it, involves a substitution of pain or punishment for reason in the adjudication of political and social ends.

The third point is ubiquitous but nonetheless important. A policy of terror assumes the social system to be inherently law-abiding, not only as a rational goal but as an ongoing functional prerequisite. It also presumes that the desire to return to the rationality of the maintenance of a system and its goals helps those engaged in terror reach their ends. Again, civil liberties is confronted here as an ongoing mechanism to which one wants to return, considering the state of terror as a temporary aberration.

The fourth point is that terrorism as a policy is anti-democratic and violates a sense of civil liberties as democratic liberties, because the terrorists' requests, demands, or ultimatums are addressed to a leadership structure rather than to the people. Terrorism demands instantaneous decision-making and consequently places a very great strain on the conventional legal mechanisms which require due process and a strong evidentiary base to take action. As a result, terrorism is an appeal to elites.

A fifth point that is both most disturbing and yet difficult to define analytically is that terror generally involves a violation of the civil liberties of those who are non-participants or non-combatants. Terrorists usually have as a foil those people who are innocent of any crime. Whatever else civil libertarians believe, they do mean to hold people responsibile for having committed no specific criminal acts. To them terrorist acts are clear and evident violations of civil freedoms of both individuals and collectivities.

THE DANGERS OF COUNTERTERRORISM

The increase in the amount of terrorism, spontaneous or organized, inevitably invites countermeasures. These extend from increased security checks, greater police surveillance, improved search and seizure measures to changes in the legal code like the restoration of capital punishment. At the same time, organizational and ideological forms also change. In place of criminology there emerges a new emphasis on victimology; in place of national organizations dedicated to civil liberties there arise organizations dedicated to maintaining civil order. Consequently, the costliest aspect of the increased resort to terrorist solutions to political problems is not the destruction of physical property; it is the decimation of the social and political fabric — the complex series of norms and laws upon which conflict resolution ultimately rests.

The seeming procrastination and reticence of national and international legislative bodies to curb terrorism seem to derive from some inchoate appreciation of the political costs involved. To be sure, when particular societies are attacked by terrorists, caution often is discarded. Yugoslavs highly resistant to formal condemnations of Palestinian terrorists are outraged by American passivity in the face of Croatian nationalist hijackings. Soviet officials, even more resistant to the idea of a United Nations ban on skyjackings, can hardly contain their sense of outrage at Jews who confiscate planes to escape to Israel. Syrians who are quite willing to see citizens of Tel Aviv randomly blown up, hang the representatives of the P.L.O. when they perform similar acts in Damascus. However, when all is said and done, it is easier to stretch the notion of tolerable limits within civil society than to establish inelastic legislation that would do more to escalate the levels and perhaps amounts of terrorism than lead to international pacification and tranquility. The idea of legislation as a magical cure-all, or even a limiting element on terrorist actions, is itself of dubious worth — a conceptual palliative more than a pragmatic solution. To address the consequences of terrorism and leave untouched its causes is not only to insure higher levels of punishment but also increased sophistication in terrorist crimes.

In 1968, President Lyndon Johnson established a major task force, the Commission on the Causes and Prevention of Violence. Analyses of historical and social causation proceeded smoothly enough, but the Commission encountered problems mainly at the policy level: What could be done to prevent violence in the future? In form if not in substance, the problem of violence then was similar to the issue raised by terrorism now. At a meeting in 1968 of the National Commission on Causes and Prevention of Violence, I said:

> . . . the destruction of the anti-war movement, whether in its abstract universalist or pacifist form, or in its nasty, brutish, or opportunistic form would represent a far greater loss to the integrity of American democracy than any silence in the streets of our major cities or quiescence in the hubs of our major universities. Obedience is not tranquility. Seething heavily is not the same as breathing easily. The anti-war movement has caused destruction in government operations, increased the cost of domestic military preparedness, stimulated disaffiliation from major parties, and has been a general nuisance for an already burdened police force. But these are costs that can be borne by a society still capable of distinguishing between national concern and national celebration. Those who want law and order, of whom there are many, as well as those who want lawlessness

and disorder, of whom there are a few, must weigh carefully the premium price to be paid in a punitive state in which a rage for order displaces a rationality of innovation. That price would be nothing short of a total militarization of the nation.

A society without terrorism is quite possible to achieve. Fascist systems manage quite adequately to reduce terrorism by a series of devices: mass organizations in which membership is compulsory; block-by-block spying networks; mandatory police identification certificates; clear delineations of "friends" and "enemies" of the regime. With the increased sophistication of computerization techniques, such mechanisms for social and personal control are increasingly available. The question remains: Does a citizenry wish to pay such a premium price for social tranquility? One might consider the quantum of violence within a society as a crucial indicator of genuine social health.

Beyond serving as a potential beacon light on social maladies, the potential for terror also is a lively reminder that state force has its counter. There is no need to try to settle the question of causation, i.e., whether state force precedes the violence of its opponents. The hardware in the hands of the state is almost always greater, more pervasive, and more devastating than the disruptive possibilities available to terrorists. One need only consider the activities of the C.I.A. and the F.B.I. to see how damaging to the body politic state force can become and how ineffectual those efforts to forestall terrorism were.

American intelligence operations involve hundreds of thousands of individuals and require the expenditure of billions of dollars. They are carried out by a complex community of organizations among which functions interact and overlap. As the Senate committee investigating activities of the C.I.A. and F.B.I. noted: "The task of democratic government is to reconcile conflicting values." The fundamental question faced by a democratic society is how to reconcile the clash between secrecy and democratic government itself. Secrecy is an essential part of intelligence activities. However, secrecy undermines the capacity of the United States to deal effectively with the principal issues of American intelligence addressed by the Select Senate Committee on Intelligence Activities. In its final report of 1976 the Committee states that

the very effort to deal with problems of terror, violence, and domestic intranquility has led to this kind of incredible malaise within the legal system, whereby the entire country has been rendered under the control of a paralegal system, a paramilitary system, in terms of dealing effectively with threats of violence.

The question of civil liberties is not simply examined from the point of view of the terrorists but from that of the counterterrorist as well. One need only remember Watergate to see how counterterrorist activities can erode our civil liberties.

A POLITICAL SOCIOLOGY OF TERRORISM

To make sense of the subject of terrorism, one must introduce a concept based upon qualitative micropolitics or the large-scale examinations of specific issues to balance the current emphasis on quantitative macropolitics, or the small-scale analysis of large-scale issues. Social researchers are obligated to discuss large-scale political events not only in aggregate numerical terms but in impact terms. We are obligated to demonstrate the discreet nature of terrorism as it affects particular and specific actors in any political dramaturgy. Only through a linkage of the qualitative to the quantitative, of micropolitics to macropolitics can a holistic sense of terrorism be framed.

If we discuss terrorism in terms of the number of people killed by design or by accident, there clearly is no comparison to the genocidal behavior of Stalin in Russia and Hitler in Germany. The state has nearly unlimited power to terrorize entire communities, ethnic or racial groups, and, of course, religious networks. If terrorism is mentioned simply in terms of lives dispatched, the holocaust in Nazi Germany, the genocidal benchmark of our century, certainly far outstrips and outranks the desultory and random performances engaged in by contemporary terrorists functioning beyond the influence of the major political systems.

If by terrorism we mean disruption of entire political systems or social organizations, then the determined but relatively impotent acts of those defined as terrorists can hardly be compared to the disruption caused by a major automobile accident on a superhighway in a densely populated area. Rarely does organized terrorism create the kinds of massive temporary breakdowns in social systems that might be occasioned by a power failure in a big city. I have always been surprised how impotent any transitory disruption of modern society is. What is really involved in a definition of terrorism is the symbolic meaning of terrorism and its support systems. When a person or group are assassinated or kidnapped because of their national origins or religious affiliations, the action speaks to the entire fabric of attitudes of one group toward another. Consequently, although the numbers involved in terrorism are usually quite limited, the calibrations are unusually large. Moreover, terrorism involves death and destruction by design, and it is clearly different from the random character of highway accidents or technological breakdowns.

If one argues that terrorism is a special method for hastening historical change, does anyone really know what scheme historical timetables follow? The conventional Marxist rhetoric about speeding up or slowing down history presumes a normal rate of historical change which has eluded almost any kind of empirical test. It is therefore perfectly appropriate for terrorists or anybody else to argue that they help to shape the course of historical events. On the other hand, the question of measurements is just as much a problem for terrorists as it is for pacifists. Ultimately, both must appeal to the same muse of history, rarely with telling or convincing effect.

Some people dogmatically and in the face of experience insist that Marx said that one cannot make a successful revolution without realizing the full potential for growth of the old social system. They are wrong to persist in believing that Marx's statement constitutes a revolutionary prohibition to social action. The problem remains empirical: What constitutes the full realization of a past social order? To employ Marxism as a determinism is to ignore those elements in radical doctrine that are based on the will of the human actor to shape the outcome of social and political drama. In this sense, terrorists score very low on a determinism scale and very high on a voluntarism scale. They are not, however, deprived of either ideology or doctrine. They uniquely believe that individual acts, sometimes with collective sponsorship, can alter the course of history in ways defined exclusively by their own revolutionary wills. Those more concerned with "scientific" socialism assume a high level of social determinism, of history acting behind the backs of human actors, and therefore of events moving in a certain inexorable pattern, whatever an individual wills. This determinism can also be viewed as a strategic option. As a result, the difference between terrorist and pacifist visions of the revolutionary process represents a philosophical option or series of options; neither provides anything resembling empirically verifiable propositions about the world. The great danger of those who claim that terrorism is simply a form of either political or psychological madness is that each psychologism will end up as a metaphysical denial, if not a metaphysical pathos, of the value of political action. Ultimately, the role of action in changing the course of human events, not any single strategic set of options, must be examined. Those who argue against terrorism simply because of its promulgation of acts or deeds are at least in as difficult a bind empirically as those who argue that every act performed changes the course of historical events.

What is required is a kind of qualitative micropolitics, an empirical test for measuring the continuity between the Anarch at one end, and the Behemoth at the other. To properly understand terrorism, it is necessary to measure the quantum of force utilized by any given society, or state within such a society, as a social indicator and characterization of that society. The amount of violence engaged in by individuals to effect their desired ends is one such measurement. The amount of violence engaged in by the armed forces and police units of the state to prevent social change from occurring represents the opposite pole on the same measurement of change. In addition, we must measure the types of violence, e.g., skyjacking and assassination at one end, letter-bombs and demonstrations at intermediary levels, and the tossing of rotten eggs or oranges at the lower end of the scale.

The weakness in the Anarchist position inheres in its imbalance. Taking a life in the name of social justice carries no corresponding recognition of the rights of a state to take a life in the name of social order. At the same time, the state invariably has chosen to exercise a monopoly on life-taking activities, decreeing as illegal all other forms of life-taking by individuals. The state decries in the name of social order any uncontrolled or spontaneous forms of terrorism. At the extremes, we have a mutual definition that life-taking is a monopoly of the individual Anarch or of the collective Behemoth, but from an operational point of view, there is little to choose between them. We have a problem of social accounting at one level and moral constraint at another. For the most part, our researches have focused too exclusively on who is taking a life and far too lightly on the life that has been taken. Perhaps a shift in emphasis would lessen the quantum of violence, but such speculative assumptions are for a different essay and a different time.

The problem is not so much terrorism as who has the monopoly on the use of force. The tendency has been to seek mechanisms to obstruct terror and remove it from its sources either in state authority or anti-state power. As a result, we are left with a self-defeating concept that narrows and distorts scientific analysis. Let us take as one illustration a problem that arises in some forms of quantitative macropolitical approaches. One might speak of the basically unsuccessful results of the use of terror to overthrow state authority. Suppose we measure success not by the coup d'etat but by the temporary disruption of the normal administrative activities of political systems. Would the same results obtain? The question is rhetorical. The question of success and failure rates of terror becomes far more sobering, although the numbers involved may be infinitesimally small. For example, can one really deny that the assassinations of John F. Kennedy and Robert Kennedy, preceded by the assassination of Martin Luther King, Jr. and followed by the attempted assassination of Governor George Wallace, changed the structure, and not just the style, of American presidential politics in the past decade? One might well argue that the series of legitimacy crises that led up to Watergate were a direct, traceable consequence of these single acts of assassination and terrorism.

Although assassination attempts represent only a small number of assaults upon political leaders, they are clearly consequential acts in macropolitical terms. The very nature of the political process was profoundly interfered with, if not interrupted, by these largely successful assassination efforts. One runs a severe risk of becoming politically blase by adopting a computer-like approach to terrorism and by assuming that numerically small aggregates are not really significant, without at the same time defining who is subject to terrorism and assassination. If we connect aggregate data to flesh and blood and take seriously the qualitative traumas involved in terrorist assassinations of a president, a candidate for presidency, a leading figure within the black liberation movement espousing nonviolence, and an attempt on the life of a major figure in Southern conservative political thought, then the essentials of American political history can be seen to be inextricably connected with terrorism. As a result, it seems premature to label terrorist activities "unsuccessful," simply because of the limited numbers involved. They have involved the elimination of one man in Dallas, another in Memphis, Tennessee, and another in Los Angeles.

In questions of terrorism, the measurement of success cannot simply be its ability to topple the social order but rather its ability to loosen that order symbolically by weakening the legitimating capacities of elected officials, casting doubt on our concept of the rights of a society and the obligations of a state. In traveling, for example, the act of boarding an airplane involves an acceptance of commonplace procedures which only a few short years ago would have been deemed a direct violation of civil liberties. To board an airplane one has to have all luggage examined and one's own person scanned or frisked. A separate section in the airport is designated for only passengers who have boarding passes. The ordinary pattern of greetings on departure or arrival by loved ones is no longer permitted. When arriving at a destination, one can no longer place luggage in a locker in most airports, bus stations, and rail terminals. Restrictions on locker storage are a consequence of a solitary bomb left in a locker at LaGuardia Airport in 1975. Contrary to what many have spoken of as exhibitionist tendencies of terrorists, no one has yet claimed responsibility for the LaGuardia bombing. The self-celebration or self-attribution on the part of terrorists is itself not an axiomatic property of terrorists but is subject to great variation. Anonymity, like publicity, may have real and symbolic consequences. Most people probably accept frisking and new baggage procedures as a necessary and acceptable cost of safe flight. Nevertheless, one has a perfect right, even a duty, to raise questions about these new social costs of travel; certainly one has the right to enquire about the permanence or transitory nature of these new surveillance procedures.

In any evaluation, one has to locate the consequences of terrorism if one wants to use the rhetoric of terrorism; one cannot simply reduce the problem of violence to one of how many people are killed in a given time or place. The paucity of numbers involved in terrorism, although important, is not necessarily or invariably crucial. The failure to distinguish what is important symbolically from what at the same time may be trivial numerically casts serious doubt on a purely quantitative analytic framework. The social impact of terrorism rather than the aggregate levels of terror should become the central focus in any system of analytic measurement.

Oversimplifying, too many people presume that terrorism serves to demoralize and demobilize populations and to disintegrate societies generally. Terrorism in many instances may serve as an integrative mechanism binding people together in a common cause. The Israeli raid on the Uganda airport, in which 103 people hijacked from an Air France flight in June 1976 were liberated, was widely thought to have galvanized and unified Israeli society as no other event had since the Six-Day

War in 1967. As a result, sporadic acts of terror like the raid mobilized sentiments in such a way as to guarantee the very survival of the system that the terrorists had aimed to destroy. The ubiquity of terrorism extends beyond definitions. The word has failed to generate a scientific or legal consensus because the results of terror have proven so contradictory.

There are several important considerations having special meaning for those in the social science community who work in political science, sociology, economics, or psychology. The central issue is what might be called anticipatory socialization. Social scientists need to work within intellectual parameters that presuppose not only the existence of terrorism but a structure of the world in anticipation of heightened terrorism, involving consequently a heightened response to terrorism. Under the prompting of special bureaus like the Atomic Energy Commission and the National Aeronautic and Space Administration, many proposals have been made by sophisticated groups of social scientists dealing with the potential of terrorism in America in the nuclear age. Research was conducted on events that have never happened and perhaps cannot happen, i.e., the ability of small bands of terrorists to steal atomic weapons or fissionable materials in order to hold the country for "ransom." Serious doubts exist that terrorists, even if successful in obtaining fissionable material, would have either the scientific or technological capability to produce atomic weapons. Without presuming expertise on the commercial nuclear industry as an attractive target for terrorist designs, anticipatory research on nuclear terrorism may invite a tightening of counterterrorist techniques that, if fully enacted, would end democratic safeguards to individual rights.

It seems reasonable that social scientists might engage in anticipatory research of potential terrorism, but a problem exists in the word, "potential." A high risk is implicit in the research on the prevention of events that have not happened. Such research does not plumb events that have not happened, but researchers can develop structures of analysis that are self-fulfilling. What results from anticipatory research is an antiterrorist industry that will directly impinge on civil rights and that presumably deals with charges against crimes which may or may not be committed. If the social science community lends itself and its analytic capacities to the study of the potential dangers of terrorism, merging its rage with futurology and with the needs of administrative bodies, the threat to civil liberties is menacing.

Risk is the nature of the democratic system, because the range of permissible acts is itself an operational guideline to democracy. It is in the nature of the system to permit modes of uncontrolled and experimental behavior. To insist that mechanisms must be created to prevent acts of terror omits the role of political marginality in constructive social change. It is in the nature of a pluralistic society to indicate when an attack on terror is more risky than the randomization of the terrorism itself. There may be little else than an algebraic equation involved: at what point is the threshhold of terror so high as to involve immediate response by authorities? On the other hand, we have been drastically confused about the difference between events and a general theory or system of response. It is certainly legitimate for a society to respond to the threat of immediate and dangerous situations. It is not fair, within the context of civil liberties, to have a systemic, built-in structure to anticipate every form of terrorist behavior. That structure will inevitably destroy the stability of pluralism and critical thinking.

One fear that the current emphasis in research on terrorism invites is that the social sciences may become a servant of policy and of policy-making groups without having a check against those groups. Rather than having a dialogue, social scientists may not be heard or consulted by policy-makers. On the other hand, social scientists must be careful not to assume that social science means futurology and nothing but futurology. We have, for example, some serious methodological problems that require attention.

Good social science must not begin with the assumption of the correctness of one's own clientele and the incorrectness of others'. We must consider that we do not know who our friends or our adversaries are at any given moment. The vagaries of history being what they are, today's battlefield companions may be tomorrow's antagonists. Moreover, we are not entirely certain about the correctness and incorrectness of goals and values, even if we do agree on instrumentalities or the lack of instrumentalities. We always have to assume in good social research that we are dealing with an interaction process. So much of what is called social science assumes an asymmetry of analysis that occurs because of the purchased character of much social research. That research is purchased, bought, and sponsored must caution us against the problem of moral as well as methodological asymmetry. American social Scientists, in particular since the Project Camelot days of counterinsurgency and civic action programs, should be extremely conscious and cognizant of this problem and must not repeat the errors of only a generation ago.

Terrorism may not be an analyzable concept unto itself. Terror is often a tactical function of situational frameworks. Terrorism may be part of an instrumental network based on proximate ends and may denote nothing over and above that instrumentality. We have no assurance, despite the size and scope of the literature on terror, that we really have an independent variable. A great deal of evidence indicates that terror is a dependent variable. The simple rotating of factors involving violent behavior is not going to determine a fruitful line of scientific inquiry. Factor rotation will only cloud the question of independence and dependence in terms of levels of explained variances. One has to measure the strength of factors, not merely list and compute them.

American civilization has an innate capacity to convert everything into an industry. Beyond the question of whether we are creating a terrorism industry is a problem in the algebra and bookkeeping of terrorism. At what point does a viable, open society assume the potential for deviance? Historically, deviant behavior, marginal behavior, and even terrorist behavior are highly consonant and congruent with rapid degrees of industrialization and modernization. If we completely succeed in eliminating what we are now calling terror, what are the consequences for the potential overall economic growth of the society itself, and what are the consequences for the liberties of individuals in that society? Both of these questions seem to be questions of ethics and accounting. Until these questions are addressed empirically as well as valuationally, one has to decide to maximize security or to maximize liberty.

Rather than search for avenues of definitional precision (a search legal theorists have done without notably reducing the actual quantum of terror), the social scientist might pay close attention to the role of terrorism as a strategy and tactic rather than as a principle and premise. A terrorist does not represent a systematic analyst, nor does a terrorist necessarily represent terrorism as a world view unto itself. Terrorism becomes a method to establish claims to justice, to seek new societies, and to release frustrations that cannot be meliorated through normal political channels. Consequently, the solution to the problem of terror is invariably beyond the framework of counterterror and discussions of it. Responses to terror must be accompanied by a strengthening of the social fabric as a whole and specifically of the economic order. That strengthening cannot be reduced to increased surveillance; it clearly entails real changes in the social system like new weightings in the distribution of wealth, power, and status.

If we extrapolate terrorism from the social fabric in which it is found, terrorism loses its specific meaning, and efforts to predict "the next round of terror" or the "next contagion" remain a formal exercise largely devoid of content. We require a qualitative micropolitical analysis to complement a quantitative macropolitical analysis. Without such complementary analyses, we will remain immersed in a one-sided picture. By remaining limited in our analyses, we do a profound injustice to the herculean research which has been done on those who dispense terrorism as well as those who are its recipients. We need information on terrorism, but what we also need is a theoretical framework in which terrorism does not elicit the fears, doubts, and recriminations that the word itself clearly invites.

Martha Crenshaw Hutchinson:
Defining Future Threat: Terrorism and Nuclear Proliferation

George Quester has already defined the danger of what he called "micro-proliferation," the use of nuclear materials or weapons by non-governmental terrorist organizations. (1) We urgently need to think about how to deal with the possible intersection of two current lines of development in world politics: 1. terrorism, primarily a political phenomenon and 2. a growing dependence on nuclear energy, a technological phenomenon. Paradoxically, terrorism is usually considered as a "weapon of the weak," because groups who employ the extraordinary violence we label terrorism are resourceless by conventional standards. On the other hand, nuclear power is the hallmark and symbol of "super power" in international relations.

The specter of micro-proliferation or nuclear terrorism is an ambiguous and ill-defined danger that may exist in the future. As yet we have been alarmed only by hoaxes and warnings, but the fear that some incident of nuclear terrorism might occur is strong. How are we to assess the credibility and magnitude of such a future threat? Why does the threat exist? Exactly what is the danger we fear? What is the solution to the problem? What are governments doing to cope with the threat, and what sort of policies should they follow?

Why does the threat of nuclear terrorism exist? The threat depends upon the concurrence of two conditions: 1. growth of the civilian nuclear power industry and 2. its vulnerability to theft or attack by small groups. These conditions and the quantity and the quality of nuclear growth are permissive or enabling causes of nuclear terrorism. If commercial nuclear power were not spreading rapidly and widely, and if proliferation did not involve the acquisition of complete nuclear fuel cycles (not just power reactors), the threat might remain remote. However, nuclear growth has led to insecurity, and vulnerability is further magnified as the number of conspicuous and appropriate targets for terrorism increases. Until recently, we recognized the danger of the proliferation of international weapons, but encouraged the civilian use of nuclear energy for peaceful purposes. Now many nations perceive that any nuclear development constitutes a liability, not only for the developer but for the entire world.

Technically, the vulnerability of nuclear fuel cycles (or power systems) is due to the presence of "special nuclear materials," primarily highly enriched uranium and plutonium, in amounts that are "critical" enough to construct some kind of explosive device. Neither substance is used in the types of commercial power reactors built today, although they may be available in experimental or research reactors or weapons production. (2) However, plutonium is present in spent reactor fuel and is presently stored because reprocessing spent fuel into new fuel is not yet done commercially. Moreover, reactors of the future may use special nuclear materials as fuel; in fact, the liquid-metal, fast breeder reactor will produce more plutonium than it consumes, thereby providing its greatest utility. Reliance on plutonium for fuel may increase if a suspected natural uranium shortage develops. The most vulnerable aspects of the fuel cycle, in which highly enriched uranium and plutonium are found in basically usable form, occur in fuel reprocessing and fabrication and at uranium enrichment plants, and shipping and storage areas. (3) The projected spread of these facilities will of course increase vulnerability to terrorism on a global scale.

Predictions of future insecurity also depend on a substantial reliance upon nuclear power for the world's future energy needs. There are doubts as to the economic feasibility and the safety of nuclear energy, and the possibility exists that less risky and cheaper alternatives may be found. At present, however, there is no indication that the trend toward dependence on nuclear power will not continue.

Despite the limited amounts of special nuclear materials in contemporary fuel cycles, present nuclear facilities are vulnerable to terrorism. Since 1967, the risk of terrorism has been amply documented by governmental and private studies in the United States. (4) Despite greatly enhanced security precautions taken as a result of internal and external criticism, both the United States civilian and military programs (especially weapons located abroad) are considered insecure. Although it is almost impossible to acquire specific information on the security of foreign nuclear programs (no evidence exists of foreign public debates comparable to those in the United States), they are generally considered more vulnerable than United States programs. The recognition of present danger supports the assumption of enhanced insecurity in the future.

In explaining the existence of a threat of nuclear power, we need to ask ourselves what we mean by security *from* what and vulnerability *to* what? Terrorism, the systematic use or threat of extraordinary violence by non-governmental individuals to obtain political objectives, has expanded in the post-war world. Terrorist exploitation of nuclear power would be a new tactical gloss on an old strategy; the basic causes and patterns of terrorism will remain fundamentally unchanged. The motivations which now inspire terrorism are not likely to disappear; in fact, they may increase. If political frustration and alienation grow, if terrorism continues to appear to be successful, available, and an easy way to satisfy grievances, then at some time the idea of nuclear terrorism will occur to those individuals who have been inspired by the convenience of machine guns and letter bombs, the vulnerability of air transportation, and the ease of kidnapping diplomats and businessmen.

That nuclear terrorism is likely to be a new means to old ends does not exclude the possibility of new motivations for terrorism. However, since the nineteenth century when terrorism against governments first became a technique of modern political protest and until terrorism spread from internal war to world politics, the causes of motivations for terrorist activity have remained relatively constant, while the permissive causes or opportunities for new forms of violence have grown. Recently, with the development of the mass communications media, the motives for terrorism have been diffused worldwide. Terrorism has almost become a respectable revolutionary strategy. The awareness that the discontent of others has found expression in terrorist violence encourages new terrorism. The publicity given to terrorism may make groups aware not only of strengths but also of grievances previously ignored. The communication of information about terrorism can create new expectations and new hopes. However, although new motives may enter the game, the phenomenon of terrorism remains basically the same.

Precisely what is it that threatens us? Why and how would a terrorist organization use or threaten nuclear violence? The number of possible scenarios of nuclear terrorism is undoubtedly infinite, but we can derive clues to the potential nuclear terrorist from past patterns of terrorist behavior and the special characteristics required for using nuclear power. We must, however, remain aware of the fearful inventiveness of the terrorists which makes future violence difficult to predict. Given the characteristics of terrorist groups, their usual purposes, and their methods, what would make nuclear power an attractive weapon for terrorists? If it was attractive, what might result?

The terrorist organization is by definition a non-governmental individual group with transnational organizational ties that cross national boundaries, an internal opposition movement, or a government bureaucracy acting independently, composed of military personnel or police. The factors which normally inhibit the conduct of government — responsibility to public opinion or organized interests, bureaucratic politics, reputation, or international legality or morality — would probably not constrain the actions of terrorists. Nor would terrorists, unless they represent a particular ethnic group or regional area, likely have a recognized geographic territory or national population against which a government could threaten retaliation. (5)

There are no ethnic or geographical restrictions on the origins of potential terrorist groups. In the past, groups have been organized in industrial as well as developing states and on all continents. Only in Communist states, excluding Yugoslavia, do we see no terrorism originating. Terrorism, like nuclear power, is becoming a world phenomenon.

In order to handle nuclear materials, to build some sort of explosive device, to seize a power plant, or otherwise to exploit nuclear power, some terrorists must acquire technical and scientific qualifications. The spread of knowledge is a largely uncontrollable transnational force, spurred by national ambitions for economic development and modernization. The skills of nuclear technology are a by-product of the diffusion of nuclear power. Since an American college chemistry student, using only publicly available information, was able to design a workable atomic bomb, technical requirements obviously will not pose a serious obstacle to the would-be nuclear terrorist. According to Theodore Taylor, construction of a nuclear explosive is no more complex than the manufacture of heroin. (6)

The terrorist group capable of stealing nuclear material, building a bomb, attacking a nuclear facility or shipment, or dispersing plutonium in a building, would not have to be extremely large. One person could conceivably build a very crude bomb; a team of about five technically proficient people could apparently build a bomb quite efficiently and safely. (7) The United States Atomic Energy Commission based its physical protection regulations on the arbitrary criterion of resistance to an armed attack of twelve to fifteen people. Undoubtedly, an exceedingly small organization could present a credible treat, especially if the group had connections with industry or government to simplify theft or attack.

However, nuclear violence would have to be a well-organized and carefully planned operation, much more so than past acts of terrorism (not that some acts have not been painstakingly planned and executed). The perpetrators would have to be a stable and cohesive group, capable of maintaining a conspiratorial unity for at least several months. If explosives had to be constructed from surreptitiously stolen materials, the operation would be quite time-consuming. For building a bomb, estimates range from a few weeks to over a year, depending on the number of people involved, their skill, experience, and resources, and the reliability and accuracy of the bomb. No matter what form it took, an act of nuclear terrorism could not be the result of a hasty or impromptu decision.

Financial resources would also be required by terrorists who intended to build a bomb. One estimate indicates that three or four people at an expense of $30,000 could in a year build a device that would almost certainly explode. A less reliable explosive could be devised by people willing to spend $10,000. (8) The necessary laboratory equipment is easily purchased at an unprohibitive expense for many existing terrorist groups, but nuclear terrorism need not require building a bomb.

Therefore, only a well-established and reasonably well-financed terrorist organization would be likely to detonate some kind of nuclear explosive, however crude. A less unified or well-provided group could mount less spectacular threats, such as attacking or seizing a nuclear shipment or plant or stealing and distributing plutonium; these threats would be more likely, because they are simpler to make. Nevertheless, no act of nuclear terrorism would be easy, and advance planning would be essential.

The most important characteristic of the potential nuclear terrorist is a willingness to take high risks. Any act of nuclear violence, including theft or sabotage, would be more risky in personal terms than any other form of terrorism, even given extensive proliferation and vulnerability. Most terrorists are apparently rational individuals, who undertake a campaign of terrorism, because the benefits to be gained exceed the estimated risks and costs. To calculate the cost-benefit ratio favorably, terrorists must feel competent about their abilities; (9) they must think that they have a chance of succeeding. Their success depends on what their goals are. Propensity for accepting risk is also related to the amount of their commitment to political values, which are also reflected in the nature of the objectives of the terrorist. Risk-taking is closely related to terrorist goals.

Regardless of the ideological bias of the terrorist group — revolutionary, nationalist, separatist, reactionary, anarchist — the objectives of terrorism can be conveniently categorized as 1. strategic and 2. tactical. Strategic goals are long-run, general, and often relatively imprecise. Tactical goals are short-run bargaining demands which are a means to strategic ends. The use of violence and threats for purposes of bargaining is a new development in the general pattern of terrorism.

The strategic aims of terrorism involve the disruption of the political status quo, on a national or international level. Terrorists seek to define and dramatize a cause through publicity. They do not necessarily want the approval of an audience of domestic or world public opinion; attention may be obtained at the expense of creating hostility. The terrorist group attempts to create insecurity and disorientation in the "enemy," who may be a government, a social class, or an entire national, social, or ethnic group. Discrediting a government by demonstrating the impotence of the authorities faced with terrorist violence is a way of increasing instability. Provoking a government to unpopular and disruptive repressive measures can also be a part of the strategy of terrorists.

The tactical goals of terrorism are expressed in specific demands for definite concessions from governments or multi-national corporations. Extortionate demands have included the payment of a monetary ransom, the release of prisoners, the publication of ideological statements, provision of food or medical supplies, safe transport to a country of asylum, and immediate and visible policy changes. Terrorists often demand acts of symbolic value in terms of their long-run goals.

The means selected by future nuclear terrorists will be logically related to their goals as well as to the accessibility of nuclear power. People who discount the risk of nuclear terrorism argue that because terrorists could obtain and use other equally destructive conventional explosives at much less cost, there is no

304 TERRORISM: INTERDISCIPLINARY PERSPECTIVES

reason for a nuclear threat. (10) Their argument overlooks the publicity value of the use of nuclear violence. If the present international prohibitions on the use of nuclear force holds in the future, the political and psychological effects of even minor nuclear violence, although incomparable in physical destructiveness to strategic nuclear war, would be infinitely greater than the impact of conventional explosives. Similarly, the dispersal of plutonium would have consequences disproportionate to the actual number and timing of deaths caused. (11) The creation of emotional reactions out of all proportion to actual deaths or damage caused by violence is an essential characteristic of terrorism.

Skeptics also argue that because past terrorists have avoided large-scale explosions causing more than a hundred casualties, despite an ability to do so through conventional means, future terrorists will not want to risk incurring popular opprobrium and hostility by, for example, exploding a nuclear device in a city. (12) It seems naive to trust the good-will and humanitarian instincts of terrorists to prevent mass casualties. The argument, although ostensibly based on past experience, overlooks a definite trend toward greater destructiveness accompanying the availability of more sophisticated weapons and explosives. The lessons of the past indicate that the trend toward greater harm will continue. If in the future states have broken the prohibition against the coercive use of nuclear power, then terrorists would also be tempted to adopt comparable means of coercion. The effects and the effectiveness of terrorism must be seen in context. Nuclear war would drastically alter the context of terrorism by lessening the dramatic impact of nuclear terrorism and by making greater than conventional destructiveness necessary in order to impress an audience, especially a universal one.

Past terrorists have not avoided acts which might alienate many people. A single act of terrorism usually has many effects, depending on the identity and reaction of different audiences. Although terrorism is not generally indiscriminate, it may be indiscriminate against a targeted group. If the direct audience is the "enemy" — a social group hostile to the terrorists' aims — then mass casualties within that group would not necessarily be undesirable. Imagine, for example, a not implausible world in the future when the gap between rich and poor countries has grown rapidly. The anti-American, anti-imperialist, and anti-Western motives which have led to terrorism in the past are stronger, deeper, and wider. A terrorist group from a poor state might feel few qualms about causing additional American deaths that might increase their popularity in their poor, home state.

The means of terrorism are closely related to ends. Given the goals described, the methods of nuclear terrorism would fall into two types: 1. destructive, one-step acts serving primarily strategic goals and 2. complicated bargaining moves, implementing both general aims and specific demands.

Destructive terrorism is characterized by many casualities in an enemy group and less frequently acts of sabotage involving impressive damage. Bombings, often without prior warning, are common. Terrorists determined on using nuclear power could attempt theft and detonation of a nuclear weapon, theft of nuclear materials to construct and explode a bomb, sabotage of a nuclear facility or cargo to cause notable damage like the radioactive contamination of the surroundings or incapacitation of a plant, or theft and dispersal of radioactive or toxic substances like plutonium. Either overt or covert theft is possible, although covert theft would intensify the surprise effect of subsequent violence. Presumably groups aspiring to general national or international sympathy would select material targets to avoid human casualties. However, an organization seeking attention at any price or hostile to the audience to be affected (especially the people who would identify with or feel sympathetic toward the victims) would be insensitive to human deaths.

In bargaining during terrorism, a threat of violence is intended as the opening move in a give-and-take situation. Usually by seizing hostages, the terrorists attempt to acquire the status with which to bargain with a government or corporation. The seizure of hostages is an initial act of violence which makes the threat of further violence credible and gives the terrorists a means of rewarding a government or corporation if it accedes to the terrorists' demands. Terrorists who threaten nuclear violence if an ultimatum is not met must establish credibility, although the magnitude of the threat will be indisputable. Several ways exist to demonstrate the believability of a threat. First, nuclear material could be stolen overtly through an armed attack or in a manner that could subsequently be demonstrated to the authorities and to the public. On the basis of clear evidence of possession, a threat would probably be quite effective whether or not a bomb were actually constructed. If the time between theft and communication of a threat were long enough, the terrorists' claim of having built a bomb would be plausible. On the other hand, lengthening the period between theft and threat increases the risk for the terrorists if the government detects the loss of material. If plutonium were stolen, the problem of "critical time" would not exist.

Stealing enough material to build two bombs, or a large amount of plutonium, would be a difficult way to establish credibility of terrorists. The terrorists could explode, perhaps in an unpopulated area, a first bomb as proof of intent and determination. They might threaten to explode a second with worse consequences in order to deter pursuit from the authorities. A very small amount of plutonium could be dispersed in surroundings of low population density; then the magnitude of the threat might be escalated by communicating an intention to use additional plutonium in a crowded area next time. Bluffs are also conceivable.

Obviously a terrorist group could invent innumerable and various strategies and tactics, many of which need not involve the construction of an atomic bomb. What could the terrorists demand of governments? What concessions would be worth the risks of attempted nuclear extortion?

Bargaining demands could be symbolically related to nuclear power. A group could demand a halt to nuclear development. Other demands might be unrelated; while the potential violence would be extraordinary, the demands would not need to be. Since the United States has consistently refused to meet terrorist demands, a determined group might calculate that in order to force ordinary concessions, they would have to escalate their threat to nuclear dimensions. The United States has often been a third party target of transnational terrorism; terrorists have seized American hostages in a foreign country to force the host government to meet their demands. Nuclear terrorism to create coercion and bargaining is possible, but it does not seem necessary, because terrorists have been successful using conventional means.

Although destruction for immediate effect appears to be dangerous from the victims' point of view, bargaining during terrorism has its own perils. Once terrorists would announce a nuclear threat, especially publicly, tension would be acute. Terrorists evidently believe that they can control the risks inherent in a public situation of conflict, but the dangers of miscalculation or accident under pressure would be immense.

The major responsibility for coping with the threat of nuclear terrorism lies with governments. Not only are all matters of internal and external security the proper functions of government, but also the growth of nuclear industry has been promoted and regulated by governments in all countries.

Consequently, nations bear some responsibility for the existence of the danger.

Preventing nuclear terrorism is not considered to be worth the cost of abandoning nuclear power as a source of energy. The question of a current policy response is framed around limiting, not halting, civilian nuclear development and improving physical security first. Governments are primarily concerned with controlling expansion and limiting vulnerability. They are also more interested in diverting nuclear power developed by the civilian sector to military uses than they are with the threat of terrorism.

Extensive criticism from inside and outside the United States government has made policymakers sensitive to the dangers involved in the civilian nuclear power industry. Frequent hoaxes and false alarms have publicized these dangers. Since 1973, the government has imposed stringent security requirements upon the nation's commercial licensees. These include design requirements for physical barriers, lighting, and exits, trained guards; security checks for personnel; detection procedures at exits; materials accountability for inventories; and an obligatory capability to respond to attacks and to establish liaison with government authorities. Transported nuclear materials have also received increased protection; armed guards ride with truck and train shipments and maintain radio communications *en route*. Military security has also been upgraded sharply in recent years; the Department of Defense budget in fiscal year 1976 provided $34 million for nuclear weapons security at Army sites in Europe.

Because both international interdependence and the nature of terrorist threat equalize state vulnerability, nuclear energy is a crucial foreign policy issue, dealt with on unilateral, bilateral, and multilateral levels, both formally and informally. The most visible interaction occurs in one formal institution, the International Atomic Energy Agency (I.A.E.A.), which has the dual responsibility of promoting the development of peaceful atomic energy and preventing weapons proliferation. To prevent diversion for military purposes, its authority to enforce safeguards on civilian programs was reinforced by the 1968 Non-Proliferation Treaty (N.P.T.) which requires non-nuclear weapon states signing it to submit to I.A.E.A. safeguards. Nuclear weapon states can export nuclear materials only under safeguards. Because not all nuclear weapon states are party to the treaty and since the successful Indian diversion of material for a bomb, some doubt exists as to whether the I.A.E.A. performs adequately.

While preventing weapons proliferation is one of the

I.A.E.A.'s main responsibilities, preventing micro-proliferation is definitely a secondary task. Because of the sensitivities of sovereign states about internal security, the I.A.E.A. has no authority to enforce measures against non-governmental diversion or attack. In 1972 and in 1975, the I.A.E.A. convened experts to recommend physical protection standards for member states, but these recommendations are only guidelines; they are not binding. They merely symbolize the existence of concern among some of the I.A.E.A.'s 106 members.

The control of civilian nuclear exports is also the subject of international activity. However, the forum for international policymaking on exports is informal, and membership is restricted. No institutions have been created or treaties proposed, but a limited group of seven of ten supplier states met frequently in 1975 to establish what are essentially civilian non-proliferation agreements.

The initiator of the sudden activity by supplier states was the United States, which has the greatest responsibility in the area, because it is the supplier of seventy percent of all power reactors in operation or on order worldwide, with eighty percent of all foreign purchases financed by the Export-Import Bank. (13) Attempts at control by the United States have also been prompted by the same domestic criticism that led to the tightening of security at home. Since 1974, the United States has unilaterally required a determination of adequate physical security, including on-site inspection, before critical amounts of special nuclear materials may be exported. (14) The government also requires that spent reactor fuel be reprocessed outside the recipient country to reduce the danger of diversion or misuse of extracted plutonium. The United States refuses to export reprocessing or enrichment equipment or technology.

Policy-makers and industry in the United States are afraid that unilateral export restrictions weaken the nation's competitive position, since other states, notably West Germany and France are less scrupulous in their export practices. These European suppliers will sell enrichment and reprocessing plants. An irony of international commercial competition in nuclear energy is that Framatome in France and Kraftwerk in West Germany are United States licensees and basically re-export American technology. Westinghouse owns forty-five percent of Framatome (15)

After a controversial West German deal with Brazil, the seven supplier states, urged by the United States, agreed on mutual consultations during negotiations for foreign sales and on the imposition of strict controls on the end-use of nuclear exports. (16) This de facto cartel of exporters links the Soviet Union, Japan, and the West, including France which has not signed the Non-Proliferation Treaty, in a rather delicate combination of odd partners. Not only are their negotiations conducted in the utmost secrecy, but also their agreements will probably be limited in scope. For example, the United States proposal of regional nuclear fuel centers was rejected. However, informal policy coordination demonstrates that the common interest in preventing state and non-state proliferation can occasionally transcend political and economic rivalries.

There are many other ambitious proposals to prevent nuclear terrorism immediately. Recommendations can be grouped as they relate to controlling the spread of nuclear power, improving physical protection of nuclear materials, deterring terrorism with threats, and other "positive" methods to reduce the threat.

Controlling or limiting the spread of nuclear facilities would minimize the number of targets open to violence and would simplify the protection of them. One suggestion, favored by the Ford administration, encourages the United States to support commercial uranium enrichment and fuel reprocessing, because if ample supplies were available from the United States, other countries would not have the incentive to acquire indigenous facilities. Another idea is to concentrate nuclear functions by creating regional fuel centers internationally or "nuclear parks" on domestic levels. Reprocessing, enrichment, and fuel fabrication could be done in one location, minimizing transportation and assuring centralized control. The United States favors this idea, and the I.A.E.A. is currently concluding a study of the international feasibility of it. Another possible means of limiting civilian proliferation is the encouragement of alternative sources of energy. However, this option does not appear to be very attractive to policymakers or industry.

Direct improvement of physical protection could be accomplished through an international treaty requiring uniform standards, enforced by the I.A.E.A. The I.A.E.A.'s physical protection experts recommended a formal convention on international transportation safeguards. However, any expansion of the I.A.E.A.'s authority does not seem politically feasible. New responsibilities would be costly as well. On a bilateral level, supplier states could require that nuclear facilities be designed for security or that existing security practices be improved, as the United States requires. The bilateral imposition of safeguards seems to be the direction of current momentum, although it risks arousing the ire of recipient states; to be effective the imposition of safeguards requires the cooperation of all supplier states. Almost never mentioned is the possibility that the supplier countries could provide some kind of international financial assistance for their clientele, for whom security costs in addition to the high cost of nuclear power may be prohibitive. Because most commercial nuclear exports are government-financed, security assistance, without undue interference in local affairs, is possible. At least information on efficient plant design could be communicated at low cost to a recipient state.

Another means of preventing nuclear terrorism is through deterrence. Although physical protection measures may in some sense "deter" by making an act of terrorism extremely difficult and possibly more dangerous for the terrorists, deterrence means threatening punishment to a would-be terrorist if he commits a certain transgression. Specific deterrent measures, many of which have been suggested, would include imposition of the death penalty for any theft of special nuclear materials or for an attack on a plant or shipment. These measures improve a government's intervention capabilities. In the United States, specially trained military units respond to a terrorist attack. Globally, an international police force, perhaps under the auspices of the I.A.E.A., could be mandated to respond to terrorism.

Numerous problems are involved in relying on deterrence to prevent terrorism. (17) Theoretically, a strategy of deterrence depends upon shared standards of rationality between the potential initiator of a threat and the party wanting to deter the threat. When criteria of rationality differ, it is difficult for government policy-makers to perceive a terrorist threat accurately. In their study of United States policy on deterrence of limited conflicts, Alexander George and Richard Smoke found that decision-makers frequently underestimated their opponent's willingness to take risks. (18) Because knowledge and understanding of a terrorist's goals and values are more vague than perceptions of state behavior, a faulty analysis of the terrorist adversary is very likely. Governments tend to dismiss a terrorist's propensity to take high risks as irrational, but if terrorists are irrational, then no threat of punishment would deter them. If a government really wants to deter terrorism, then it must discover what kind of threat terrorists would interpret as punishment severe enough to make the terrorists rationally cease their terrorism.

An equally serious problem in implementing a strategy of

deterrence is establishing the credibility of the deterrent threat. The strategic nuclear threat of retaliation against an aggressor's home population bears little correspondence to terrorism. A government threat to a terrorist usually involves personal harm or imprisonment and only secondarily involves the elimination of an organization as a political group or, perhaps more importantly, the destruction of the values or ideology which the terrorist believes his action supports. A terrorist may think that through his act, no matter what the future may be for himself or his comrades, the ideas he represents will continue to live.

The uncertainty of the implementation of a threat also weakens its credibility. Although the capture and punishment of a domestic terrorist may be certain, depending upon the state, international interdependence interferes with punishment of the transnational terrorist. To punish a hijacker or a hostage-taker, the United States must rely on the cooperation of other states to extradite or prosecute. Such dependence has proved unsatisfactory, and terrorists who operate transnationally probably feel sure that they may escape punishment. Consequently, unilateral deterrence cannot be effectively implemented, but mutual deterrence on a world scale is politically impossible.

Deterrence, which involves conflict and cooperation, also depends upon the adversaries' perception of a common interest that may be reflected in the outcome of a conflict. Both sides, the terrorists and the government, must compromise, but both must stand to gain something. The mutual aim of survival by avoiding nuclear catastrophe, which is at the heart of strategic deterrence, is missing. Perhaps the threats have not been horrible enough to make avoidance and survival reasons to compromise.

Terrorism may well be a threat that cannot be deterred. It is, however, dangerous to rely on deterrence as a protection against a threat of nuclear terrorism. Positive alternatives to deterrence would include maintaining an international climate of opinion in which the use of any form of nuclear weapons by states or non-states remains abhorrent and counter-productive. Another alternative, unfortunately utopian in present international relations, would be providing some peaceful means to at least recognize if not arbitrate political grievances. For example, an International Court of Justice could hear claims of non-states. Because the entire international community is now susceptible to the consequences of frustrations caused by the policies of each member, official repression which may inspire terrorism is no longer a purely domestic matter. Neither the responsibility for injustice nor its effects can be isolated. Because not all terrorism is caused by genuine political grievances, these positive proposals would not solve the problem entirely. However, the removal of one source of terrorism would diminish the imitation effect and would help remove the aura of revolutionary legitimacy which surrounds the use of terrorism.

Another area of government policy, a discussion of which inevitably sounds like a Dr. Strangelove, is contingency planning. If an incident of nuclear terrorism should occur and if all efforts at prevention and deterrence have failed, what should be the response of the threatened or attacked government? What should be the reaction of the international community? To cope with terrorist acts of either destruction or bargaining, advance planning for a coordinated response at all institutional levels of government, national and international, must be thorough and detailed. Plans should consider the proper authorities to alert at home and abroad; provisions for determining the credibility of the threat; means of reassuring or directing the population if necessary; and different policy options for various contingencies. The confusion and uncertainty in government and among the population following an unanticipated attack or threat would be immensely dangerous. Critics of a future "plutonium economy" fear that efforts to cope with nuclear terrorism will lead to serious deprivations of civil liberties. (19) An irrational and hasty response to terrorism might be more devastating than the terrorism.

Governments must learn to respond to a bargaining threat from terrorists. Refusing to negotiate would be extremely risky, and the consequences of a forceful response might be disastrous. In view of the magnitude of a terrorist threat, governments must develop skillful and well informed bargaining techniques. Attempts can be made to delay the implementation of a threat, to persuade the terrorists that execution of the threat would not be in their interests, or to offer less unacceptable alternative concessions to those demanded, including publicity. None of these bargaining attempts depend upon unequivocal surrender to terrorist demands, although governments must be prepared to consider the costs and benefits of total surrender.

Bargaining does not mean that a government must reward violence by agreeing to terrorist demands, which might indeed encourage future violence. However, a government must recognize that once a threat of nuclear terrorism is made public, choices are severely restricted, and the government may no longer be able to deny a reward to the terrorists. If terrorists actually want attention and recognition more than the specific concessions demanded, then an announcement of their threat has satisfied most of their ambitions, and the specific government response is insignificant except as it increases publicity. Governments must avoid the temptations of over-reacting. By under-reacting a government may gain bargaining leverage to persuade the terrorists that they do not want to take the mutually painful step of seeing their threat realized. Token concessions might have to be offered to allow the terrorists to retain their pride, but disaster could be avoided. Because terrorists may attempt to force a government to choose between capitulation and intervention, the government must try to increase the range of its available options.

Consideration of alternative responses to all types of nuclear terrorism is especially critical because of the potential effects of even a minor threat upon public opinion. Although popular reactions of widespread panic and terror might be avoided, the long-term results of nuclear terrorism might well be a strengthening of opposition to the use of nuclear energy and a serious loss of confidence in the government. It is psychologically conceivable that a population would blame their government for failing to protect them from terrorism more than they would blame terrorists for initiating violence.

The proliferation of both nuclear power and terrorism means that the two trends may merge at some future time. Nuclear terrorism is a political issue of high priority, yet study of it is under-developed. Understanding the significance and implications of this particular kind of violent conflict is an interdisciplinary endeavor, involving the coordination of data and insights from science and technology, psychology, sociology, and political science. Interdisciplinary research remains to be done. To explain the subject and prescribe policy responses in the area of politics, terrorism raises questions about the relevance of theories of political behavior and interaction. Traditional theories, which on domestic levels concentrate on "normal" political behavior and which internationally concern state actions, do not encompass the phenomenon satisfactorily.

That threats may exist primarily in the future also complicates an assessment of the meaning of nuclear terrorism, yet the issue provokes thought about the ambiguities of the future world we are entering. What is the meaning of political power, if a small group of individuals can not only use a nuclear weapon but also seriously force a government to obey their wishes? What is the future of the nation-state in a world characterized by micro-proliferation? Is nuclear terrorism the kind of issue which should be handled by international institutions, or should it be left to unilateral national initiatives? What kind of economic, political, and technological developments will make micro-proliferation more or less likely? Defining the future threat of nuclear terrorism exposes inadequacies in both the theory and the reality of contemporary international relations.

NOTES

(1) "What's New on Nuclear Proliferation?" paper prepared for the 1975 Aspen Workshop on Arms Control; reprinted in U.S. Congress, House, Committee on International Relations, Subcommittee on International Security and Scientific Affairs, *Nuclear Proliferation: Future U.S. Foreign Policy Implications.* Hearings, 94th Cong., 1st Sess., Washington: G.P.O., 1975, pp. 476-99. See also: Hutchinson, Martha C., "Terrorism and the Diffusion of Nuclear Power," a paper prepared for the XVII Annual Convention of the International Studies Association, Toronto, Canada, February 25-29, 1976.

(2) In 1974, 568 A.E.C.-licensed industrial facilities were authorized to process 1,041,000 pounds of plutonium or enriched uranium, but 99.8% of this material was used in 97 facilities, of which only 27 were considered vulnerable to theft. See: Senator Abraham Ribicoff's remarks in the *Congressional Record*, May 28, 1974, reproduced in U.S. Congress, Senate, Committee on Government Operations, *Peaceful Nuclear Exports and Weapons Proliferation*, Washington: G.P.O., 1975, 0. 497.

(3) For an excellent discussion of the vulnerabilities of different types of fuel cycles, see: Mason Willrich and Theodore B. Taylor, *Nuclear Theft: Risks and Safeguards*, Cambridge: Ballinger Publishing Co., 1974.

(4) See: list of reports, some classified, cited by Theodore B. Taylor in "Diversion by Non-governmental Organizations," in Mason Willrich, ed., *International Safeguards and Nuclear Industry*, Baltimore: John Hopkins Press, 1973, p. 177. The earliest public report was apparently the "Lumb Report," Ad Hoc Advisory Panel on Safeguarding Special Nuclear Material, *Report to the Atomic Energy Commission*, March 10, 1967, excerpts reprinted in *Peaceful Nuclear Exports*, pp. 563-72. The biographical study of Ted Taylor in *The New Yorker*, "The Curve of Binding Energy," XLIX, No. 41-43, Dec. 3, 10, and 17, 1973, also publicized the issue. Other critical studies are U.S. Comptroller General, Reports to the Congress, "Improvements

Needed in the Program for the Protection of Special Nuclear Material," Nov. 7, 1973, and "Protecting Special Nuclear Material in Transit," April 12, 1974, G.A.O., Reports B-164105, both in *Peaceful Nuclear Exports*, pp. 1170-1225; and the "Special Safeguards Study," the "Rosenbaum Report," done for A.E.C., placed in the *Congressional Record*, April 30, 1974, and reprinted in *Peaceful Nuclear Exports*, pp. 467-90.

(5) Obviously some terrorist groups do have constituencies, which they may or may not represent accurately. For example, Israeli retaliation against Palestinian refugee camps is an attempt to strike at the terrorists' home base, but governments cannot count on such circumstances, nor are the links between terrorists and constituency formally recognized.

(6) There is substantial disagreement on the question of whether amateurs could build some sort of explosive device. See, however: Willrich and Taylor, Chapter 6, pp. 107-20; remarks by Senator Ribicoff in the *Congressional Record*, May 28, 1974, citing an A.E.C. experiment with two physicists, reprinted in *Peaceful Nuclear Exports*, pp. 491-97; and the transcript of NOVA's "The Plutonium Connection," *Congressional Record*, Vol. 121, No. 39, March 11, 1975, p. S3620.

(7) See: E. M. Kinderman, "Plutonium: Home Made Bombs?" a paper presented at the Conference on Nuclear Public Information, Information-3, organized by the Atomic Industrial Forum, March, 1972, in *Peaceful Nuclear Exports*, pp. 25-26; and a statement by Theodore B. Taylor before the Subcommittee on International Finance of the Senate Committee on Banking, Housing, and Urban Affairs, July 15, 1974, in *Peaceful Nuclear Exports*, p. 983.

(8) See: the New York *Times* interview with the student who designed the bomb for NOVA, Feb. 27, 1975, p. 12.

(9) The A.E.C. noted that the terrorist's decision to attack a particular target will depend on how competent the individual thinks he is, which is a psychological factor difficult to judge objectively. See: *Proposed Final Environmental Statement* on the liquid metal fast breeder reactor, Dec. 1974, WASH 1535, Vol. IV, Section 7.4.3., excerpted in *Peaceful Nuclear Exports*, p. 605.

(10) See for example: a statement by the manager of the A.E.C. safeguards program at Los Alamos, in Robert B. Leachman and Philip Althoff, *Preventing Nuclear Theft*, New York: Praeger, 1972, p. 275; and the I.A.E.A. Inspector General's statement to the New York *Times*, June 20, 1975, p. 8.

(11) A gram of plutonium dispersed without warning in a building could cause seventy deaths, although not immediately. See: Bernard L. Cohen, "The Hazards in Plutonium Dispersal" (which discounts the danger), March, 1975, in *Peaceful Nuclear Exports*, especially pp. 1294-95, 1300, and 1302.

(12) See: Brian Jenkins, "Will Terrorists Go Nuclear?" discussion paper No. 64, California Seminar on Arms Control and Foreign Policy, October, 1975.

(13) See: U.S. Congress, Senate, Committee on Government Operations, *Facts on Nuclear Proliferation*, a handbook prepared by the Congressional Research Service of the Library of Congress. Washington: G.P.O., 1975, p. 198; also the New York *Times*, Aug. 17, 1975, p. 36.

(14) These requirements were first implemented in sales to West Germany in 1975. See: U.S. Congress, Senate, Committee on Government Operations, *The Export Reorganization Act — 1975*, Hearings, 94th Cong., 1st Session, Washington: G.P.O., 1975, pp. 74-75 and 227; and *Peaceful Nuclear Exports*, pp. 687-713.

(15) The New York *Times*, Aug. 17, 1975, p. 36.

(16) The seven major supplier states are Canada, France, the United States, Great Britain, Japan, the Soviet Union, and West Germany. See: the New York *Times*, Feb. 24, 1976, pp. 1 and 8.

(17) Fred C. Iklé, Director of the U.S. Arms Control and Disarmament Agency, has cited "the core of the problem" as our reliance on deterrence: "Our principal approach in preventing the use of nuclear destructive devices, that is to say, the approach of nuclear deterrents [sic], would not be applicable to these threats, in all likelihood." Testimony in the Export Reorganization Act hearings, p. 12.

(18) *Deterrence in American Foreign Policy: Theory and Practice*, New York: Columbia University Press, 1974, pp. 64 and 505.

(19) See: statement on "The Plutonium Economy" and the supporting background report by a Committee of Inquiry chaired by Margaret Mead and René Dubos for the National Council of Churches of Christ in the U.S.A., September, 1975.

Selected Bibliography

Aaron, Harold R., "The Anatomy of Guerrilla Terror," *Infantry*, Vol. 58, March-April, 1967, p. 14.

"A.B.C.'s Grim T.V. First: Coverage of Terrorist Raid at Munich Olympics," *Newsweek*, Vol. 80, September 18, 1972, pp. 67-68.

Adamic, Louis, *Dynamite: The Story of Class Violence in America*, New York: Viking, 1934.

Adelson, Alan, *S.D.S.: A Profile*, New York: Scribner's, 1972.

Adkins, E.H., Jr., "Protection of American Industrial Dignitaries and Facilities Overseas," *Security Management*, Vol. 18, No. 3, July, 1974, pp. 14, 16, 55.

Adu-Lughad, Ibrahim, "Unconventional Violence and International Politics," *American Journal of International Law*, Vol. 67, 1973, p. 100.

Aggarwala, Narinder, "Political Aspects of Hijacking," *International Conciliation*, No. 585, 1971, pp. 7-27.

Ahmad, Egbal, "The Theory and Fallacy of Counterinsurgency," *Nation*, Vol. 213, 1971, pp. 70-85.

"Aids to the Detection of Explosives — A Brief Review of Equipment for Searching out Letter Bombs and Other Explosive Devices," *Security Gazette*, Vol. 17, No. 2, February, 1975, pp. 48-49, 61.

Aines, Ronald C., *The Jewish Underground against the British Mandate in Palestine*, Thesis, Union College, 1973.

Aircraft Piracy Amendments of 1973 (Debate and Vote in the Senate), *Congressional Record*, daily ed., Vol. 120, March 12, 1974, pp. S3502-3506.

"Airport Security Searches and the Fourth Amendment," *Columbia Law Review*, Vol. 71, 1971, pp. 1039-58.

Akehurst, Michael, "Arab-Israeli Conflict and International Law," *New Zealand Universities Law Review*, Vol. 5, 1973, p. 231.

Akers, E.R. and V. Fox, "The Detroit Rioters and Looters Committed to Prison," *Journal of Criminal Law, Criminology and Police Science*, Vol. 35, 1964, p. 105.

Alexander, Robert J., *The Bolivian National Revolution*, New Brunswick, New Jersey: Rutgers University Press, 1958.

Alexander, Yonah, *The Role of Communications in the Middle East Conflict: Ideological and Religious Aspects*, New York: Praeger, 1973.

_____, *Terrorism: National, Regional, and Global Perspectives*, with a foreword by Arthur J. Goldberg, New York: Praeger, 1976.

Alexander, Yonah, and Nicholas N. Kittrie, *Crescent and Star: Arab-Israeli Perspectives on the Middle East Conflict*, New York: AMS Press, 1972.

Ali, Tariq, ed., *The New Revolutionaries: A Handbook of the International Radical Left*, New York: William Morrow, 1969.

Allbach, D. M., "Countering Special-Threat Situations," *Military Police Law Enforcement Journal*, Vol. 2, No. 2, Summer Quarterly, 1975, pp. 34-40.

Allen, Rodney F. and Charles H. Adair, eds., *Violence and Riots in Urban America*, Worthington, Ohio: Jones Publishing, 1969.

Allon, Yigal, *Shield of David*, New York: Random House, 1970.

Alper, Benedict S. and Jerry F. Boren, *Crime: International Agenda*, with a Foreword by William Clifford, Lexington, Mass.: Lexington Books; D. C. Heath, 1972.

Alsina, Geronimo, "The War and the Tuparamos," *Bulletin Tricontinental*, August 1972, pp. 29-42.

Alves, Márcio Moreira, *A Grain of Mustard Seed*, Garden City, N.Y.: Doubleday Anchor, 1973.

_____, "Kidnapped Diplomats: Greek Tragedy on a Latin Stage," *Commonweal*, Vol. 92, 1970, pp. 311-14.

Anable, David, "Terrorists in New York Threatened U.S.-Soviet Links," *Christian Science Monitor*, April 5, 1976, p. 4.

"Anarcho-Nihilism," *Economist*, Vol. 237, No. 6635, 1970, pp. 2-33.

Andel, A. M. von, "Media en Gijzeling (Media and the Taking of Hostages)," *Algemeen Politieblad*, Vol. 124, No. 16 August 2, 1975, pp. 384-386.

Anderson, Jack, "Urban Guerrilla Operations Feared," Washington

Post, April 23, 1974.

Anderson, W., *Age of Protest*, Pacific Palisades, Calif.: Goodyear Publishing, 1969.

Andics, Hellmut, *Rule of Terror*, New York: Holt, Rinehart & Winston, 1969.

"And Now, Mail-a-Death," *Time*, October 2, 1972, 28 ff.

Andreski, Stanislav, *Parasitism and Subversion: The Case of Latin America*, New York: Pantheon, 1967.

Annual of Power and Conflict, 1974-75: A Survey of Political Violence and International Influence, London: Institute for the Study of Conflict, 1976.

"Anti-Soviet Zionist Terrorism in the U.S.," *Current Digest of the Soviet Press*, Vol. 23, 1971, pp. 6-8.

Antonius, George, *The Arab Awakening*, Beirut: Khayat, 1955.

"Approaches to the Problems of International Terrorism — Symposium, 10," *Journal of International Labor and Economics*, Vol. 10, 1976, p. 483

"Arab Terrorism," *Jewish Frontier*, Vol. 36, 1969, pp. 13-16.

Archinard, André, "La Suisse et les infractions non aérliennes commises à bord des aéronefs civils," *A.S.D.A. Bulletin S.V.I.R.* No. 3, 1968, pp. 3-9; No. 1, 1969, pp. 2-10; No. 2, 1969, pp. 1-12.

Arendt, Hannah, *The Origins of Totalitarianism*, New York: Harcourt, Brace & World, 1966.

_____, "Reflections on Violence," *Journal of International Affairs*, Vol. 23, No. 1, 1969, pp. 1-35.

_____, *On Revolution*, New York: Viking, 1963.

_____, *On Violence*, New York: Harcourt, 1969.

Arey, James A., *The Sky Pirates*, New York: Scribner's, 1972.

"Argentina: Revolutions within the Revolution," *Latin America*, Vol. 5, No. 54, 1971, pp. 337-38.

Ariel, Dan, *Explosion!* Tel Aviv: Olive Books, 1972.

Aron, Raymond, *History and the Dialectic of Violence: An Analysis of Sartre's "Critique de la Raison Dialectique"*, Translation by Garry Cooper, London: Blackwell, 1975.

Ashab, Naim, "To Overcome the Crisis of the Palestinian Resistance," *World Marxist Review*, Vol. 15, No. 5, 1972, pp. 71-78.

"As Violence Spreads, United States Goes on Guard," *U.S. News and World Report*, November 2, 1970, p. 15.

Atwater, J., "Time to Get Tough with Terrorists," *Reader's Digest*, Vol. 102, April 1973, pp. 89-93.

Avineri, Sholomo, ed., *Israel and the Palestinians: Reflections on the Clash of Two National Movements*, New York: St. Martin's, 1971.

Avner [Pseud.], *Memoirs of an Assasin*, New York: Yoseloff, 1959.

Avrich, Paul, *The Russian Anarchists*, Princeton, N.J.: Princeton University Press, 1967.

Avsiel, Ehud, *Open the Gates! The Dramatic Personal Story of "Illegal" Immigration to Israel*, London: Weidenfeld & Nicolson, 1975.

Azad, Abul Kalam, *India Wins Freedom*, Calcutta: Orient Longmans, 1959.

Azar, Edward E. and Thomas J. Sloan, *Dimensions of Interaction: A Source Book for the Study of the Behavior of 31 Nations from 1948 through 1973*, Pittsburgh: International Studies Association, 1975.

Baccelli, Guido Rinaldi, "Pirateria aerea: realtrà effettiva e disciplina giuridica," *Diritto aereo*, Vol. 9, No. 35, 1970, pp. 150-60.

Bagts, Alfred, *A History of Militarism, Civilian and Military*, London: Hollis & Carter, 1959.

Bain, Chester A., *Vietnam: The Roots of Conflict*, Englewood Cliffs, N.J.: Prentice-Hall, 1967.

Bander, Edward J., ed., *Turmoil on the Campus*, New York: H. W. Wilson, 1970.

Bandura, Albert, *Aggression: A Social Learning Analysis*, Englewood Cliffs, N.J.: Prentice-Hall, 1973.

Barner, Don, "P.L.O. at U.N., What Now?" *New Outlook*, Vol. 17, No. 9, 1974, pp. 62-66.

Barnett, Correlli, *The Collapse of British Power*, New York: Morrow, 1972.

Barrie, G.N., "Crimes Committed Aboard Aircraft," *South African Law Journal*, Vol. 83, 1968, pp. 203-8.

Barron, John, *K.G.B.: The Secret Work of Soviet Secret Agents*, New York: Reader's Digest Press, 1974.

Bartos, M., "International Terrorism," *Review of International Affairs*, Vol. 23. April 20, 1972, p. 25.

"Basques: Business and Bombs," *Time*, Vol. 103 January 1974, pp. 48-49.

Bassiouni, M. Cherif, *Criminal Law and Its Processes*, Springfield, Ill.: Thomas, 1970.

_____, "Ideologically Motivated Offenses and the Political Offense Exceptions in Extradition: A Proposed Judicial Standard for an Unruly Problem," *DePaul Law Review*, Vol. 19, 1969, p. 217.

_____, "International Extradition: An American Experience and a Proposed Formula," *Revue Internationale de Droit*

Penal, Vol. 39, 1968, p. 3.

_____, "International Extradition in the American Practice and World Public Order," *Tennessee Law Review*, Vol. 36, 1969, p. 1.

_____, ed., *International Terrorism and Political Crimes*, Third Conference on Terrorism and Political Crimes, held in Syracuse, Sicily, Springfield, Ill.: Thomas, 1975.

_____, *The Law of Dissent and Riots*, Springfield, Ill.: Thomas, 1971.

Bassiouni, M. C. and V. P. Nanda, *A Treatise on International Criminal Law, Jurisdiction, and Cooperation*, Springfield, Ill.: Thomas, 1973.

Baudovin, Jean, *Terrorisme et Justice*, Montreal: Editions du Jour, 1970.

Bauer, Yehuda, *From Diplomacy to Resistance: A History of Jewish Palestine, 1939-1945*, Philadelphia: Jewish Publication Society, 1970.

Baumann, Carol Edler, *The Diplomatic Kidnappings: A Revolutionary Tactic of Urban Terrorism*, The Hague: Martinus Nijhoff, 1973.

Bayer, Alan E. and Alexander W. Astin, "Violence and Disruption on the U.S. Campus, 1968-1969," *Educational Record*, Vol. 50, 1969, p. 337.

Bayo, Alberto, *150 Questions to a Guerrilla*, translation by R. I. Madigan and Angel de Lumus Medina, Montgomery, Ala.: Air University, n.d.

Beaton, L., "Crisis in Quebec," *Round Table*, No. 241, 1971, pp. 147-52.

Beckett, J. C., "Northern Ireland," *Journal of Contemporary History*, Vol. 6, No. 1, 1971, pp. 121-34.

Begin, Menachem, *The Revolt*, New York: Henry Schuman, 1951.

"Behind the Terror Bombings," *U.S. News & World Report*, March 30, 1970, p. 15.

Bell, J. Bowyer, "Assassination in International Politics: Lord - Moyne, Count Bernadotte, and the Lehi," *International Studies Quarterly*, No. 1, 1972, pp. 59-82.

_____, "The Gun in Europe," *New Republic*, November 22, 1975, p. 1.

_____, *The Long War: Israel and the Arabs since 1946*, Engelwood Cliffs, N.J.: Prentice-Hall, 1969.

_____, *The Myth of the Guerrilla: Revolutionary Theory and Malpractice*, New York: Knopf, 1971.

_____, *The Profile of a Terrorist*, New York: Columbia

Institute of War and Peace Studies, n.d.

_____, *The Secret Army: The I.R.A. 1916-1974*, Cambridge: Massachusetts Institute of Technology Press, 1974.

_____, *Transnational Terror*, Washington, D.C.: American Enterprise Institute for Public Policy Research, 1975.

Ben-Sak, Joseph D., ed., *The Future of Collective Violence: Societal and International Perspectives*, New York: Humanities, 1974.

Bennett, George, *The Concept of Empire: Burke to Atlee, 1774-1947*, New York: Barnes & Noble, 1962.

Bennett, Richard Lawrence, *The Black and Tans*, Boston: Houghton Mifflin, 1959.

Bennett, R. K., "Brotherhood of the Bomb," *Reader's Digest*, December 1970, pp. 102-6.

_____, "Terrorists among Us: An Intelligence Report," *Reader's Digest*, October 1971, p. 115-20.

Bennett, W. T., Jr., "U.S. Initiatives in the United Nations to Combat International Terrorism," *International Lawyer*, Vol. 7, 1973, p. 752.

Benson, Mary, *South Africa: The Struggle for a Birthright*, London: Penguin, 1966.

Beqiraj, Mehmet, *Peasantry in Revolution*, Ithaca: Center for International Studies, Cornell University, 1966.

Berger, Peter L. and Richard J. Heuhaus, *Movement and Revolution*, Garden City, N.Y.: Doubleday, 1970.

Berkman, Alexander, *Now and After: The A.B.C. of Communist Anarchism*, New York: Vanguard, 1929.

_____, *Prison Memoirs of an Anarchist*, New York: Schocken, 1970.

Berkowitz, B. J. et al, *Superviolence: The Civil Threat of Mass Destruction Weapons*, Santa Barbara, Calif.: A.S.C.O.N. Corporation, 1972.

Berkowitz, Leonard, *A Social Psychological Analysis*, New York: McGraw-Hill, 1962.

Bern, Major H. von Dach, *Total Resistance*, Boulder, Colo: Panther, 1965.

Berson, L., *Case Study of a Riot: The Philadelphia Story*, New York Institute of Human Relations, 1966.

Besedin, Alexander, "Against Air Piracy," *New Times*, November 2, 1970, pp. 24-25.

Bettleheim, Bruno, *The Informed Heart*, New York: Free Press, 1960.

Bienen, Henry, *Violence and Social Change*, Chicago: University of Chicago Press, 1968.

"Biggest Blast," *Newsweek*, September 7, 1970, p. 33.

Binder, David, "U.S. Is Said to Plan a New Approach on Terrorism," New York *Times*, March 27, 1976, p. 3.

Bingham, Jonathan B. and Alfred M. Bingham, *Violence and Democracy*, New York: World, 1971.

Black, Cyril E. and Thomas P. Thornton, *Communism and Revolution*, Princeton: Princeton University Press, 1964.

"Black Men and Bombs," *Ebony*, Vol. 25, May 1970, pp. 49-50.

Blanchard, W. H., *Rousseau and the Spirit of Revolt*, Ann Arbor: University of Michigan Press, 1967.

Bloomfield, Louis M. and Gerald F. Fitzgerald, *Crimes against Internationally Protected Persons: Prevention and Punishment: An Analysis of the U.N. Convention*, New York: Praeger, 1975.

"Blowing up Bridges," *Newsweek*, February 7, 1972, p. 28.

"Blown up," *Economist*, January 16, 1971, p. 16.

Blumenthal, Monica D., Robert L. Kahn, Frank M. Andrews and Kendra B. Head, *Justifying Violence: Attitudes of American Men*, Ann Arbor, Mich.: Institute for Social Research, 1972.

Bocca, Geoffrey, *The Secret Army*, Englewood Cliffs, N.J.: Prentice-Hall, 1968.

Boesel, David and Peter H. Rossi, eds., *Cities under Siege: An Anatomy of the Ghetto Riots, 1964-1968*, New York: Basic Books, 1971.

"Bomb at the Golden Arch," Washington *Star-News*, August 20, 1975.

"Bombing Fallout," *Business Week*, November 22, 1969, p. 44.

"Bombing Incidents — 1972," *F.B.I. Law Enforcement Bulletin*, April 1973, p. 21.

"Bomb Jitters," *Newsweek*, March 30, 1970, p. 23.

"Bomb Plots: Warning on Terror War," *U.S. News & World Report*, October 26, 1970, p. 36.

"Bomb Research Center," New York *Morning Telegraph*, December 8, 1971.

"Bomb Threats," *Environment*, October 1974, p. 21.

Bond, James, "Application of the Law of War to Internal Conflicts," *Georgia Journal of International and Comparative Law*, Vol. 3, 1973, p. 345.

_____, *The Rules of Riot: Internal Conflict and the Law of War*, Princeton, N.J.: Princeton University Press, 1974.

Borisov, J., *Palestine Underground: The Story of Jewish Resistance*, New York: Judea Publishing, 1947.

Boston, Guy D.; Marvin Marcus and Robert J. Wheaton, *Terrorism: A Selected Bibliography*, Washington, D.C.:

National Criminal Justice Reference Service, March 1976.

Bowen, D. and L. H. Masotti, *Civil Violence: A Theoretical Overview*, Cleveland, Ohio: Case Western Reserve Civil Violence Research Center, 1968.

Boyle, Robert P., "International Action to Combat Aircraft Hijacking," *Lawyer of the Americas*, Vol. 4, 1972, pp. 460-73.

Bozakis, Christos L., "Terrorism and the Internationally Protected Persons in the Light of the I.L.C.'s Draft Articles," *International and Comparative Law Quarterly*, Vol. 23, 1974, p. 32.

Brach, Richard S., "The Inter-American Convention on the Kidnapping of Diplomats." *Columbia Journal of Transnational Law*, Vol. 10, 1971 pp. 392-412.

Bradford, A. L., "Legal Ramifications of Hijacking Airplanes," *American Bar Association Journal*, Vol. 48, 1962, pp. 1034-39.

Brandon, Henry, "Were We Masterful . . .," *Foreign Policy*, No. 10, 1973, pp. 158-70.

Bravo, Navarro M., "Apoderamiento ilicito de aeronaves en vuelo," *Revista española de derecho internacional*, Vol. 22, 1969, pp. 788-809.

Brennan, Ray, *Castro, Cuba, and Justice*, Garden City, N.Y.: Doubleday, 1959.

Breton, J. M., "Piraterie aerienne et droit international public," *Revue générale de droit international public*, Vol. 75, 1971, pp. 392-445,

Brinton, Crane, *The Anatomy of a Revolution*, Englewood Cliffs, N.J.: Prentice-Hall, 1965.

Brissenden, P. F., *The I.W.W.: A Study of American Syndicalism*, New York: Columbia University, 1920.

Brodie, T. G., *Bombs and Bombings*, Springfield, Ill.: Thomas, 1972.

Broehl, Wayne G., *The Molly Maguires*, Cambridge: Harvard University Press, 1964.

Brogan, Dennis W., *The Price of Revolution*, New York: Harper, 1951.

Brown, Richard M., *Strain of Violence: Historical Studies of American Violence and Vigilantism*, London: Oxford University Press, 1975.

Browne, Jeffrey T., *International Terrorism: The American Response*, School of International Service, Washington, D.C.: The American University, December 1973.

Browne, Malcolm W., *The New Face of War*, Indianapolis: Bobbs-Merrill, 1965.

Bunting, Brian, *The Rise of the South African Reich*, London: Penguin, 1964.

Burckhardt, Jacob, *Force and Freedom*, New York: Pantheon; Random House, 1943.

Burke, E., *Reflections on the Revolution in France*, London: Dent, 1910.

Burki, S. J., "Social and Economic Determinants of Political Violence: A Case Study of the Punjab," *Middle East Journal*, Vol. 25, 1971, pp. 465-80.

Burnham, J., "Notes on Terrorism," *National Review*, October 13, 1972, p. 1116.

Burns, Alan, *In Defense of Colonies*, London: Allen & Unwin, 1957.

Burton, Anthony M., *Urban Terrorism*, New York: Macmillan, 1975; Free Press, 1976.

"Busing and Strikes: Schools in Turmoil," *Time*, September 15, 1975, p. 35.

Callanan, Edward F., "Terror in Venezuela," *Military Review*, Vol. 49, 1969, pp. 49-56.

Caloyanni, M. A., "The Proposals of M. Laval to the League of Nations for the Establishment of an International Permanent Tribunal in Criminal Matters," *Transactions of the Grotius Society*, Vol. 21, 1936, p. 77.

_____, "Le Terrorisme et la création d'une cour répressive internationale," *Revue de droit international*, Vol. 15, 1935, pp. 46-71.

Calvert, Peter, "The Diminishing Returns of Political Violence," *New Middle East*, Vol. 56, May 1973, p. 25.

_____, *Revolution*, New York: Praeger, 1970.

_____, *A Study of Revolution*, Oxford: Clarendon Press, 1970.

Campbell, J. S. and J. R. Sahid, *Law and Order Reconsidered*, Washington, D.C.: Government Printing Office, 1969.

Camus, Albert, *Neither Victims nor Executioners*, Chicago: World Without War, 1968.

Carlton, David and Carlo Schaerf, eds., *International Terrorism and World Security*, New York: Wiley, 1975.

Carr, E. H., *Studies in Revolution*, New York: Grosset & Dunlap, 1964.

Carr, Gordon, *The Angry Brigade, A History of Britain's First Urban Guerrilla Group*, London: Gollancz, 1975.

Carter, April, David Haggett and Adam Roberts, *Non-Violent Action: A Selected Bibliography*, London: Housmans, 1970.

Chailand, Gerard, *The Palestinian Resistance*, Baltimore: Penguin, 1972.

Chakhotin, S., *The Rape of the Masses*, New York: Haskell, 1971.
Chalmers, D. M., *Hooded Americanism*, New York: Quadrangle, 1968.
Chambard, Claude, *The Maquis: A History of the French Resistance Movement*, Indianapolis: Bobbs-Merrill, 1976.
Chappell, Duncan and John Monahan, eds., *Violence and Criminal Justice*, Lexington: Lexington Books; D. C. Heath, 1975.
Charles, Russell and Robert E. Hildner, "Urban Insurgency in Latin America: Its Implications for the Future," *Air University Review*, Vol. 22, September-October 1971, pp. 54-64.
Chase, L. J., ed., *Bomb Threats, Bombings and Civil Disturbances: A Guide for Facility Protection*, Corvallis, Oregon: Continuing Education Publications, 1971.
Chaturvedi, S. C., "Hijacking and the Law," *Indian Journal of International Law*, Vol. 11, 1971, pp. 89-105.
Chisholm, Henry J., *The Function of Terror and Violence in Revolution*, Thesis, Georgetown University, 1948.
Chorley, Katherine, *Armies and the Art of Revolution*, London: Faber & Faber, 1943.
Choucri, Nazli and Robert C. North, *Nations in Conflict*, San Francisco: W. H. Freeman, 1945.
Clark, Dennis, "Which Way the I.R.A.?" *Commonweal*, No. 13, 1973, pp. 294-97.
Clark, Lorne S., "The Struggle to Cure Hijacking," *International Perspectives*, January-February 1973 pp. 47-51.
Clark, Michael K., *Algeria in Turmoil*, New York: Praeger, 1959.
Clutterbuck, Richard, *Living with Terrorism*, London: Faber & Faber, 1975.
_____, *Protest and the Urban Guerrilla*, London: Abelard-Schuman, 1973.
Clyne, P., *Anatomy of Skyjacking*, London: Abelard-Schuman, 1973.
Coblentz, S. A., *The Militant Dissenters*, South Brunswick, N.J.: Barnes, 1970.
Cobo, Juan, "The Roots of 'Violencia,' " *New Times*, August 5, 1970, pp. 25-27.
Cohen, Geula, *Women of Violence: Memoirs of a Young Terrorist, 1943-1948*, London: Hart-Davis, 1966.
Cole, George F., *Politics and the Administration of Justice*, Beverly Hills, Calif.: Sage Publications, 1973.
Colebrook, Joan, "Israel with Terrorists," *Commentary*, Vol. 58, No. 1, July 1974, p. 30.

BIBLIOGRAPHY 327

Collier, Richard, *The Great Indian Mutiny*, New York: Dutton, 1964.

Collins, L., "Orgy of Killing: Algeria's European Secret Army Organization," *Newsweek*, Vol. 59, January 29, 1962, p. 42.

"Comment, Constitutional and Statutory Basis of Governors' Emergency Powers," *Michigan Law Review*, Vol. 64, 1965, p. 1290.

Conant, R., *The Prospects for Revolution: A Study of Riots, Civil Disobedience and Insurrection in Contemporary America*, New York: Harper's Magazine Press, 1971.

Conquest, Robert, *The Great Terror*, New York: Macmillan, 1968.

_____, *The Soviet Police System*, New York: Praeger, 1968.

"The Convention for the Prevention and Punishment of Terrorism," *British Yearbook of International Law*, Vol. 19, 1938, p. 214.

Convention to Prevent and Punish the Acts of Terrorism Taking the Form of Crimes against Persons and Related Extortions That Are of International Significance, *Serie Sobre Tratados*, Vol. 37, Washington, D.C.: Pan American Union, February 2, 1971.

Coogan, Tim Patrick, *The I. R. A.* New York: Praeger, 1970.

Cooley, John K., "China and the Palestinians," *Journal of Palestinian Studies*, Vol. 1, No. 2, 1972, pp. 19-34.

_____, "Moscow Faces a Palestinian Dilemma," *Mid East*, Vol. 11, No. 3, 1970, pp. 32-35.

Cooper, H. H. A., "Terrorism and the Intelligence Function," *Chitty's Law Journal*, Vol. 73, March 1976, p. 24.

_____, "The Terrorist and His Victims," *Victimology*, Vol. 1, No. 2, June 1976.

Cosyns-Verhaegen, R., *Actualite du Terrorisme: Selection Bibliographique (Present Day Terrorism: Bibliographical Selection)*, Wavre, Belgium: Centre D'Information et de Documentation de la L. I. L., 1973.

Craig, Alexander, "Urban Guerrillas in Latin America," *Survey*, Vol. 17, No. 3, 1971, pp. 112-28.

Cranston, Maurice, "Sartre and Violence," *Encounter*, July 1967.

Crime and Justice in America, 1967-1968, Washington, D.C.: Congressional Quarterly, 1968.

Critchley, T. A., *Conquest of Violence: Order and Liberty in Britain*, New York: Schoken Books, 1970.

Crosby, John, *An Affair of Strangers*, New York: Stein & Day, 1975.

Cross, Colin, *The Fall of the Empire*, New York: Coward-McCann, 1969.

Cross, James Eliot, *Conflict in the Shadows*, New York: Doubleday, 1963.

Crotty, William J., *Assassination and the Political Order*, New York: Harper & Row, 1971.

Crozier, Brian, "Anatomy of Terrorism," *Nation*, Vol. 188, 1959, pp. 250-52.

_____, *Annual of Power and Conflict, 1973-1974: A Survey of Political Violence and International Influence*, London: Institute for the Study of Conflict, 1974.

_____, *Annual of Power and Conflict, 1974-1975: A Survey of Political Violence and International Influence*, London: Institute for the Study of Conflict, 1975.

_____, *The Rebels: A Study of Post-War Insurrections*, London: Chatto & Windus, 1960.

_____, *South-East Asia in Turmoil*, Baltimore: Penguin, 1965.

_____, "Transnational Terrorism," *Annual of Power and Conflict*, Vol. 1972-1973, 1973.

_____, *Study of Conflict*, London: Institute for the Study of Conflict, 1974.

_____, *Ulster: Politics and Terrorism*, London: Institute for the Study of Conflict, 1973.

"Curbing Terrorism," *Christian Science Monitor*, January 16, 1976, p. 32.

Curtis, Lynn A., *Violence, Race and Culture*, Lexington, Mass.: Lexington Books, 1975.

Curtis, Michael et al, eds., *The Palestinians: People, History, Politics*, Edison, N. J.: Transaction Books, 1975.

Da Cunha, Euelides, *Rebellion in the Backlands*, Chicago: University of Chicago Press, 1944.

Dadrian, V., "Factors of Anger and Aggression in Genocide," *Journal of Human Relations*, Vol. 19, 1971, pp. 394-417.

Daigon, Arthur, *Violence — U.S.A.*, New York: Bantam, 1975.

Dallin, Alexander and George W. Breslauer, *Political Terror in Communist Systems*, Stanford: Stanford University Press, 1970.

Dasgupta, S., "Violence: Development and Tensions," *International Journal of Group Tensions*, Vol. 1, 1971, pp. 114-129.

Davies, Donald M., "Terrorism: Motives and Means," *Foreign Service Journal*, September 1962, p. 14.

Davies, James C., "The Circumstances and Causes of Revolution: A Review," *Journal of Conflict Resolution*, June 1967, p. 11.

_____, "Toward a Theory of Revolution," *American Sociological Review*, Vol. 27, 1962, pp. 5-14.

_____, ed. *When Men Revolt and Why*, New York: Free Press, 1971.

Davis, Angela, *An Autobiography*, New York: Random House, 1974.

Davis, Jack, *Political Violence in Latin America*, London: International Institute for Strategic Studies, 1972.

Davis, M., *Jews Fight Too!*, New York: Jordan, 1945.

Davison, W. Phillips, *International Political Communication*, New York: Praeger, 1965.

_____, "Some Observations on Viet Cong Operations in the Villages," *Rand Abstracts*, RM 5367, September 1968, p. 2.

Deakin, T. J., "Legacy of Carlos Marighella," *F.B.I. Law Enforcement Bulletin*, Vol. 43, No. 10, October 1974, pp. 19-25.

"Death Comes in Small Parcels," *Economist*, December 1971, p. 56.

"Death Penalty for Terrorists?" *Christian Century*, Vol. 9, March 21, 1973, p. 333.

Debray, R., *L'Indesirable*, Parks: Le Seuil, 1975.

Debray, R., *Revolution on the Revolution*, New York: Monthly Review Press, 1967.

de Gramont, Sanche, "Moslem Terrorists in a New Job," *New York Herald Tribune*, July 9, 1962, pp. 1-2.

De Grazia, Sebastian and Livio C. Stecchini, *The Coup d'etat: Past Significance and Modern Technique*, China Lake, Calif.: U. S. Ordinance Test Station, 1965.

Dekel, Ephraim (Krasner), *Shai: Historical Exploits of Haganah Intelligence*, New York: Yoseloff, 1959.

Delaume, G. R., "Jurisdiction over Crimes Committed Abroad: French and American Law," *George Washington Law Review*, Vol. 21, 1952, p. 173.

De Mott, Benjamin, "Seven Days in May: The Teacher in Apocalypse," *Change*, Vol. 2, 1971, p. 55.

Denaro, J. M., "In-flight Crimes, the Tokyo Convention and Federal Judicial Jurisdiction," *Journal of Air Law and Commerce*, Vol. 35, 1969, pp. 171-203.

Derber, M., "Terrorism and the Movement," *Monthly Review*, Vol. 22, February 1971, p. 36.

Dershowitz, Alan M., "Terrorism and Preventive Detention: The Case of Israel," *A Commentary Report*, 1970, pp. 3-14.

Des Pres, Terrence, *An Anatomy of Life in the Death Camps*, New York: Oxford University Press, 1976.

Dewitt, Howard A., *Images of Ethnic and Radical Violence in California Politics, 1917-1930: A Survey*, San Francisco: R. and E. Research Associates, 1975.

De Wolf, L. Harold, *Crime and Justice in America: A Paradox of Conscience*, New York: Harper & Row, 1975.

Dies, M., *Martin Dies' Story*, New York: Bookmailer, 1963.

Dillon, Martin and Denis Lehane, *Political Murder in Northern Ireland*, Baltimore: Penguin, 1974.

Dinstein, Yoram, "Criminal Jurisdiction over Aircraft Hijacking," *Israel Law Review*, Vol. 7, 1972, pp. 195-206.

_____, "Terrorism and Wars of Liberation Applied to the Arab-Israeli Conflict: An Israeli Perspective," *Israel Yearbook on Human Rights*, Vol. 3, 1973, p. 78.

Dionisopoulog, P. A., *Rebellion, Racism and Representation*, DeKalb: Northern Illinois University Press, 1970.

"Dir Yassin," *West Asia Affairs*, Summer 1969, pp. 27-30.

Dishon, Daniel, ed., *Middle East Record*, Vol. 4, 1968, Tel Aviv: Israel Universities Press, 1973.

Dixon, C. A. and D. Heilbrunn, *Communist Guerrilla Warfare*, New York: Praeger, 1954.

Dobson, Christopher, *Black September: Its Short, Violent History*, New York: Macmillan, 1974.

"Document on Terror," *News from behind the Iron Curtain*, Vol. 1, 1952, pp. 44-57.

Domestic Terrorist Matters, Washington, D.C.: F.B.I., 1974.

Donnedieu de Vabres, H., "La répression internationale du terrorisme; les conventions de Genève," *Revue de droit international et de législation comparée*, Vol. 19, 1938, pp. 37-74

Dortzbach, Karl and Debbie, *Kidnapped*, New York: Harper & Row, 1975.

Douglas, William O., *Points of Rebellion*, New York: Vintage, 1970.

Downton, J. V., *Rebel Leadership*, New York: Free Press, 1973.

"Draft Convention for the Prevention and Punishment of Certain Acts of International Terrorism," *Department of State Bulletin*, Vol. 67, October 16, 1972, p. 431.

Draper, Theodore, *Castro's Revolution: Myths and Realities*, New York: Praeger, 1962.

_____, "The Ethical and Juridical Status of Constraints in War," *Military Law Review*, Vol. 55, 1972, p. 169.

Drapkin, Israel and Emilio Viano, eds., *Victimology: A New Focus:* Pt. 2: "Mass Violence and Genocide." Lexington, Mass.: Lexington Books; D. C. Heath, 1975.

Dror, Yehezkel, *Crazy States: A Counterconventional Strategic Problem*, Tel Aviv: Department of Defense, 1973.

Dubois, Jules, *Fidel Castro*, Indianapolis: Bobbs-Merrill, 1959.

Duchene, F., *Civil Violence and the International System: Part One*, London: Institute for Strategic Studies, 1971.

Duff, Ernest A. and John F. McCamant, *Violence and Repression in Latin America: A Quantitative and Historical Analysis*, New York: Macmillan, 1976.

Dugard, John, "International Terrorism," *International Affairs*, Vol. 50, No. 1, 1974, pp. 67-81.

_____, "Towards the Definition of International Terrorism," *American Journal of International Law*, Vol. 67, No. 5, 1973, pp. 94-100.

Duncan, Patrick, *South Africa's Rule of Violence*, London: Methuen, 1964.

Eave, L., "Political Terrorism: Hysteria on the Left," *New York Times Magazine*, April 12, 1970, pp. 25-27.

Eayrs, James, *Diplomacy and Its Discontents*, Toronto: University of Toronto Press, 1971.

Eckstein, Harry, ed., *Internal War*, New York: Free Press, 1964.

Edwardes, Michael, *Red Year: The Indian Rebellion of 1857*, London: Hamish Hamilton, 1973.

Edwards, Lyford P., *The Natural History of Revolution*, New York: Free Press, 1963.

Efforts Continue to Check Arab Terrorism, Washington, D.C.: Embassy of Israel, 1973.

Efrat, Edgar S., ed., *Introduction to Sub-Saharan Africa*, Lexington/Toronto: Xerox College Publishing, 1973.

Eggers, William, *Terrorism: The Slaughter of Innocents*, Chatsworth, Calif.: Major Books, 1975.

Einaudi, Luigi R., ed., *Beyond Cuba: Latin America Takes Charge of Its Future*, New York: Crane, Russak, 1974.

Elliff, John T., *Crime, Dissent and the Attorney General*, Beverly Hills, Calif.: Sage Publications, 1971.

Ellis, Albert and John Gullo, *Murder and Assassination*, New York: Stuart Lyle, 1971.

Ellul, Jacques, *Violence: Reflections from a Christian Perspective*, translation by Cecilia Gaul, New York: Seabury, 1969.

El-Rayyes, Riad N. and Dunia Nahas, eds., *Guerrillas for Palestine: A Study of the Palestinian Commando Organization*, Beirut: An-Nahar Press Services, 1974.

Emerson, Rupert, *From Empire to Nation: The Rise to Self-Assertion of Asian and African People*, Cambridge, Mass.: Harvard University Press, 1960.

Endleman, Shalom, *Violence in the Streets*, New York: Quadrangle, 1968.

Engdahl, David E., "Soldiers, Riots and Revolution: The Law

and History of Military Troops in Civil Disorders," *Iowa Law Review*, Vol. 57, 1971, p. 1.

Epstein, D. G., "Combating Campus Terrorism," *Police Chief*, Vol. 38, No. 1, January 1971, pp. 46-47, 49.

Erskine, Hazel, "Fear of Violence and Crime," *Public Opinion Quarterly*, Vol. 38, 1974, p. 131.

Esson, D.M.R., "The Secret Weapon — Terrorism," *Army Quarterly*, Vol. 78, 1959, p. 167.

Eustathiades, C., La Cour pénale internationale pour la répression du terrorisme et le problème de la responsabilité internationale des états, *Revue Générale de droit international public*, Vol. 43, 1936, pp. 385-415.

Evans, Alona E., "Aircraft Hijacking: Its Cause and Cure," *American Journal of International Law*, Vol. 63, 1969, pp. 695-710.

_____, "Aircraft Hijacking: What Is Being Done," *American Journal of International Law*, Vol. 67 October 1973, pp. 641-671.

_____, "Aircraft Hijacking: What Is to Be Done?" *American Journal of International Law*, Vol. 66, 1972, pp. 819-22.

_____, "Jurisdiction — Fugitive Offender — Forcible Abduction — Ker-Frisbie Rule — Treaties — Extradition," *American Journal of International Law*, Vol. 69, 1975, p. 406.

_____, "A Proposed Method of Control," *Journal of Air Law and Commerce*, Vol. 37, 1971, pp. 171-81.

_____, "Reflections upon the Political Offenses in International Practice," *American Journal of International Law*, Vol. 57, 1963, p. 1.

Fairbairn, G., *Revolutionary Guerilla Warfare — The Countryside Version*, Middlesex, England: Penguin, 1974.

Faleroni, Alberto S., "What is an Urban Guerrilla?" *Military Review*, Vol. 47, 1969, p. 94.

Falk, Richard A., "Terror, Liberation Movements, and the Processes of Social Change," *American Journal of International Law*, Vol. 63, 1969, pp. 423-27.

Fallaci, Oriana, "A Leader of Fedayeen: 'We Want a War Like the Vietnam War': Interview with George Habash," *Life*, June 12, 1970, pp. 32-34.

Fanon, Franz, *Towards the African Revolution: Political Essays*, Translation by Haakon Chevalier, New York: Grove, 1967.

_____, *The Wretched of the Earth*, New York: Grove, 1968.

Fawcett, J. E. S., "Kidnappings Versus Government Protection," 1970, pp. 359-62.

Fearey, Robert A., International Terrorism, *Department of State Bulletin*, Vol. 74 March 29, 1976, pp. 394-403.

Feierabend, Ivo, R. L. Feierabend, and T. R. Gurr, eds., *Anger, Violence, and Politics: Theories and Research*, Englewood Cliffs, N.J.: Prentice-Hall, 1972.

Feller, S. Z., "Comment on Criminal Jurisdiction over Aircraft Hijacking," *Israel Law Review*, Vol. 7, 1972, pp. 207-14.

Felt, Edward, *Urban Revolt in South Africa, 1960-1964: A Case Study*, Evanston, Ill.: Northwestern University Press, 1971.

Fenello, Michael J., "Technical Prevention of Air Piracy," *International Conciliation*, No. 585, 1971, pp. 28-41.

Fenwick, C. G., " 'Piracy' in the Caribbean," *American Journal of International Law*, Vol. 55, 1961, pp. 426-28.

Feraoun, Mouloud, *Journal 1955-1962*, Paris: Seuil, 1962.

Ferguson, J. Halcro, *The Revolutions of Latin America*, London: Thames & Hudson, 1963.

Ferreira, J. C., *Carlos Marighella*, Havana: Tricontinental, 1970.

Firestone, Joseph M., "Continuities in the Theory of Violence," *Journal of Conflict Resolution*, Vol. 18, 1974, p. 117.

Fitzgerald, Charles P., *Revolution in China*, New York: Praeger, 1952.

Fitzgerald, G. F., "Development of International Rules Concerning Offences and Certain Other Acts Committed on Board Aircraft," *Canadian Yearbook of International Law*, Vol. 1, 1963, pp. 230-51.

_____, "Offences and Certain Other Acts Committed on Board Aircraft: The Tokyo Convention of 1963," *Canadian Yearbook of International Law*, Vol. 2, 1964, pp. 191-204.

_____, "Toward Legal Suppression of Acts against Civil Aviation," *International Conciliation*, No. 585, 1971, pp. 42-78.

Fitzgibbon, Russell H., "Revolution in Latin America: A Tentative Prognosis, *Virginia Quarterly Review*, Spring 1963, p. 39.

Flacks, R., "The Liberated Generation: A Exploration of the Roots of Student Protest," *Journal of Social Issues*, Vol. 23, 1967, p. 52.

Fogelson, Robert M., *Violence as Protest: A Study of Riots and Ghettos*, Garden City, N.Y.: Doubleday, 1971.

Forman, J., *The Making of Black Revolutionaries*, New York: Macmillan, 1972.

Fortas, Abe, *Concerning Dissent and Civil Disobedience*, New York: The New American Library, 1968.

Franck, Thomas M. and Bert B. Lockwood, "Preliminary

Thoughts towards an International Convention on Terrorism," *American Journal of International Law*, Vol. 68, 1974, p. 4.

Franjeck, S., "How Revolutionary Is the Palestinian Resistance: A Marxist Interpretation," *Journal of Palestine Studies*, Vol. 1, No. 2, 1972, pp. 52-60.

Frank, Gerold, *The Deed*, New York: Simon & Schuster, 1963.

_____, "The Moyne Case: A Tragic History," *Commentary*, December 1945, pp. 64-71.

Franklin, W. M., *Protection of Foreign Interests*, New York: Greenwood, 1969.

Freedman, Robert Owen, *Soviet Policy toward the Middle East since Nasser*, New York: Praeger, 1975.

Freeman, Thomas [Pseud.], *The Crisis in Cuba*, Derby, Conn.: Monarch Books, 1963.

Friedlander, R. A., "Terrorism," *Barrister*, Vol. 2, Summer 1975, p. 10.

Friedman, W., "Some Impacts of Social Organization on International Law," *American Journal of International Law*, Vol. 50, 1956, pp. 475-513.

Friedmann, W., "Terrorist and Subversive Activities," *American Journal of International Law*, Vol. 50, 1956, p. 475.

Friedrich, Carl, ed., *Revolution*, New York: Atherton, 1966.

_____, "Uses of Terror," *Problems of Communism*, Vol. 19, November 1970, p. 46.

Fromkin, David, "Strategy of Terrorism," *Foreign Affairs*, Vol. 53, 1975, p. 683.

Fromm, Erich, *The Anatomy of Human Destructiveness*, New York: Rinehart & Winston, 1973.

Gablonski, Edward, *Terror from the Sky: Airwar*, Garden City, N.Y.: Doubleday, 1971.

Galula, David, *Counterinsurgency Warfare: Theory and Practice*, New York: Praeger, 1964.

Galyean, T. E., "Acts of Terrorism and Combat by Irregular Forces: An Insurance 'War Risk,'" *California Western International Law Journal*, Vol. 4, 1974, p. 314.

Gann, L. H., *Guerrillas in History*, Stanford: Hoover Institute, 1971.

Garcia-Mora, Manuel R., "Crimes against Humanity and the Principle of Nonextradition of Political Offenders," *Michigan Law Review*, Vol. 62, 1964, p. 927.

_____, "The Crimes against Peace," *Fordham Law Review*, Vol. 34, 1965, p. 1.

_____, "Criminal Jurisdiction over Foreigners for Treason and Offenses against the Safety of the State Committed upon

Foreign Territory," *University of Pittsburgh Law Review*, Vol. 19, 1958, p. 567.

_____, *International Law and Asylum As a Human Right*, Washington, D.C.: Public Affairs Press, 1956.

_____, *International Responsibility for Hostile Acts of Private Persons against Foreign States*, The Hague: Martinus Nijhoff, 1962.

_____, "The Nature of Political Offenses: A Knotty Problem of Extradition Law," *Virginia Law Review*, Vol. 48, 1962, p. 122.

_____, "Present Status of Political Offenses in the Law of Extradition and Asylum," *University of Pittsburgh Law Review*, Vol. 14, 1953, p. 371.

Garson, G. David, "Force vs. Restraint in Prison Riots," *Crime and Delinquency*, Vol. 18, 1972, p. 411.

Gaucher, Roland, *The Terrorists: From Tsarist Russia to the O.A.S.*, translation by P. Spurlin, London: Secker & Warburg, 1968.

Gellner, J., *Bayonets in the Streets: Urban Guerrilla at Home and Abroad*, Ontario: Collier-Macmillan Canada, 1974.

Gerassi, F., ed., *Venceremos!* New York: Simon & Schuster, 1968.

Gerassi, Marysa N., "Uruguay's Urban Guerrillas," *Nation*, Vol. 209, No. 10, 1969, pp. 306-10.

Gervasi, Frank, "Terror in Palestine," *Collier's*, August 11, 1945, pp. 64-65.

Geschwender, James A., "Explorations in the Theory of Social Movements and Revolutions," *Social Forces*, December 1968, p. 67.

"Getting away with Murder," *Economist*, November 4, 1972, pp. 15-16.

Giap, Vo-nguyen, *People's War, People's Army: The Viet-Cong Insurrection Manual for Underdeveloped Countries*, New York: Praeger, 1962.

_____, *The South Vietnam People Will Win*, Hanoi: Foreign Languages Publishing House, 1966.

Gilio, M. E., *The Tupamaro Guerrillas*, New York: Ballantine, 1970.

_____, *The Tupamaro Guerrillas*, translation by Anne Edmondston and with an Introduction by Robert J. Alexander, New York: Saturday Review Press, 1972.

_____, *The Tupamaros*, London: Secker & Warburg, 1972.

"The Girl Who Almost Killed Ford," *Time*, September 15, 1975, p. 8.

Gitlin, Jan, *The Conquest of Acre Fortress*, Tel-Aviv: Hardar, 1962.

Gittings, John, *The Role of the Chinese Army*, London: Oxford University Press, 1967.

Glaser, S., "Terrorisme International et ses Divers Aspects," *Revue Internationale de Droit Compare*, Vol. 25, 1973, p. 825.

Glubb, John Bagot, *A Soldier with the Arabs*, London: Hadder & Stoughton, 1957.

Goldberg, Yona, *Haganah or Terror*, New York: Hechalutz, 1947.

Goldenberg, Boris, *The Cuban Revolution and Latin America*, New York: Praeger, 1965.

Goldstein, Jeffrey H., *Aggression and Crimes of Violence*, London: Oxford University Press, 1975.

Goodsell, James N., "Terrorism in Latin America," *Commentator*, March 1966, pp. 9-11.

Gonzalez, Lapeyre E., *Aspectos Juridicas del Terrorismo*, Montivideo: Fernandez, 1972.

Gott Richard, *Guerrilla Movements in Latin America*, London: Thomas Nelson, 1970.

_____, "Latin American Guerrillas," *Listener*, Vol. 84, 1970, pp. 437-40.

Graham, Hugh S. et al, eds., *Violence: The Crisis of American Confidence*, Baltimore: Johns Hopkins University Press, 1972.

Graham, Hugh D. and Ted R. Gurr, eds., *Violence in America: Historical and Comparative Perspectives*, Washington, D.C.: National Commission of the Causes and Prevention of Violence, 1969.

Great Britain, Committee of Privy Counsellors Appointed to Consider Authorized Procedures for the Interrogation of Persons Suspected of Terrorism, *Report*, London: H. M. Stat. Off., 1972.

"Greece Takes Tougher Stance Following Airport Terrorism," *Aviation Week*, Vol. 99, August 13, 1973, p. 26.

Green, G. *The Hostage Heart*, Chicago: Playboy Press, 1976.

_____, *Terrorism: Is It Revolutionary?* New York: Outlook Publications, 1970.

Green, L. C., "International Law and the Suppression of Terrorism," edited by G. W. Bartholomew, *Malaya Law Review Legal Essays*, 1975.

_____, *The Nature and Control of International Terrorism*, Atlanta: University of Atlanta Department of Political Science, 1974.

Greene, T. N., ed., *The Guerrilla: And How to Fight Him*, New

York: Praeger, 1962.

Greer, Herb, "Grim Argument," *Encounter*, Vol. 46, No. 4, 1976, p. 50.

Griffith, Samuel B., II, *The Chinese People's Liberation Army*, New York: McGraw-Hill, 1967.

Grimshaw, Allen, "Changing Patterns of Racial Violence in the United States," *Notre Dame Lawyer*, Vol. 40, 1965, p. 534.

_____, *Racial Violence in the United States*, Chicago: Aldine, 1970.

Grivas, G., *Guerrilla Warfare and E.O.K.A.'s Struggle*, London: Longman's, 1964.

Grodsky, M., "Protection of Dignitaries," *International Police Academy Review*, Vol. 6, No. 4, October 4, 1972, pp. 1-6.

Gross, Leo, "International Terrorism and International Criminal Jurisdiction," *American Journal of International Law*, Vol. 67, July 1973, pp. 508-511.

Grundy, Kenneth W., *Guerrilla Struggle in Africa: An Analysis and Preview*, New York: Grossman, 1971.

"Guerilla Warfare," *Encyclopedia Britannica*, Vol. 8, 1974, p. 459.

Guevara, Ché Ernesto, *Reminiscences of the Cuban Revolutionary War*, translation by V. Ortiz, New York: Monthly Review Press, 1968.

_____, *Ché Guevara on Guerrilla Warfare*, translation by Harries-Clichy Peterson, New York: Praeger, 1961.

_____, *Guerrilla Warfare*, New York: Random, 1961.

_____, *Obra Revolucionaria*, 4th ed., Mexico: Ediciones Era, 1971.

Guillén, Abraham, *Philosophy of the Urban Guerrilla*, translation by D. C. Hodges, New York: Morrow, 1973.

Guiness, Os, *Violence — Crisis or Catharsis?* Rev. ed., Downers Grove, Ill.: Inter-Varsity, 1974.

Gunn, John Charles, *Violence*, New York: Praeger, 1973.

Gurion, Itzhak, *Triumph on the Gallows*, New York: Brit Trmpeldor of America, 1950.

Gurr, Ted Robert, "A Causal Model of Civil Strife: A Comparative Analysis Using New Indices," *American Political Science Review*, Vol. 62, 1968, p. 1104.

_____, *New Error-Compensated Measures for Comparing Nations: Some Correlates of Civil Violence*, Princeton, N.J.: Center of International Studies, 1970.

_____, "Psychological Factors in Civil Violence," *World Politics*, January 1968, p. 20.

_____, *Why Men Rebel*, Princeton: Princeton University Press, 1970.

Gurr, Ted and Charles R. Ruttenberg, *The Conditions of Civil Violence: First Tests of a Causal Model*, Princeton, N.J.: Center of International Studies, 1970.

Guzmán, Campos et al., *La Violencia en Colombia*, Bogotá: Ediciones Tercer Mundo, 1963.

Haas, Ernest, et al, *Conflict Management by International Organizations*, Morristown, N.J.: General Learning Press, 1972.

Hacker, Frederick, *Terror and Terrorism*, New York: Norton, 1976.

Hackey, Thomas, ed., *The Problem of Partition: Peril to World Peace*, New York: Rand McNally, 1972.

_____, *Voices of Revolution: Rebels and Rhetoric*, Dryden Press, 1973.

Hakman, Nathan, "Political Trials in the Legal Order: A Political Science Prospect," *Journal of Public Law*, Vol. 21, No. 1, 1972 pp. 73-127.

Halperin, Ernst, *Terrorism in Latin America*, Beverly Hills, Calif.: Sage Publications, 1976.

Hamer, John, "Protection of Diplomats," *Editorial Research Reports*, VII, October 3, 1973, pp. 759-776.

Hannay, William A., "International Terrorism: The Need for a Fresh Perspective," *International Lawyer*, Vol. 8, No. 2, 1974, pp. 268-84.

Hansen, Emmanuel, *Frantz Fanon: Social and Political Thought*, Columbus: Ohio State University Press, 1976.

Harkabi, Yehoshafat, *The Arabs' Position in Their Conflict with Israel*, Jerusalem: Israel Universities Press, 1972.

Harris, John, *The Indian Mutiny*, London: Hart-Davis MacGibbon, 1973.

Harris, Thomas, *Black Sunday*, New York: Putnam, 1975.

Hartley, Norman, *The Viking Process*, New York: Simon & Schuster, 1975.

Hastings, Adrian, *Wiriyamu*, London: Search Press, 1974.

Hayden, Tom, *Rebellion in Newark*, New York: Random House, 1967.

Haykal, Muhammed Hasanayn, *The Road to Ramadan*, New York: Quadrangle, 1975.

Healy, R. J., *Design for Security*, New York: Wiley, 1968.

Heaps, W. A., *Riots, U.S.A., 1765-1965*, New York: Seabury, 1970.

Heilbrunn, Otto, *Partisan Warfare*, New York: Praeger, 1962.

Hempstone, I., *Rebels, Mercenaries, and Dividends: The Katanga Story*, New York: Praeger, 1962.

Hermann, W. W., *Riot Prevention and Control — Operations Research Response*, Springfield, Va.: National Technical Information Service, 1968.

Hewitt, Warren E., "Respect for Human Rights in Armed Conflicts," *New York University Journal of International Law and Politics*, Vol. 4, 1971, p. 41.

Hibbs, Douglas A., *Mass Political Violence: A Cross-national Causal Analysis*, New York: Wiley, 1973.

Higham, R., ed., *Bayonets in the Streets; The Use of Troops in Civil Disturbances*, Lawrence: University of Kansas Press, 1969.

Hillquist, Morris, *Loose Leaves from a Busy Life*, New York: Macmillan, 1934.

Hilsman, Roger, "Internal War: The New Communist Tactic," *Military Review*, Vol. 42, April 1962, p. 11.

Hirano, R., "Convention on Offences and Certain Other Acts Committed on Board Aircraft of 1963," *Japanese Annual of International Law*, No. 8, 1964, pp. 44-52.

Hirsch, Arthur I. and David Otis, "Aircraft Piracy and Extradition," *New York Law Forum*, Vol. 16, 1970, pp. 392-419.

Hobsbawm, Eric J., "Pentagon's Dilemma: Goliath and the Guerrilla," *Nation*, July 10, 1975, pp. 20-21.

——————, *Primitive Rebels*, Manchester: Manchester University Press, 1959.

Hodges, Donald Clark, *National Liberation Fronts: 1960-1970*, New York: Morrow, 1972.

——————, *Philosophy of the Urban Guerrilla*, New York: Morrow, 1973.

Hoffacker, Lewis, "The U.S. Government Response to Terrorism: A Global Approach," *Department of State Bulletin*, Vol. 70 March 18, 1974, pp. 274-278.

Hofstadter, Richard and Michael Wallace, eds., *American Violence: A Documentary History*, New York: Knopf, 1970.

Hopper, Rex D., "The Revolutionary Process: A Frame of Reference for the Study of Revolutionary Movements," *Social Forces*, March 1950, p. 28.

Horlick, Gary N., "The Developing Law of Air Hijacking," *Harvard International Law Journal*, Vol. 12, 1971, pp. 33-70.

Horn, Carl von, *Soldiering for Peace*, New York: McKay, 1967.

Horn, F. Stanley, *Invisible Empire: The Story of the Ku Klux Klan, 1866-1871*, Boston: Houghton Mifflin, 1939.

Horowitz, Irving L., "Political Terrorism and State Power," *Journal of Political and Military Sociology*, Vol. 1, Spring 1973, p. 147.

_____, *The Struggle Is the Message: The Organization and Ideology of the Anti-War Movement*, Berkeley: Glendessary Press, 1970.

Horowitz, Irving L., ed., *The Anarchists*, New York: Dell Publishing, 1964.

Horowitz, J., de Castro and Gerassi, eds., *Latin American Radicalism*, New York: Vintage, 1969.

Horrell, Muriel, *Terrorism in South Africa*, Johannesburg: South African Institute of Race Relations, 1968.

Hosmer, Stephen T., *Viet Cong Repression and Its Implications for the Future*, Lexington: Heath Lexington Books, 1970.

Hostage-Taking: Problems of Prevention and Control, Montreal: International Centre for Comparative Criminology, October 1976.

Howard, A. J., "Urban Guerrilla Warfare in a Democratic Society," *Medicine Science and the Law*, Vol. 12, No. 4, October 1972, pp. 231-243.

Howard, Bruce, "Living with Terrorism," Washington *Post*, July 18, 1976, pp. C1, C4.

Howe, Irving, "Political Terrorism: Hysteria on the Left," New York *Times Magazine*, April 12, 1970, pp. 25-27.

Howe, Irving and Carl Gershman, *Israel, the Arabs and the Middle East*, New York: Quadrangle, 1972.

"How Israelis Started the Terror by Post," London: *The Sunday Times*, September 24, 1962, pp. 3-11.

Hruska, Roman L., "Aircraft Piracy Amendments of 1972 Remarks in the Senate," *Congressional Record*, daily ed. Vol. 119, February 15, 1973, pp. S1183-A1186.

Hubbard, D. G., "Bringing Skyjackers down to Earth: Views of a Psychiatrist," *Time*, October 4, 1971, pp. 64-65.

Huberman, Leo and Paul M. Sweezy, *Cuba: Anatomy of a Revolution*, 2nd ed., New York: Monthly Review Press, 1960.

Huberman, L., and P. M. Sweezy, eds., *Regis Debray and the Latin American Revolution*, New York: Monthly Review 1968.

Huddleston, Sidney, *France: The Tragic Years*, Belmont, Mass. Western Islands, 1965.

Hudson, Michael C., "The Palestinian Arab Resistance Movement Its Significance in the Middle East Crisis," *Middle East Journal*, Vol. 23, 1969, pp. 291-301.

_____, "The Proposed International Criminal Court," *American Journal of International Law*, Vol. 32, 1938, pp. 549-54.

Hugh, Davis Graham and Ted Robert Gurr, eds., *Violence in*

America: Historical and Comparative Perspectives, New York: Bantam, 1970.

Huntington, I. P., *Civil Violence and the International System: Part Two.* London: Institute for Strategic Studies, 1971.

Hurewitz, Jacob C., *The Struggle for Palestine*, New York: Greenwood, 1968.

Hussain, Mehmood, *The Palestine Liberation Organization: A Study in Ideology and Tactics*, New York: International Publications Service, 1975.

Hutchinson, Martha Crenshaw, "The Concept of Revolutionary Terrorism," *Journal of Conflict Resolution*, Vol. 16, No. 3, 1972, pp. 383-95.

Hyams, Edward, *Terrorists and Terrorism*, New York: St. Martin's, 1974.

Hyde, Douglas Arnold, *The Roots of Guerrilla Warfare*, Chester Springs, Pa.: Dufour Editions, 1968.

The I.C.A.O. and Arab Terrorist Operations: A Record of Resolutions, Jerusalem: Ministry for Foreign Affairs, 1973.

Iglitzin, Lynne, *Violent Conflict in American Society*, New York: Chandler Publishers, 1972.

Inter-American Judicial Committee, "Draft Protocol on Terrorism," *International Legal Materials*, Vol. 9, 1970, p. 1177.

International Association of Chiefs of Police, *Civil Disorders — After-Action Reports*, Washington, D.C.: N.C.J.R.S. Microfiche Program, 1968.

"Is America by Nature a Violent Society?" New York *Times Magazine*, April 28, 1969, pp. 24, 25.

Jabber, F., "The Arab Regimes and the Palestinian Revolution, 1967-71." *Journal of Palestinian Studies*, Vol. 2, No. 2, 1973, pp. 79-101.

Jack, H. A., "Terrorism: Another U.N. Failure," *America*, October 20, 1973, pp. 282-85.

Jackson, Sir Geoffrey, *Surviving the Long Nights: An Autobiographical Account of a Political Kidnapping*, New York: Vanguard, 1974.

Jacobs, P., *Prelude to Riot*, New York: Random House, 1968.

Jacobson, Peter M., "From Piracy on the High Seas to Piracy in the High Skies: A Study of Aircraft Hijacking," *Cornell International Law Journal*, Vol. 5, 1972, pp. 161-87.

Janowitz, Morris, *Social Control of Escalated Riots*, Chicago: University of Chicago Center for Public Study, 1968.

"Japan's United Red Army," *Newsweek*, Vol. 79, June 12, 1972, p. 59.

Jaszi, O. and J. D. Lewis, *Against the Tyrant: The Tradition and*

Theory of Tyrannicide, Glencoe, Ill.: Free Press, 1957.

Jay, M., "Politics of Terror," *Partisan Review*, Vol. 38, 1971, p. 72.

Jeffries, Charles, *Transfer of Power: Problems of the Passage to Self-Government*, London: Pall Mall, 1960.

Jenkins, Brian Michael, *The Five Stages of Urban Guerrilla Warfare*, Santa Monica, Calif.: Rand, 1971.

_____, "International Terrorism: A Balance Sheet," *Survival*, Vol. 17, July-August 1975, pp. 158-164.

_____, *International Terrorism: A New Mode of Conflict*, Los Angeles: Crescent Publications, 1975.

_____, *Soldiers Versus Gunmen: The Challenge of Urban Guerrilla Warfare*, Santa Monica, Calif.: Rand, 1974.

_____, *Terrorism Works — Sometimes*, Santa Monica: Rand, April 1974.

_____, "Urban Violence in Africa," *American Behavioral Scientist*, Vol. 2, No. 4, 1968, p. 37.

Jenkins, B. M. and J. Johnson, *International Terrorism: A Chronology, 1968-1974*, Santa Monica, Calif.: Rand Corporation, 1975.

Johnson, Chalmers A., *Revolutionary Change*, Boston: Little, Brown, 1966.

Johnson, John J., *The Military and Society in Latin America*, Stanford: Stanford University Press, 1964.

Johnson, K. F., "Guatemala— from Terrorism to Terror,' *Conflict Studies*, No. 23, May 1972, pp. 4-17.

_____, "On the Guatemalan Political Violence," *Politics and Society*, Vol. 4, Fall 1973, p. 55.

Johnson, P., "Age of Terror," *New Statesman*, Vol. 88, 1974 p. 763.

_____, "The Resources of Civilisation," *New Statesman*, October 31, 1975, p. 531.

_____, "Wrath of the Righteous," *New Statesman*, Vol. 87 June 1974, p. 871.

Joll, James, *The Anarchists*, New York: Grossett & Dunlap 1964.

Joyner, Nancy D., *Aerial Hijacking as an International Crime* Dobbs Ferry, New York: Oceana, 1974.

Judicial Conference of the District of Columbia, *The Administra tion of Justice under Emergency Conditions in the District o Columbia: Report to the Judicial Conference, District o Columbia Circuit*, Washington, D.C.: 1973.

Justice, Blair, *Violence in the City*, Fort Worth, Tex.: Texa Christian University Press, 1973.

Kadi, Leila S., ed., *Basic Political Documents: Documents of th*

Armed Palestinian Resistance Movement, Beirut: Palestine Liberation Organization Research Center, 1969.

Kaplan, Morton A., ed., *The Revolution in World Politics*, New York: Wiley, 1962.

Kapsis, R. et al., *The Reconstruction of a Riot: A Case Study of Community Tensions and Civil Disorder*, Waltham, Mass: Lemberg Center for the Study of Violence, 1966.

Karagueuzian, Dikran, *Blow It Up!* Boston: Gambit, 1971.

Karber, P. O., "Urban Terrorism: Baseline Data and a Conceptual Framework," *Social Science Quarterly*, Vol. 52, 1971, p. 521.

Katz, Doris, *The Lady Was a Terrorist*, New York: Shiloni, 1953.

Katz, Donald R., "Riots of Spring," *The New Republic*, May 8, 1976, p. 14.

Katz, Samuel, *Days of Fire: The Secret History of the Irgun Zvai Leumi*, Garden City, N.Y.: Doubleday, 1968.

_____, *Days of Fire: The Secret Story of the Making of Israel*, London: Allen, 1968.

Kautsky, Karl, *Terrorism and Communism: A Contribution to the Natural History of Revolution*, translation by W. H. Kerridge, London: Allen & Unwin, 1920.

Kelley, C. M., *Statement on Terrorism*, Washington, D.C.: N.C.J.R.S. Microfiche Program, May 31, 1974.

"Kelley Discounts F.B.I.'s Link to a Terrorist Group," New York *Times*, January 12, 1976, p. 24.

Kelly, George A. and Linda B. Miller, *Internal War and International Systems: Perspectives on Method*, Center for International Affairs: Harvard University, 1969.

Kelly, Joseph B., "Assassination in Wartime," *Military Law Review*, Vol. 30, October 1965, p. 101.

Kelly, R. J., *New Political Crimes and the Emergence of Revolutionary Nationalist Ideology*, Chicago: Rand-McNally, 1973.

Kelman, Herbert C., "Violence without Moral Restraint: Reflections on the Dehumanization of Victims and Victimizers," *Journal of Social Issues*, Vol. 29, 1974, p. 25.

Khan, Rahmatullah, "Hijacking and International Law," *Africa Quarterly*, Vol. 10, 1971, pp. 398-403.

"Kidnapping Incidents," *Bulletin of the International Commission of Jurists*, December 1967, pp. 24-33.

"Killing Cops: The New Terror Tactics," *U.S. News*, Vol. 69, August 31, 1970, pp. 11-13.

Kimche, David, *The Secret Roads*, New York: Farrar, Straus and Cudahy, 1955.

Kimche, J., "Can Israel Contain the Palestine Revolution?" *Conflict Studies*, No. 13, June 1971.

Kirchheimer, Otto, "Confining Conditions and Revolutionary Breakthroughs," *American Political Science Review*, December 1965, p. 59.

Kirkham, J. F. and S. Levy, *Assassination and Political Violence*, National Commission on the Causes and Prevention of Violence. Washington: U.S. Government Printing Office, 1969.

Kitson, Frank, *Low Intensity Operations: Subversion, Insurgency, Peace-Keeping*, London: Faber, 1972.

Klein, Milton M., "The Fact of Violence in America: A Historical Perspective," *Social Education*, Vol. 37, 1973, p. 540.

Knohl, Dov, *Siege in the Hills of Hebron: The Battle of the Etzion Bloc*, New York: Yoseloff, 1958.

Knorr, Klaus, "Unconventional Warfare: Strategy and Tactics in Internal Political Strife," *The Annals of the American Academy of Political and Social Science*, May 1962, p. 346.

Kohl, J. and J. Litt, *Urban Guerrilla Warfare in Latin America*, Cambridge: Massachusetts Institute of Technology Press, 1974.

Kornilov, Y., "Meetings with the Fedayeen," *New Times*, No. 42, 1972, pp. 24-25.

Krieger, David, "Terrorists and Nuclear Technology," *Bulletin of the Atomic Scientists*, Vol. 31, No. 6, 1975, pp. 28-34.

Kropotkin, P., *Memoirs of a Revolutionist*, New York: Houghton Mifflin, 1899.

Kruger, R., "Notwendigkeit und Zulassigkeit einer gesetalichen Regelung der bewussten Totung bei polizeilichem Schusswaffengebrauch (Need for the Justifiability of Legislation Regulating Deliberate Killing with Firearms by the Police)," Part 1, *Kriminalistik*, Vol. 29, No. 9 September 1975, pp. 385-389.

_____, "Notwendigkeit und Zulassigkeit einer gestzlichen Regelung dur bewussten Totung bei polizeilichem Schusswaffengebrauch (Need for the Justifiability of Legislation Regulating Deliberate Killing with Firearms by the Police)," Part 2, *Kriminalistik*, Vol. 29, No. 10 October 1975, pp. 441-444.

Kuhn, H. D., "Theology of Violence?" *Christianity Today*, Vol. 13, November 22, 1968, pp. 49-50.

Kuhn, Philip A., *Rebellion and Its Enemies in Late Imperial China*, Cambridge: Harvard University Press, 1970.

Kumar, Mahendra, *Violence and Nonviolence in International*

Relations, New Delhi: Thompson Press, 1975.

Kuriyama, Y., "Terrorism at Tel Aviv Airport and a "New Left" Group in Japan," *Asian Survey*, Vol. 13, March 1973, p. 336.

Kuroda, Yasumasa, "Young Palestinian Commandos in Political Socialization Perspective," *Middle East Journal*, Vol. 26, 1972, pp. 253-70.

Kutner, Luis, "Constructive Notice: A Proposal to End International Terrorism," *New York Law Forum*, Vol. 19, 1973, p. 325.

Lachica, Edwards, "Japan Using Diplomacy to Fight Terrorists," Washington *Star-News*, March 10, 1975.

Lador-Lederer, J. J., "A Legal Approach to International Terrorism," *Israel Law Review*, Vol. 9, 1974, pp. 194-220.

Laffin, John, *Fedayeen*, New York: Macmillan, 1973.

Lambrick, H. T., *The Terrorist*, London: Rowman, 1972.

Lapp, Ralph E., "The Ultimate Blackmail," New York *Times*, February 4, 1973, p. 13.

Laqueur, Walter, "Coming to Terms with Terror," *Times Literary Supplement*, April 2, 1976, p. 362.

_____, "The Futility of Terrorism," *Harper's*, March 1976, p. 99.

_____, *Guerrilla*, Boston: Little, Brown, 1976.

_____, "Guerrillas and Terrorists," *Commentary*, Vol. 58, No. 4, October 1974, pp. 40-48.

Lasky, Melvin J., "Ulrike Meinhof and the Baader-Meinhof Gang," *Encounter*, June 1975, p. 9.

Lasswell, Harold A. and Daniel Lerner, eds., *World Revolutionary Elites: Studies in Coercive Ideological Movements*, Cambridge: Massachusetts Institute of Technology Press, 1965.

Lasswell, Harold A. and Myres McDougal, "Enterprise: Toward a World Public Order of Human Dignity," *Virginia Journal of International Law*, Vol. 14, 1974, p. 535.

"Latin America and Revolution," *Christian Century*, November 17, 1965, pp. 1409-12.

"Latin America in Revolution," *America*, April 27, 1968, pp. 562-87.

"Latin America: Revolution without Revolutionaries," *Nation*, August 22, 1966, pp. 145-49.

Lauterpacht, H., "Revolutionary Activities by Private Persons against Foreign States," *American Journal of International Law*, Vol. 22, 1928, p. 105.

"Law Enforcement Faces the Revolutionary-Guerrilla Criminal," *F.B.I. Law Enforcement Bulletin*, Vol. 39, No. 12, December

1970, pp. 20-22, 28.

Lawrence, John, *The Seeds of Disaster*, New York: Taplinger, 1968.

Lawrence, T.E., *Seven Pillars of Wisdom: A Triumph*, Garden City: Doubleday, 1935.

Lefevure, Georges, *The Great Fear of 1789*. New York: Pantheon; Random House, 1973.

Legum, C., "How to Curb International Terrorism," *Current History*, Vol. 147, 1973, pp. 3-9.

Leiden, Carl and Karl M. Schmitt, eds., *The Politics of Violence*, Englewood Cliffs, N.J.: Prentice-Hall, 1968.

Leites, Nathan and Charles Wolf, Jr., *Rebellion and Authority: An Analytic Essay on Insurgent Conflicts*, Chicago: Markham, Lieuwen, Edwin, 1970.

Lejeune, Anthony, comp., *The Case for South West Africa*, London: Tom Stacey, 1971.

Lens, Sidney, *Radicalism in America*, New York: Thomas Y. Cromwell, 1966.

Lerner, Max, "Assassination," *Encyclopedia of the Social Sciences*, New York, 1933.

Lesch, Mosely, *The Politics of Palestinian Nationalism*, Los Angeles, Calif.: University of California Press, 1973. Lewis,

Lewis, Flora, "The Anatomy of Terror," New York *Times*, November 18, 1956, p. 67.

LiBonachea, Ramon, *The Cuban Insurrection*, Brunswick, N.J.: Marta San Martin, 1974.

Lifton, Robert Jay, *History and Human Survival*, New York: Random House, 1970.

Lincoln, James H., *The Anatomy of a Riot: A Detroit Judge's Report*, New York: McGraw-Hill, 1968.

Lissitzyn, Oliver J., "International Control of Aerial Hijacking: The Role of Values and Interests," *Proceedings of the American Society of International Law*, 1971, pp. 80-86.

Little, Tom, "The Nature of the Palestinian Resistance Movement," *Asian Affairs*, Vol. 57, 1970, pp. 157-69.

_____, "New Arab Extremists — A View from the Arab World," *Conflict Studies*, No. 4 May 1970, pp. 5-22.

Lopez Gutierrez, Juan J., "Should the Tokyo Convention of 1963 Be Ratified?" *Journal of Air Law and Commerce*, Vol. 31, 1965, pp. 1-21.

Lorch, Netanel, *The Edge of the Sword: Israel's War of Independence 1947-1949*, New York: Putnam, 1961.

Lowi, T. J., *Politics of Disorder*, New York: W. W. Norton, 1971.

Lowry, D., "Ill-Treatment, Brutality and Torture: Some Thoughts upon the 'Treatment' of Irish Political Prisoners," *DePaul Law Review*, Vol. 22, 1973, p. 553.

Loy, Frank E., "Some International Approaches to Dealing with Hijacking of Aircraft," *International Lawyer*, Vol. 4, 1970, pp. 444-52.

Lum, Dyer D., *A Concise History of the Great Trial of the Chicago Anarchists*, Chicago: Socialistic Publishing Co., 1887.

Lupsha, Peter, "Explanation of Political Violence: Some Psychological Theories," *Politics and Society*, Vol. 2, 1971, pp. 88-104.

MacCarthy, J. M., ed., *Limerick's Fighting Story*, Tralee, Ireland: Anvil, 1966.

MacDonald, John M., *Psychiatry and the Criminal: A Guide to Psychiatric Examinations for the Criminal*, 3rd ed., Springfield, Ill.: Thomas, 1976.

Mack, John A. and Hans-Jurgen Kerner, eds., *The Crime Industry*, with a foreword by Marvin E. Wolfgang, Lexington, Mass.: Lexington Books; D. C. Heath, 1975.

Maclean, Donald, *British Foreign Policy: The Years since Suez*, New York: Stein & Day, 1970.

Mac Stiofan, Sean, *Revolutionary in Ireland*, London: G. Cremonesi, 1975.

Mahoney, H. T., "After a Terrorist Attack — Business As Usual," *Security Management*, Vol. 19, No. 1, March 1975, pp. 16, 18, 19.

Mailer, Norman, *Miami and the Siege of Chicago: An Informal History of the Republican and Democratic Conventions of 1968*, New York: Signet, 1968.

Malawer, Stuart S., "United States Foreign Policy and International Law: The Jordanian Civil War and Air Piracy," *International Problems*, Vol. 10, 1971, pp. 31-40.

Malik, Sushman, "Legal Aspects of the Problem of Unlawful Seizure of Aircraft," *Indian Journal of International Law*, Vol. 9, 1969, pp. 61-71.

Mallin, Jay, ed., *Terror and Urban Guerrillas: A Study of Tactics and Documents*, Coral Gables, Fla.: University of Miami Press, 1971.

_____, *Terror in Viet Nam*, Princeton, N.J.: D. Van Nostrand, 1966.

_____, "Terrorism As a Political Weapon," *Air University Review*, Vol. 22, 1971, pp. 45-52.

_____, "Terrorism in Revolutionary Warfare," *Strategic Review*, Vol. 2, Fall 1974, p. 48.

Mallison, W. T., Jr. and S. V. Mallison, "Concept of Public

Purpose Terror in International Law, Doctrines and Sanctions to Reduce the Destruction of Human and Material Values," *Howard Law Journal*, Vol. 18, 1973, p. 12.

Malloy, James M., *Bolivia: The Uncompleted Revolution*, Pittsburgh: University of Pittsburgh Press, 1970.

Malmborg, K. E., "New Developments in the Law of International Aviation: The Control of Aerial Hijacking," *Proceedings of the American Society of International Law*, 1971, pp. 75-80.

Mankiewicz, R. H., "The 1970 Hague Convention," *Journal of Air Law and Commerce*, Vol. 37, 1971, pp. 195-210.

Mansergh, Nicholas, *The Commonwealth Experience*, London: Weidenfeld & Nicolson, 1969.

Mao Tse-tung, *Basic Tactics*, New York: Praeger, 1966.

_____, *On Guerrilla Warfare*, New York: Praeger, 1961.

Marcuse, H., *Counterrevolution and Revolt*, Boston: Beacon Press, 1972.

Mardor, Munya, *Haganah*, New York: New American Library, 1966.

_____, *Strictly Illegal*, London: Robert Hale, 1964.

Marighella, Carlos, *For the Liberation of Brazil*, Harmondsworth: Penguin, 1972.

_____, *Minimanual of the Urban Guerrilla*, Havana: Tricontinental, n.d.

Martin, Bill, "The Politics of Violence: The Urban Guerrilla in Brazil," *Ramparts*, October 1970, p. 35.

Martines, Lauro, ed., *Violence and Civil Disorder in Italian Cities*, Berkeley: University of California Press, 1972.

Martinez, Codo Enrique, "Continental Defense and Counter insurgency," *Military Review*, Vol. 50, No. 4, 1970, pp. 71-74.

_____, "The Urban Guerrilla," *Military Review*, Vol. 51, No. 8, 1971, pp. 3-10.

Martz, John D., *Colombia: A Contemporary Political Survey*, Chapel Hill: University of North Carolina Press, 1962.

Masotti, Louis H. and Don R. Bowen, eds., *Riots and Rebellions: Civil Violence in the Urban Community*, Beverly Hills: Sage Publications, 1968.

Masotti, Louis H. and J. R. Corsi, *Shoot-Out in Cleveland, Black Militants and the Police*, Washington, D.C.: Government Printing Office, 1969.

Mather, Berkely, *With Extreme Prejudice*, New York: Scribners, 1976.

Mathews, A. S., "Terrors of Terrorism," *South African Law*

Journal, Vol. 91, August 1974, p. 381.

Mathur, L. P., *Indian Revolutionary Movement in the United States of America,* Delhi: S. Chand, 1970.

Max, Alphonse, *Guerrillas in Latin America,* The Hague: International Documentation and Information Centre, 1971.

May, Rollo, *Power and Innocence: A Search for the Sources of Violence,* New York: Norton, 1972.

May, W. F., "Terrorism as Strategy and Ecstasy," *Social Research,* Vol. 41, Summer 1974, p. 277.

Meron, T., "Some Legal Aspects of Arab Terrorists Claim to Privileged Combatancy," *Mordisk Tidsakrift for International Ret,* Vol. 40, 1970, p. 47.

McDougal, Myres and Harold Lasswell, "The Identification and Appraisal of Diverse Systems of Public Order," *American Journal of International Law,* Vol. 53, 1959, p. 1.

McGee, Henry W., Jr., "Arrest in Civil Disturbances: Reflections on the Use of Deadly Force in Riots," *Rutgers Law Review,* Vol. 22, 1968, p. 717.

McKnight, G., *Mind of the Terrorist,* London: Michael Joseph, 1974.

McLellan, Vin and Paul Avery, *The Voices of Guns: The Definitive and Dramatic Story of the 22-Month Career of the Symbionese Liberation Army,* New York: Putnam, 1976.

McMahon, John P., "Air Hijacking: Extradition as a Deterrent," *Georgetown Law Journal,* Vol. 58, 1970, pp. 1135-52.

McWhinney, E. W., et al, *Aerial Piracy and International Law,* Leiden: Sijthoff; Dobbs Ferry, New York: Oceana, 1971.

Medzini, Roni, "China and the Palestinians," *The New Middle East,* No. 32, 1971, pp. 34-40.

Melo, Artemio Luis, "La inviolabilidad diplomática y el caso del Embajador Von Spreti," *Revista de derecho internacional y ciencias diplomáticas,* Vol. 19, Nos. 37-38, 1970, pp. 147-56.

Mendelsohn, A. I., "In-flight Crime: The International and Domestic Picture under the Tokyo Convention," *Virginia Law Review,* Vol. 53, 1967, pp. 509-63.

Mercader, A. and J. de Vera, *Tupamaros: Estrategia y Acción,* Montevideo: Editorial Alfa, 1969.

Meridor, Yaacov, *Long Road to Freedom,* New York: United Zionists Revisionists, 1961.

Merleau-Ponty, Maurice, *Humanism and Terror: An Essay on the Communist Problem,* Boston: Beacon, 1969.

Meron, Theodor, "Some Legal Aspects of Arab Terrorists' Claim to Privileged Combatancy," *Nordisk Tidaskrift for international ret,* Vol. 40, Nos. 1-4, 1970, pp. 47-85.

Meyrowitz, H., "Statut des Guerrilleros dans le Droit International," *Journal du Droit International*, Vol. 100, October-December 1973, p. 875.

Miller, Michael J. and Susan Gilmore, *Revolution at Berkley*, New York: Dial, 1965.

Milte, Kerry, "Terrorism and International Order," *The Australian and New Zealand Journal of Criminology*, Vol. 8, June 1975, p. 101.

Minogue, Kenneth, "The Doctrine of Violence," *Times Literary Supplement*, November 7, 1975, p. 1318.

Molnar, Andrew R. et al, *Undergrounds in Insurgent, Revolutionary, and Resistance Warfare*, Washington, D.C.: The American University Special Operations Research Office, 1963.

Monboisse, R.M., *Blueprint of Revolution: The Rebel, the Party, the Techniques of Revolt*, Springfield, Ill.: Thomas, 1970.

_____, *Crowd Control and Riot Prevention*, Sacramento Calif.: Office of State Printing, 1964.

Montgomery, de J.E.G., "The Barbary States in the Law of Nations," *Transactions of the Grotius Society*, Vol. 4, 1918 p. 87.

Moody, T. W. and F. Y. Martin, eds., *The Course of Irish History*, New York: Weybright & Tally, 1967.

Moore, Barrington M., Jr., *Terror and Progress in the U.S.S.R.* Cambridge, Mass.: Harvard University Press, 1954.

Moore, J. W., "Terrorism and Political Crimes in International Law," *American Journal of International Law*, Vol. 67, 1973 p. 87.

Morehouse, Ward, III, "U.S. Border Watch for Terrorists," *Christian Science Monitor*, March 26, 1976, p. 2.

Morente, Frederico Quintero, "Terrorism," *Military Review* Vol. 45, 1965, p. 55.

Morris, Michael, *Terrorism*, Cape Town: Timmins, 1971.

Morris, Roger, "Patty Hearst and the New Terror," *New Republic*, Vol. 173, November 22, 1975, p. 8.

Morton, Marian J., *Terrors of Ideological Politics*, Cleveland: Cas Western Reserve, 1972.

Moss, Robert, "International Terrorism and Western Societies," *International Journal*, Vol. 28, No. 3, 1973, p. 418.

_____, "The War against Terrorism," *London Daily Telegraph*, December 11, 1974.

_____, *Urban Guerrillas*, London: Temple Smith, 1972.

_____, "Urban Guerrillas in Latin America," *Conflic*

Studies, Vol. 8, October 1970, pp. 4-15.

_____, "Urban Guerrillas in Uruguay," *Problems of Communism*, Vol. 20, No. 5, 1971, pp. 14-23.

_____, *The War for the Cities*, New York: Coward, 1972.

Mphahlele, Ezekiel, *The African Image*, Rev. ed., New York: Praeger, 1974.

"Mr. Wilson's Irish Question," *New Statesman*, Vol. 88, December 1974, p. 814.

Mueller, Claus, *The Politics of Communication: A Study in the Political Sociology of Language, Socialization, and Legitimation*, London: Galaxy Books; Oxford University Press, 1975.

Mukherjee, Uma, *Two Great Indian Revolutionaries*, Calcutta: Firma K. L. Mukhopadhyay, 1966.

Murphy, John F., "International Legal Controls of International Terrorism: Performance and Prospects," *Illinois Bar Journal*, Vol. 63, April 1975, p. 444.

Mydans, Carl and Shelley Mydans, *The Violent Peace*, New York: Atheneum, 1968.

Naipaul, V. S., *Guerrillas*, New York: Knopf, 1975.

Najmuddin D., "Kidnapping of Diplomatic Personnel," *Police Chief*, Vol. 40, No. 2, February 1973, pp. 18, 20, 22, 23.

Nasser Terror Gangs: The Story of the Fedayeen, Jerusalem: Ministry for Foreign Affairs, 1956.

Nasution, Abdul Haris, *Fundamentals of Guerrilla Warfare*, New York: Praeger, 1965.

Neale, William D., "Oldest Weapon in the Arsenal: Terror," *Army*, August 1973, p. 10.

Neier, Aryeh, *Crime and Punishment*, New York: Stein & Day, 1976.

Nekhlek, E.A., "Anatomy of Violence: Theoretical Reflections on Palestinian Resistance," *Middle East Journal*, Vol. 25, 1971, pp. 180-200.

"Neo-Fascism on Trial: Italian Social November Party and Rightist Terrorism," *Time*, Vol. 101, May 21, 1973, pp. 49-50.

"New Way to War on Innocents: Swissair Crash," *Newsweek*, Vol. 75, March 9, 1970, p. 32.

Nieburg, H. L., *Political Violence: The Behavioral Process*, New York: St. Martin's, 1969.

Niezing, John, ed., *Urban Guerrilla*, Rotterdam: Rotterdam University Press, 1976.

Nkrumah, Kwame, *Handbook of Revolutionary Warfare*, New York: International Publishers, 1972.

Nolin, Thierry, *La Haganah: L'armée Secrète d'Israel*, Paris: Ballard, 1971.

Nomad, Max, *Aspects of Revolt: A Study in Revolutionary Theories and Techniques*, New York: Noonday, 1959.

"No More Tribute for Terror," *Time*, March 22, 1971, p. 31.

Northedge, F. S., *The Use of Force in International Relations*, New York: Free Press, 1974.

Note, "Convention to Prevent and Punish Acts of Terrorism," *American Journal of International Law*, Vol. 65, 1971, p. 898.

Note, "Developments in the Law: The National Security Interest and Civil Liberties," *Harvard Law Review*, Vol. 85, 1972, p. 1130.

Note, "Riot Control: The Constitutional Limits of Search, Arrest and Fair Trial Procedure," *Columbia Law Review*, Vol. 68, 1968, p. 85.

Note, "Riot Control and the Fourth Amendment," *Harvard Law Review*, Vol. 81, 1968, p. 638.

Note, "Riot Control and the Use of Federal Troops," *Harvard Law Review*, Vol. 81, 1968, p. 638.

Nussbaum, Peter D., *The Administration of Justice under Emergency Conditions*, New York: Criminal Justice Coordinating Council; The Vera Institute of Justice, 1969.

O'Ballance, Edgar, *The Indo-China War, 1945-1954: A Study in Guerrilla Warfare*, London: Faber & Faber, 1964.

_____, *The Red Army of China*, London: Faber & Faber, 1962.

O'Brion, Leon, *Dublin Castle and the 1916 Rising*, New York: New York University Press, 1971.

O'Farrell, Patrick, *Ireland's English Question*, London: Batsford, 1971.

O'Flaherty, Liam, *The Terrorist*, London: Archer, 1926.

O'Mara, Richard, "New Terror in Latin America: Snatching the Diplomats," *Nation*, Vol. 210, No. 17, 1970, pp. 518-19.

Oppenheimer, Martin, *The Urban Guerrilla*, Chicago: Quadrangle, 1969.

Osanka, Franklin Mark, *Modern Guerrilla Warfare: Fighting Communist Guerrilla Movements 1941-1961*, New York: Free Press, 1962.

Osmond, Andrew, *Saladin!* New York: Doubleday, 1976.

Paige, Jeffery M., "Political Orientation and Riot Participation," *American Sociological Review*, Vol. 36, 1972, p. 810.

Palmer, Stuart, *Violent Society*, New Haven, Conn.: College and University Press, 1972.

Panhuys, Haro F. van, "Aircraft Hijacking and International Law," *Columbia Journal of Transnational Law*, Vol. 9, 1970, pp. 1-22.

Panikkar, Sardar K. M., *Asia and Western Dominance*, London: Allen & Unwin, 1959.

Paret, Peter and John W. Shy, *Guerrillas in the 1960's*, Rev. ed., New York: Praeger, 1962.

Parker, Thomas F., ed., *Violence in the United States*, New York: Facts on File, 1974.

Parrilli, R. E. F., "Effects of Castrismo and the Guevarismo on Leftist Thought in Latin America," *Revista de Derecho Puertorriqueñe*, Vol. 12, 1972, p. 69.

Parry, Albert, *Terrorism: From Robespierre to Arafat*, New York: Vanguard, 1976.

Paske, Gerald H., "Violence, Value, and Education," *Teachers College Record*, Vol. 71, 1969, p. 51.

Paust, Jordan J., "Some Thoughts on 'Preliminary Thoughts' on Terrorism," *American Journal of International Law*, Vol. 68, 1974, pp. 502-03.

_____, "A Survey of Possible Legal Responses to International Terrorism: Prevention, Punishment and Cooperative Action," *Georgia Journal of International and Comparative Law*, Vol. 5, 1975, p. 431.

_____, "Terrorism and the International Law of War," *Military Law Review*, Vol. 64, 1974, p. 1.

Payne, Pierre Stephen Robert, *The Terrorists: The Story of the Forerunners of Stalin*, New York: Funk & Wagnalls, 1967.

_____, *Zero: The Story of Terrorism*, New York: Day, 1950.

Pella, Vespasian V., "La Répression des Crimes Contre la Personnalité de l'État," *Recueil des Cours de l'Académie de Droit International de la Haye*, Vol. 3, 1930, pp. 677-831.

_____, "La Repression du Terrorisme et la Creation d'Une Cour Internationale," *Nouvelle Revue de Droit International Prive*, Vol. 5, p. 785; Vol. 6, p. 120, 1939.

Pepinsky, Harold E., *Crime and Conflict*, New York: Academic Press; Harcourt Brace Jovanovich, 1976.

Pepitone, Albert, "The Social Psychology of Violence," *International Journal of Group Tensions*, Vol. 2, 1972, pp. 19-32.

Peres, Shimon, *David's Sling*, New York: Random House, 1970.

Peters, R., "Terrorists at Work: Report from Argentina," *National Review*, July 28, 1964, p. 63.

Peterson, Edward A., "Jurisdiction-Construction of Statute-Aircraft Piracy." *Journal of Air Law and Commerce*, Vol. 30, 1964, pp. 292-95.

_____, "Urban Guerrilla Warfare," *Military Review*, March 1972, p. 82.

Phillips, R. Hart, *Cuba: Island of Paradox*, New York: McDowell, Obolensky, 1959.

Pike, Douglas, *The Viet-Cong Strategy of Terror*, Saigon: U.S. Mission, Viet Nam, 1970.

Plastrik, S., "On Terrorism," *Dissent*, Vol. 21, Spring 1974, p. 143.

Platt, Anthony M., ed., *The Politics of Riot Commissions, 1917-1970: A Collection of Official Reports and Critical Essays*, New York: Macmillan, 1971.

"P.L.O. Threatens to Hit Israeli Targets in United States," Washington *Post*, March 13, 1975, p. 8.

Pomeroy, William J., *Guerrilla Warfare and Marxism*, New York: International Publishers, 1968.

Popper, F. J., "Internal War As a Stimulant of Political Development," *Comparative Political Studies*, Vol. 3, January 1971, p. 413.

"Portrait of a Terrorist," *Science Digest*, Vol. 75, June 1974, p. 70.

Porzicanski, A. C., *Uruguay's Tupamaros: The Urban Guerrilla*, New York: Praeger, 1973.

Possony, Stefan T., ed., *The Lenin Reader*, Chicago: Regenery, 1966.

Poulantzas, Nicholas M., "The Hague Convention for the Suppression of Unlawful Seizure of Aircraft (December 16, 1970)," *Nederlands tijdschrift voor internationaal recht*, Vol. 18, No. 1, 1971, pp. 25-75.

_____, "Hijacking or Air Piracy?" *Nederlands juristenblad*, No. 20, 1970, pp. 566-74.

_____, "Hijacking v. Piracy: A Substantial Misunderstanding Not a Quarrel over Semantics," *Revue Héllenique de droit international*, Vol. 23, Nos. 1-4, 1970, pp. 80-90.

_____, "Some Problems of International Law Connected with Urban Guerrilla Warfare: The Kidnapping of Members of Diplomatic Missions, Consular Offices and Other Foreign Personnel," *Annales d'etudes internationales*, Vol. 3, 1972, pp. 137-67.

Powell, W., *The Anarchist Cookbook*, New York: Lyle Stuart, 1971.

Powers, Thomas, *Diana: The Making of a Terrorist*, Boston: Houghton Mifflin, 1970.

Price, D. L., "Ulster-Consensus and Coercion, Part 2: Security Force Attrition Tactics," *Conflict Studies*, No. 50, October 1974, pp. 7-24.

Priestland, Gerald, *The Future of Violence*, London: Hamilton, 1974.

"Private Sector," *Economist*, January 25, 1975, p. 38.

Pryce-Jones, David, *The Face of Defeat: Palestinian Refugees and Guerrillas*, London: Weidenfeld & Nicholson, 1972.

Pulsifer, Roy and Robert Boyle, "The Tokyo Convention on Offences and Certain Other Acts Committed on Board Aircraft," *Journal of Air Law and Commerce*, Vol. 20, 1964, pp. 305-54.

Pustay, John S., *Counterinsurgency Warfare*, New York: Free Press, 1965.

Pye, Lucien W., *Guerrilla Communism in Malaya: It's Social and Political Meaning*, Princeton: Princeton University Press, 1956.

Quandt, William D., Fuad Jabber and Ann Mosely Leach, *The Politics of Palestinian Nationalism*, Berkeley: University of California Press, 1973.

Radovanovic, L., "The Problem of International Terrorism," *Review of International Affairs*, Vol. 23, October 1972, p. 5.

Rafat, Amir, "Control of Aircraft Hijacking: The Law of International Civil Aviation," *World Affairs*, Vol. 134, 1971, pp. 143-56.

Rapoport, David C., *Assassination and Terrorism*, Toronto: Canadian Broadcasting System, 1971.

Rauch, Elmer, "The Compatability of the Detention of Terrorists Order (Northern Ireland) with the European Convention for the Protection of Human Rights," *New York University Journal of International Law and Politics*, Vol. 6, 1973, p. 1.

Rayne, F., "Executive Protection and Terrorism," *Top Security*, Vol. 1, No. 6, October 1975, pp. 220-225.

Reed, David, *111 Days in Stanleyville*, New York: Harper & Row, 1965.

Regush, Nicholas M., *Pierre Vallieres: The Revolutionary Process in Quebec*, New York: Dial, 1973.

Rein, Bert, "A Government Perspective," *Journal of Air Law and Commerce*, Vol. 37, 1971, pp. 183-93.

Reisman, W. M., "Private Armies in a Global War System: Prologue to Decision," *Virginia Journal of International Law*, Vol. 14, 1973, p. 1.

Repression, Violence et Terreur: Rebellions au Congo, Brussels: Centre de Recherche et d'Information Socio-Politiques, 1969.

Revel, Jean-Francois, *Without Marx or Jesus: The New American Revolution Has Begun*, Garden City, N.Y.: Doubleday & Co., 1971.

Rhan, M. A., *Guerrilla Warfare: Its Past, Present and Future*, Karachi, India: Rangrut, 1960.

Richardson, Lewis Fry, *Statistics of Deadly Quarrels*, edited by

Quincy Wright and C. C. Lienau, Pittsburgh: Boxwood Press, 1960.

Riedel, M. and T. P. Thornberry, *Crime and Delinquency — Dimensions of Deviance*, New York, Praeger, 1974.

Rivers, Charles R. and Kenneth A. Switzer, *Violence*, Rochelle Park, N.J.: Hayden, 1976.

Robinson, Donald B., *The Dirty Wars*, New York: Delacorte, 1968.

Rojo, R., *My Friend Ché*, New York: Dial, 1969.

"The Role of International Law in Combating Terrorism," *Current Foreign Policy*, January 1973, pp. 1-7.

Romaniecki, Leon, *The Arab Terrorists in the Middle East and the Soviet Union*, Jerusalem: Soviet and East European Research Center of the Hebrew University of Jerusalem, 1973.

_____, "The Soviet Union and International Terrorism," *Soviet Studies*, Vol. 26, No. 3, July 1974, p. 417.

Ropp, Theodore, *War in the Modern World*, Rev. ed., New York: Collier, 1962.

Rose, T., ed., *Violence in America: A Historical and Contemporary Reader*, New York: Random House, 1969.

Rosenbaum, H. Jon and Peter C. Sederberg, "Vigilantism: An Analysis of Establishment Violence," *Comparative Politics*, Vol. 6, 1974, p. 541.

Rostow, Eugene B., "Illegality of the Arab Attack on Israel of October 6, 1973," *American Journal of International Law*, Vol. 69, 1975, p. 272.

Rotberg, R. J. and Ali A. Mazrui, eds., *Protest and Power in Black Africa*, New York: Oxford University Press, 1970.

Roucek, Joseph S., "Sociological Elements of a Theory of Terror and Violence," *American Journal of Economics and Sociology*, Vol. 21, Spring 1962, pp. 165-172.

Roux, J. A., "Le Projet de convention internationale pour la répression des crimes présentant un danger public," *Revue international de droit pénal*, Vol. 12, 1935, pp. 99-130.

Rovine, Arthur W., "The Contemporary International Legal Attack on Terrorism," *Israel Yearbook on Human Rights*, Vol. 3, 1973, pp. 9-38.

Rude, G., *The Crowd in History*, New York: Wiley, 1964.

Ruppenthal, Kare M., "World Law and the Hijackers," *Nation*, February 3, 1969, pp. 144-46.

Russell, Charles A. and Robert E. Hildner, "Urban Insurgency in Latin America: Its Implications for the Future," *Air University Review*, Vol. 22, No. 6, 1971, pp. 55-64.

Russell, D. E. H., *Rebellion, Revolution, and Armed Force*, New York: Academic Press; Harcourt Brace Jovanovich, 1974.

Russin, Joseph M., "The Transformation of Patricia Hearst," Washington *Post*, June 23, 1974, pp. 1, 5.

Sacks, A., *The Violence of Apartheid*, 2nd ed., London: International Defense and Air Fund, 1970.

Saldaña, I., "Le Terrorisme," *Revue international de droit pénal*, Vol. 13, 1936, pp. 26-37.

Sale, Kirkpatrick, *S.D.S.* New York: Random House, 1973.

_____, "The Political Underground is Small and Often Violent," New York *Times*, May 10, 1975.

Samuels, Alec, "Crimes Committed on Board Aircraft: Tokyo Convention Act, 1967," *British Yearbook of International Law*, Vol. 42, 1967, pp. 271-77.

_____, "The Legal Problems: An Introduction," *Journal of Air Law and Commerce*, Vol. 37, 1971, pp. 163-70.

Sandor [Pseud.], *The Coming Struggle for South Africa*, London: The Fabian Society, 1963.

Santos, M. Barbero, "Delitos de Bandolerismo, Rebelion Militar y Terrorismo Regulados por ed Secreto de 21 Septiembre de 1960," *La Justicia*, Vol. 33, January 1974, p. 43.

Sarkesian, Sam C., ed., *Revolutionary Guerrilla Warfare*, Chicago: Precedent Publishing, 1975.

The Savage Kinship: A Chronology of the Use of Violence for Political Ends in Arab Countries, Jerusalem: Carta, 1973.

Saywell, John T., *Quebec 70: A Documentary Narrative*, Toronto: University of Toronto Press, 1971.

Schechtman, Joseph B., *The Mufti and the Fuehrer*, London: Yoseloff, 1965.

_____, *Rebel and Statesman: The Jabotinsky Story*, New York: Yoseloff, 1956, 1961.

Schiff, Zeev and Raphael Rothstein, *Fedayeen: Guerrillas against Israel*, New York: McKay, 1972.

_____, *Fedayeen: The Story of the Palestinian Guerrillas*, London: Vallentine, Mitchell, 1972.

Schloesing, E., "La Repression Internationale du Terrorisme," *Revue Politique et Parlementaire*, Vol. 841, April 1973, p. 50.

Schuman, S. I., ed., *Law and Disorder — The Legitimation of Direct Action As an Instrument of Social Policy*, Detroit: Wayne State University Press, 1971.

Schwarzenberger, Georg, "Terrorists, Hijackers, Guerrilleros and Mercenaries," *Current Legal Problems*, Vol. 24, 1971, pp. 257-82.

"Scope and Limit of a Fedayeen Consensus," *Wiener Library Bulletin*, 1970/71, pp. 1-8.

Search and Destroy: A Report by the Commission of Inquiry into the Black Panthers, New York: Metropolitan Applied Research Center. 1973.

Sears, D. D. and J. B. McConahay, *Politics of Violence: The New Urban Blacks and the Watts Riot*, Boston: Houghton Mifflin, 1973.

Segre, Dan and J. H. Adler, "The Ecology of Terrorism," *Encounter*, Vol. 40, 1973, pp. 17-24.

Semple, Robert B., Jr., "Police Toughening Anti-terrorist Tactics," New York *Times*, December 25, 1975, p. 1.

Shaffer, Helen B., "Political Terrorism," *Editorial Research Reports*, Vol. 1, 1970, pp. 341-60.

Sharabi, Hisham B., *Nationalism and Revolution in the Arab World*, Princeton: Van Nostrand, 1966.

Shaw, P. D., "Extortion Threats: Analytic Techniques and Resources," *Assets Protection*, Vol. 1, No. 2, 1975, pp. 5-16.

Shay, R., *The Silent War*, Salesbury: Galaxy, 1971.

Sheehan, William M., "Hijacking and World Law," *World Federalist*, U.S. Edition, Vol. 16, 1970, pp. 14-15, 19.

Shepard, Ira M., "Air Piracy: The Role of the International Federation of Airline Pilots Associations," *Cornell International Law Journal*, Vol. 3, 1970, pp. 79-91.

Short, J. F. and M. E. Wolfgang, *Collective Violence*, Chicago: Aldine, 1972.

Shubber, Sami, "Is Hijacking of Aircraft Piracy in International Law?" *British Yearbook of International Law*, Vol. 43, 1968-69, pp. 193-204.

Shulman, Alix K., *Red Emma Speaks*, New York: Random House, 1972.

Silver, Isidore, "Toward Theory of the Political Defense," *Catholic Lawyer*, Vol. 18, No. 3, 1972, pp. 206-36.

Silverman, Jerry M. and Peter M. Jackson, "Terror in Insurgency Warfare," *Military Review*, Vol. 50, 1970, pp. 61-70.

Silvert, Kalman H., *Reaction and Revolution in Latin America*, New Orleans: Hauser, 1961.

Simp, Howard R., "Terror," *U.S. Naval Institute Proceedings*, Vol. 96, 1970, pp. 64-69.

"Since Jordan — The Palestinian Fedayeen," *Conflict Studies*, No. 38, September 1973, pp. 3-18.

Sinclair, Andrew, *Guevara*, London: William Collins, 1970.

Singer, J. David and Melvin Small, *The Wages of War, 1816-1965: A Statistical Handbook*. New York: John Wiley, 1972.

Singh, Baljit, *Theory and Practice of Modern Guerrilla Warfare*, New York: Asia Publishing House, 1971.

Singh, Khushwant and Satindra Singh, *Ghadar 1915: India's First Armed Revolution*, New Delhi: R. K. Publishing House, 1966.

Skobnick, Jerome, ed., *The Politics of Protest*, New York: Ballantine, 1969.

_____, *The Politics of Protest: A Report*, Washington, D.C.: Government Printing Office, 1969.

Skolnick, Joseph M., Jr., "An Appraisal of Studies of the Linkage between Domestic and International Conflict," *Comparative Political Studies*, Vol. 6, 1974, p. 485.

"S.L.A. Shoots It Out," *Economist*, May 25, 1974, p. 64.

Smith, Colin L., *Carlos: Portrait of a Terrorist*, London: Deutsch, 1976.

_____, "Probable Necessity of an International Prison in Solving Aircraft Hijacking," *International Lawyer*, Vol. 5, 1971, pp. 269-78.

Smith, D., "Scenario Reality: A New Brand of Terrorism," *Nation*, March 30, 1974, pp. 392-94.

Smith, McKeithen, R. N., "Prospects for the Prevention of Aircraft Hijacking through Law," *Columbia Journal of Transnational Law*, Vol. 9, 1970, pp. 60-80.

Smith, R. D. and R. Kobetz, *Guidelines for Civil Disorders and Mobilization Planning*, Gaithersburg, Md.: International Association of Chiefs of Police, 1968.

Sobel, L. A., *Political Terrorism*, New York: Facts on File, 1975.

Solzhenitsyn, Alexander, *The Gulag Archipelago*, New York: Harper & Row, 1973.

Sorel, Georges, *Reflections on Violence*, New York: Collier, 1961.

Sottile, A., "Le Terrorisme International," *Recueil des cours de l'Académie de droit international de la Haye*, Vol. 3, 1938, pp. 87-184.

"Soviet Airliner Hijacked to Turkey," *Current Digest of the Soviet Press*, Vol. 22, 1970, pp. 6-7.

Spegele, Roger, *Terrorism in Unconventional Warfare*, Thesis, University of California, 1964.

Sperber, M., "Violence from Below," *Survey*, Vol. 18, Summer 1972, p. 189.

Sponsler, T. H., "International Kidnapping," *International Lawyer*, Vol. 5, 1971, p. 27.

Standing, P. D., *Guerrilla Leaders of the World*, London: Cassell, 1913.

Stechel, Ira, "Terrorist Kidnapping of Diplomatic Personnel,"

Cornell International Law Journal, Vol. 5, 1972, pp. 189-217.

Stephen, J. E., "Going South: Air Piracy and Unlawful Interference with Air Commerce," *International Lawyer,* Vol. 4, 1970, pp. 433-43.

Stevenson, John, R., "International Law and the Export of Terrorism," *Record of the Association of the Bar of the City of New York,* Vol. 27, 1972, p. 716.

Stewart, Anthony Terence Quincey, *The Ulster Crisis,* London: Faber & Faber, 1967.

Stone, Lawrence, "Theories of Revolution," *World Politics,* Vol. 18, 1966, p. 159.

Storr, Anthony, *Human Destructives,* New York: Basic Books, 1972.

Strafford, David, "Anarchists in Britain Today," *Government and Opposition,* Vol. 6, No. 3, 1971, pp. 346-53.

Strauss, Harlan, "Revolutionary Types," *Journal of Conflict Resolution,* Vol. 14, 1973, p. 307.

A Study: Viet Cong Use of Terror, Saigon: U.S. Mission in Viet Nam, 1967.

Stumper, A., "Considerations a Propos de l'Affaire Baader-Meinhof," *Revue de Droit Penal et de Criminologie,* Vol. 54, October 1973, p. 33.

Stupack, Ronald J. and D. C. Booher, "Guerrilla Warfare: A Strategic Analysis in the Superpower Context," *Journal of Southeast Asia and the Far East,* November 2, 1970, pp. 181-96.

Suchlicki, Jaime, *University Students and Revolution in Cuba, 1920-1968,* Coral Gables: University of Miami Press, 1969.

Sugg, Carolyn, ed., *Violence,* Paramus, N.J.: Paulist-Newman, 1970.

Sulzberger, C. L., "The Antiterrorist League," New York *Times,* April 14, 1976, p. 39.

_____, "Strategy of Terrorism," New York *Times,* November 23, 1975, Sec. 4, p. 17.

Sundberg, J. W. F., "The Case for an International Criminal Court," *Journal of Air Law and Commerce,* Vol. 37, 1971, pp. 211-27.

Syrkin, Marie, "Political Terrorism," *Midstream,* Vol. 18, No. 9, 1972, pp. 3-11.

Szabo, M. O., "Political Crimes: A Historical Perspective," *Denver Journal of International Law and Politics,* Vol. 2, 1972, p. 7.

Taber, Robert, *The War of the Flea,* New York: Lyle Stuart, 1965.

Tanham, George Kilpatrick, *Communist Revolutionary Warfare*, New York: Praeger, 1961.

Tannenbaum, Frank, *Peace by Revolution: Mexico after 1910*, New York: Columbia University Press, 1933.

Tanter, Raymond and Manus Midlarsky, "A Theory of Revolution," *Journal of Conflict Resolution*, Vol. 9, 1967, p. 264.

Taulbee, J. L., "Retaliation and Irregular Warfare in Contémporary International Law," *International Lawyer*, Vol. 7, 1973, p. 12.

Taylor, Charles L. and Michael C. Hudson, *World Handbook of Political and Social Indicators*, 2nd ed., New Haven: Yale University Press, 1972.

Taylor, Karl K. and Fred W. Soady, Jr., ed., *Violence: An Element of American Life*, Boston: Holbrook, 1972.

Taylor, Telford, *Nuremberg and Vietnam: An American Tragedy*, New York: Quadrangle, 1970.

Teixeira, Bernardo, *The Fabric of Terror: Three Days in Angola*, New York: Devin-Adair, 1965.

Terekhov, Vladimir, "International Terrorism and the Fight against It," *New Times*, No. 11, 1974, pp. 20-22.

"Terror through the Mails," *Economist*, September 23, 1972, pp. 15-16.

"The Terrorism Act of South Africa," *Bulletin of the International Commission of Jurists*, June 1968, pp. 28-34.

"Terrorist Acts against United Nations Missions," *United Nations Chronicle*, Vol. 8, 1971, p. 61.

"Terrorism Curbs Enacted in Bonn," *New York Times*, January 17, 1976, p. 8.

"Terrorism in Latin America," *Atlas*, Vol. 20, No. 10, 1971, pp. 18-21.

"Terrorism on the Left," *Newsweek*, March 23, 1970, p. 26.

"Terrorism and Marxism," *Monthly Review*, Vol. 24, November 1972, pp. 1-6.

"Terrorism and Political Crimes in International Law, Proceedings of American Society of International Law, April 12, 1973," *American Journal of International Law*, Vol. 67, 1973, p. 87.

"Terrorism: The Proposed U.S. Draft Convention," *Georgia Journal of International and Comparative Law*, Vol. 3, 1973, p. 430.

Terrorism: Statistics and Techniques — An F.B.I. Special Study, Washington, D.C.: U.S. Department of Justice, January 12, 1973.

"Threat for Bicentennial Year — Terrorists Getting Ready," *U.S. News and World Report*, Vol. 79, No. 3, July 21, 1975, pp. 23-27.

Tiewul, S. A., "Terrorism: A Step towards International Control," *Harvard International Law Journal*, Vol. 14, 1973, p. 585.

Tilly, Charles, "The Analysis of a Counter-Revolution," *History and Theory*, Vol. 3, 1963, p. 30.

Tilly, Charles and James Rule, *Measuring Political Upheavel*, Princeton: Center for International Studies, Princeton University. 1965. Research Monograph No. 19.

Tobin, R. L., "More Violent Than Ever: Preoccupation with Bad News in the Mass Media," *Saturday Review*, Vol. 51, November 9, 1968, pp. 79-80.

Todd, Ian, *Ghosts of the Assassins*, New York, Seemann, 1976.

Toplin, Robert Brent, *Unchallenged Violence: An American Ordeal*, Westport, Conn.: Greenwood, 1975.

"Trail of the Basque Separatists," *America*, December 19, 1970, p. 532.

Tran, Tam, "Terrorisme et le droit pénal international contemporain," *Revue de droit international de sciences diplomatiques et politiques*, Vol. 45, 1967, pp. 11-25.

Treanor, G. F., *Riots and Municipalities*, Washington, D.C.: National Institute of Municipal Law Officers, 1967.

Trelease, Allen W., *White Terror: The Ku Klux Klan Conspiracy and Southern Reconstruction*, New York: Harper & Row, 1971.

"Trends in Urban Guerrilla Tactics," *F.B.I. Law Enforcement Bulletin*, Vol. 42, No. 7, July 1973, pp. 3-7.

Trotsky, Leon, *Against Individual Terrorism*, New York, Pathfinder Press, 1974.

_____, *Stalin*, New York: Harper & Brothers, 1941.

A Trust Betrayed: Namibia, New York: U.N. Office of Public Information, 1974.

Tuckerman, A., "U.N.: New Look for 1972: Debate on Terrorism," *Nation*, October 2, 1972, p. 258.

Tupamaros, *Actus Tupamaros*, Buenos Aires: Schapire, 1971.

Turi, Robert T. et al., *Descriptive Study of Aircraft Hijacking*, Huntsville, Texas: Institute of Contemporary Corrections and the Behavioral Sciences, 1972.

Tuttle, W. M., *Race Riot — Chicago in the Red Summer of 1919 — Studies in American Negro Life*, Boston: Atheneum, 1970.

Uris, Leon, *Trinity*, New York: Doubleday, 1976.

U.S. Army, *Civil Disturbances and Disasters*, Washington, D.C.:

Government Printing Office, 1968.

U.S. Congress, *Terrorism*, Washington, D.C.: Government Printing Office, 1974.

U.S. Congress, House, Committee on Foreign Affairs, Subcommittee on International Organizations and Movements, *Problems of Protecting Civilians under International Law in the Middle East Conflict*; Washington, D.C.: Government Printing Office, 1974.

U.S. Congress, House, Committee on Foreign Affairs, Subcommittee on the Near East and South Asia, *International Terrorism*, Washington, D.C.: Government Printing Office, 1974.

U.S. Congress, House, Committee on Internal Security, *Terrorism*, Washington, D.C.: Government Printing Office, 1974.

_____, *Terrorism: A Staff Study*, Washington, D.C.: Government Printing Office, 1974.

U.S. Congress, Senate Committee on the Judiciary, Subcommittee to Investigate the Administration of the Internal Security Act and Other Internal Security Laws, *Assaults on Law Enforcement Officers*, Washington, D.C.: Government Printing Office, 1970.

_____, *Terrorist Activity*, Washington, D.C.: Government Printing Office, 1974.

_____, *Trotskyite Terrorist International*, Washington, D.C.: Government Printing Office, 1975.

U.S. Department of State, *The Role of International Law in Combating Terrorism*, Washington, D.C.: Government Printing Office, 1973.

U.S. Department of State, Bureau of Public Affairs, Office of Media Services, *U.S. Action to Combat Terrorism*, Washington, D.C.: Government Printing Office, 1973.

U.S. Federal Bureau of Investigation, *Prevention and Control of Mobs and Riots*, Washington, D.C.: Government Printing Office, 1965.

_____, *Terrorism: Its Tactics and Techniques*, Washington, D.C.: Government Printing Office, 1973.

U.S. Kerner Commission, *Report of the National Advisory Commission on Civil Disorders*, with an Introduction by Tom Wicker, New York: Dutton, 1968.

U.S. National Advisory Commission on Civil Disorders, *Supplemental Studies*, Washington, D.C.: Government Printing Office, 1968.

U.S. National Commission on the Causes and Prevention of Violence, *To Establish Justice, to Protect Domestic Tranquility: Final Report*, New York: Bantam, 1970.

_____, *Progress Report to President Lyndon B. Johnson*, Washington, D.C.: Government Printing Office, 1969.

_____, *Staff Reports*, Washington, D.C.: Government Printing Office, 1969.

U.S. President's Commission on Campus Unrest, *Report*, Washington, D.C.: Government Printing Office, 1970.

Van Dalen, H., "Terror as a Political Weapon," *Military Police Law Enforcement Journal*, Vol. 2, No. 1, 1975, pp. 21-26.

van den Berghe, Pierre L., *South Africa: A Study in Conflict*, Middletown: Wesleyan University Press, 1965.

Van den Haag, Ernest, *Political Violence and Civil Disobedience*, New York: Harper & Row, 1972.

Van Voris, William H., *Violence in Ulster: An Oral Documentary*, Amherst: University of Massachusetts Press, 1975.

Vasilijeric, V. A., "Essai de Determination du Terrorisme en tant que Crime International," *Jugoslarenska Revija za Medunarodno Praro (Yug.)*, Vol. 20, 1973, p. 169.

Vayrynen, Raimo, "Some Aspects of Theory and Strategy of Kidnapping," *Instant Research on Peace and Violence*, No. 1, 1971, pp. 3-21.

Venter, Al J., *Africa at War*, Old Greenwich, Conn.: Devin-Adair, 1974.

_____, *The Terror Fighters*, Capetown and Johannesburg: Purnell, 1969.

Venturi, Franco, *Roots of Revolution*, New York: Grosset & Dunlap, 1966.

Viet Cong Terror Tactics in South Viet Nam, Washington, D.C.: U.S. Department of State, July 1967.

Volsky, Dmitry, "The Beirut Crime," *New Times*, No. 16, 1973, pp. 12-13.

Von Baeyer-Katte, W., Ed., *Marxism, Communism and Western Society*, Vol. 8, New York: Herder & Herder, 1973.

Vox der Mekden, Fred R., *Comparative Political Violence*, Englewood Cliffs: Prentice-Hall, 1973.

Vucinic, Milan, "The Responsibility of States for Acts of International Terrorism," *Review of International Affairs*, Vol. 23, Nos. 536-37, 1972, pp. 11-12.

Waddis, Jack, *New Theories of Revolution*, New York: International Publishers, 1972.

Wahl, Jonathan, "Responses to Terrorism: Self-Defense or Reprisal?" *International Problems*, Vol. 5, Nos. 1-2, 1973, pp. 28-33.

Wallace, Michael, "The Uses of Violence in American History," *American Scholar*, Vol. 40, 1971, p. 81.

Walter, Eugene Victor, *Terror and Resistance: A Study of Political Violence*, New York: Oxford University Press, 1969.

_____, "Violence and the Process of Terror," *American Sociological Review*, Vol. 29, 1964, p. 248.

Walzer, Michael, "The New Terrorists," *New Republic*, August 30, 1975.

_____, *The Revolution of the Saints: A Study in the Origins of Radical Politics*, Cambridge, Mass.: Harvard University Press, 1965.

Walzer, Michael, J. Bowyer Bell and Roger Morris, "Terrorism: A Debate," *New Republic*, December 22, 1975, p. 12.

Watson, Francis M., *Political Terrorism: The Threat and the Response*, Washington, D.C.: Robert B. Luce, 1976.

Weil, H. M., "Domestic and International Violence: A Forecasting Approach," *Futures*, Vol. 6, December 1974, p. 477.

Weissberg, Guenter, "United Nations Movements toward World Law," *International and Comparative Law Quarterly*, Vol. 24, 1975, p. 460.

Weller, Jac, "Guerrilla Warfare," *National Guardsman*, Vol. 24, 1970, pp. 2-8.

West, D.J., P. Wiles and C. Stanwood, *Research on Violence*, London: University of Cambridge Institute of Criminology, n.d.

Westin, A. and S. Baker, *Databanks in a Free Society: Computers, Recordkeeping and Privacy*, New York: Quadrangle, 1972.

"What Makes a Skyjacker?" *Science Digest*, Vol. 71, 1972, pp. 21-22.

Whelton, Charles, *Skyjack!* New York: Tower Publications, 1970.

"When Tradition Comes to the Aid of Terrorism," *Economist*, March 17, 1973, p. 23.

"Which Way the I.R.A.?" *Commonweal*, January 5, 1973, pp. 294-97.

White, Gillian M. E., "The Hague Convention for the Suppression of Unlawful Seizure of Aircraft," *International Commission of Jurists Review*, No. 6, 1971, pp. 38-45.

Wilkins, Roy, "The Riots of 1964: The Causes of Racial Violence," *Notre Dame Lawyer*, Vol. 40, 1965, p. 552.

Wilkinson, Paul, *Political Terrorism*, London: Macmillan, 1974.

_____, "Three Questions on Terrorism," *Government and Opposition*, Vol. 8, No. 3, 1973, pp. 290-312.

Wilson, R. S., *Cordon and Search*, Aldershat: Gale & Polden, 1949.

Winegarten, R., "Literary Terrorism," *Commentary*, March 1974, pp. 58-65.

Wohl, Paul, "New Soviet Revolutionary Stance in the Middle East," *Radio Liberty Dispatch*, May 25, 1970, p. 2.

Wolf, J. B., "Terrorist Manipulation of the Democratic Process," *Police Journal*, Vol. 48, No. 2, April-June 1975, pp. 102-112.

Wolf, Michael, "Cheerleader for the Revolution," New York *Times Magazine*, July 21, 1974, pp. 11-20.

Wolfe, Bertram D., *Three Who Made a Revolution*, New York: Dial, 1961.

Wolfgang, Marvin E. and Franco Ferranti, *The Subculture of Violence: Towards an Integrated Theory in Criminology*, London: Tavistock, 1967.

Wolin, Simon and Robert M. Slusser, eds., *The Soviet Secret Police*, New York: Praeger, 1957.

Wood, Arthur L., *Deviant Behavior and Control Strategies*, Lexington, Mass.: Lexington Books; D. C. Heath, 1974.

Woods, J., *New Theories of Revolution: A Commentary on the Views of Frantz Fanon, Regis Debray, and Herbert Marcuse*, New York: International Publishers, 1972.

Woodstock, George, *Anarchism*, New York: World, 1971.

Worthy, W., "Bombs Blast a Message of Hate: An Interview with an Admitted Bomber," *Life*, Vol. 68, March 27, 1970, pp. 24-32.

Yaari, Ehud, "The Decline of Al-Fatah," *Midstream*, May 1971, pp. 3-12.

_____, *Strike Terror*, New York: Sabra Books, 1970.

Yahalom, Dan, *Fire on Arab Terrorism*, Jerusalem: Carta, 1973.

Yahalom, Yirtah, *Arab Terror*, Tel Aviv: World Labour Zionist Movement, 1969.

Yamamoto, Soji, "The Japanese Enactment for the Suppression of Unlawful Seizure of Aircraft and International Law," *Japanese Annual of International Law*, No. 15, 1971, pp. 70-80.

Yaniv, A., *P.L.O.: A Profile*, Jerusalem: Israel Universities Study Group for Middle East Affairs, 1974.

Young, Oran R., *The Politics of Force*, New York: Free Press, 1974.

Zaar, Issac, *Rescue and Liberation*, New York: Bloch, 1954.

Zahn, G. C., "Terrorism for Peace and Justice," *Commonweal*, October 23, 1970, pp. 84-85.

Zivic, J., "The Nonaligned and the Problem of International Terrorism," *Review of International Affairs*, Vol. 24, January 1973, p. 6.

Zotiades, George B., "The International Criminal Prosecution o!

Persons Charged with an Unlawful Seizure of Aircraft,"*Revue
hellénique de droit international*, Vol. 23, Nos. 1-4, 1970,
pp. 12-37.
Zwiebach, Burton, *Civility and Disobedience*, New York:
Cambridge University Press, 1975.

Contributors

Yonah Alexander is Professor of International Studies and Director of The Institute for Studies in International Terrorism at the State University of New York at Oneonta.

H. H. A. Cooper is Staff Director of the National Advisory Committee, Task Force on Disorders and Terrorism, Washington, D.C.

Alona E. Evans is Kendall Professor of Political Science at Wellesley College.

Ernest Evans received his doctorate in political science at the Massachusetts Institute of Technology and is a staff researcher for the Senate Arms Services Committee.

Seymour Maxwell Finger is Professor of Political Science and Director of The Ralph Bunche Institute on the United Nations at the City University of New York.

Robert A. Friedlander is Associate Professor of Law in the College of Law at Lewis University.

Irving Louis Horowitz is Professor of Sociology and Political Science at Rutgers University.

Martha Crenshaw Hutchinson is Assistant Professor of Government at Wesleyan University.

Bernard Johnpoll is Professor of Political Science at the State University of New York at Albany.

Jay Mallin is Director of the Institute for Study of Change in Miami, Florida.

Joseph Margolin is Director of the Behavioral Studies Group at The George Washington University.

Edward F. Mickolus is a doctoral candidate in political science at Yale University.

James A. Miller is a doctoral candidate in international studies at American University.

Hans J. Morgenthau is Professor of Political Science at the New School for Social Research.

Jordan J. Paust is Associate Professor of Law in the Law School at the University of Houston.

David Rapoport is Professor of Political Science at the University of California in Los Angeles.

Alfred P. Rubin is Professor of International Law in the Fletcher School of Law and Diplomacy at Tufts University.

Baljit Singh is Professor of Political Science and Assistant Dean of the College of Social Science at Michigan State University.

Index

376 INDEX

state terrorism, 3
Stern Gang, 46, 54
subversion, 6, 23, 76, 82, 83, 98
Sunni, 6
Sun-Tsu, 6
Sweden, 133, 134
Symbionese Liberation Army (S.L.A.), 11, 66, 122, 164, 169
Syria, 109, 126, 170, 178, 180

tactics, 10-12, 24, 25, 32, 47, 67, 80-87, 93, 95, 100-104
Taylor, Theodore, 301
terrorism, behavioral approaches to, 270-282; conceptual model of, 65-91; definitions of, 18-25, 31; deterrence of, 106-117; history of political, 3-15, 32-37, 46-57, 92-94, 209-211; international, 30-37, 53-55, 65-91, 106-107, 121, 136; legal approaches to, 121-136, 283-297; media coverage of, 141-165, in the Middle East, 166-199, nuclear proliferation and, 283-314; as psychological warfare, 95-104; statistical approaches to, 211-269
Toscanino, 131
torture, 67
totalitarianism, 36
Tokyo Convention, 128, 136
transnational terrorism, 210
Treaty of St. Germain, 35
Trotsky, 46
Trotskyite, 161
Tupamaros, 14, 53, 84, 103, 108
Turkey, 134
tyrranicide, 32, 34

Ulrike Meinhof Action Committee, xii
United Nations, 52, 81, 116, 125, 126, 128, 129, 132, 134, 183, 190, 191; Draft Convention on International Terrorism, 110; General Assembly Convention on Prevention & Punishment of Crimes against Internationally Protected Persons, Including Diplomatic Agents, 36; Treaty of 1973, 110; U.N.E.S.C.O., 190, 196, 197
United Kingdom, 131, 142
United States, 7, 14, 24, 81, 92, 100, 102-104, 106, 111, 117, 125, 130, 133, 134, 157, 175, 183, 191, 192, 222, 225, 288, 299, 302, 307-309
unlawful seizure of aircraft, 128
Uraguay, 101, 102, 107, 108

vandalism, 5
Viet Cong, 12, 101, 102
Vietnam, 95, 98, 101, 102, 147, 177
violence, 121, 122
von Dock Bern, Major H., 98

Wallace, George, 121, 122, 144
Walters, Barbara, 159
War, Anglo-Irish (1918), 35; Civil, 68, 69; conventional and unconventional, 5, 6, 76, 82, 84, 86, 101, 102; general, 68, 69; Korean, 68; limited, 68, 69; nuclear, 68; peninsula, 32; Six Day, 52, 170, 171, 180, 294; total, 68, 69; see also: World War
Washington *Post*, 143, 149